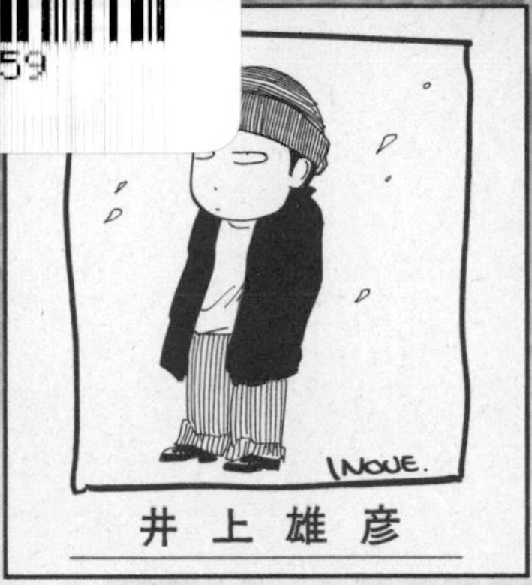
INOUE.
井上雄彦

Takehiko Inoue

1. MANY TEAMS IN THE NBA ARE CHANGING THEIR UNIFORMS. A WEAKER TEAM CAN REVAMP ITS IMAGE AS A LOSING FRANCHISE BY DOING SO, BUT I DON'T LIKE IT WHEN STRONGER TEAMS OR CHAMPIONS PUT ON NEW, TASTELESS UNIFORMS.

2. *HIGH TIME* WON THE GOOD DESIGN AWARD. THANK YOU TO EVERYBODY AT ASICS.

Takehiko Inoue's *Slam Dunk* is one of the most popular manga of all time, having sold over 100 million copies worldwide. He followed that series up with two titles lauded by critics and fans alike—*Vagabond*, a fictional account of the life of Miyamoto Musashi, and *Real*, a manga about wheelchair basketball.

SLAM DUNK
Vol. 27: Shohoku in Trouble

SHONEN JUMP Manga Edition

STORY AND ART BY TAKEHIKO INOUE

English Adaptation/Stan!
Translation/Joe Yamazaki
Touch-up Art & Lettering/James Gaubatz
Cover & Graphic Design/Matt Hinrichs
Editor/Mike Montesa

© 1990 - 2013 Takehiko Inoue and I.T. Planning, Inc.
Originally published in Japan in 1995 by Shueisha
Inc., Tokyo. English translation rights arranged with
I.T. Planning, Inc. All rights reserved.

The SLAM DUNK U.S. trademark is used with
permission from NBA Properties, Inc.

Some scenes have been modified from the original
Japanese edition.

The stories, characters and incidents mentioned in this
publication are entirely fictional.

Printed in Canada

Published by VIZ Media, LLC
P.O. Box 77010
San Francisco, CA 94107

10 9 8 7 6 5 4 3 2
First printing, April 2013
Second printing, September 2015

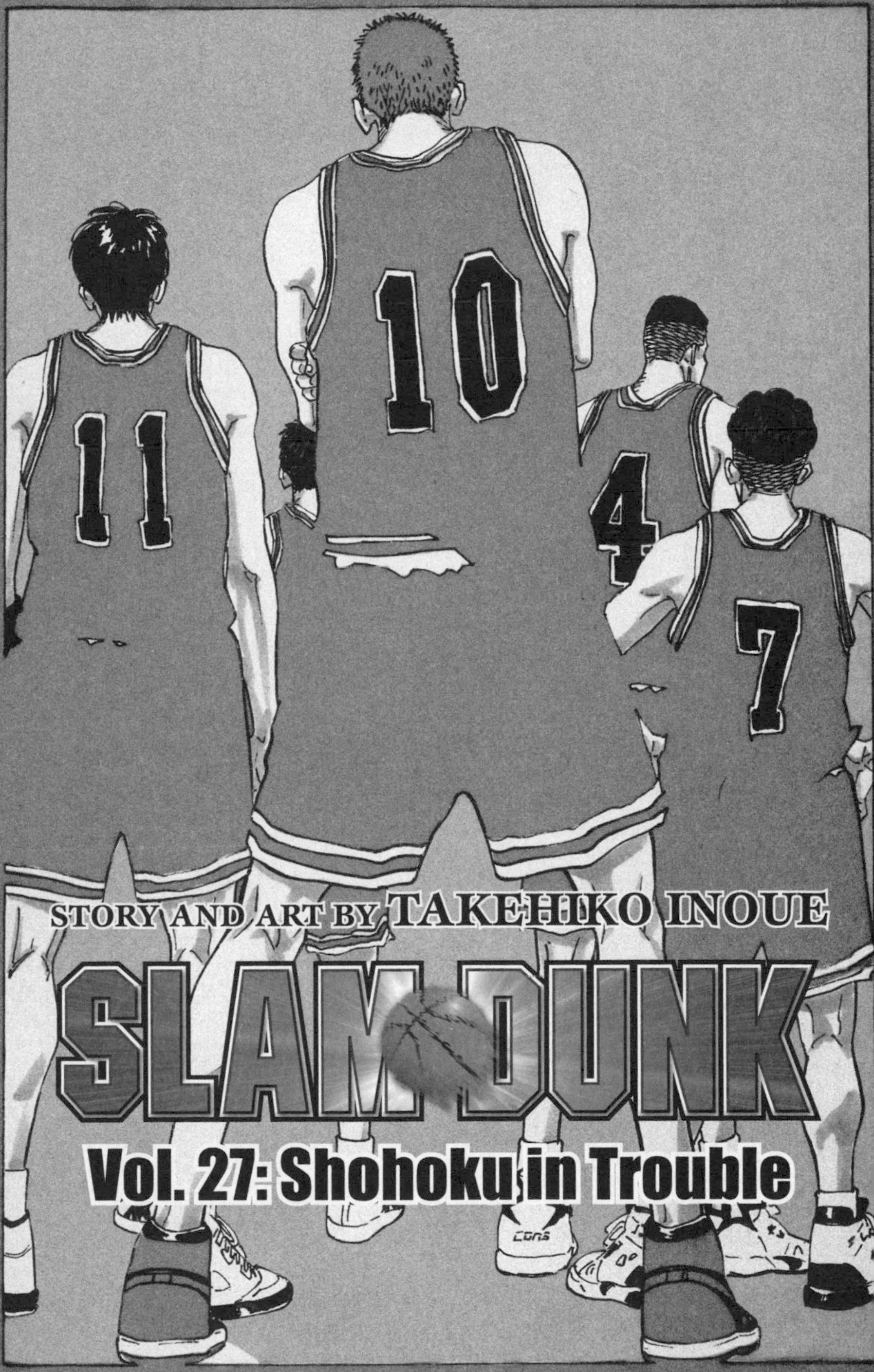

STORY AND ART BY TAKEHIKO INOUE

SLAM DUNK

Vol. 27: Shohoku in Trouble

Character Introduction

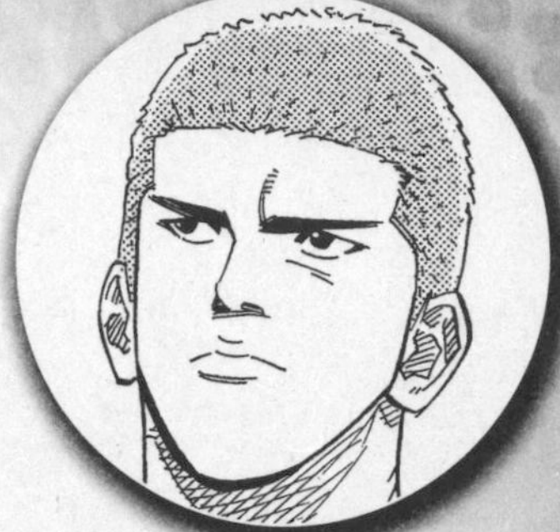

Hanamichi Sakuragi
A first-year at Shohoku High School, Sakuragi is in love with Haruko Akagi.

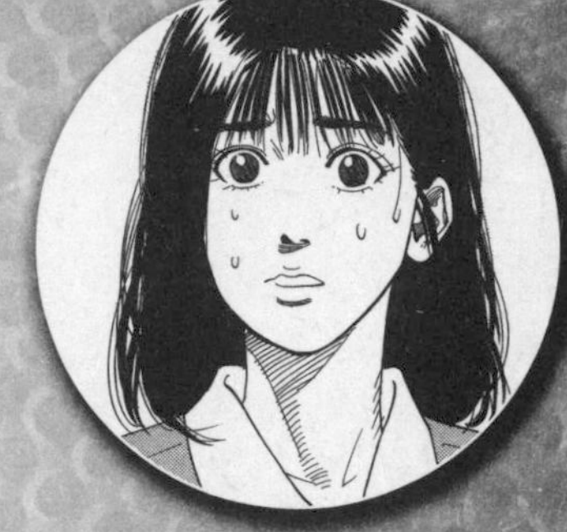

Haruko Akagi
Also a first-year at Shohoku, Takenori Akagi's little sister has a crush on Kaede Rukawa.

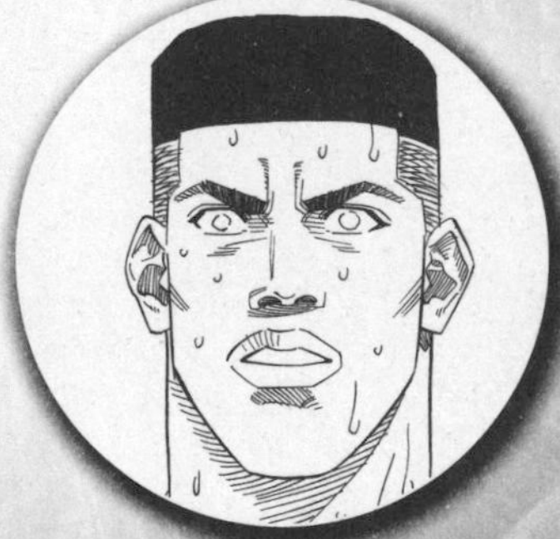

Takenori Akagi
A third-year and the basketball team's captain, Akagi has an intense passion for his sport.

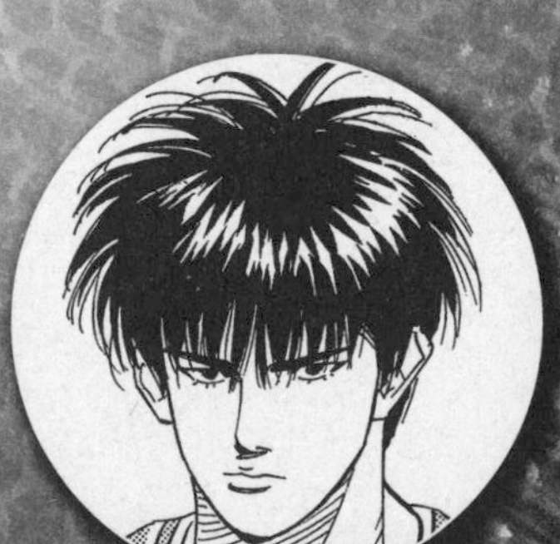

Kaede Rukawa
The object of Haruko's affection (and that of many of Shohoku's female students!), this first-year has been a star player since junior high.

Sawakita

Fukatsu

Kawata

Ryota Miyagi
A problem child with
a thing for Ayako.

Ayako
Basketball Team
Manager

Hisashi Mitsui
An MVP during
junior high.

Our Story Thus Far

Hanamichi Sakuragi is rejected by close to 50 girls during his three years in junior high. He joins the basketball team to be closer to Haruko Akagi, but his frustration mounts when all he does is practice day after day.

Shohoku advances through the Prefectural Tournament and earns a spot in the Nationals.

Shohoku advances to the second round to face Sannoh Kogyo, last year's national champions and considered by most to be the best team in the country. Miyagi and Hanamichi surprise the crowd by opening the game with an alley-oop dunk. With momentum on their side, Shohoku finishes the first half with a two-point lead. Now everything rides on how they do in the second half.

Vol. 27:
Shohoku in Trouble

Table of Contents

#234
SHOHOKU
IN TROUBLE

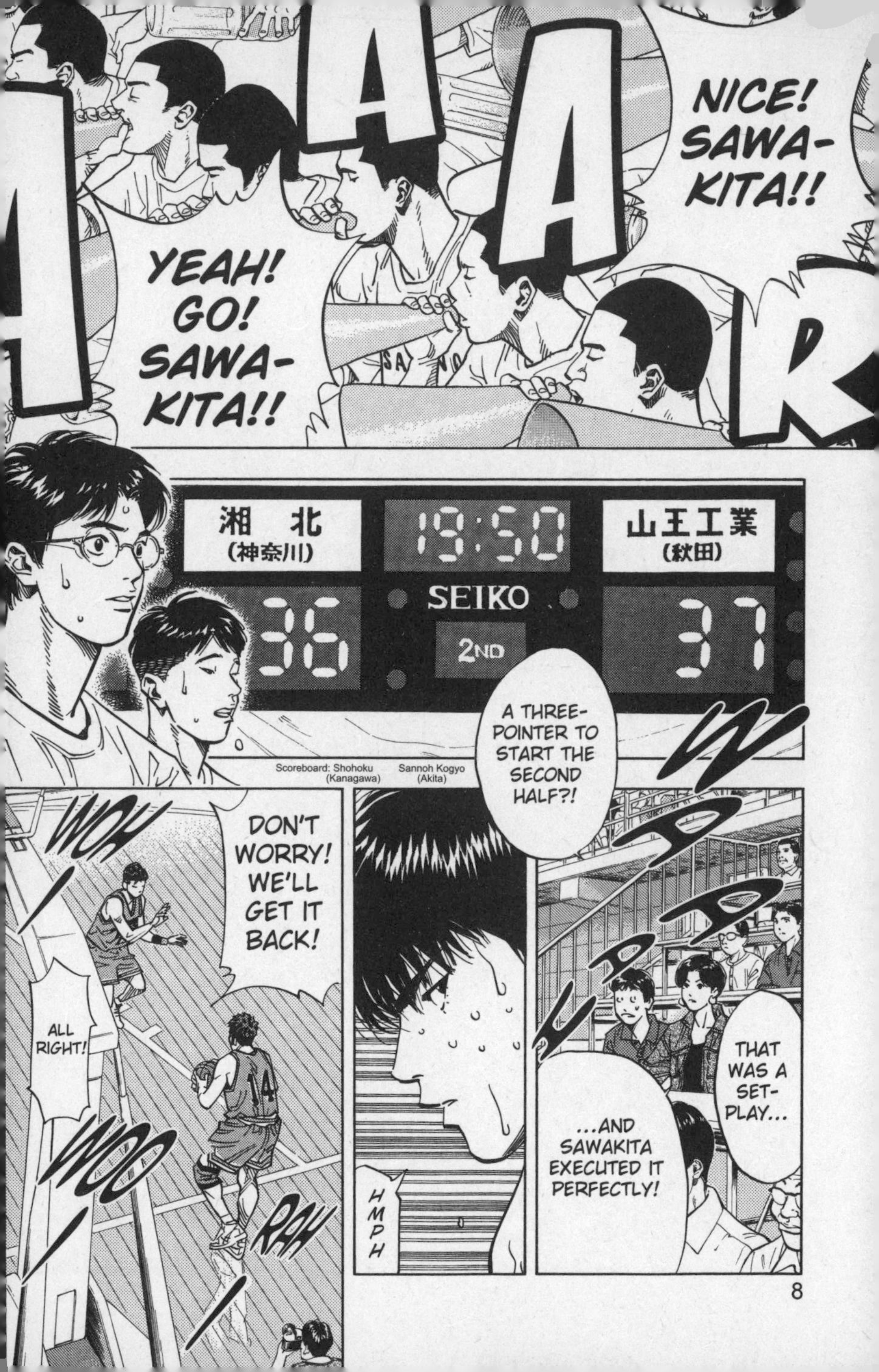
AAR
NICE! SAWA-KITA!!
YEAH! GO! SAWA-KITA!!
湘北 (神奈川)
19:50
山王工業 (秋田)
SEIKO
36
2ND
37
Scoreboard: Shohoku (Kanagawa) Sannoh Kogyo (Akita)
A THREE-POINTER TO START THE SECOND HALF?!
THAT WAS A SET-PLAY...
...AND SAWAKITA EXECUTED IT PERFECTLY!
HMPH
DON'T WORRY! WE'LL GET IT BACK!
ALL RIGHT!
WOH
WOO
RAH

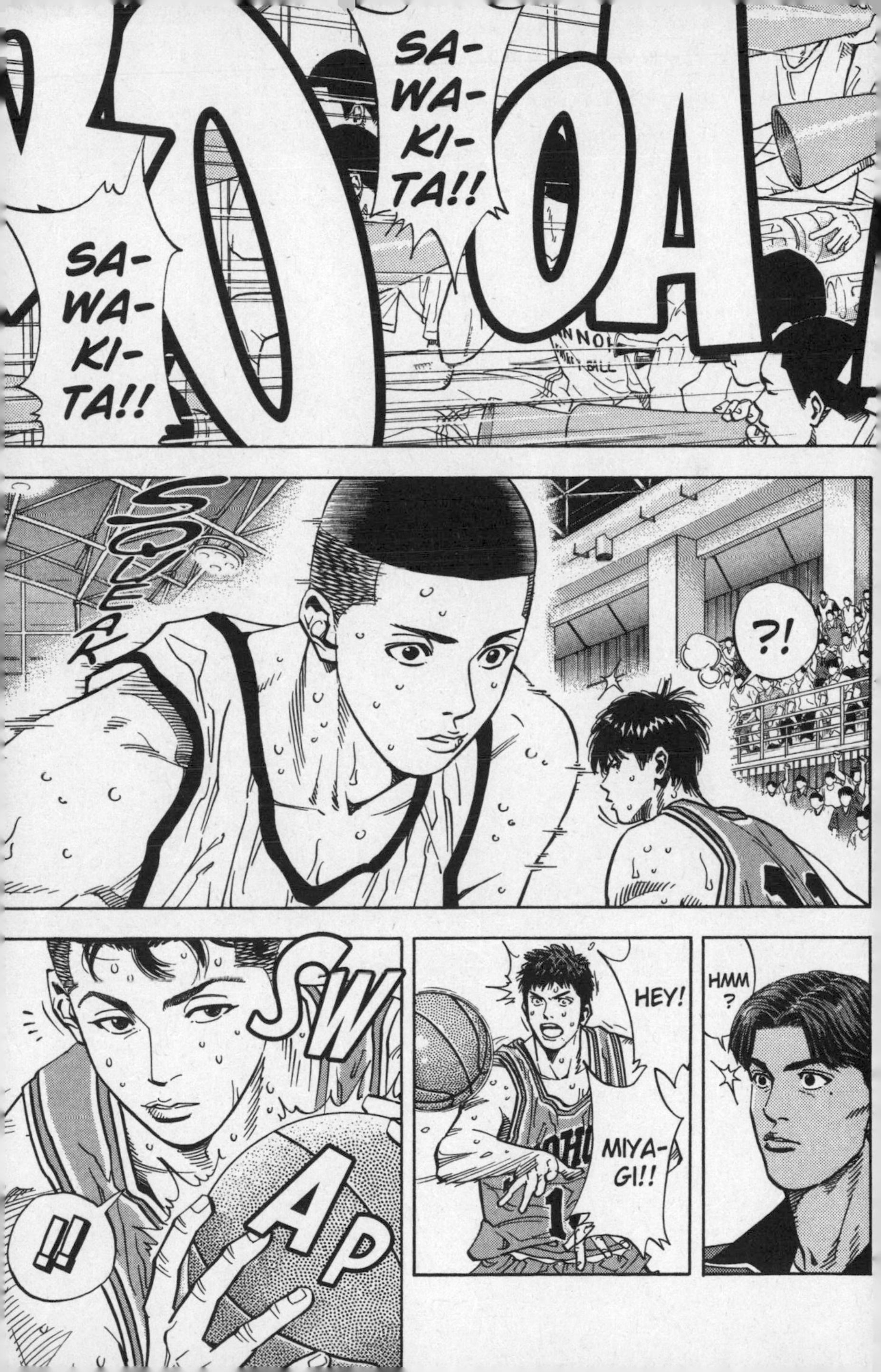
SA-WA-KI-TA!!
SA-WA-KI-TA!!
SQUEAK
?!
HMM ?
HEY!
MIYA-GI!!
SWAP
!!

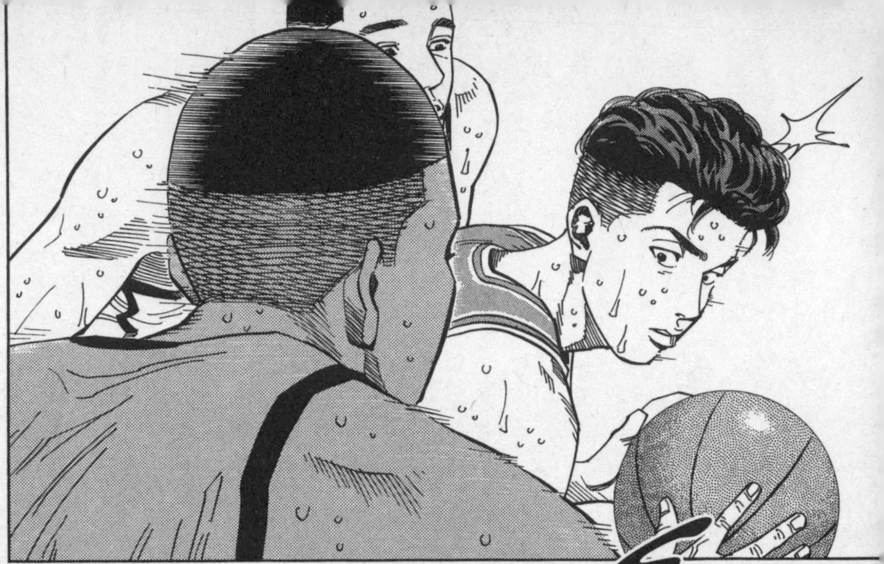

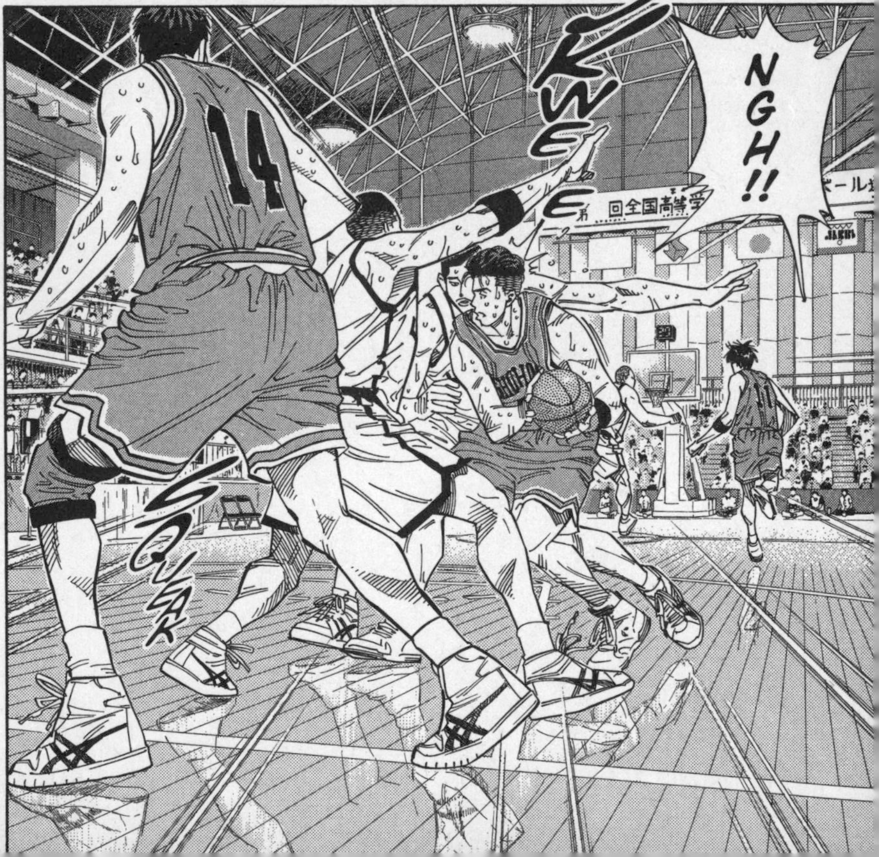
NGH!!
SKWEEE
回全国高等学
SQUEAK

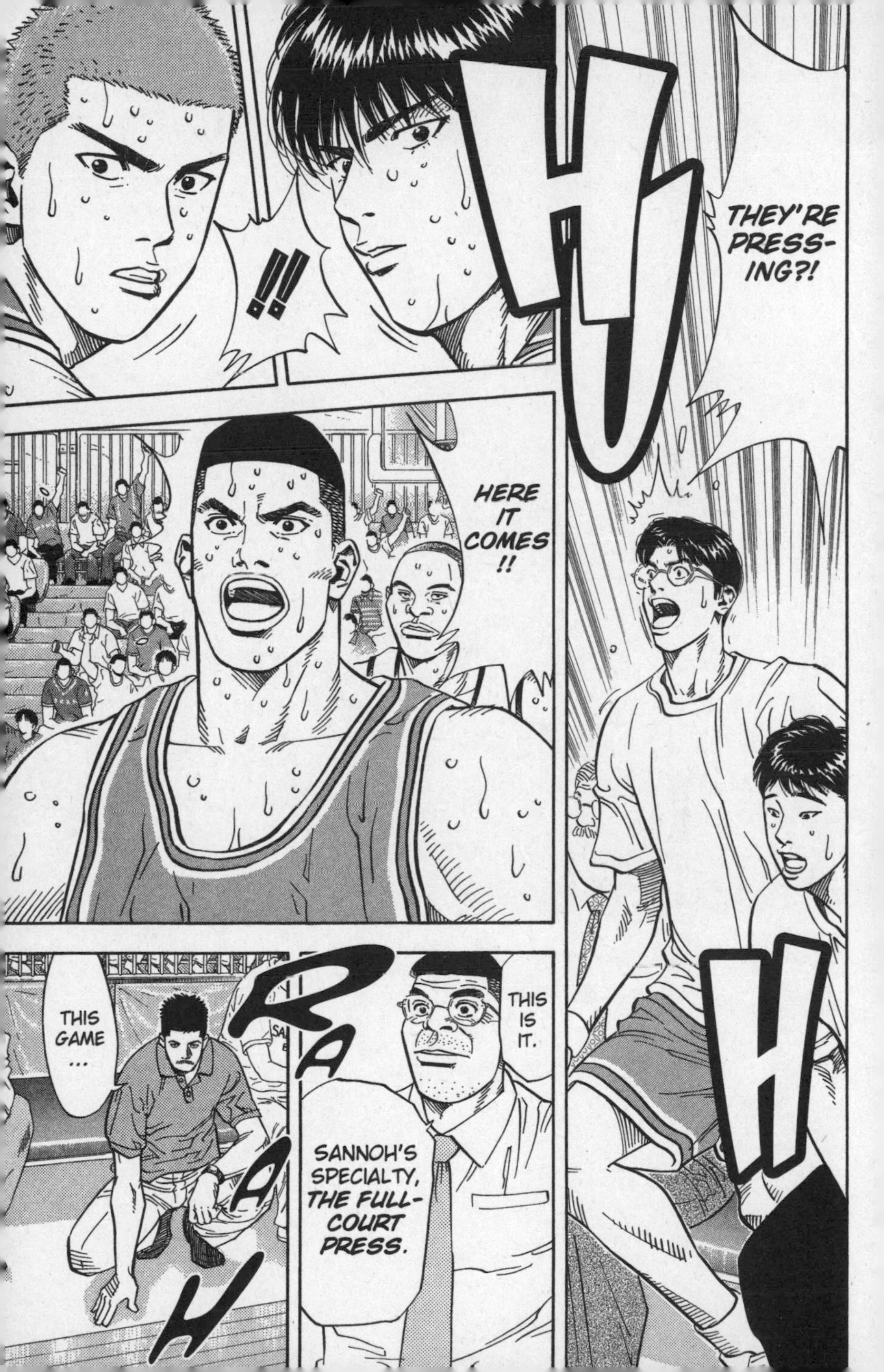
HUH
THEY'RE PRESS-ING?!
!!
HERE IT COMES !!
THIS IS IT.
SANNOH'S SPECIALTY, THE FULL-COURT PRESS.
RAAH
THIS GAME ...

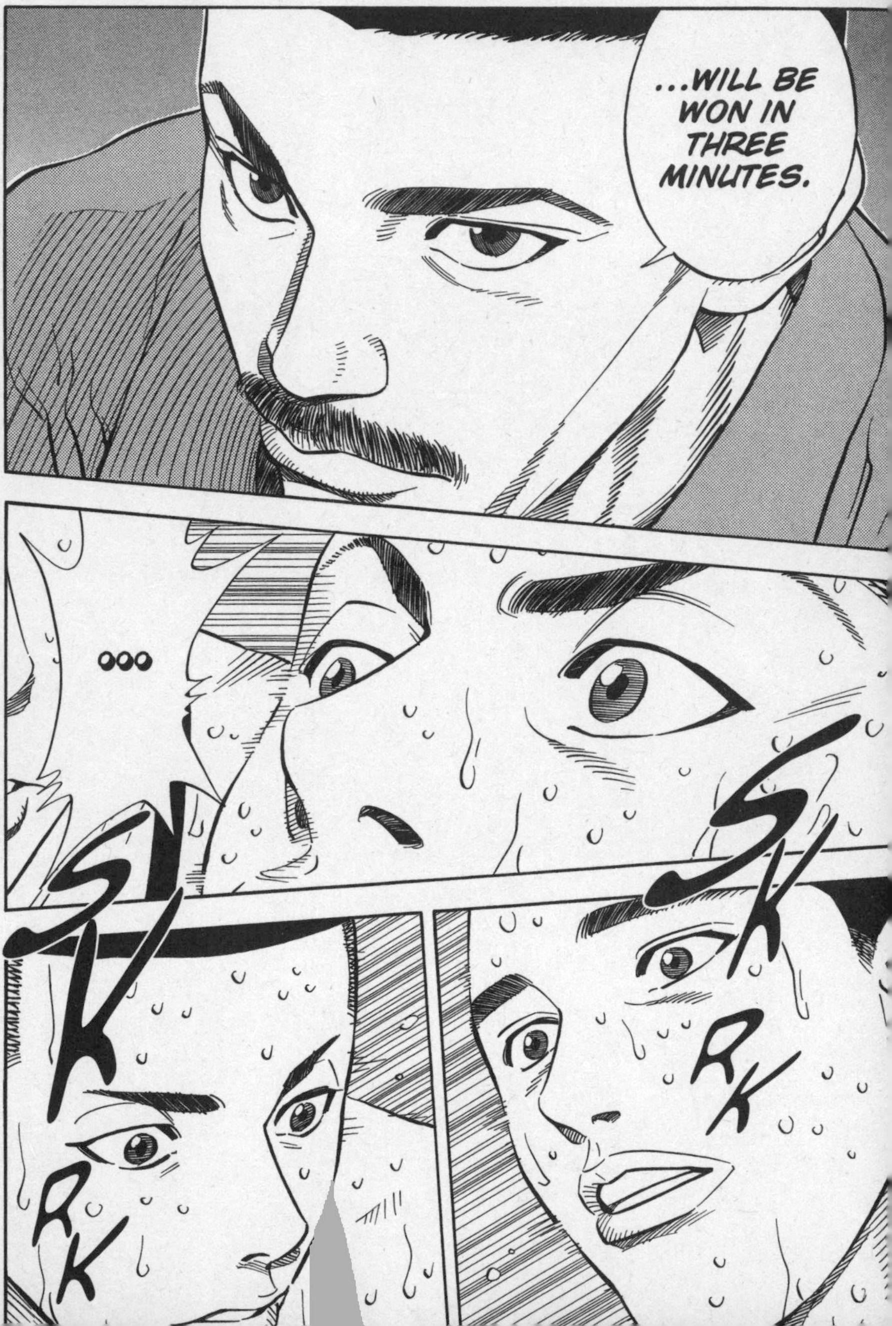
...WILL BE WON IN THREE MINUTES.
...
SKRK
SKRK

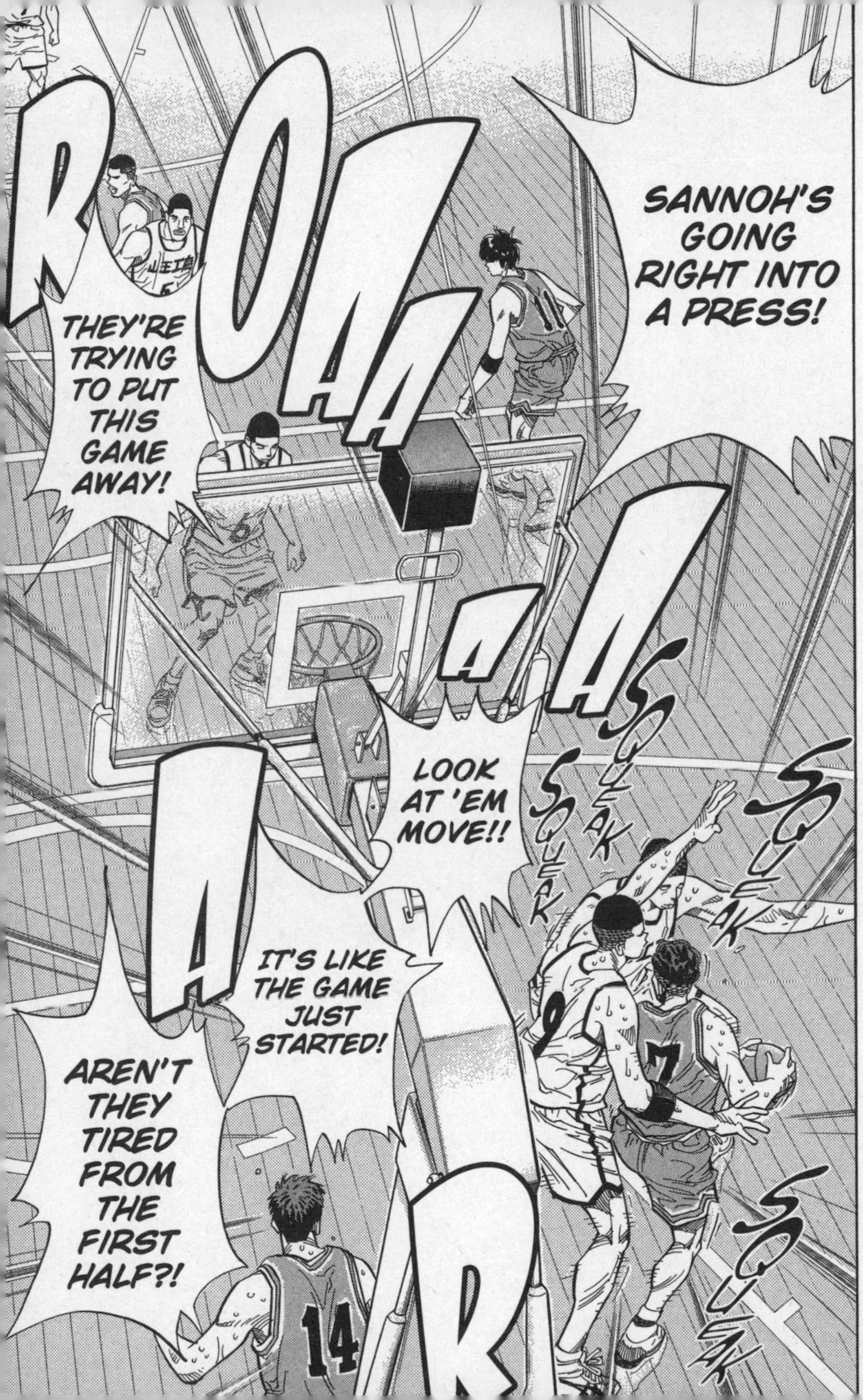
SANNOH'S GOING RIGHT INTO A PRESS!
ROAAAAAR
THEY'RE TRYING TO PUT THIS GAME AWAY!
SQUEAK
SQUEAK
SQUEAK
LOOK AT 'EM MOVE!!
SQUEAK
SQUEAK
IT'S LIKE THE GAME JUST STARTED!
AREN'T THEY TIRED FROM THE FIRST HALF?!

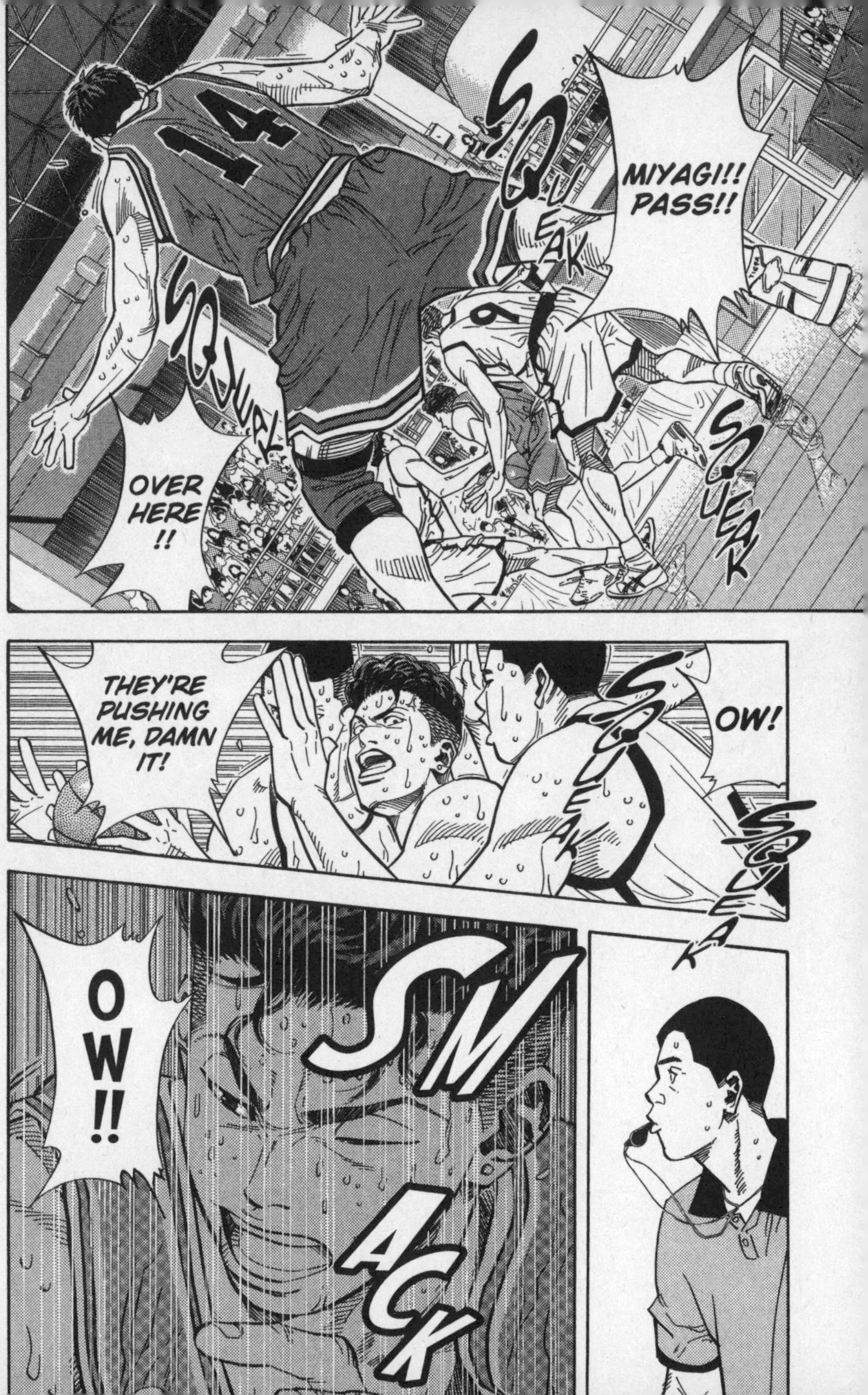
MIYAGI!! PASS!!
SQUEAK
SQUEAK
SQUEAK
OVER HERE!!
OW!
SQUEAK
SQUEAK
THEY'RE PUSHING ME, DAMN IT!
SMACK
OW!!

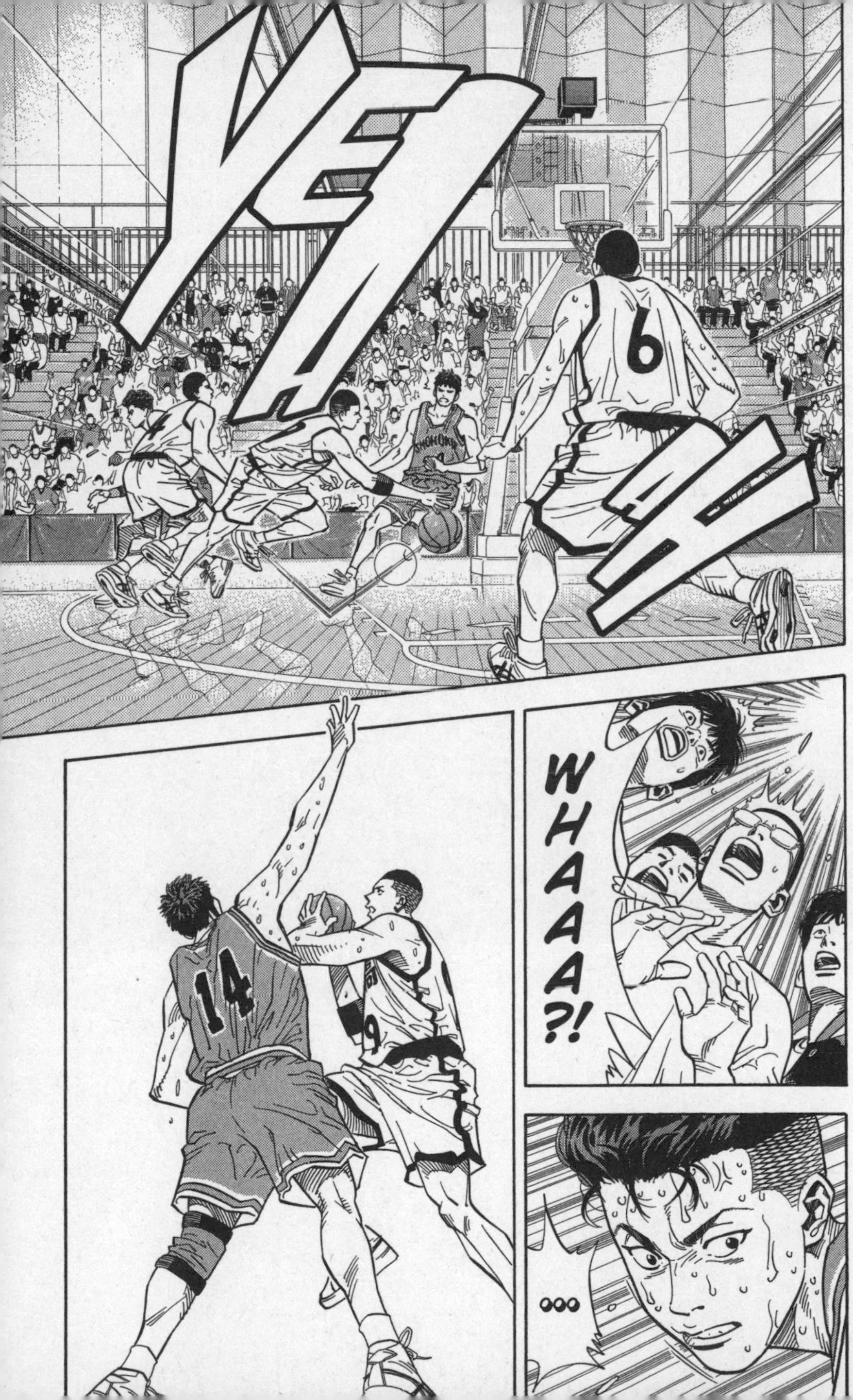
YEA
AH
WHAAAA?!
...

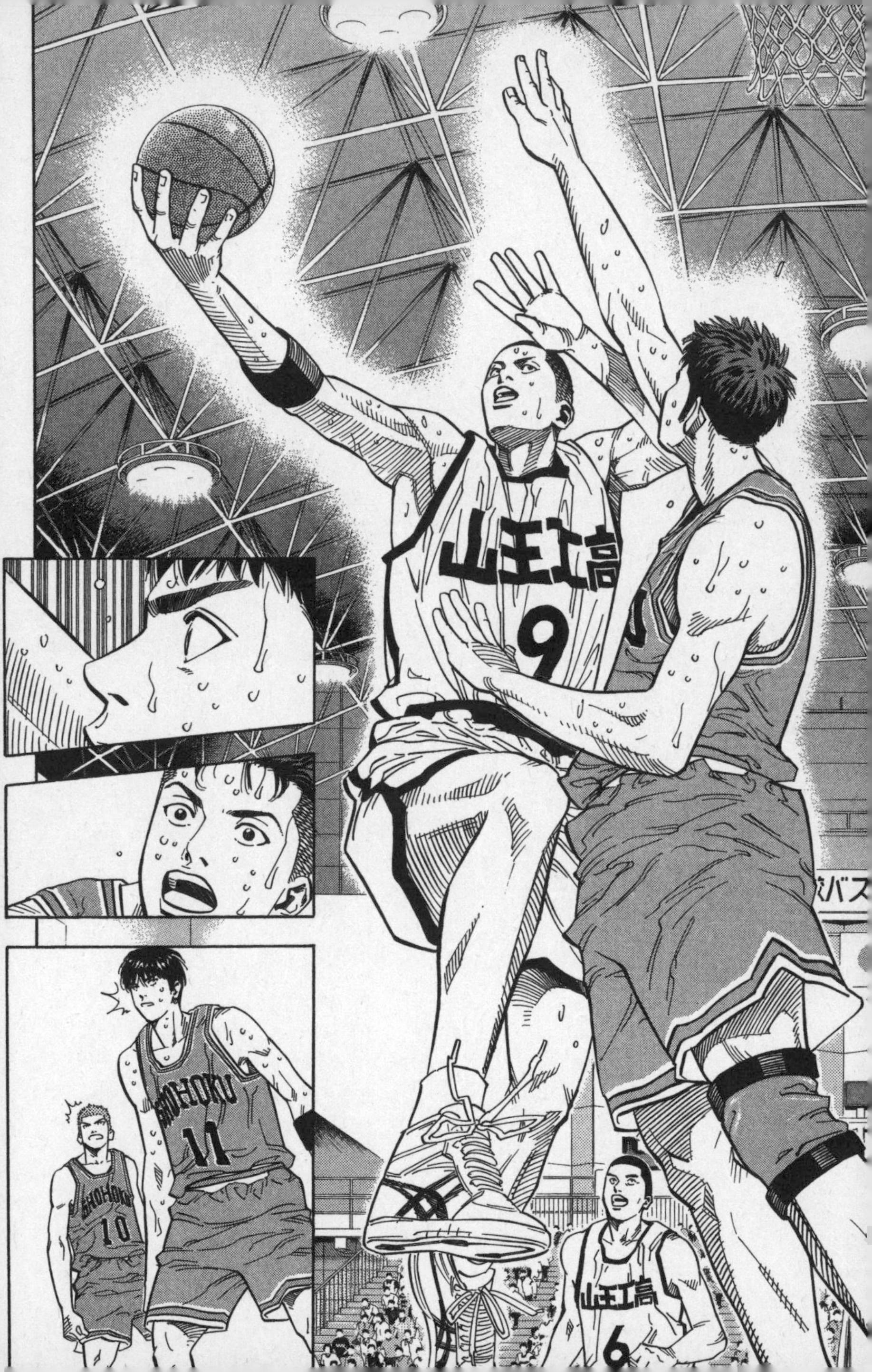

山王工高
SHOHOKU

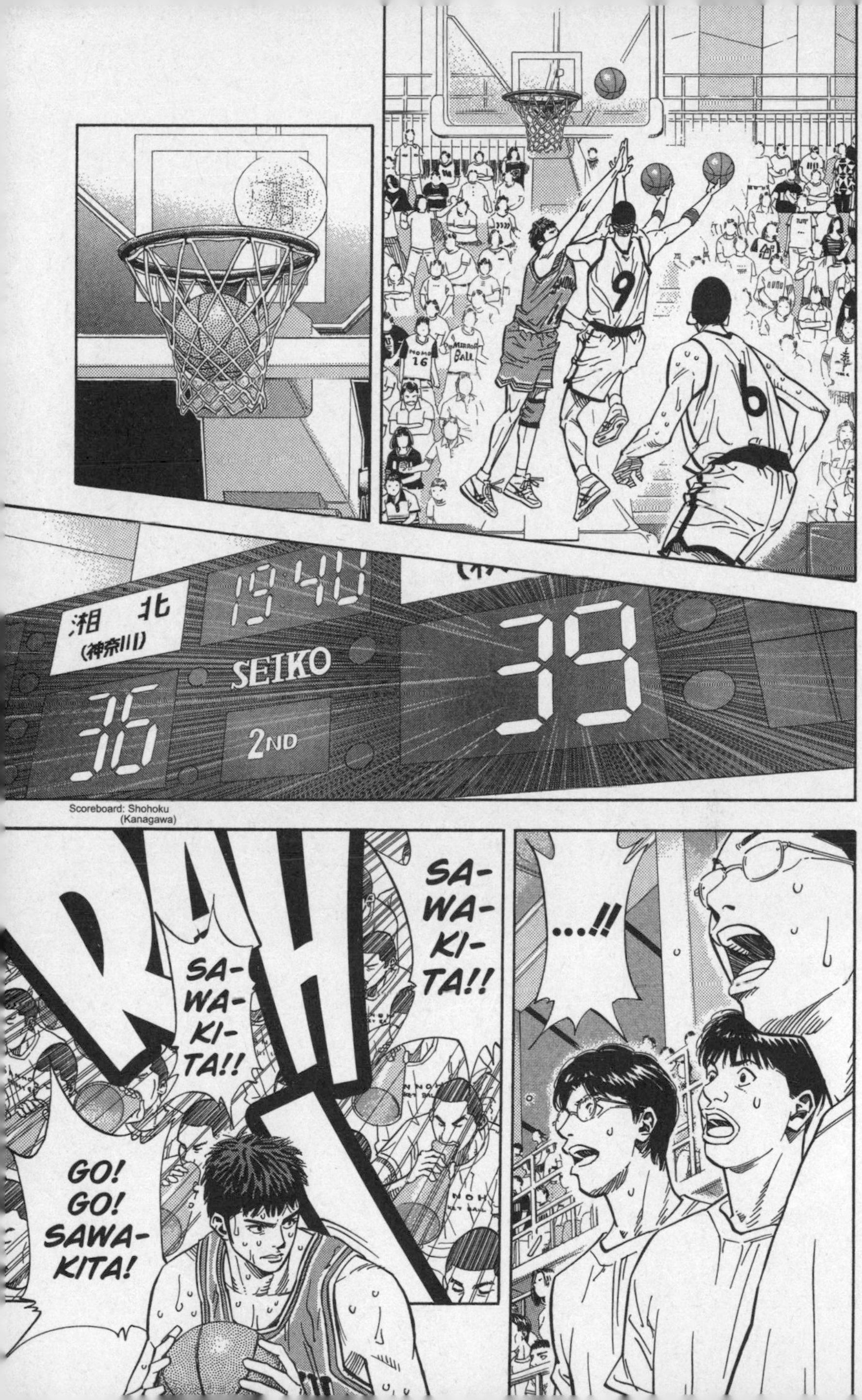
湘北
(神奈川)
1940
SEIKO
36
2ND
39
Scoreboard: Shohoku
(Kanagawa)
...!!
SA-WA-KI-TA!!
SA-WA-KI-TA!!
GO! GO! SAWA-KITA!
RAH

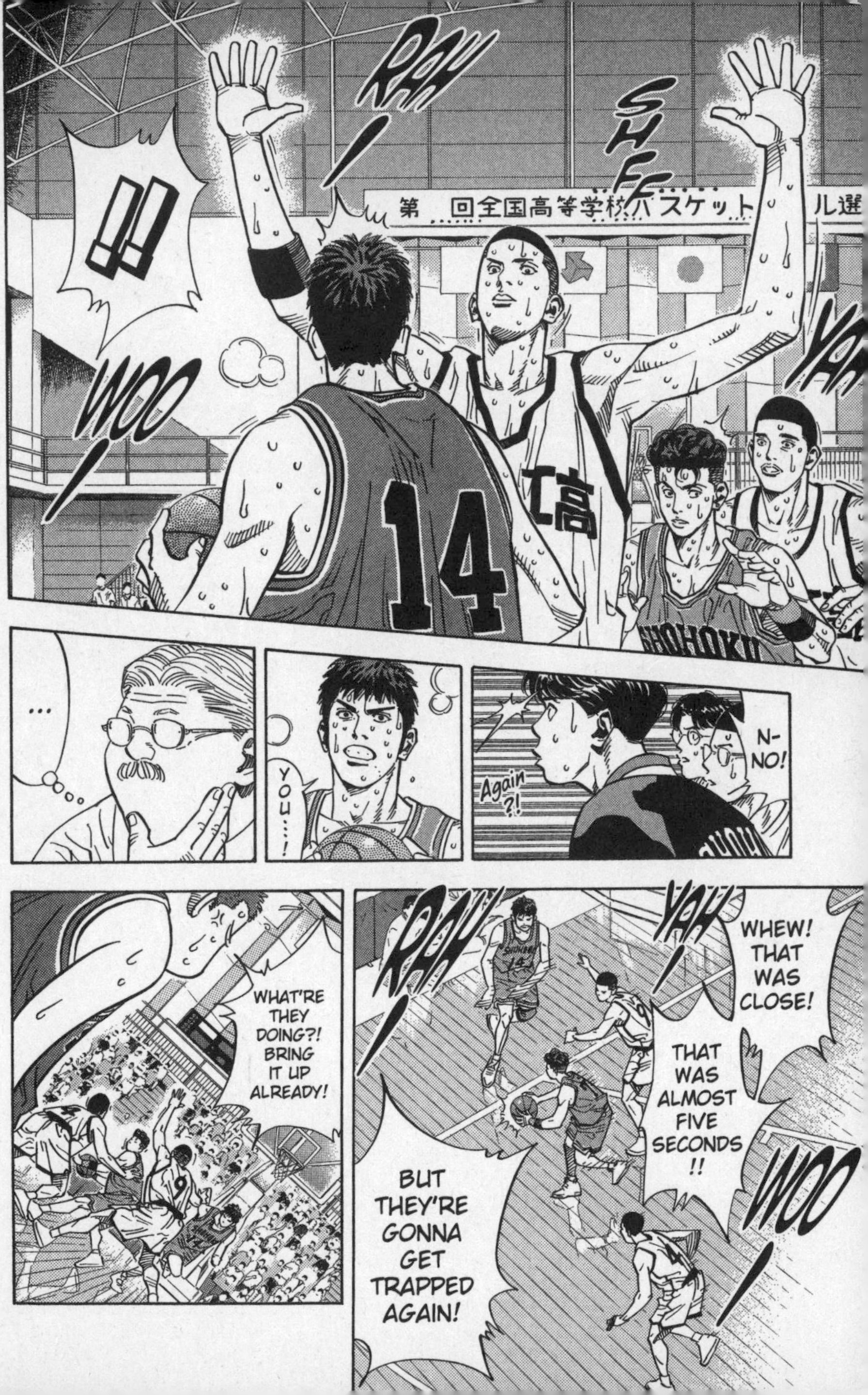
YAH!
SHFF
RAH!
第 回全国高等学校バスケット ル選
!!
WOO!
工高
14
SHOHOKU
N-NO!
Again?!
YOU...!
...
YAH!
WHEW! THAT WAS CLOSE!
THAT WAS ALMOST FIVE SECONDS!!
WOO!
RAH!
BUT THEY'RE GONNA GET TRAPPED AGAIN!
WHAT'RE THEY DOING?! BRING IT UP ALREADY!

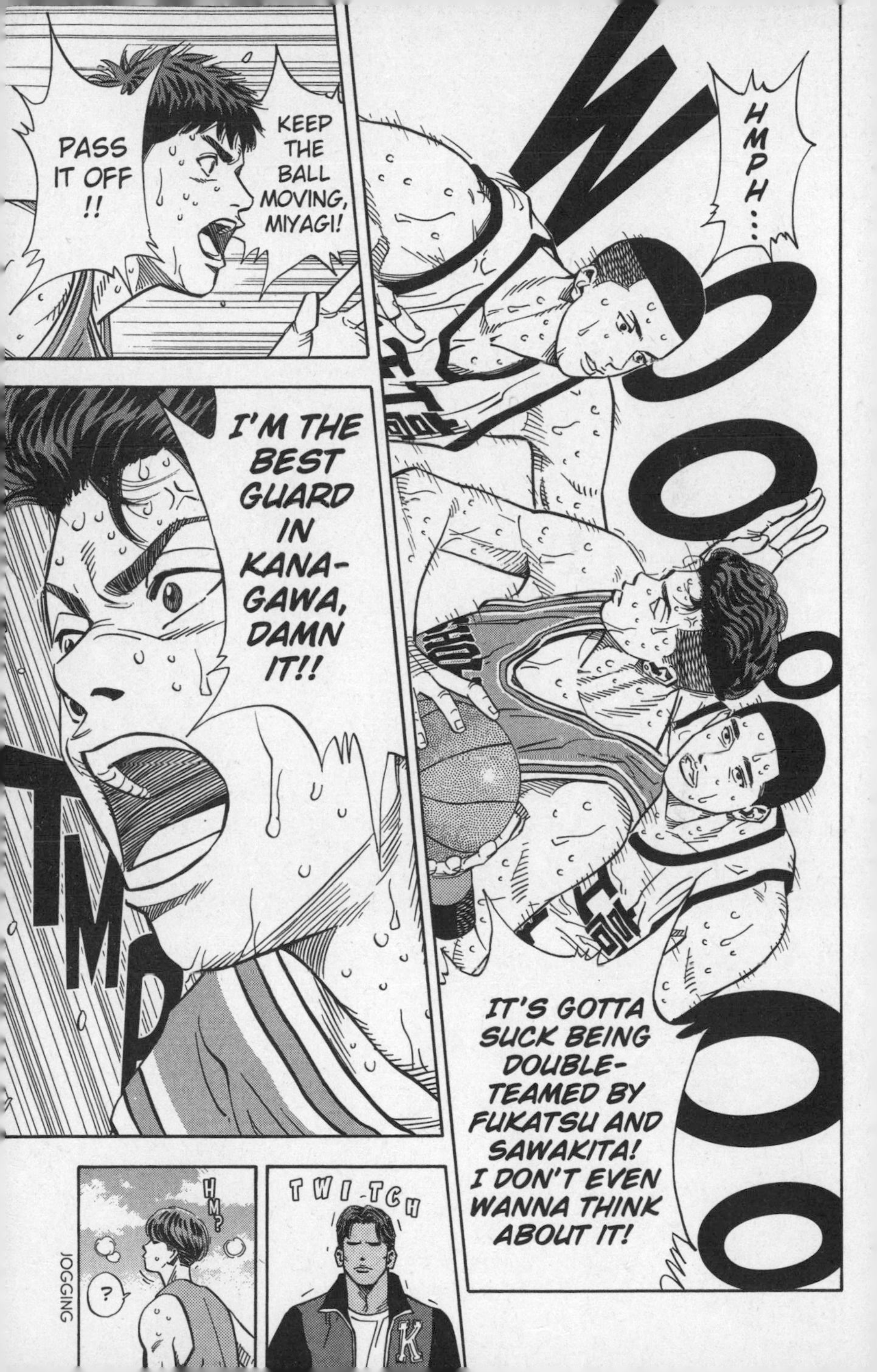
HMPH...
WOOOOOO
IT'S GOTTA SUCK BEING DOUBLE-TEAMED BY FUKATSU AND SAWAKITA! I DON'T EVEN WANNA THINK ABOUT IT!
KEEP THE BALL MOVING, MIYAGI!
PASS IT OFF !!
I'M THE BEST GUARD IN KANA-GAWA, DAMN IT!!
TMP
TWI-TCH
HMP?
?
JOGGING

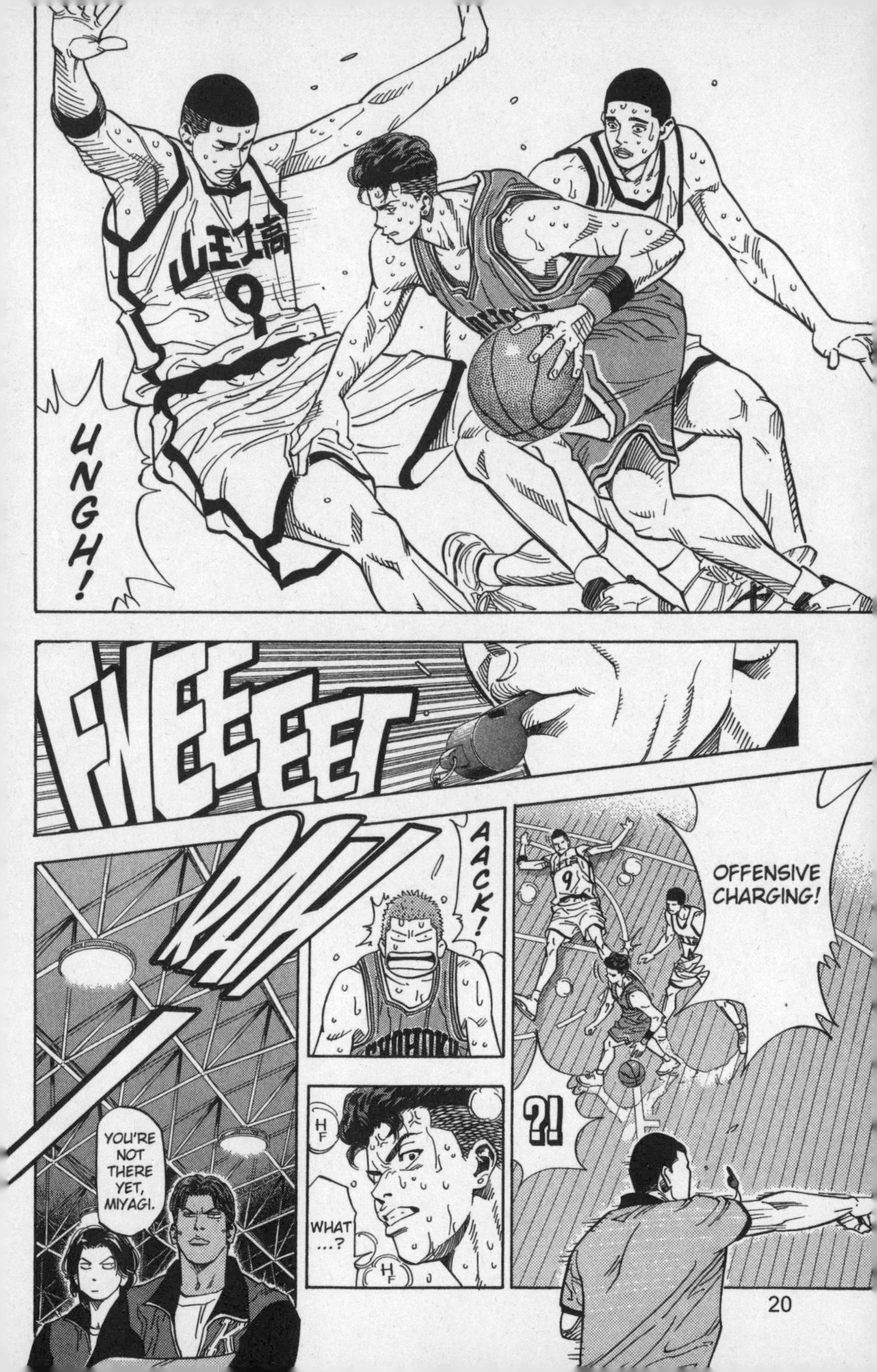
UNGH!
WHEEEET
OFFENSIVE CHARGING!
?!
AACK!
HF
WHAT ...?
HF
YOU'RE NOT THERE YET, MIYAGI.

READ THIS WAY

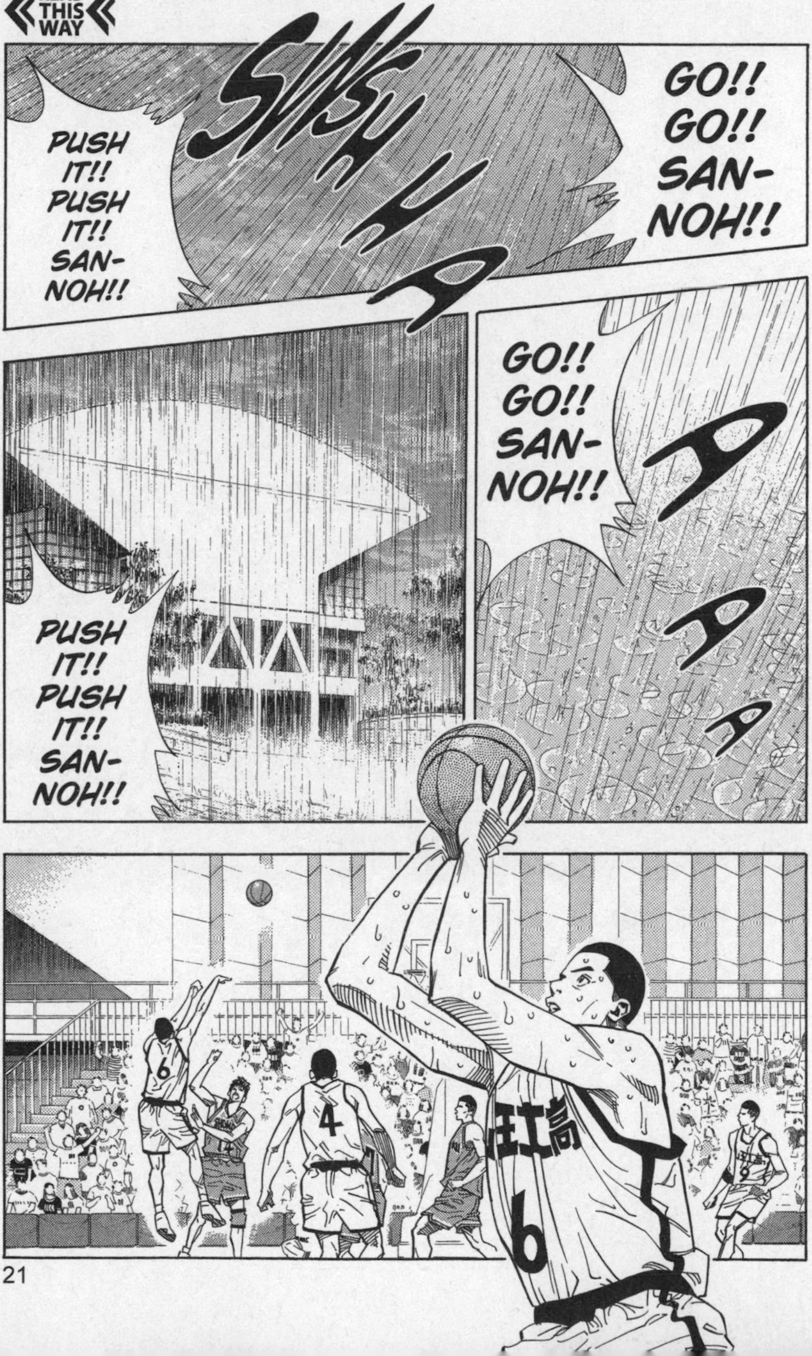
GO!! GO!! SAN-NOH!!
SWSHHA
PUSH IT!! PUSH IT!! SAN-NOH!!
GO!! GO!! SAN-NOH!!
AAA
PUSH IT!! PUSH IT!! SAN-NOH!!

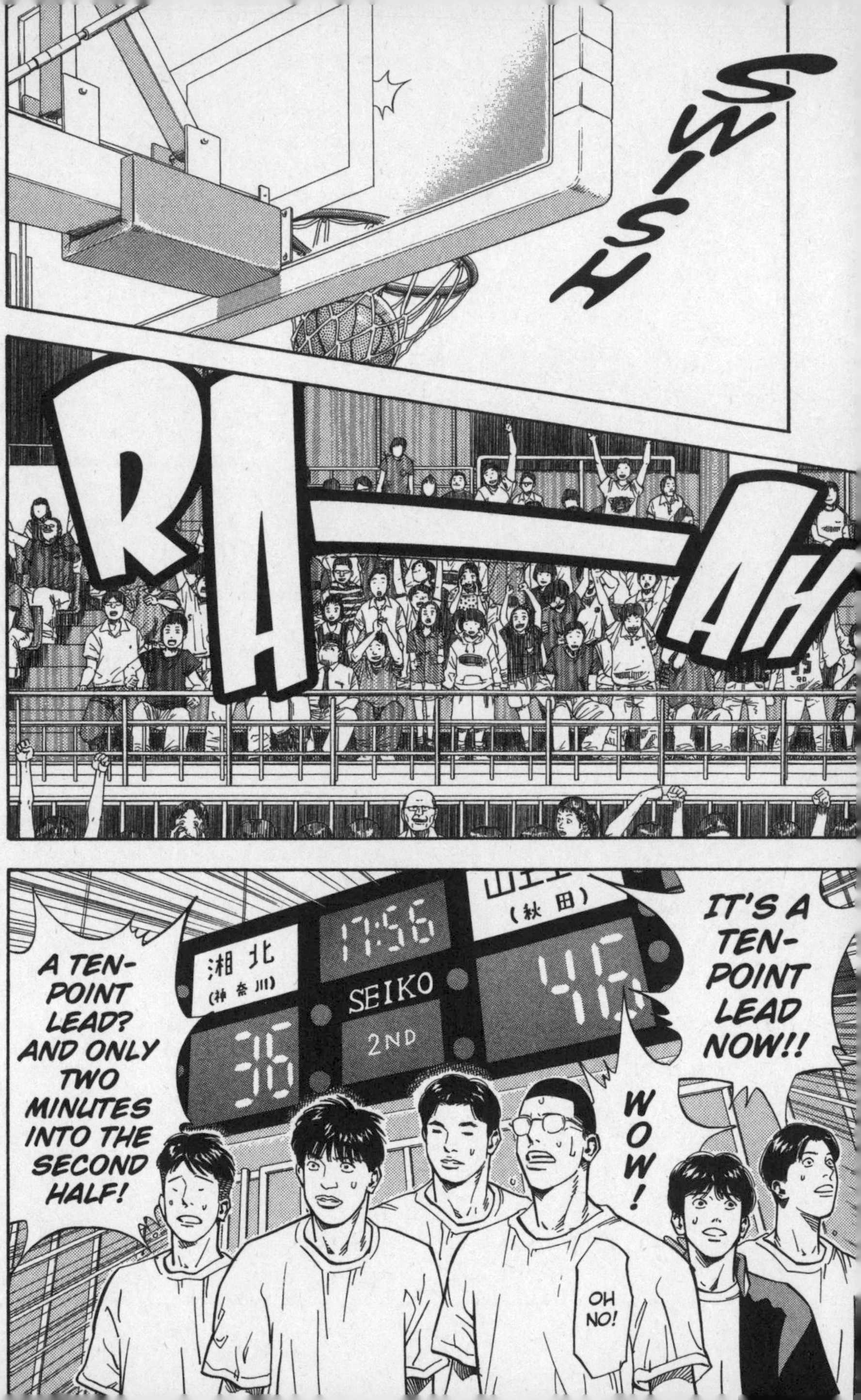
SWISH
RAAAH
IT'S A TEN-POINT LEAD NOW!!
17:56
(秋田)
湘北
(神奈川)
SEIKO
46
36
2ND
WOW!
A TEN-POINT LEAD? AND ONLY TWO MINUTES INTO THE SECOND HALF!
OH NO!

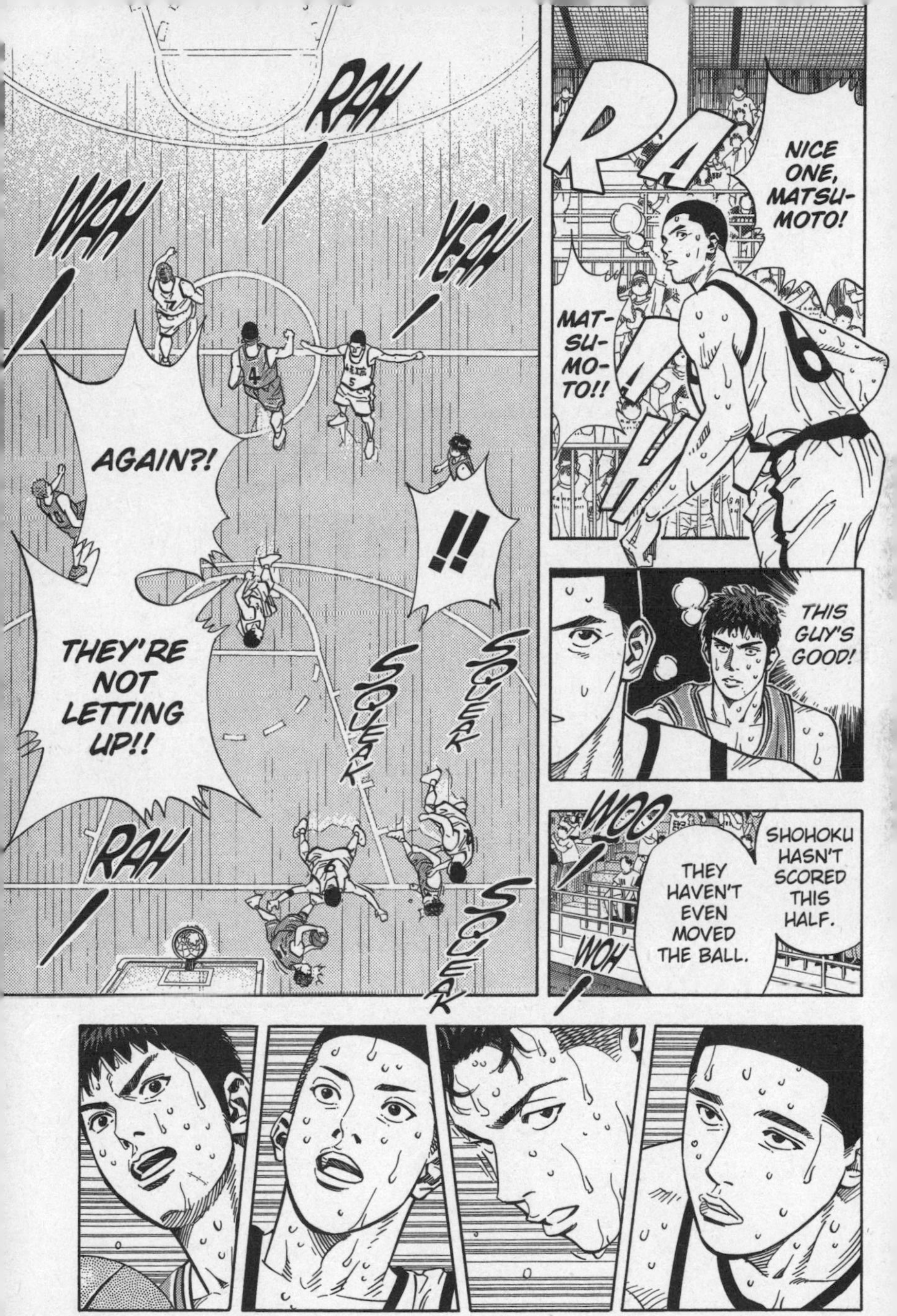
RAAH
NICE ONE, MATSUMOTO!
MATSUMOTO!!
THIS GUY'S GOOD!
SHOHOKU HASN'T SCORED THIS HALF.
THEY HAVEN'T EVEN MOVED THE BALL.
WOO!
WOH!
RAH!
YEAH!
WAH!
AGAIN?!
!!
THEY'RE NOT LETTING UP!!
SQUEAK
SQUEAK
SQUEAK
RAH!

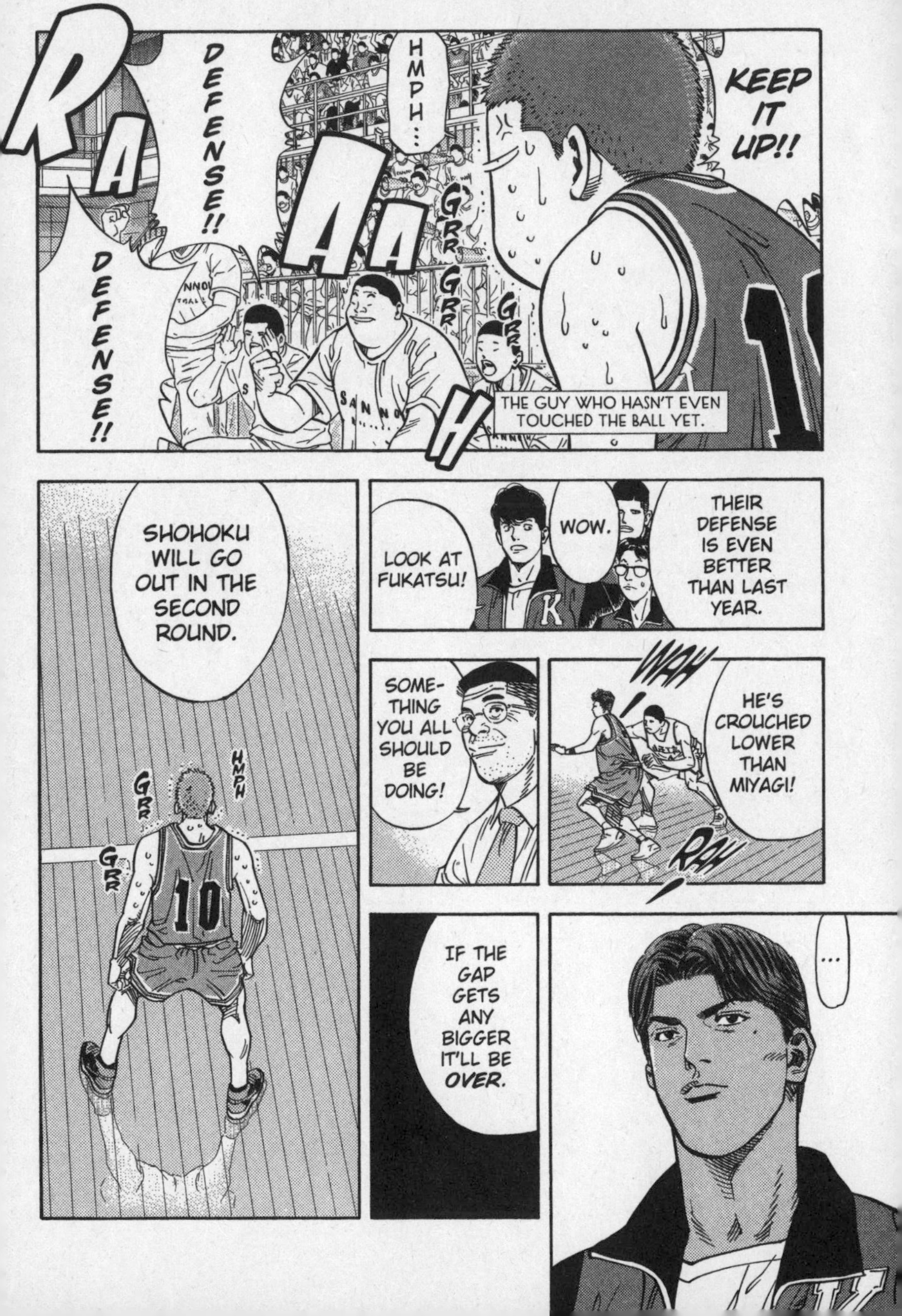
KEEP IT UP!!
HMPH...
DEFENSE!!
DEFENSE!!
RAAAAH
GRR GRR GRR
THE GUY WHO HASN'T EVEN TOUCHED THE BALL YET.
THEIR DEFENSE IS EVEN BETTER THAN LAST YEAR.
WOW.
LOOK AT FUKATSU!
WAH
HE'S CROUCHED LOWER THAN MIYAGI!
RAH
SOME-THING YOU ALL SHOULD BE DOING!
...
IF THE GAP GETS ANY BIGGER IT'LL BE OVER.
SHOHOKU WILL GO OUT IN THE SECOND ROUND.
HMPH
GRR
GRR

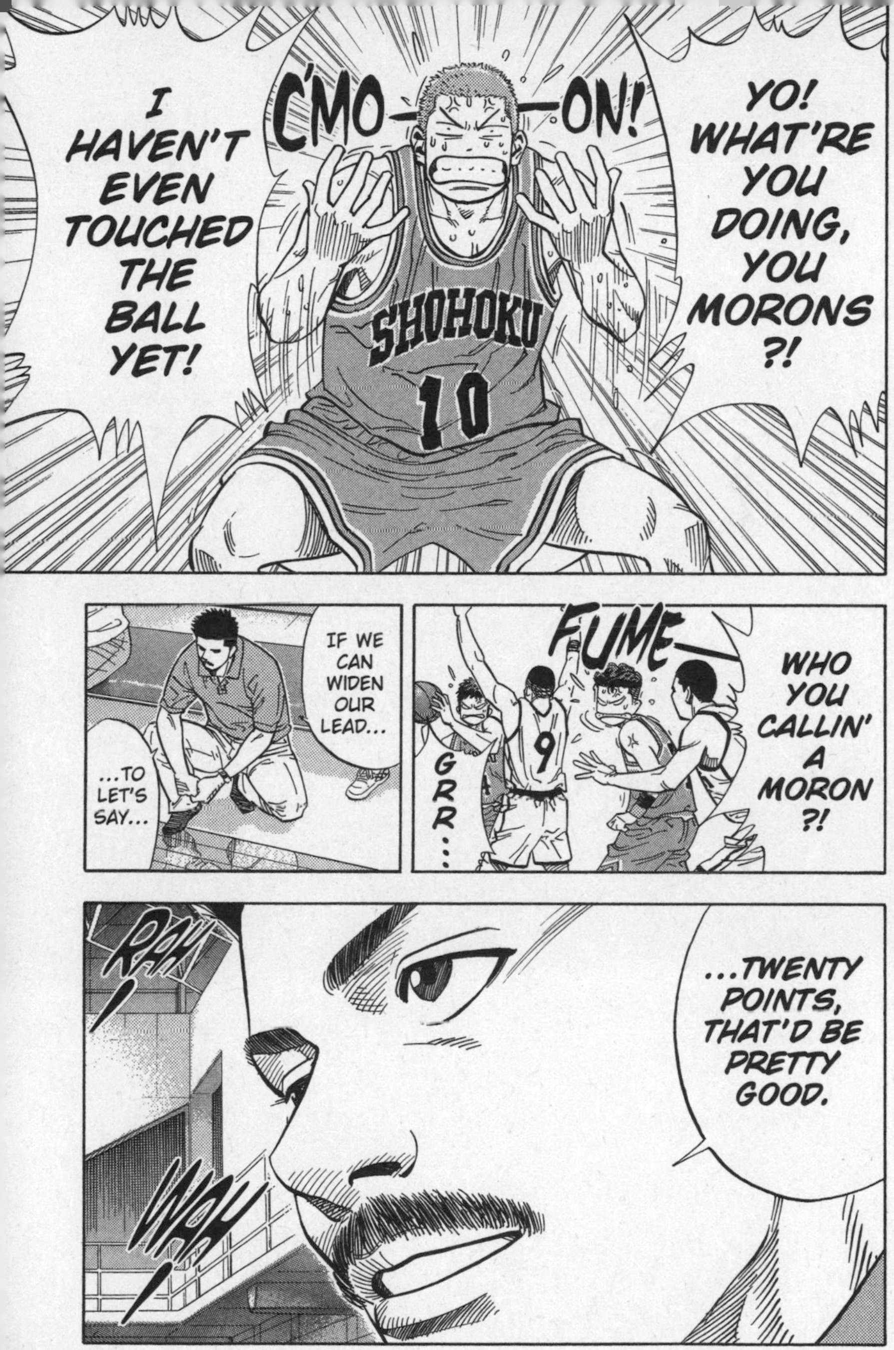
YO! WHAT'RE YOU DOING, YOU MORONS?!
C'MO—ON!
I HAVEN'T EVEN TOUCHED THE BALL YET!
FUME
WHO YOU CALLIN' A MORON?!
GRR...
IF WE CAN WIDEN OUR LEAD...
...TO LET'S SAY...
...TWENTY POINTS, THAT'D BE PRETTY GOOD.
RAH!
WAH!

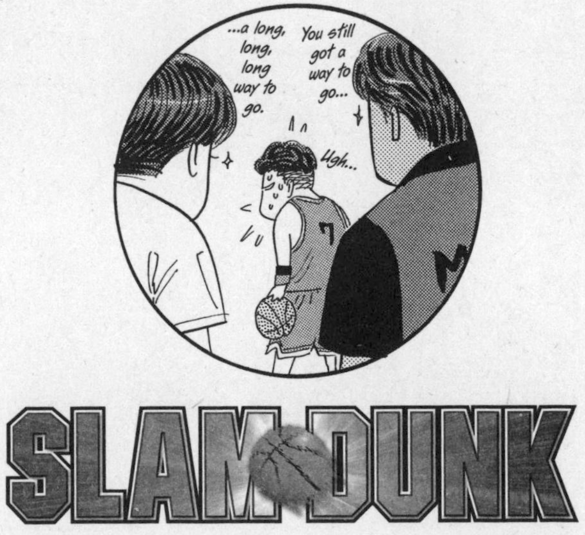
You still got a way to go...
...a long, long, long way to go.
Ugh...

SLAM DUNK

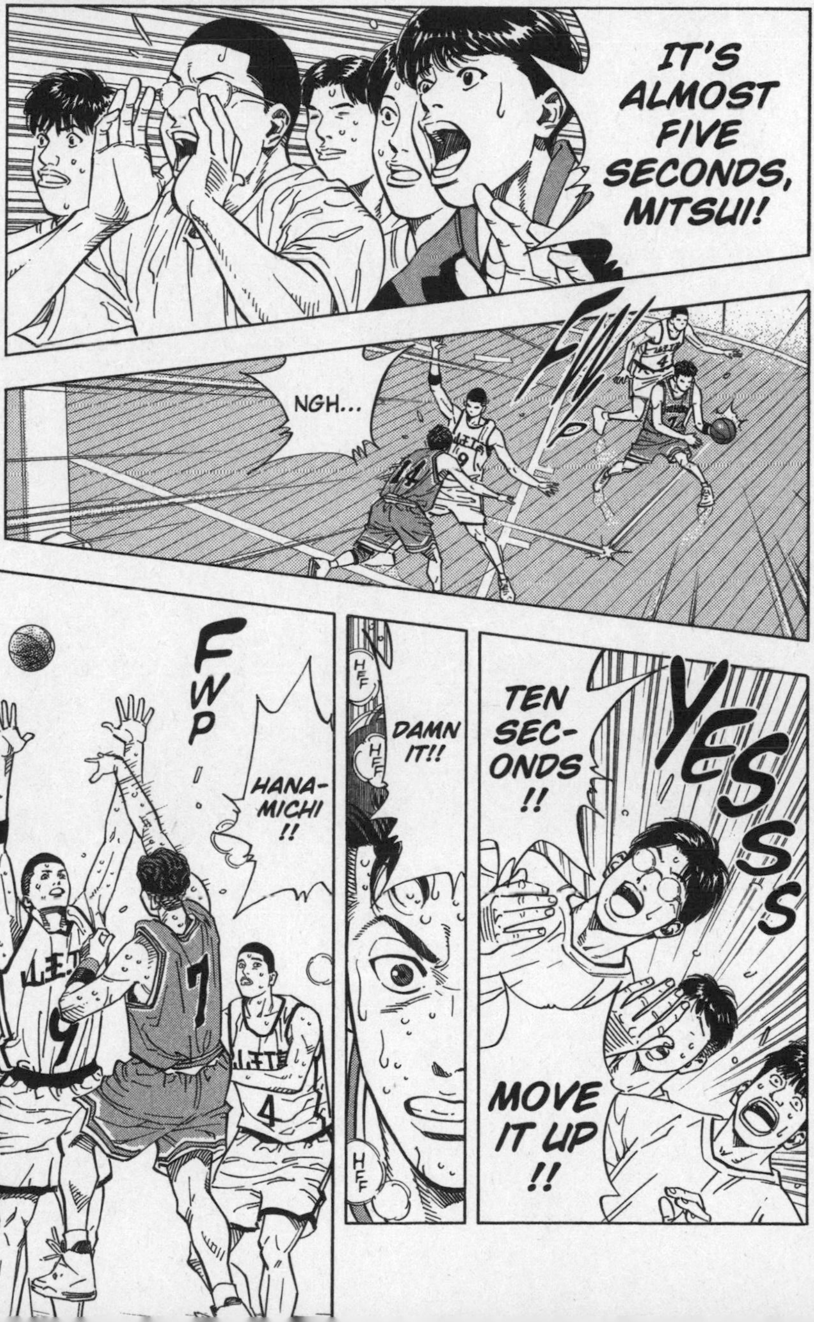
IT'S ALMOST FIVE SECONDS, MITSUI!
NGH...
TEN SECONDS!!
YESSSS
MOVE IT UP!!
HEF
DAMN IT!!
HEF
HEF
FWP
HANAMICHI!!

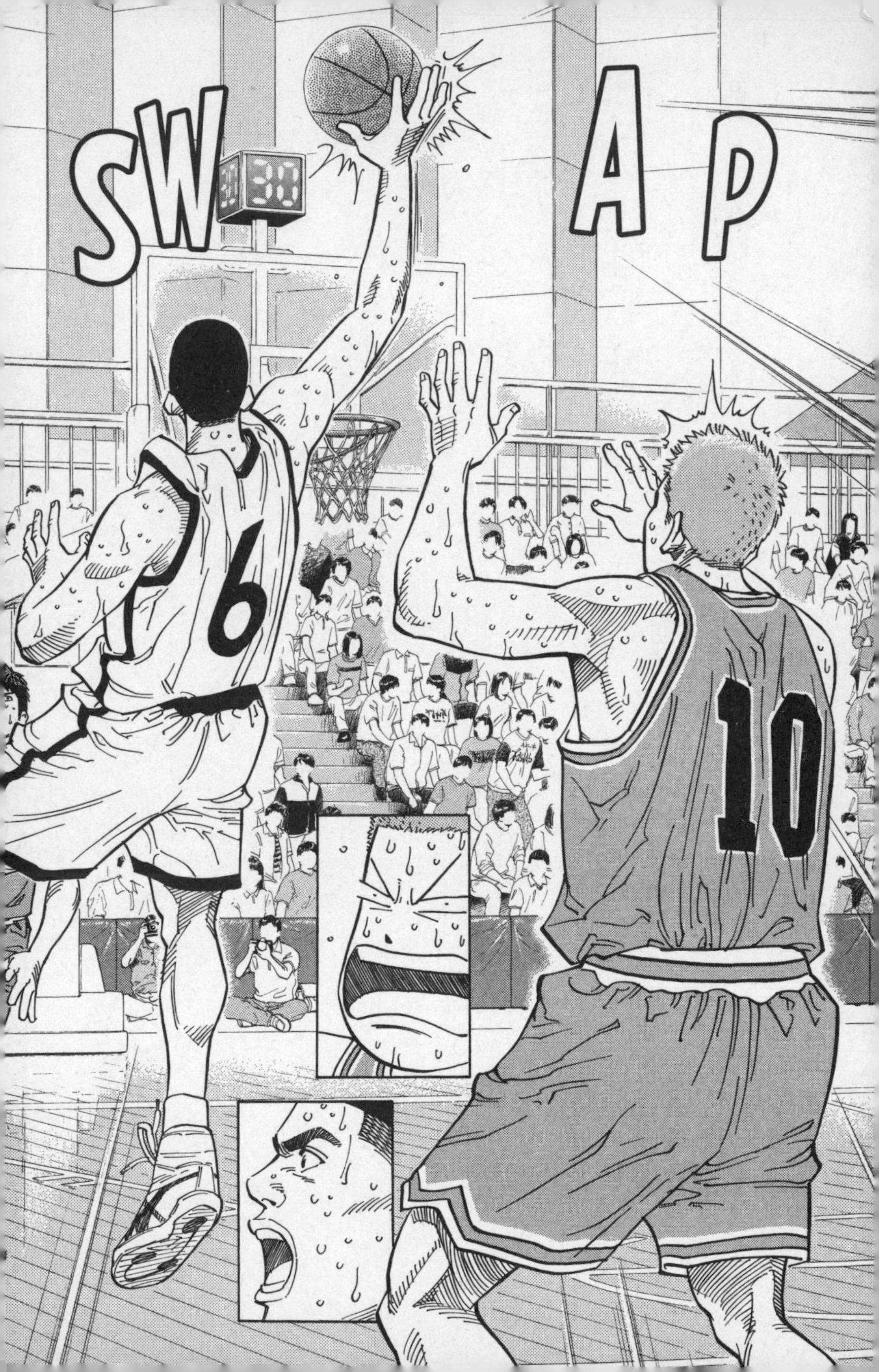
SWAP

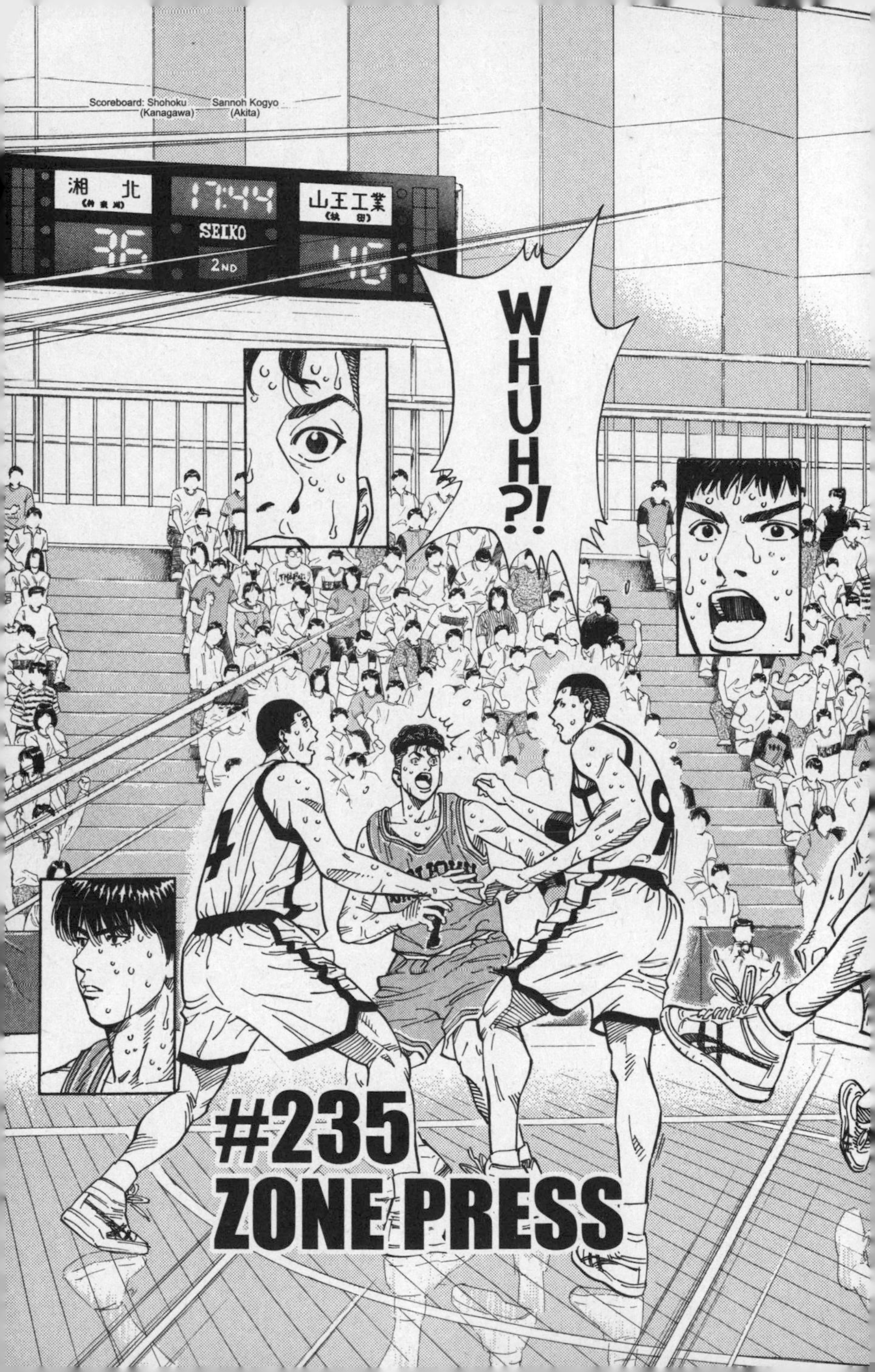
Scoreboard: Shohoku (Kanagawa) Sannoh Kogyo (Akita)
湘北
17:44
山王工業
SEIKO
36
2ND
46
WHUH?!
#235
ZONE PRESS

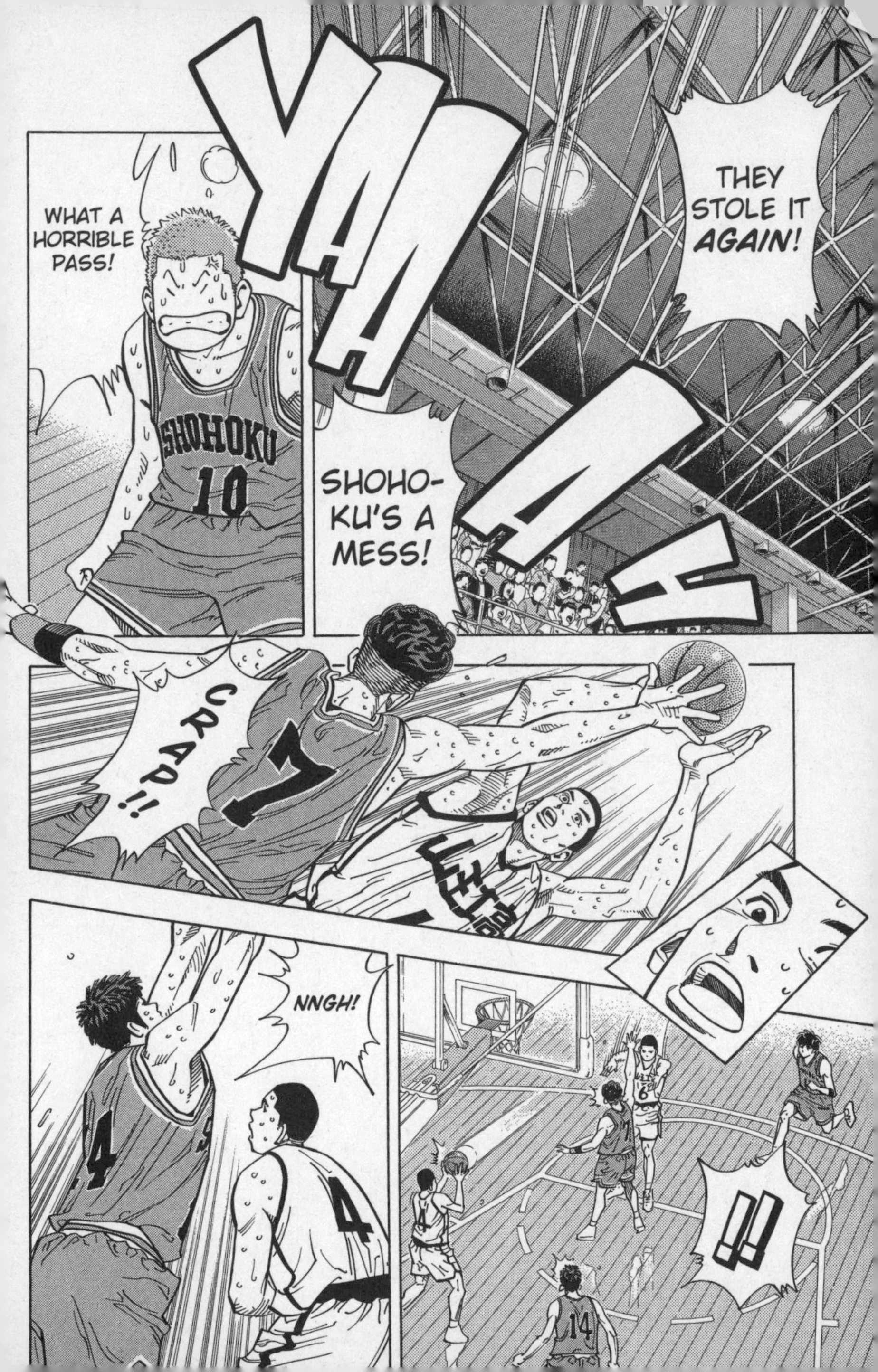
THEY STOLE IT AGAIN!
YAAAH
SHOHOKU'S A MESS!
WHAT A HORRIBLE PASS!
SHOHOKU
10
CRAP!!
7
!!
14
NNGH!
4
4

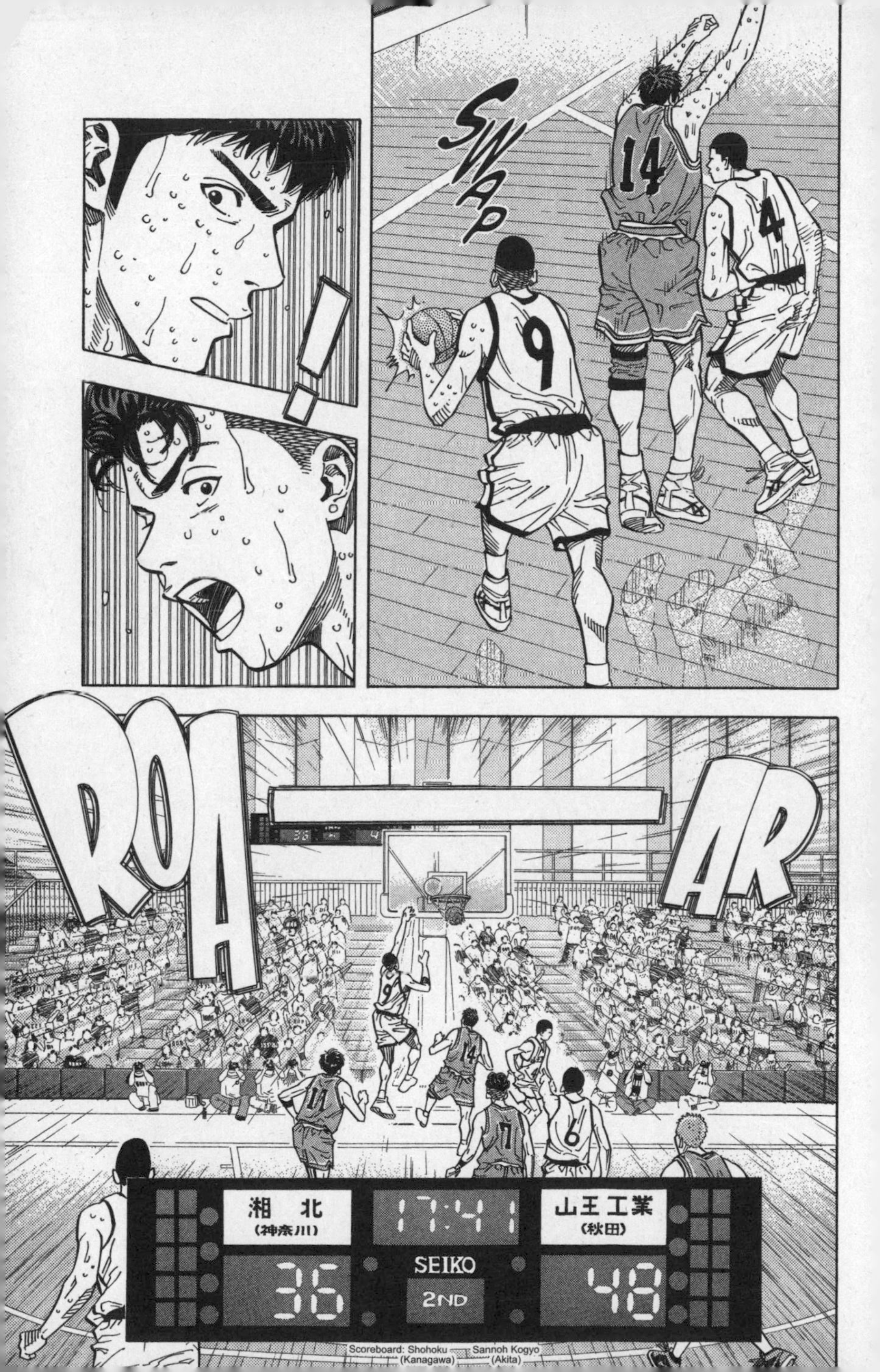
SWAP
!
ROA—AR
湘 北
(神奈川)
17:41
山王工業
(秋田)
36
SEIKO
2ND
48
Scoreboard: Shohoku (Kanagawa) — Sannoh Kogyo (Akita)

WOH
RUKAWA! MOVE DOWN!
HELP THEM MOVE THE BALL UP!
YAH
HMPH ...
WOO
4
11
6
5
7
14
9
4
7
10
THIS IS THE BASIC POSITIONING FOR THIS DEFENSE.
FIRST THEY CLOSE IN ON THE PASSER, SO HE ONLY HAS ONE PASS OPTION.
THEY THEN QUICKLY DOUBLE-TEAM THE BALL CARRIER ...
... FORCING HIM TO THE EDGE OF THE COURT.

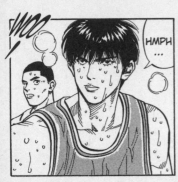

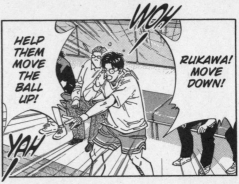

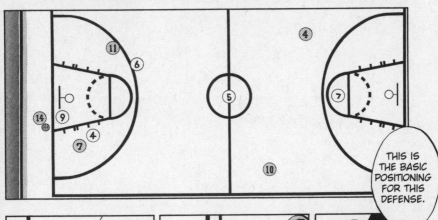

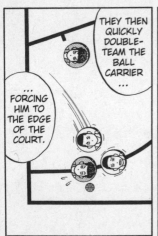

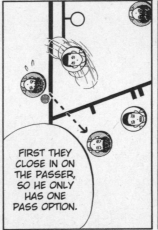

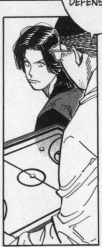

READ THIS WAY

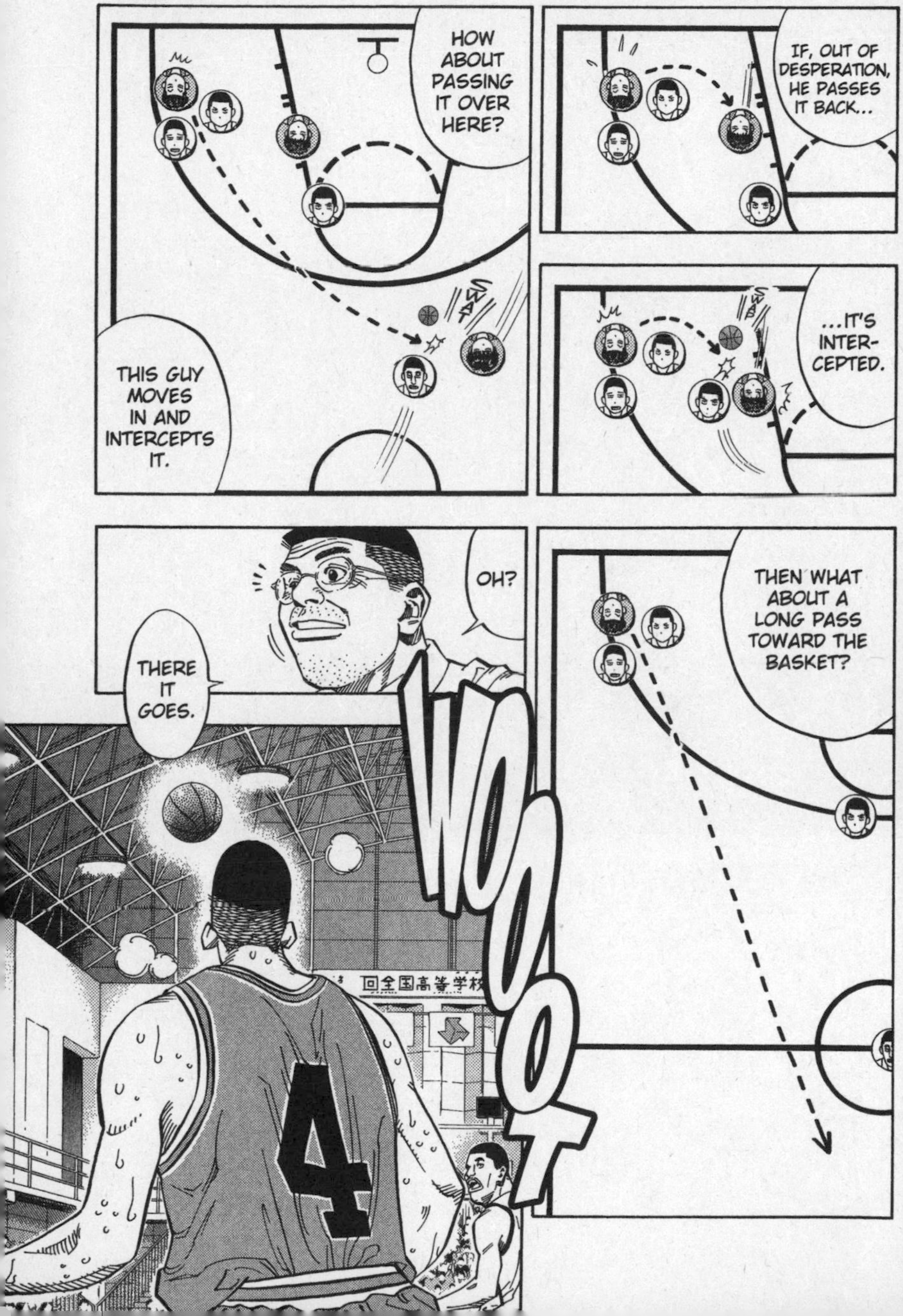
IF, OUT OF DESPERATION, HE PASSES IT BACK...
SWAP
...IT'S INTERCEPTED.
HOW ABOUT PASSING IT OVER HERE?
SWAT
THIS GUY MOVES IN AND INTERCEPTS IT.
THEN WHAT ABOUT A LONG PASS TOWARD THE BASKET?
OH?
THERE IT GOES.
WOOOOT
回全国高等学校

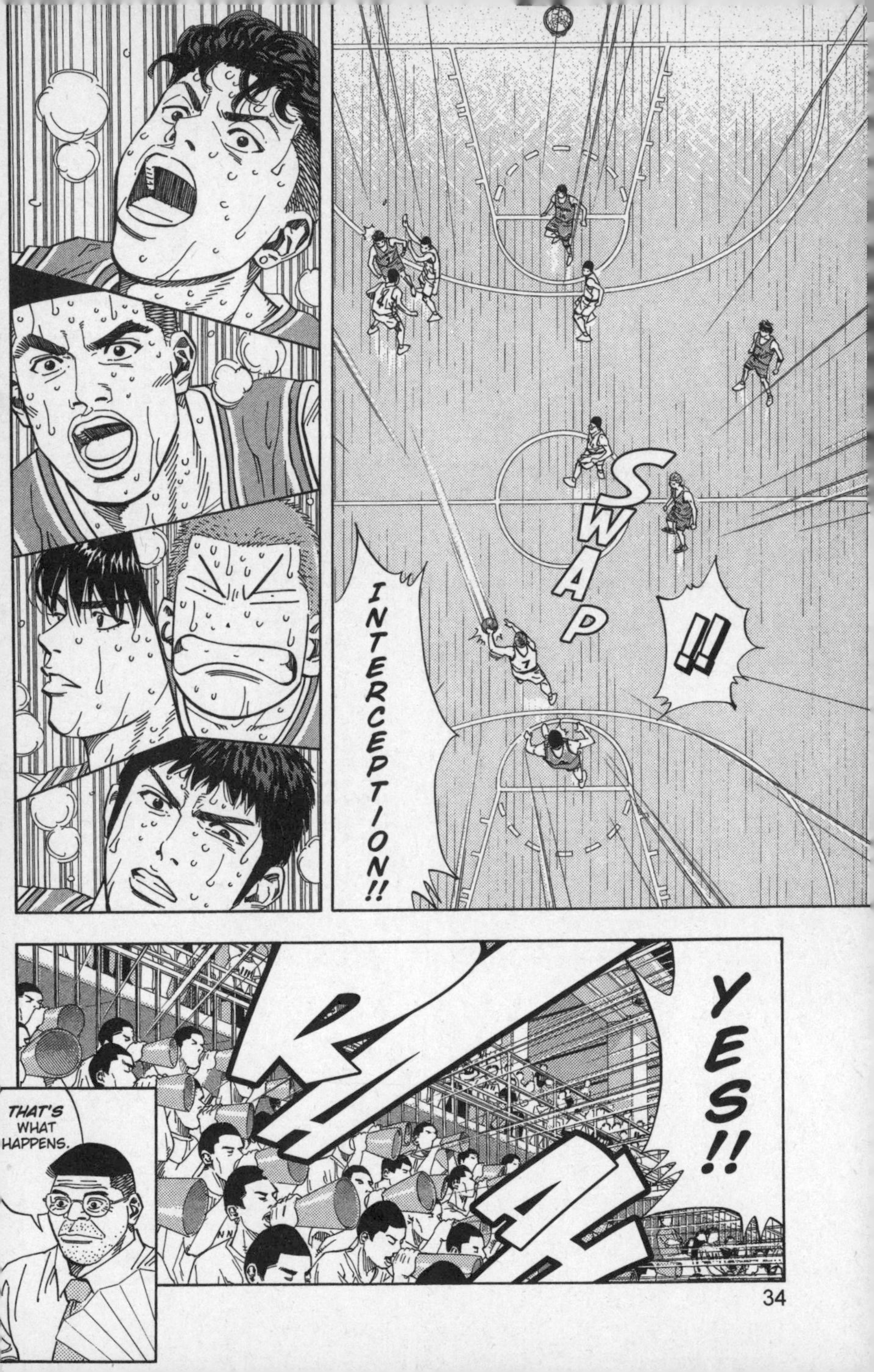
INTERCEPTION!!
SWAP
!!
YES!!
THAT'S WHAT HAPPENS.

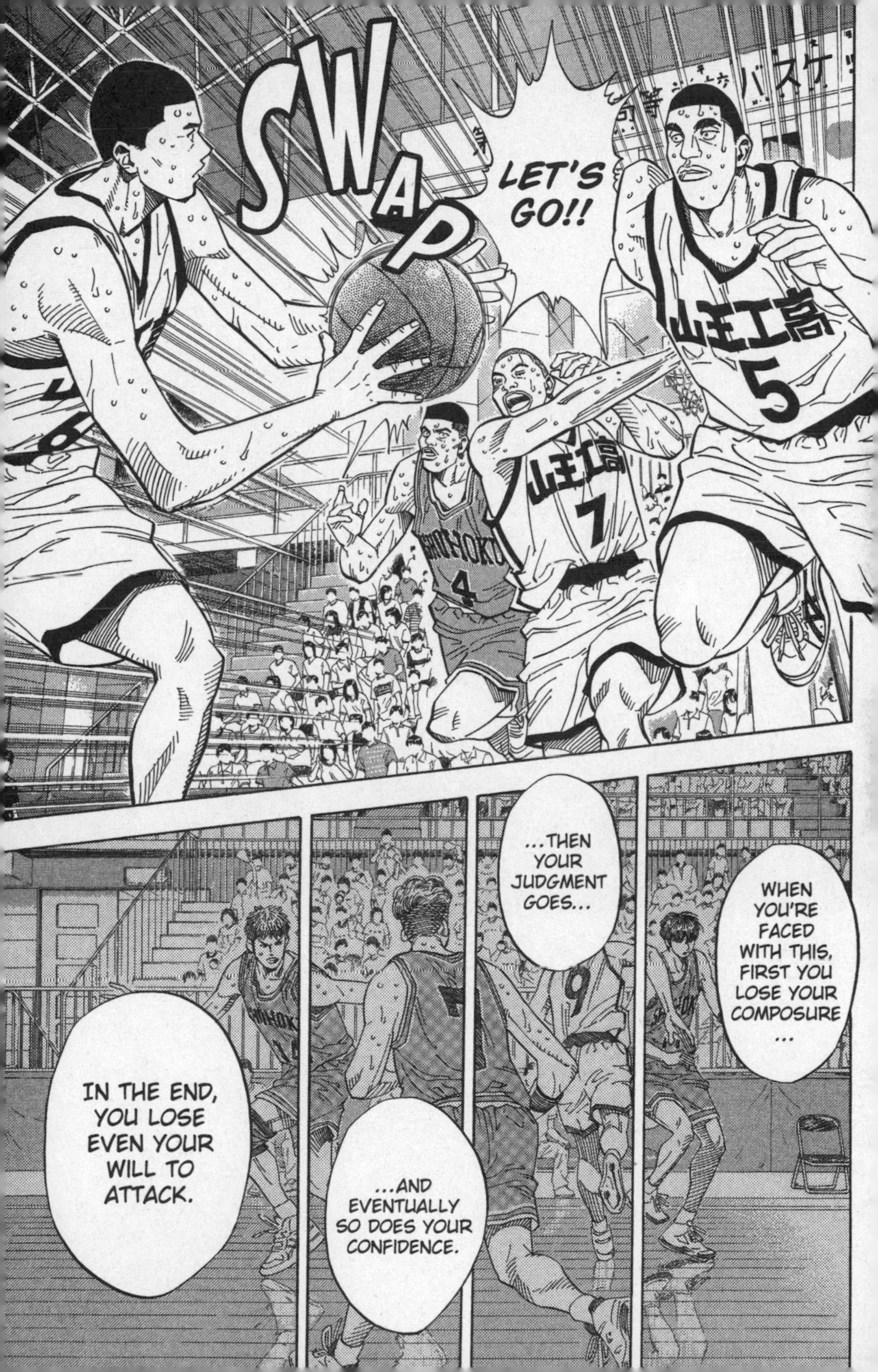
LET'S GO!!
SWAP
WHEN YOU'RE FACED WITH THIS, FIRST YOU LOSE YOUR COMPOSURE ...
...THEN YOUR JUDGMENT GOES...
...AND EVENTUALLY SO DOES YOUR CONFIDENCE.
IN THE END, YOU LOSE EVEN YOUR WILL TO ATTACK.

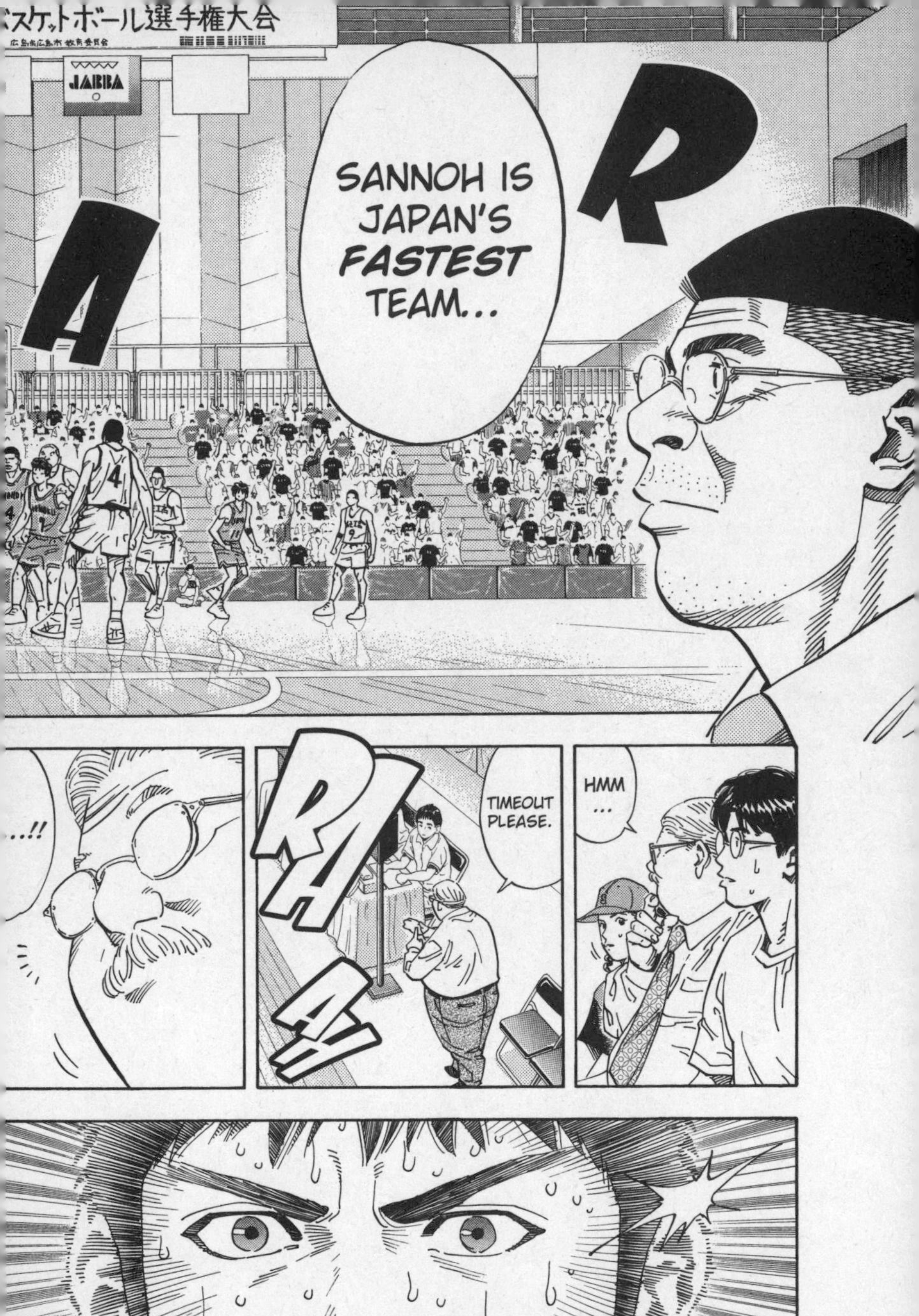
スケットボール選手権大会
JABBA
R
SANNOH IS JAPAN'S *FASTEST* TEAM...
A
HMM ...
TIMEOUT PLEASE.
RA
...!!

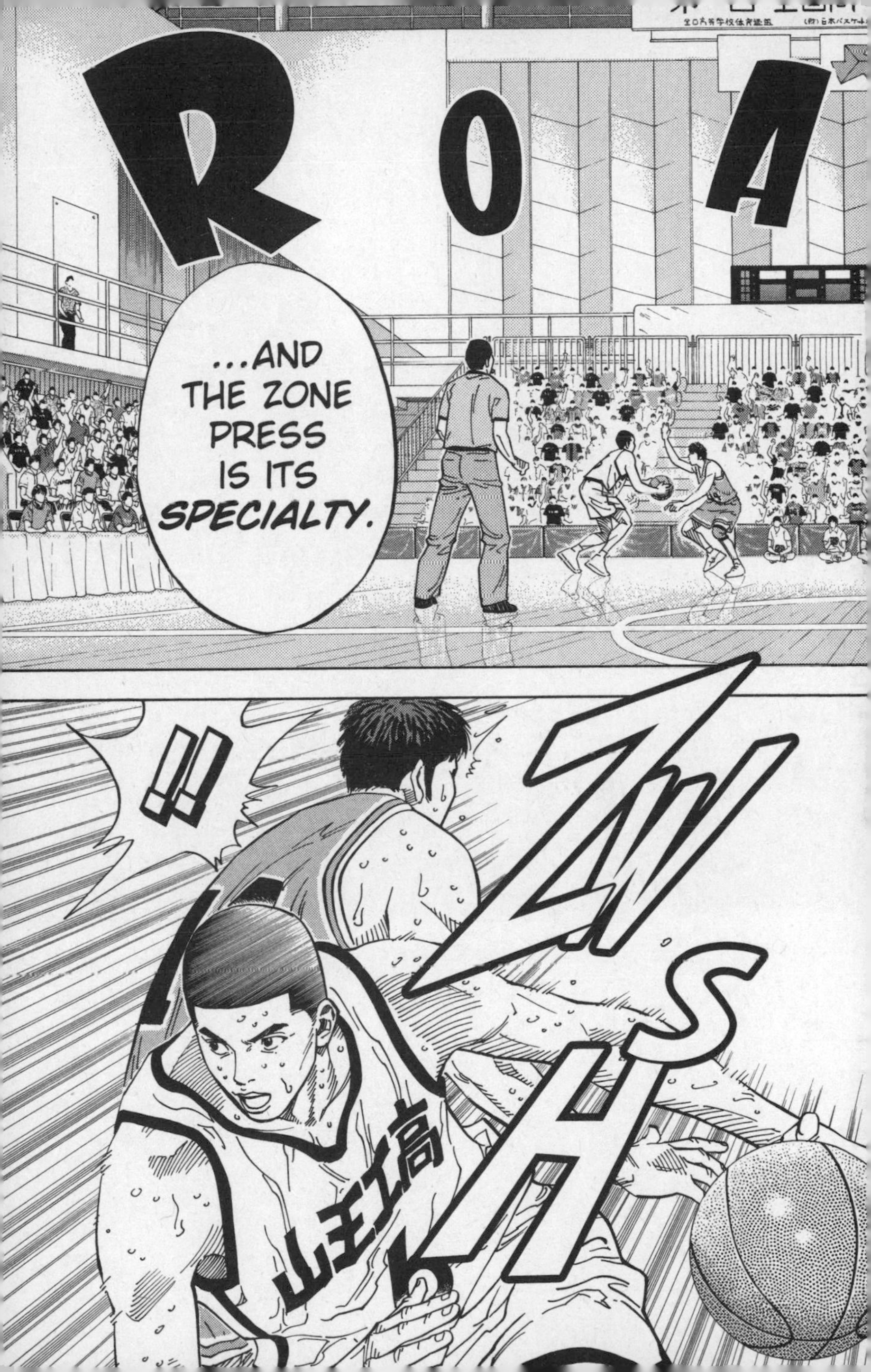
ROA
...AND THE ZONE PRESS IS ITS SPECIALTY.
ZWSH
!!
山王工高

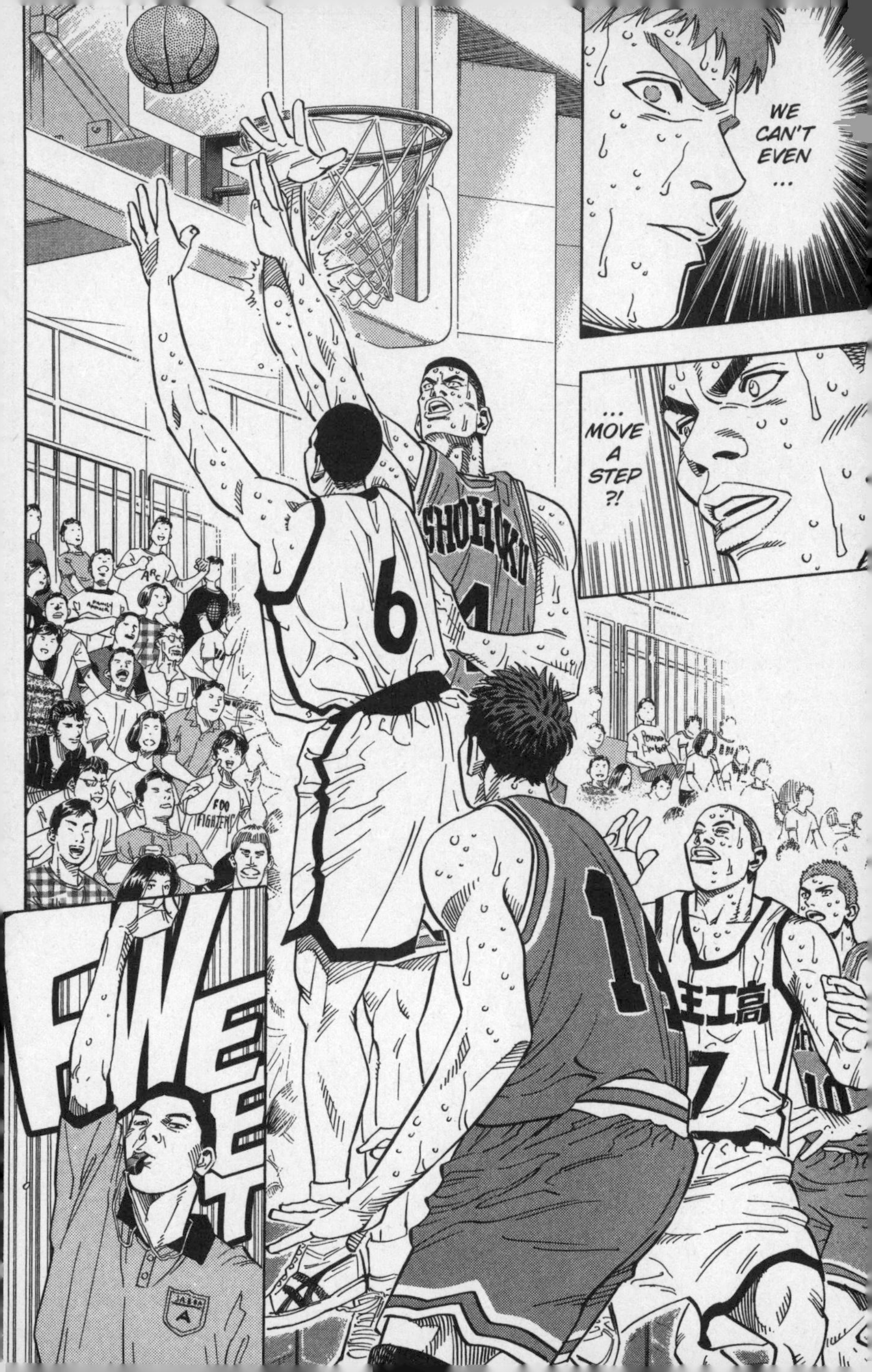
WE CAN'T EVEN ...
... MOVE A STEP ?!
FWEET

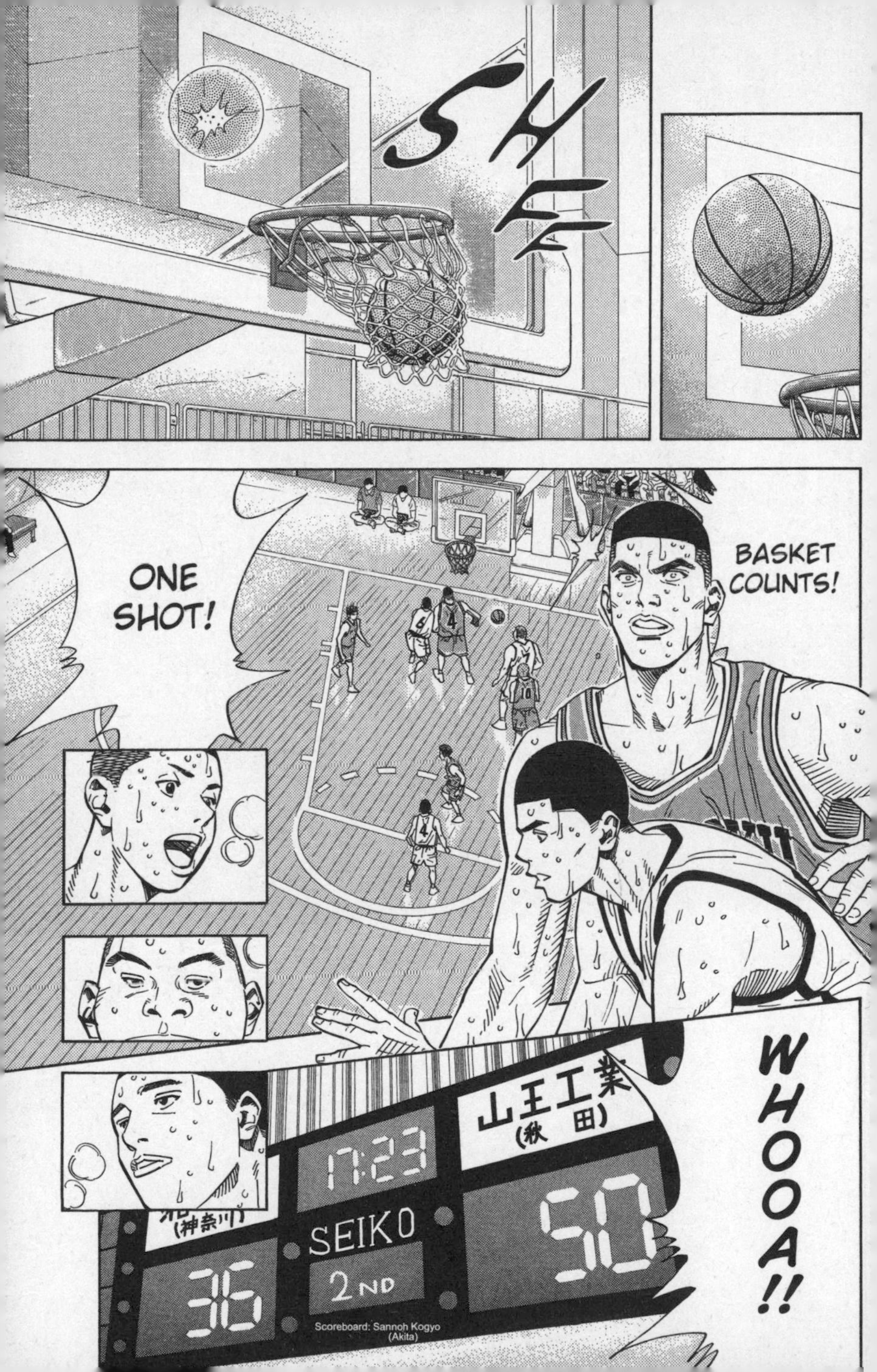
SHFF
BASKET COUNTS!
ONE SHOT!
WHOOA!!
山王工業
(秋田)
17:23
50
SEIKO
2ND
(神奈川)
36
Scoreboard: Sannoh Kogyo (Akita)

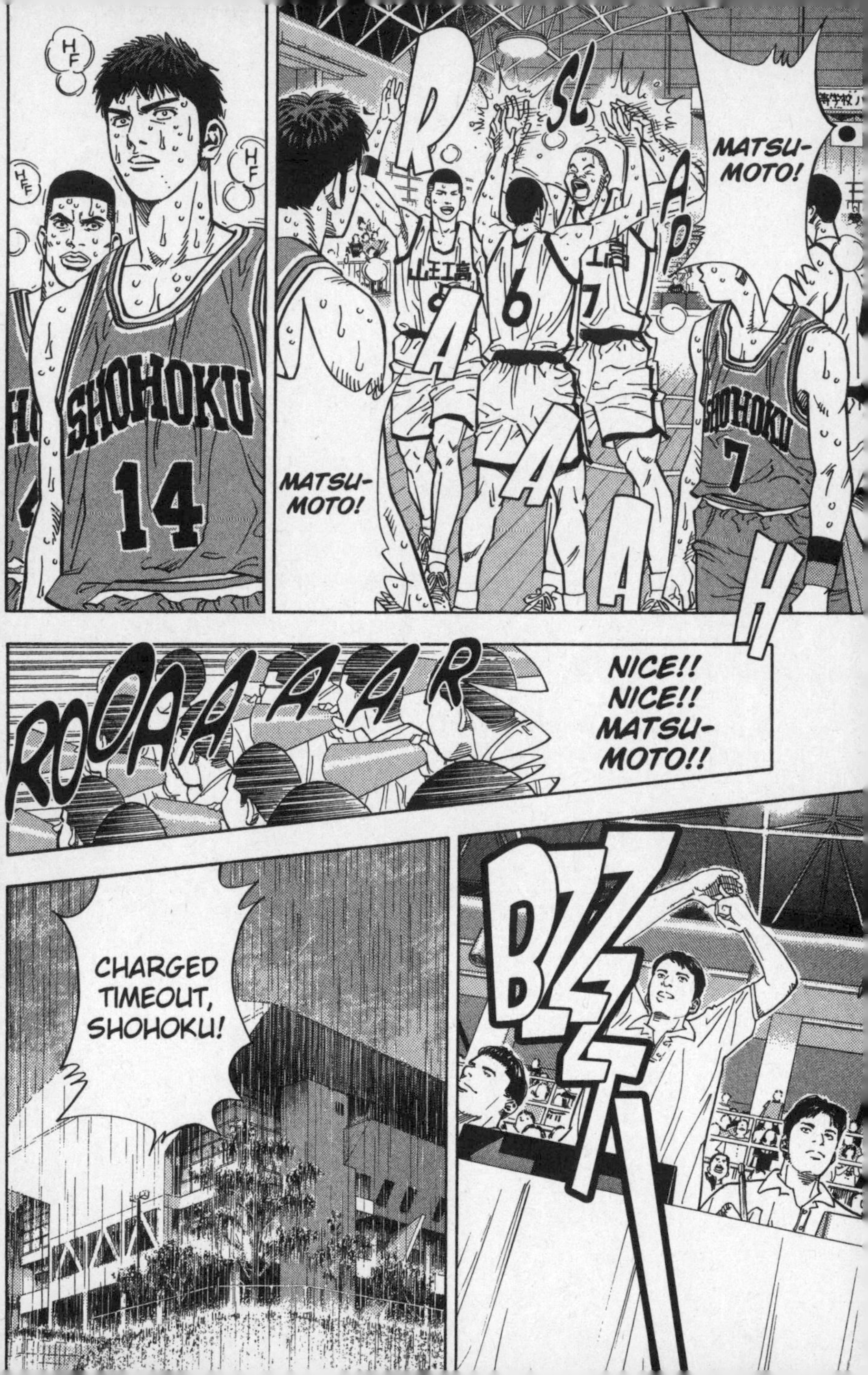
MATSU-MOTO!
SLAP
RAAAH
MATSU-MOTO!
HF
HF
HFF
NICE!! NICE!! MATSU-MOTO!!
ROOAAAAAR
BZZT
CHARGED TIMEOUT, SHOHOKU!

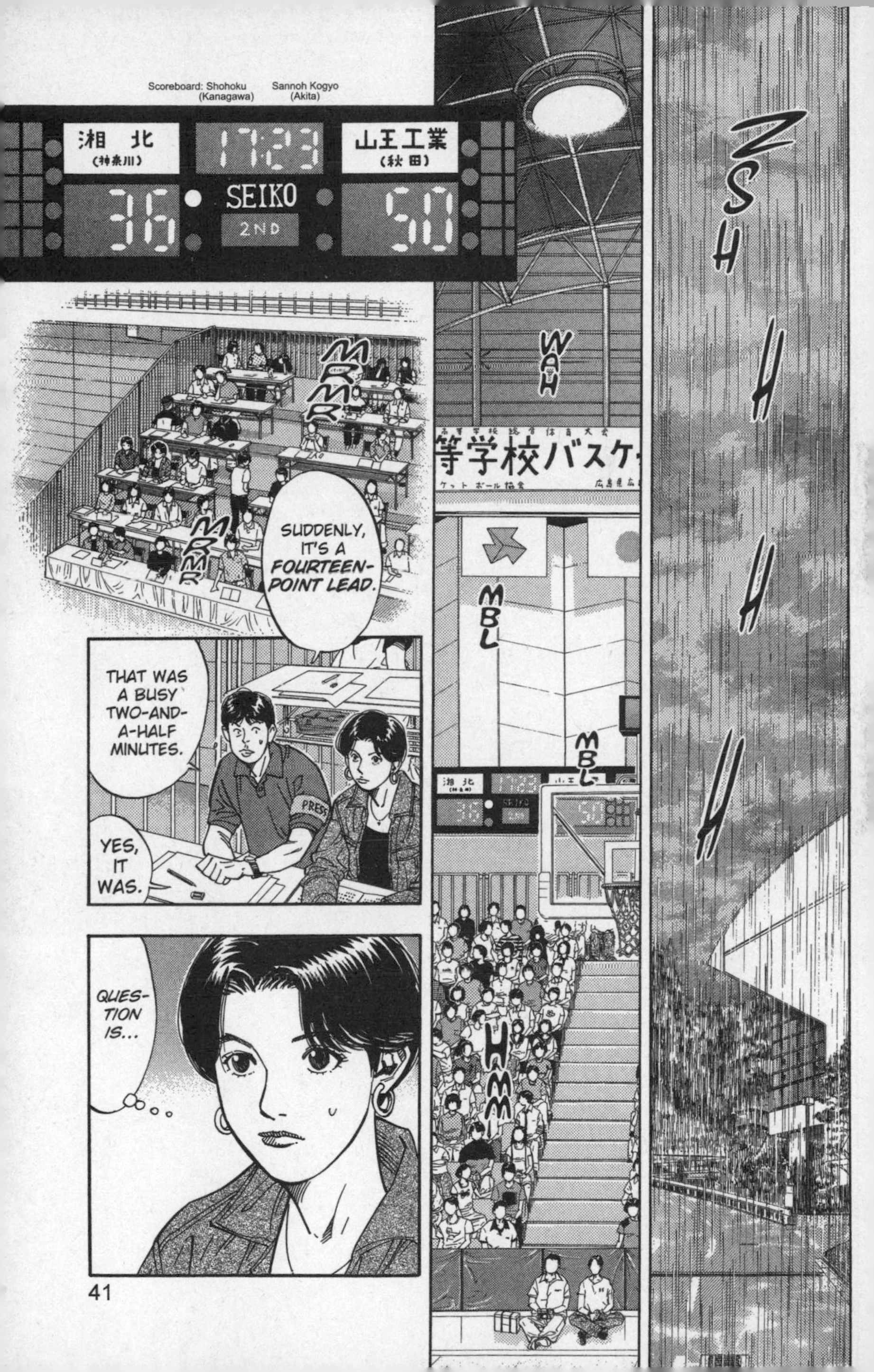
ZSHHHHHH
WAH
等学校バスケッ
MBL
MBL
HMM
Scoreboard: Shohoku (Kanagawa) Sannoh Kogyo (Akita)
湘北
(神奈川)
17:23
山王工業
(秋田)
36
SEIKO
2ND
50
MRMR
MRMR
SUDDENLY, IT'S A *FOURTEEN-POINT LEAD.*
THAT WAS A BUSY TWO-AND-A-HALF MINUTES.
YES, IT WAS.
QUESTION IS...

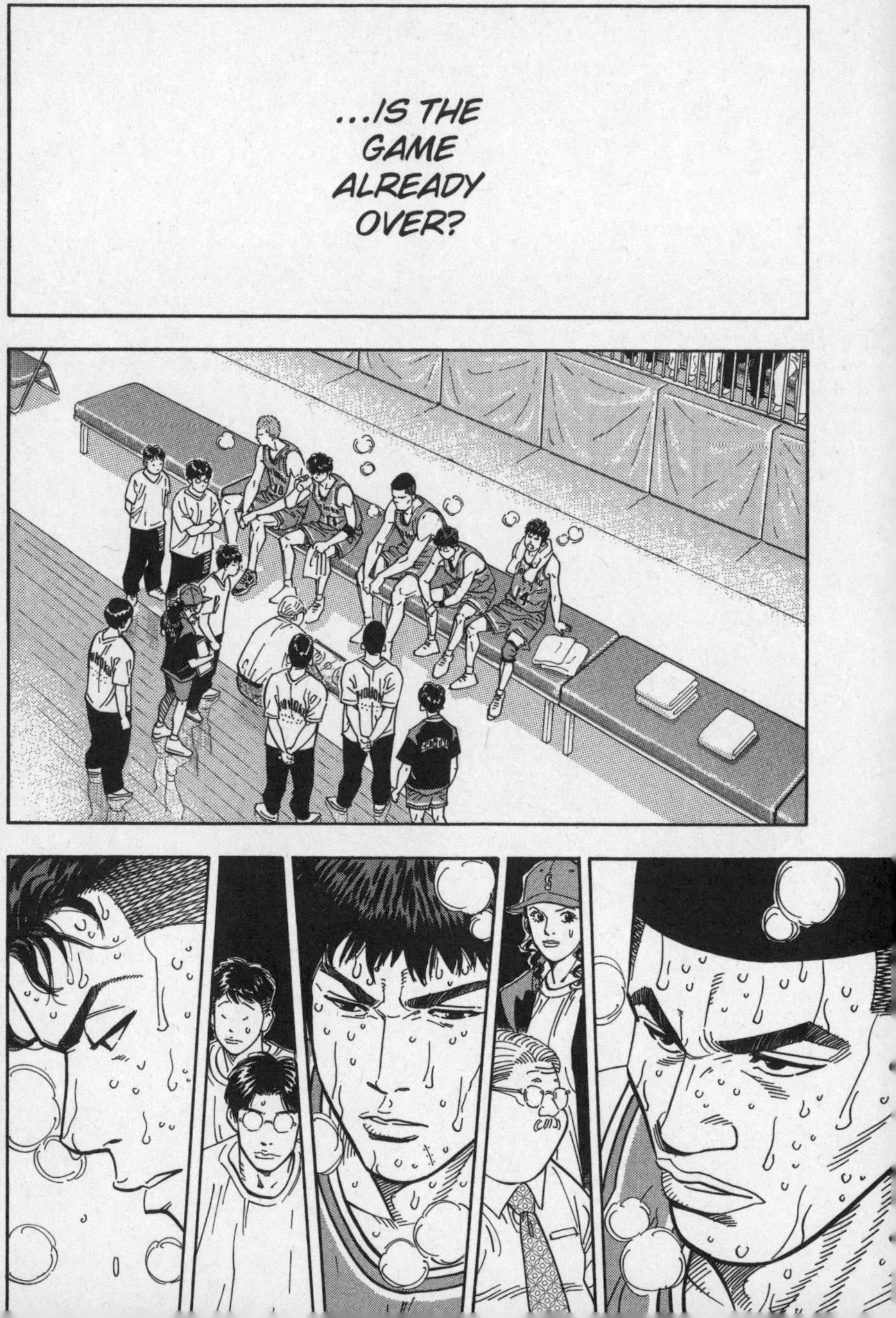
...IS THE GAME ALREADY OVER?

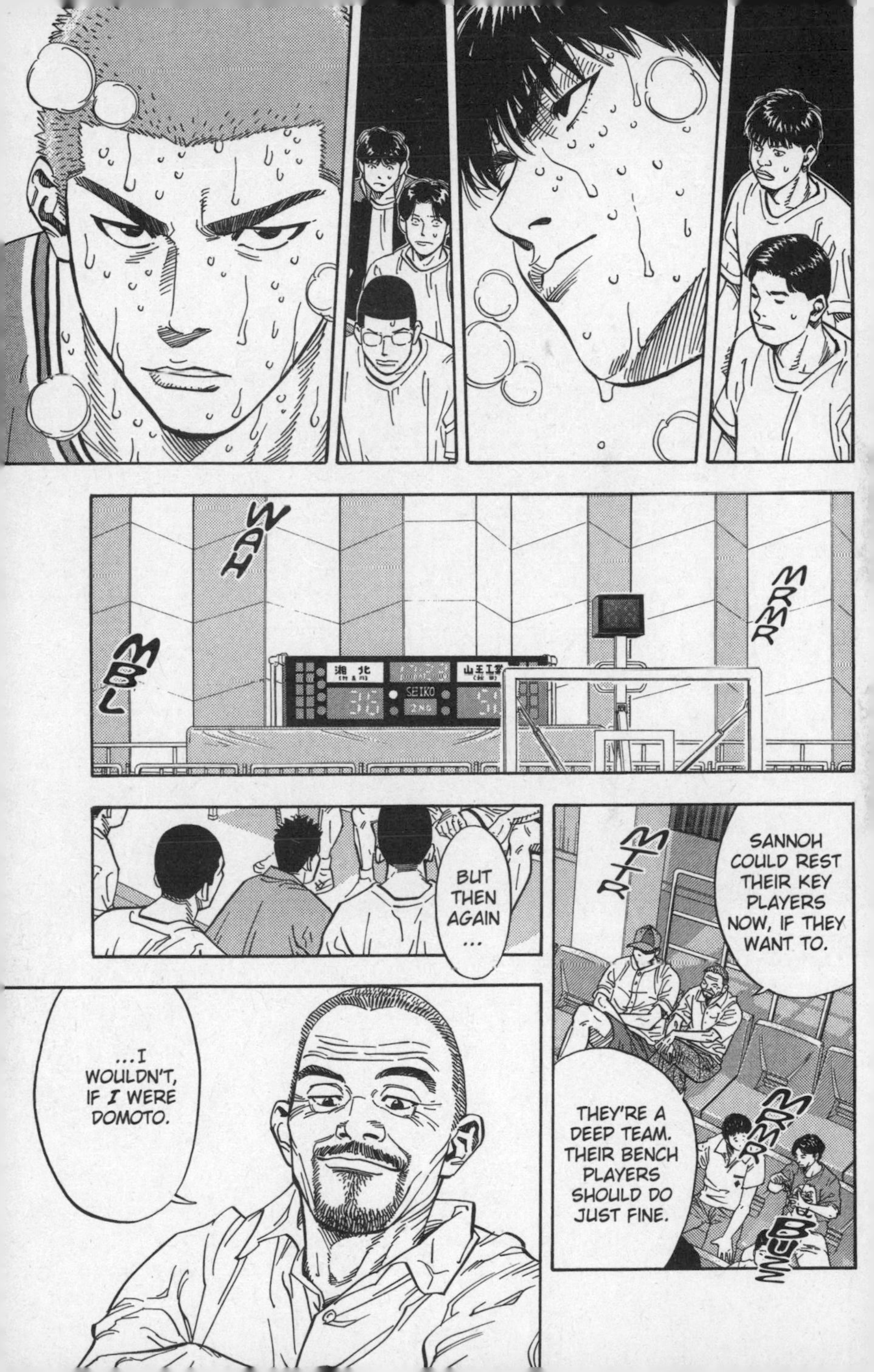
MRMR
WAH
湘北
SEIKO
MBL
MTTR
SANNOH COULD REST THEIR KEY PLAYERS NOW, IF THEY WANT TO.
THEY'RE A DEEP TEAM. THEIR BENCH PLAYERS SHOULD DO JUST FINE.
MRMR
BUZZ
BUT THEN AGAIN ...
...I WOULDN'T, IF I WERE DOMOTO.

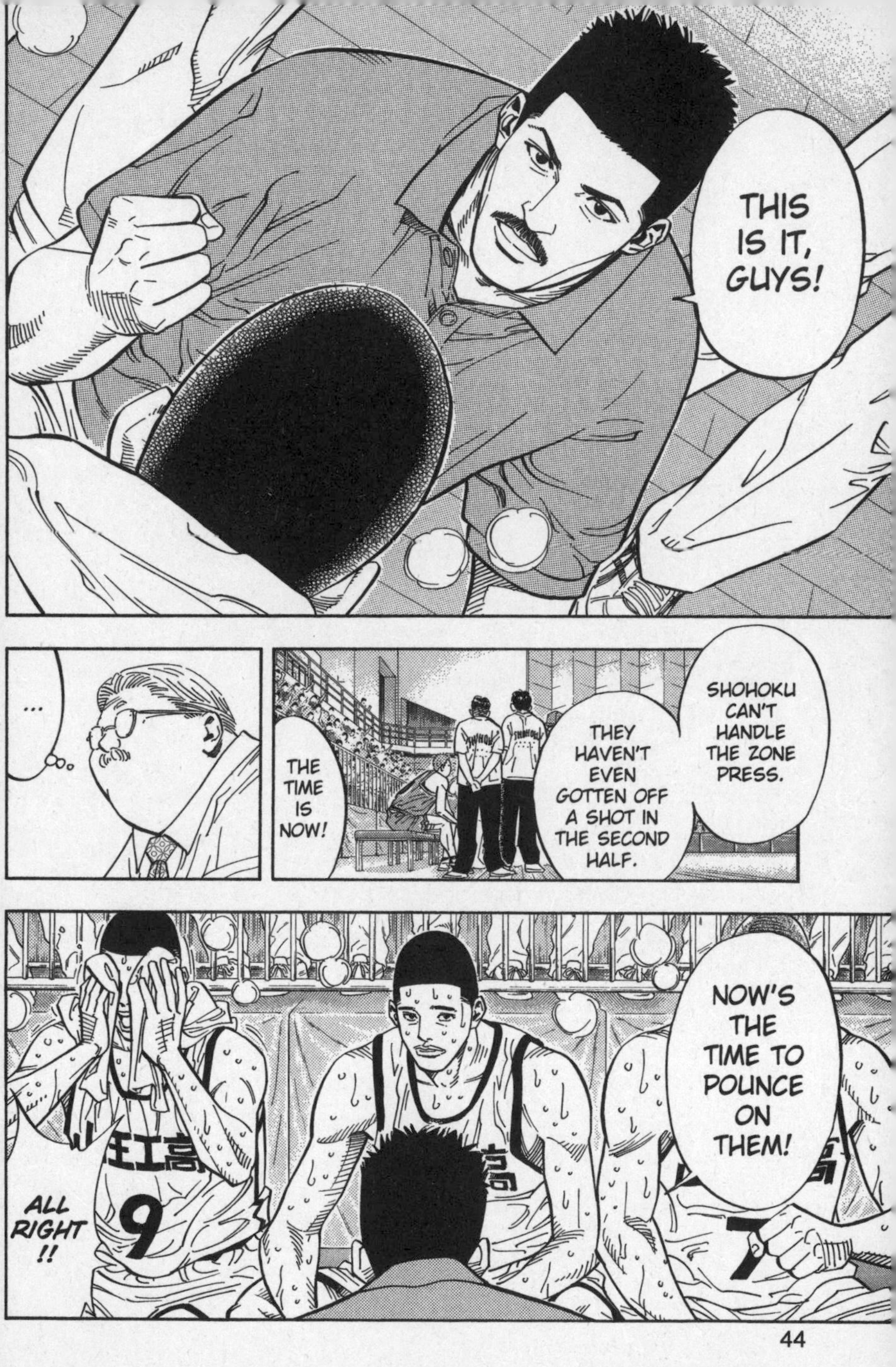
THIS IS IT, GUYS!
SHOHOKU CAN'T HANDLE THE ZONE PRESS.
THEY HAVEN'T EVEN GOTTEN OFF A SHOT IN THE SECOND HALF.
THE TIME IS NOW!
...
NOW'S THE TIME TO POUNCE ON THEM!
ALL RIGHT !!

READ THIS WAY

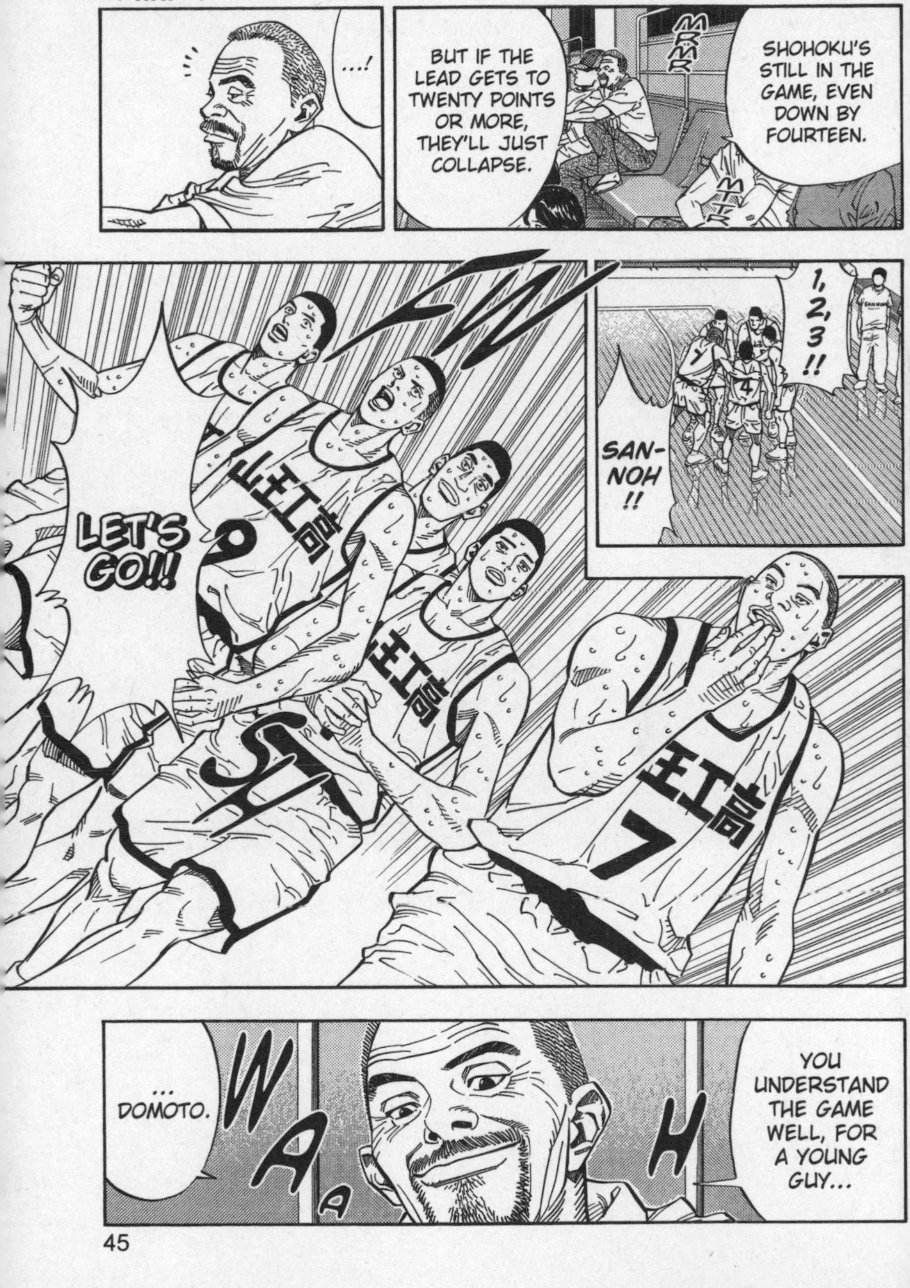
SHOHOKU'S STILL IN THE GAME, EVEN DOWN BY FOURTEEN.
BUT IF THE LEAD GETS TO TWENTY POINTS OR MORE, THEY'LL JUST COLLAPSE.
...!
1, 2, 3 !!
SAN-NOH !!
LET'S GO!!
YOU UNDERSTAND THE GAME WELL, FOR A YOUNG GUY...
WAAH
... DOMOTO.

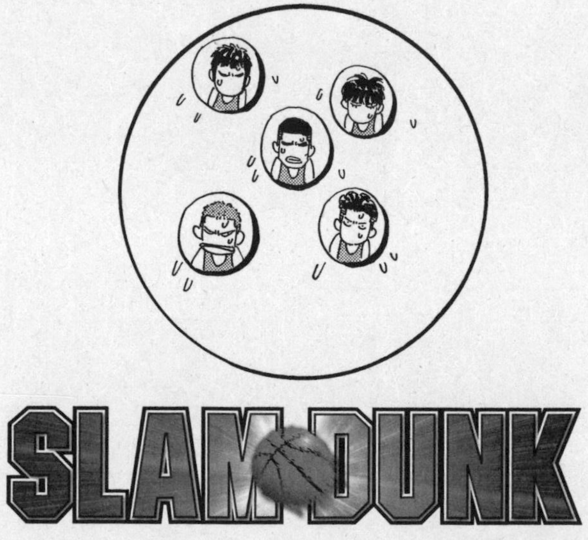

SLAM DUNK

SPEEDSTER

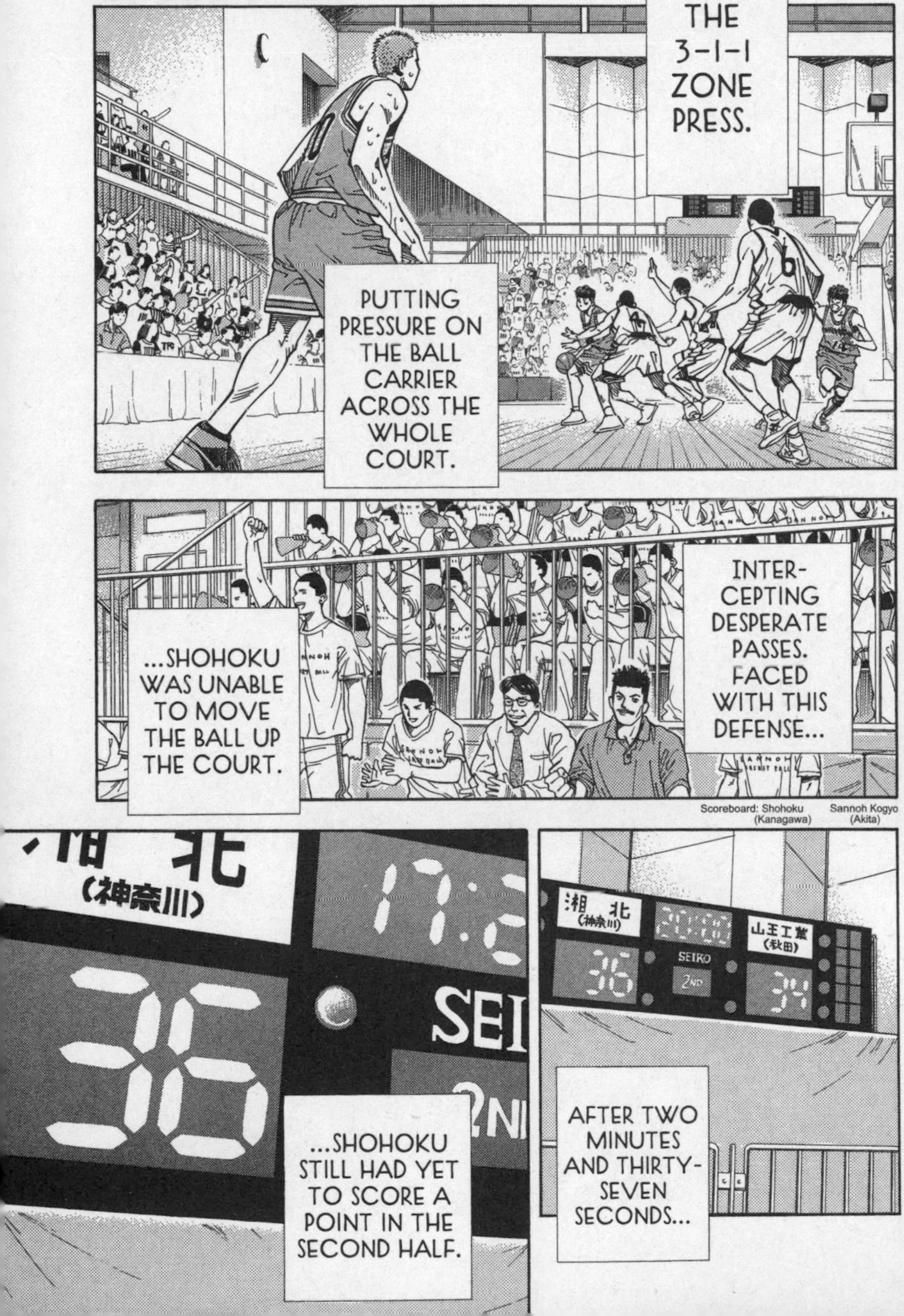
THE 3-1-1 ZONE PRESS.
PUTTING PRESSURE ON THE BALL CARRIER ACROSS THE WHOLE COURT.
INTERCEPTING DESPERATE PASSES. FACED WITH THIS DEFENSE...
...SHOHOKU WAS UNABLE TO MOVE THE BALL UP THE COURT.
Scoreboard: Shohoku (Kanagawa) Sannoh Kogyo (Akita)
AFTER TWO MINUTES AND THIRTY-SEVEN SECONDS...
...SHOHOKU STILL HAD YET TO SCORE A POINT IN THE SECOND HALF.

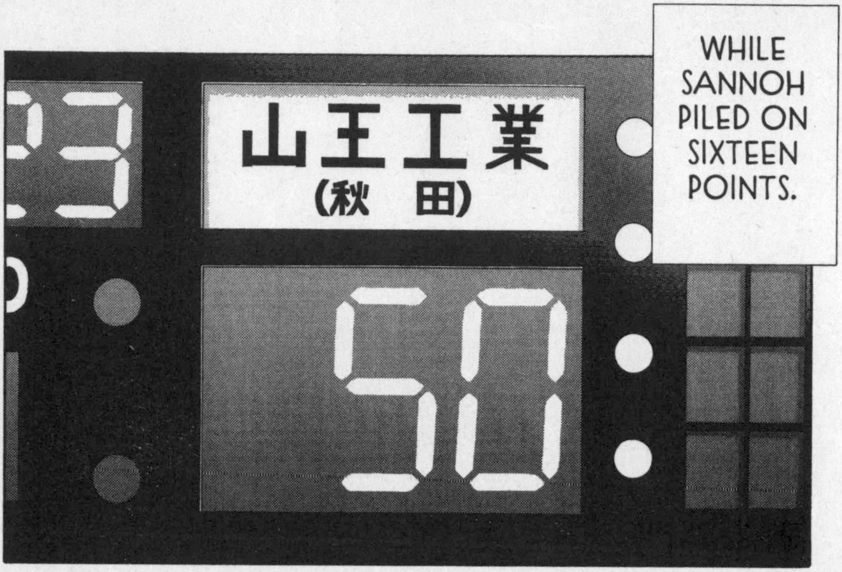
WHILE SANNOH PILED ON SIXTEEN POINTS.
山王工業
(秋田)
50

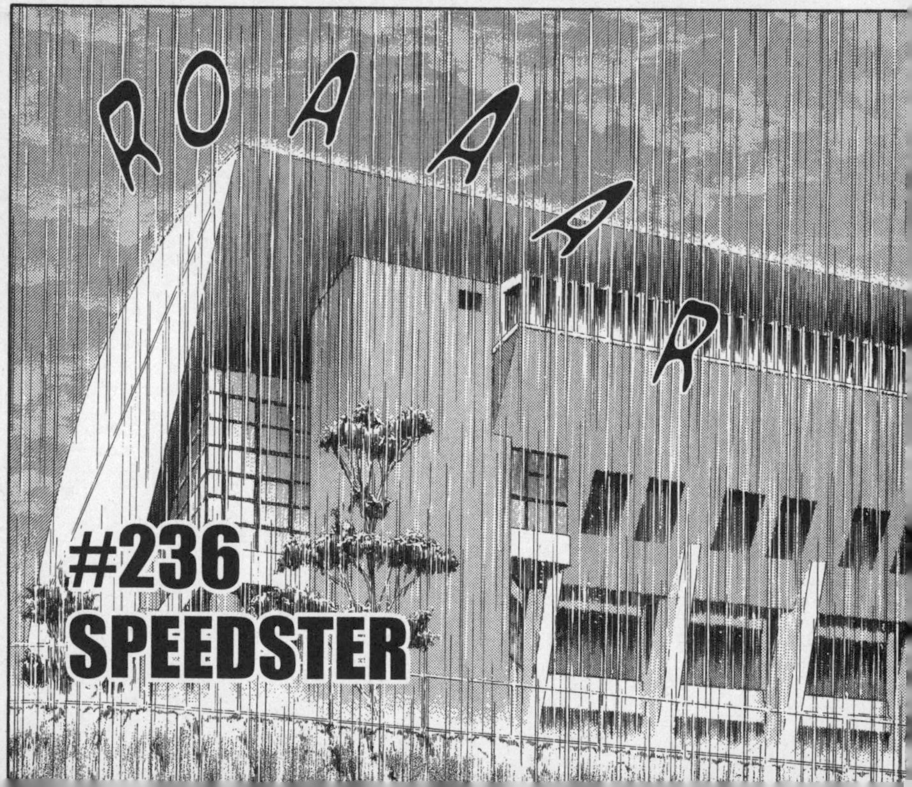
ROAAAR

#236 SPEEDSTER

READ THIS WAY

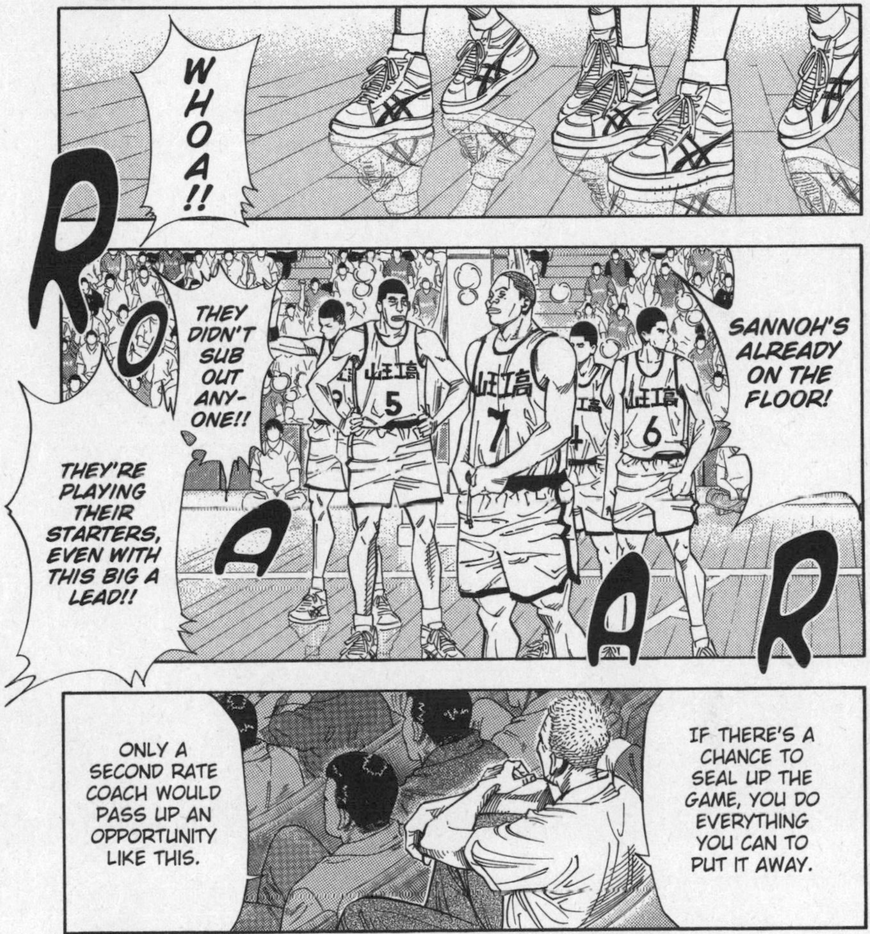
WHOA!!
ROAAR
SANNOH'S ALREADY ON THE FLOOR!
THEY DIDN'T SUB OUT ANY-ONE!!
THEY'RE PLAYING THEIR STARTERS, EVEN WITH THIS BIG A LEAD!!
IF THERE'S A CHANCE TO SEAL UP THE GAME, YOU DO EVERYTHING YOU CAN TO PUT IT AWAY.
ONLY A SECOND RATE COACH WOULD PASS UP AN OPPORTUNITY LIKE THIS.

Scoreboard: Shohoku (Kanagawa) Sannoh Kogyo (Akita)

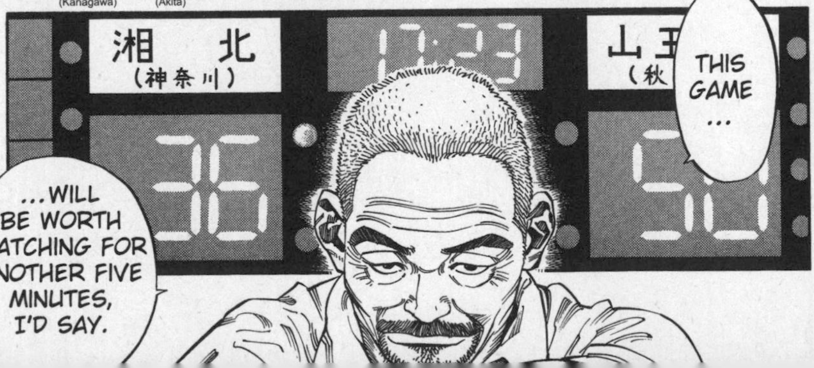
湘北
（神奈川）
17:23
THIS GAME...
...WILL BE WORTH WATCHING FOR ANOTHER FIVE MINUTES, I'D SAY.

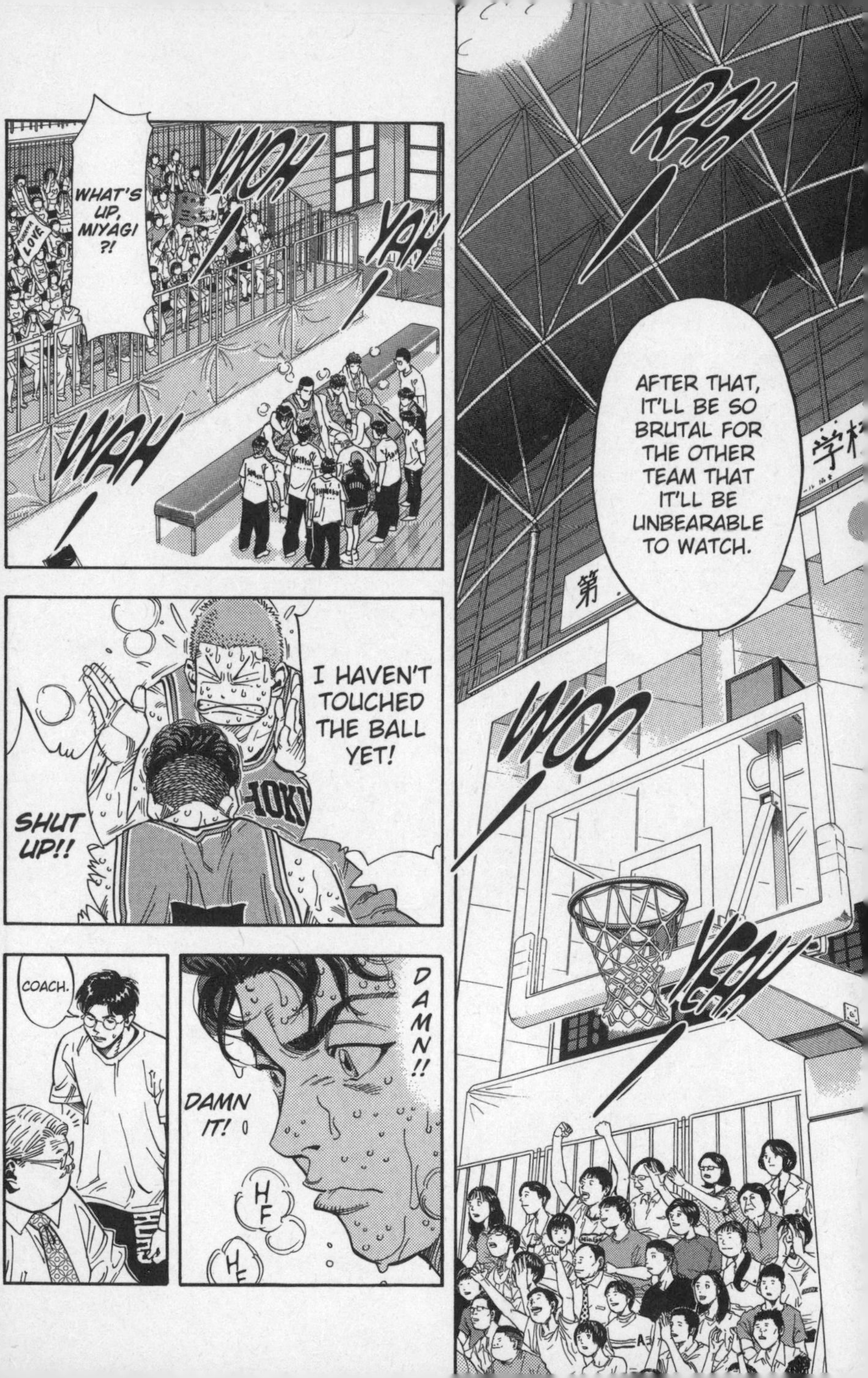
RAH!
AFTER THAT, IT'LL BE SO BRUTAL FOR THE OTHER TEAM THAT IT'LL BE UNBEARABLE TO WATCH.
WOO!
YEAH!
WOH!
YAH!
WHAT'S UP, MIYAGI?!
WAH!
I HAVEN'T TOUCHED THE BALL YET!
SHUT UP!!
DAMN!!
DAMN IT!
HF
HF
COACH.

READ THIS WAY

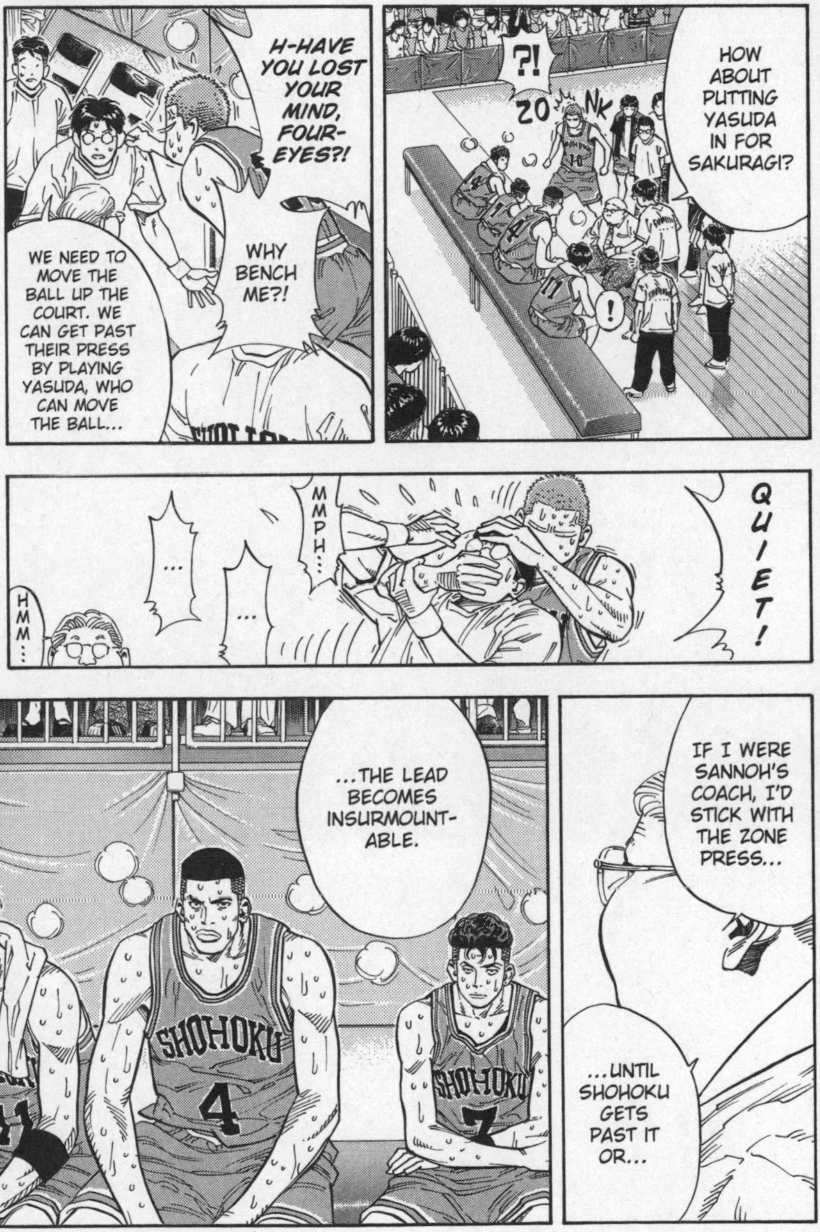

HOW ABOUT PUTTING YASUDA IN FOR SAKURAGI?
?!
ZONK
!
H-HAVE YOU LOST YOUR MIND, FOUR-EYES?!
WHY BENCH ME?!
WE NEED TO MOVE THE BALL UP THE COURT. WE CAN GET PAST THEIR PRESS BY PLAYING YASUDA, WHO CAN MOVE THE BALL...
QUIET!
MMPH...
...
...
HMM...
IF I WERE SANNOH'S COACH, I'D STICK WITH THE ZONE PRESS...
...UNTIL SHOHOKU GETS PAST IT OR...
...THE LEAD BECOMES INSURMOUNTABLE.

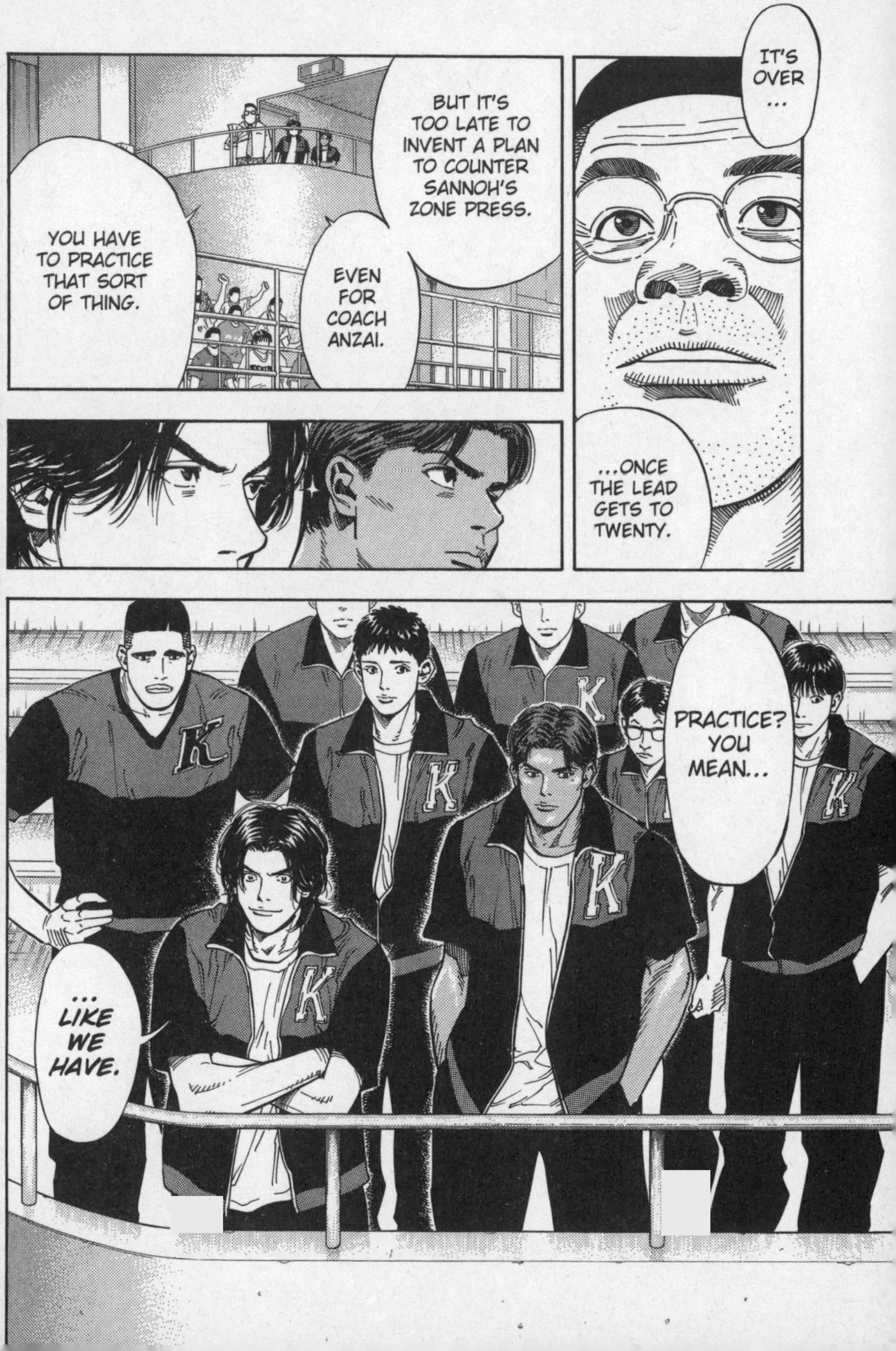

IT'S OVER ...
...ONCE THE LEAD GETS TO TWENTY.
BUT IT'S TOO LATE TO INVENT A PLAN TO COUNTER SANNOH'S ZONE PRESS.
EVEN FOR COACH ANZAI.
YOU HAVE TO PRACTICE THAT SORT OF THING.
PRACTICE? YOU MEAN...
... LIKE WE HAVE.

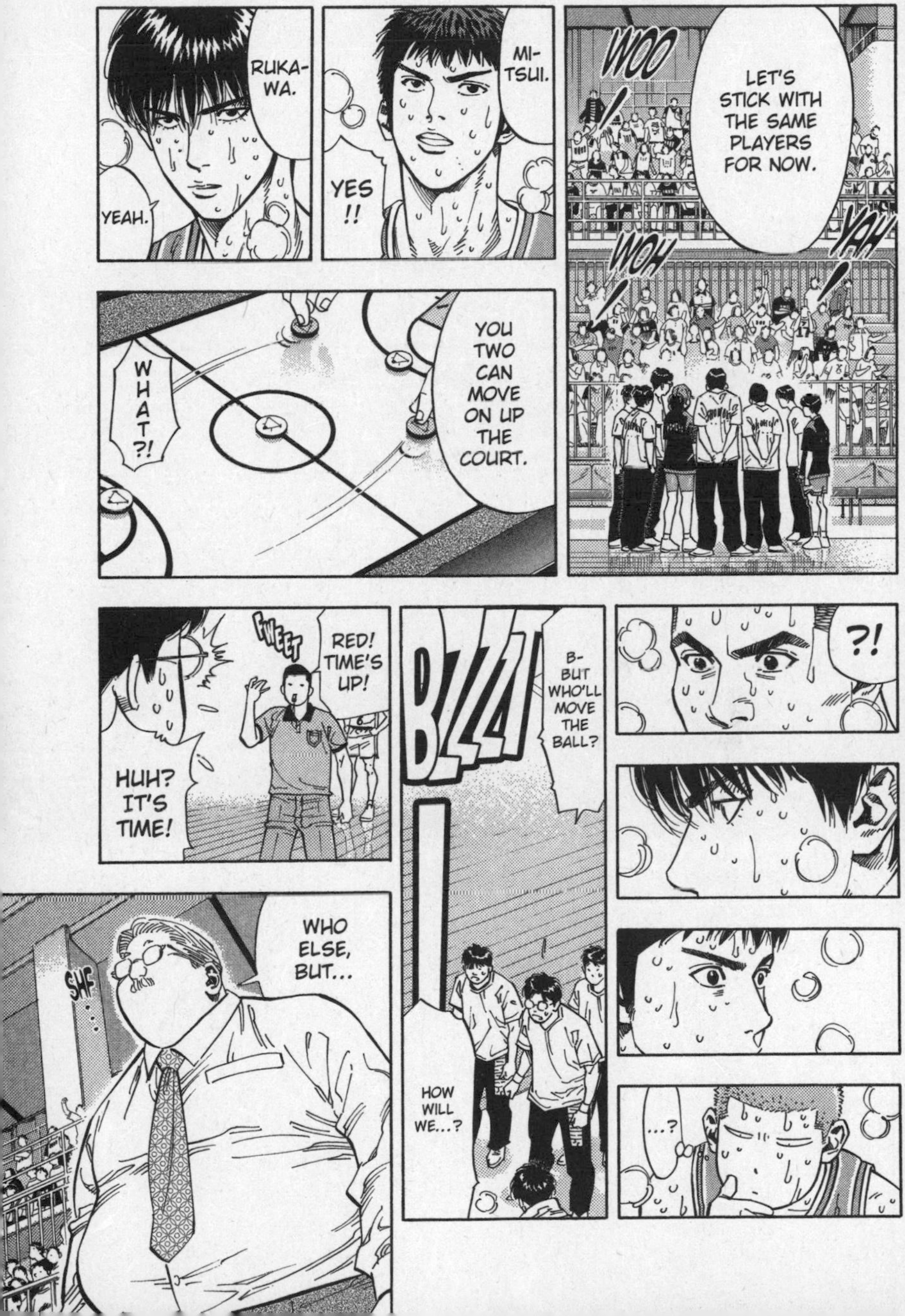
WOO
LET'S STICK WITH THE SAME PLAYERS FOR NOW.
WOH
YAH
MI-TSUI.
YES!!
RUKA-WA.
YEAH.
YOU TWO CAN MOVE ON UP THE COURT.
WHAT?!
?!
...?
BZZT
B-BUT WHO'LL MOVE THE BALL?
HOW WILL WE...?
FWEET
RED! TIME'S UP!
HUH? IT'S TIME!
WHO ELSE, BUT...
SHF...

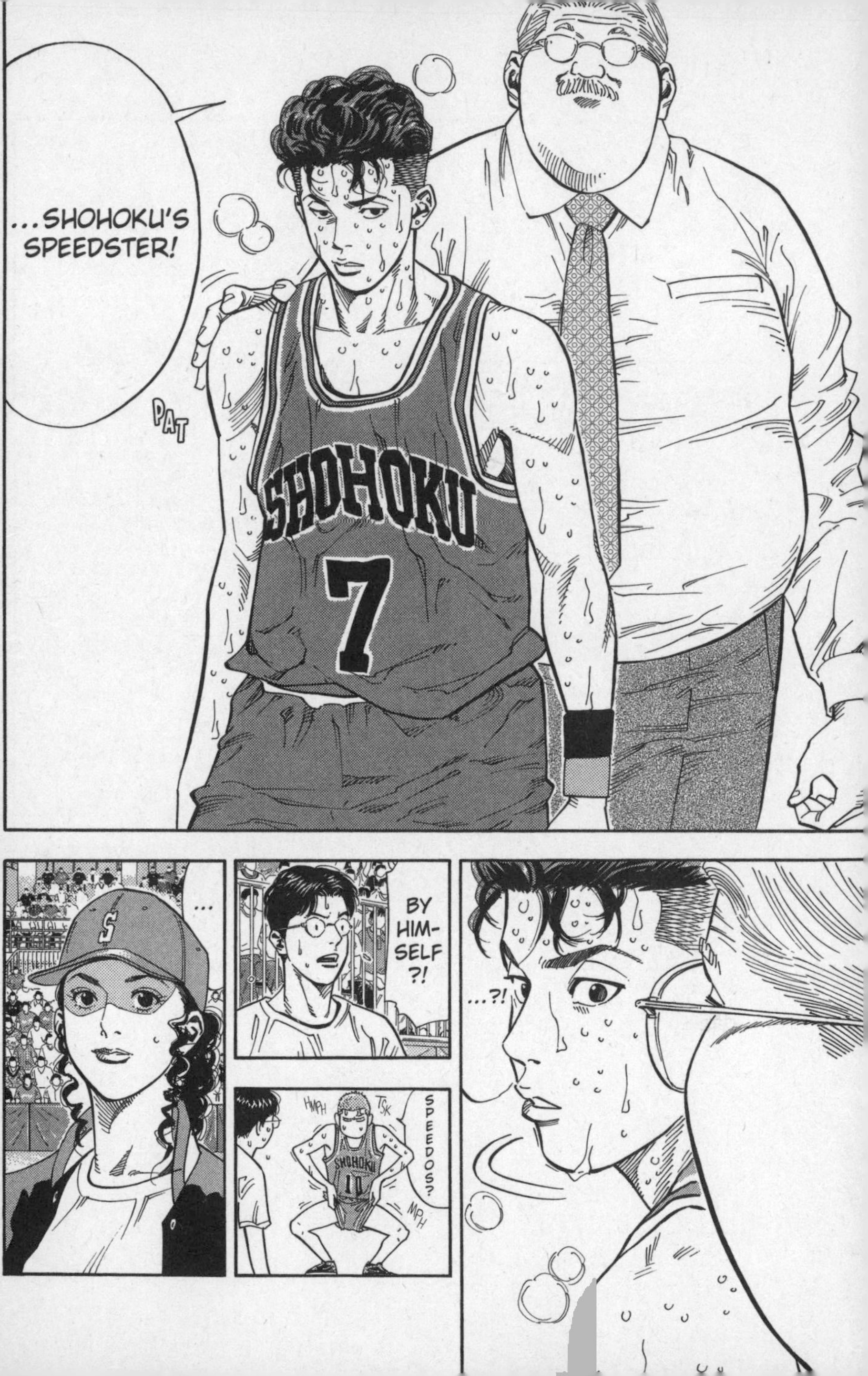
...SHOHOKU'S SPEEDSTER!
PAT
SHOHOKU
7
...?!
BY HIM-SELF ?!
SPEEDOS?
TSK
HMPH
SHOHOKU
10
MPH
...

READ THIS WAY

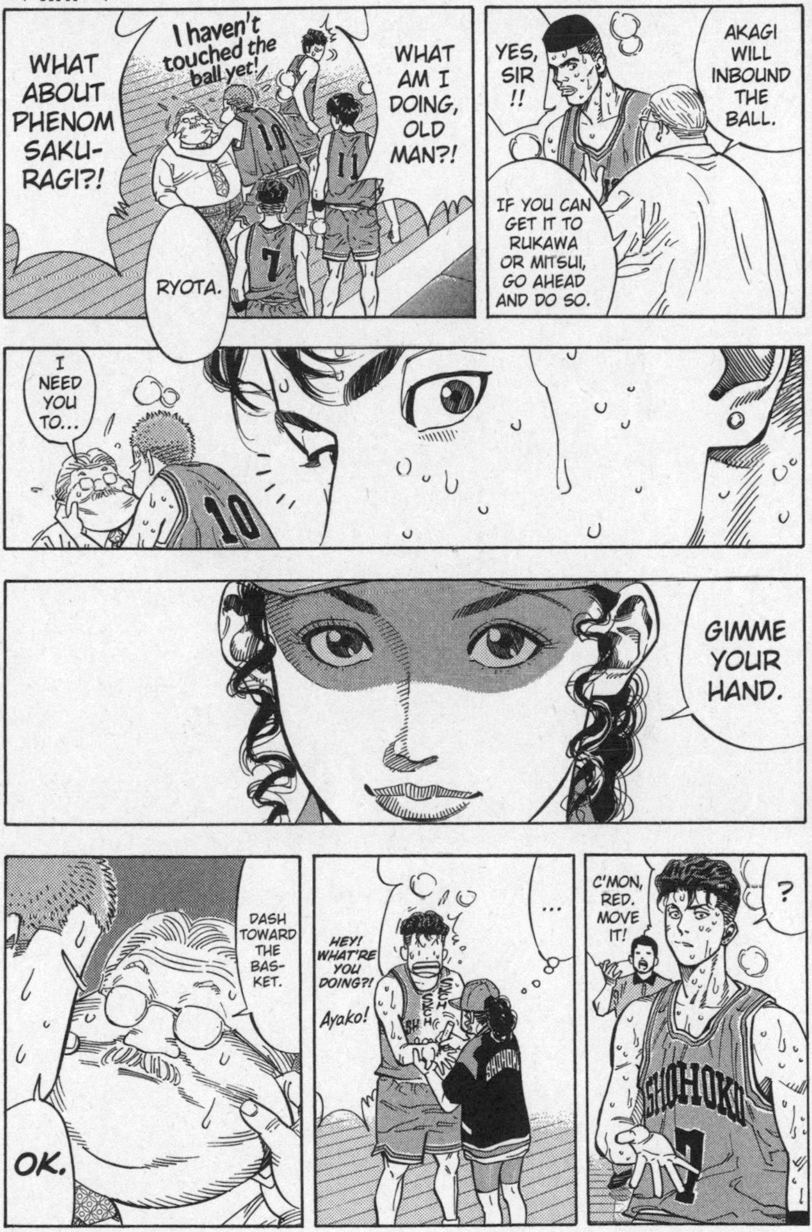
AKAGI WILL INBOUND THE BALL.
YES, SIR !!
IF YOU CAN GET IT TO RUKAWA OR MITSUI, GO AHEAD AND DO SO.
WHAT AM I DOING, OLD MAN?!
I haven't touched the ball yet!
WHAT ABOUT PHENOM SAKU-RAGI?!
RYOTA.
I NEED YOU TO...
GIMME YOUR HAND.
?
C'MON, RED. MOVE IT!
...
HEY! WHAT'RE YOU DOING?!
Ayako!
DASH TOWARD THE BAS-KET.
OK.

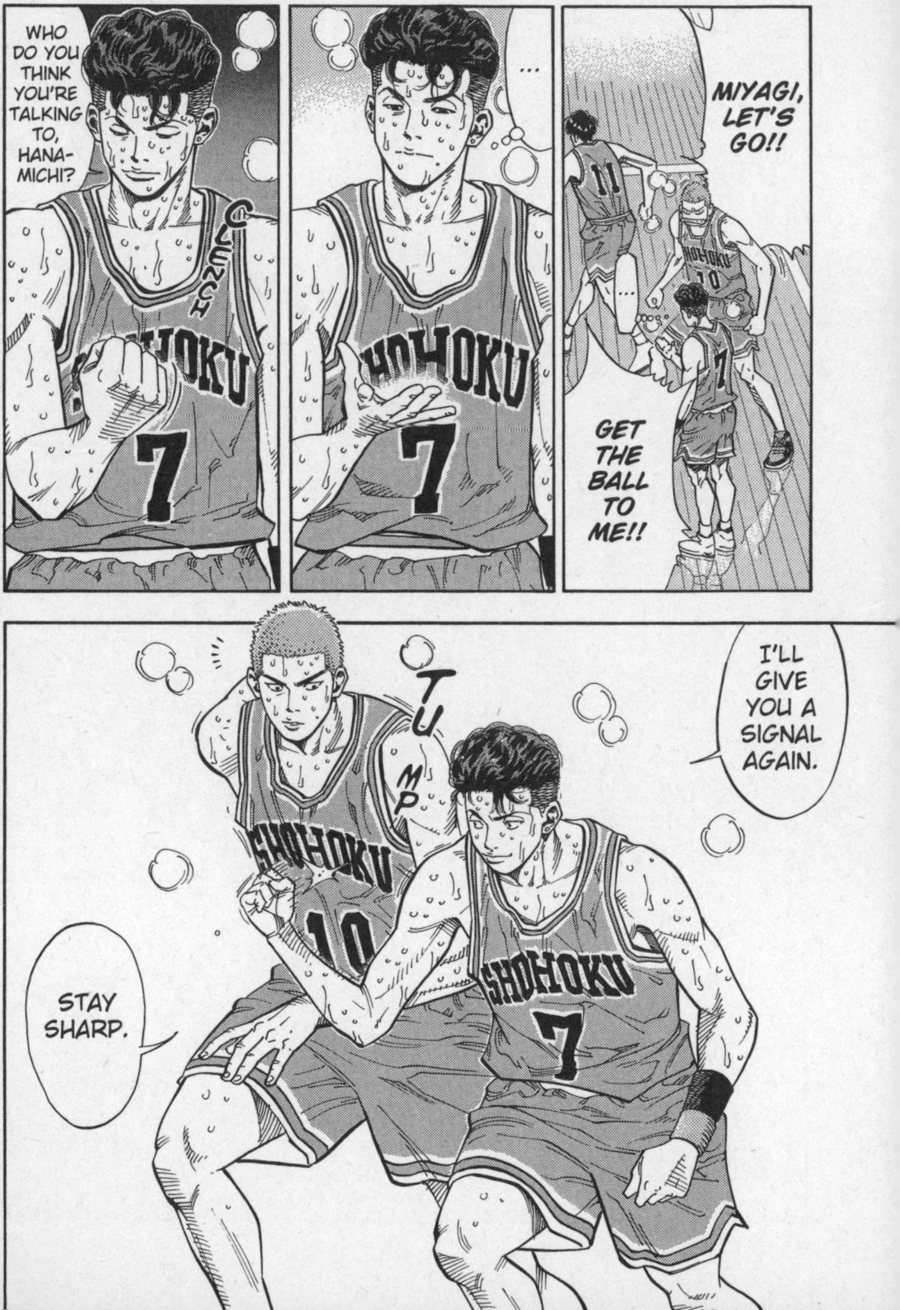
MIYAGI, LET'S GO!!
...
GET THE BALL TO ME!!
...
WHO DO YOU THINK YOU'RE TALKING TO, HANA-MICHI?
CLENCH
I'LL GIVE YOU A SIGNAL AGAIN.
TUMP
STAY SHARP.

READ THIS WAY

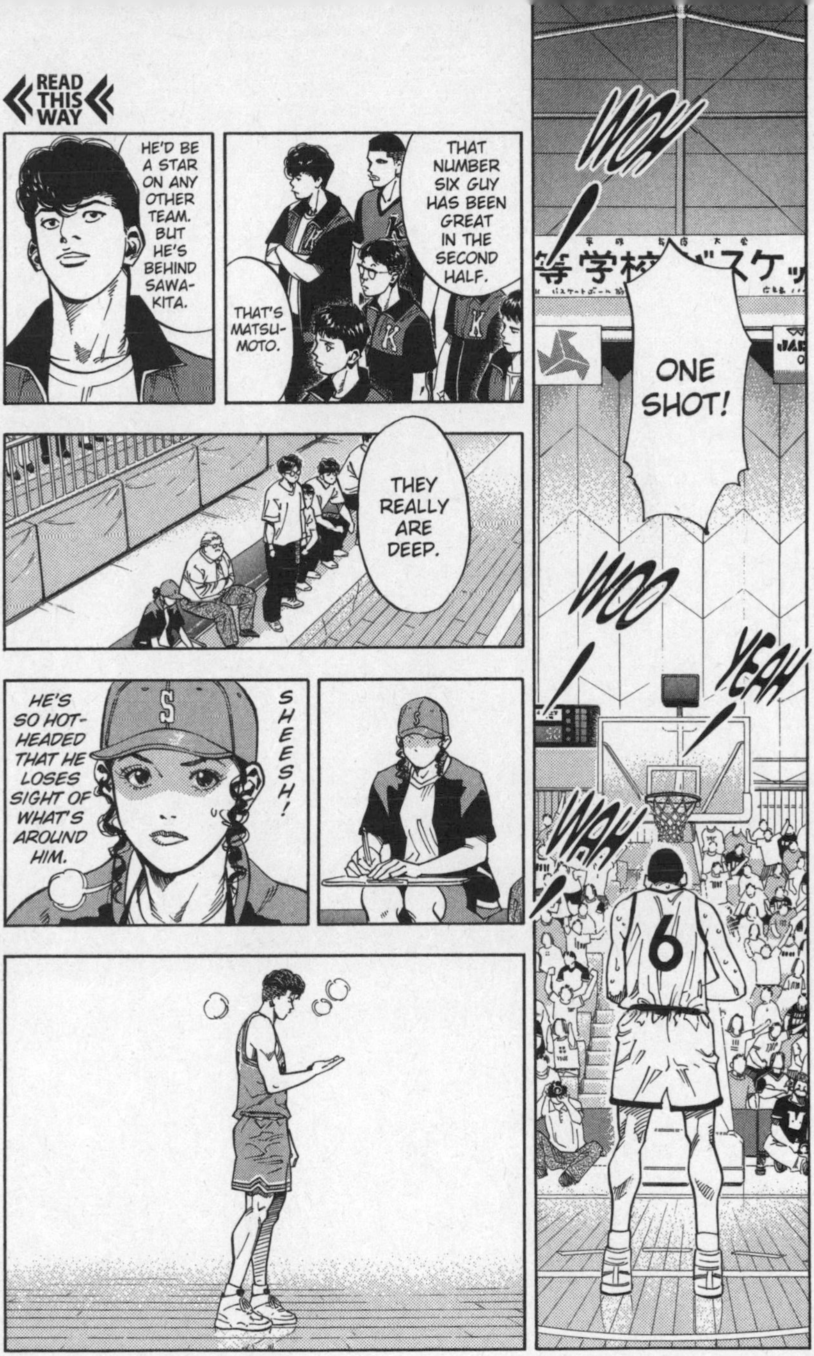

WOH!
ONE SHOT!
WOO!
YEAH!
WAH!
THAT NUMBER SIX GUY HAS BEEN GREAT IN THE SECOND HALF.
THAT'S MATSU-MOTO.
HE'D BE A STAR ON ANY OTHER TEAM. BUT HE'S BEHIND SAWA-KITA.
THEY REALLY ARE DEEP.
SHEESH!
HE'S SO HOT-HEADED THAT HE LOSES SIGHT OF WHAT'S AROUND HIM.

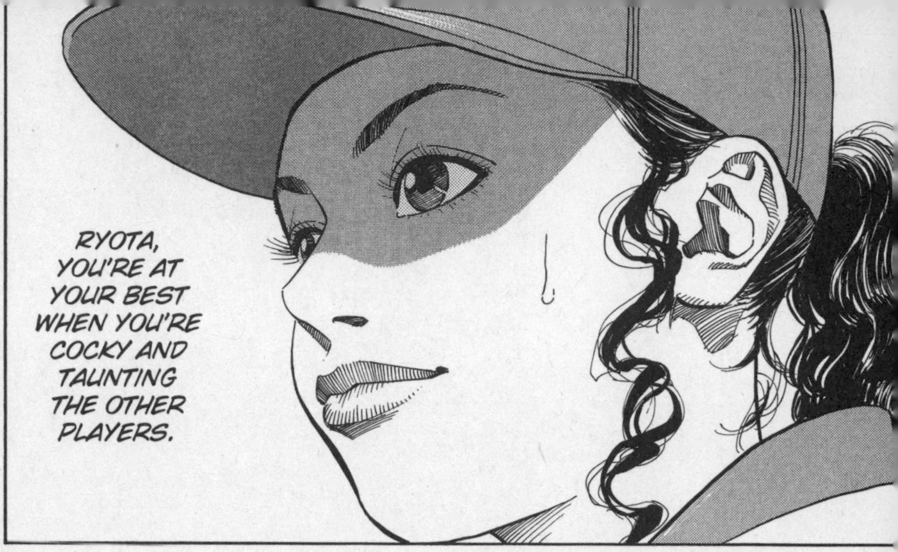
RYOTA, YOU'RE AT YOUR BEST WHEN YOU'RE COCKY AND TAUNTING THE OTHER PLAYERS.

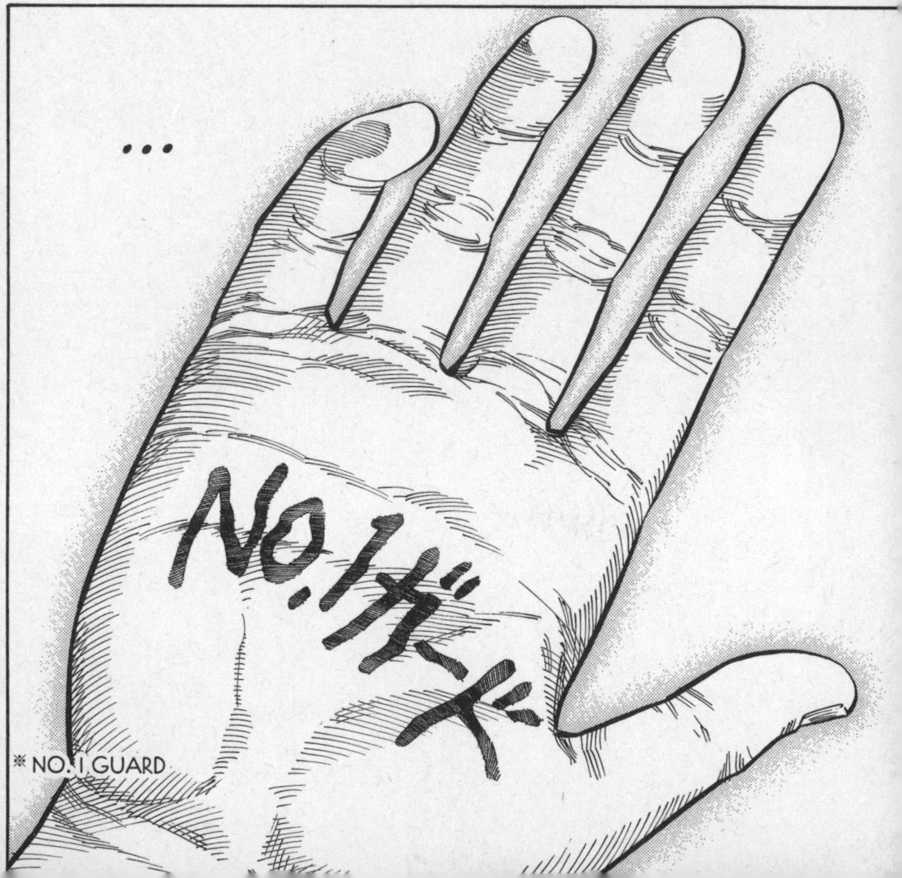
...
No.1ガード
※ NO. 1 GUARD

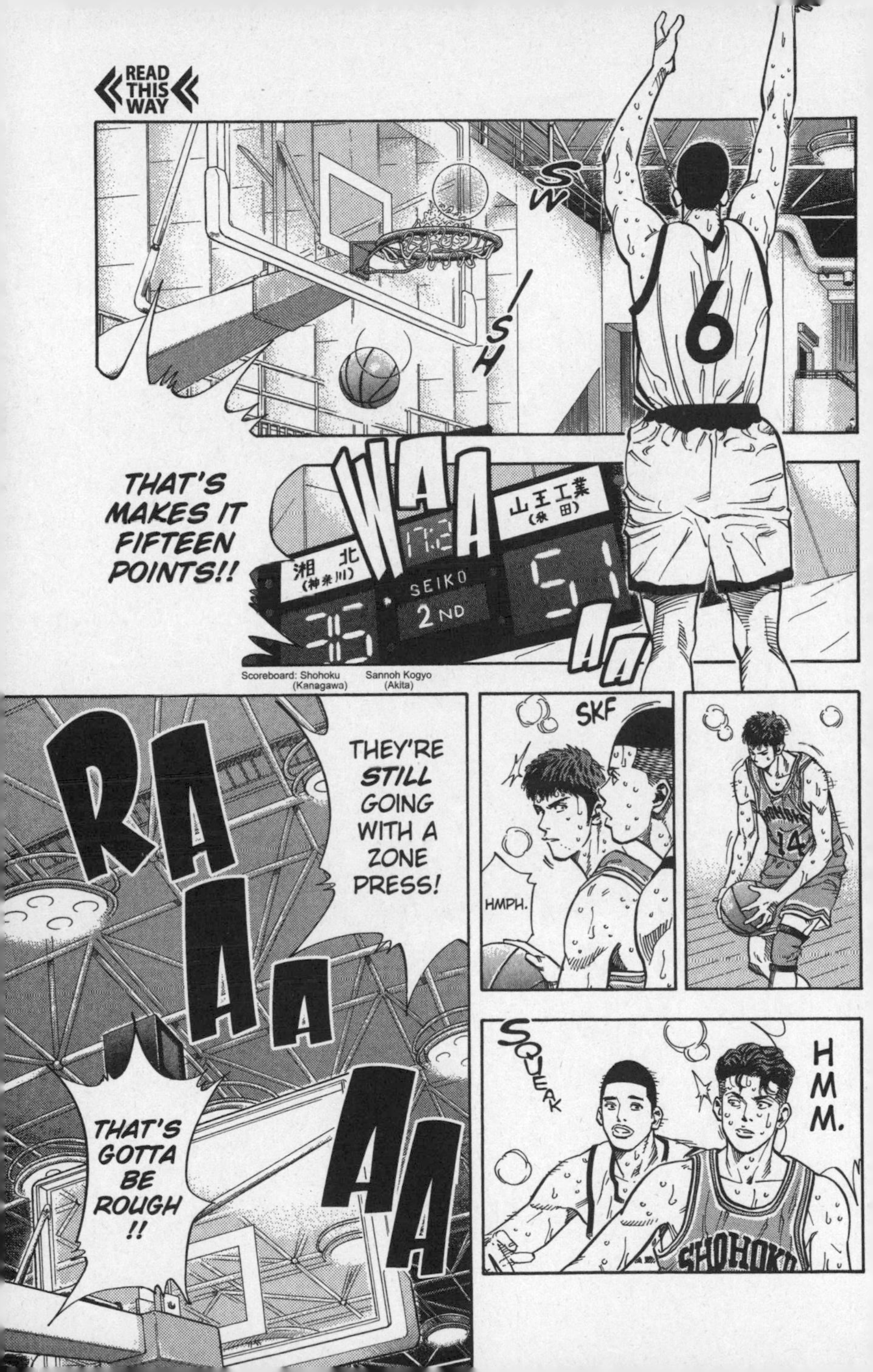
READ THIS WAY
SWISH
THAT'S MAKES IT FIFTEEN POINTS!!
WAAAA
山王工業
湘北
SEIKO
2ND
35
51
Scoreboard: Shohoku (Kanagawa) Sannoh Kogyo (Akita)
SKF
HMPH.
HMM.
SQUEAK
RAAAAAA
THEY'RE STILL GOING WITH A ZONE PRESS!
THAT'S GOTTA BE ROUGH!!

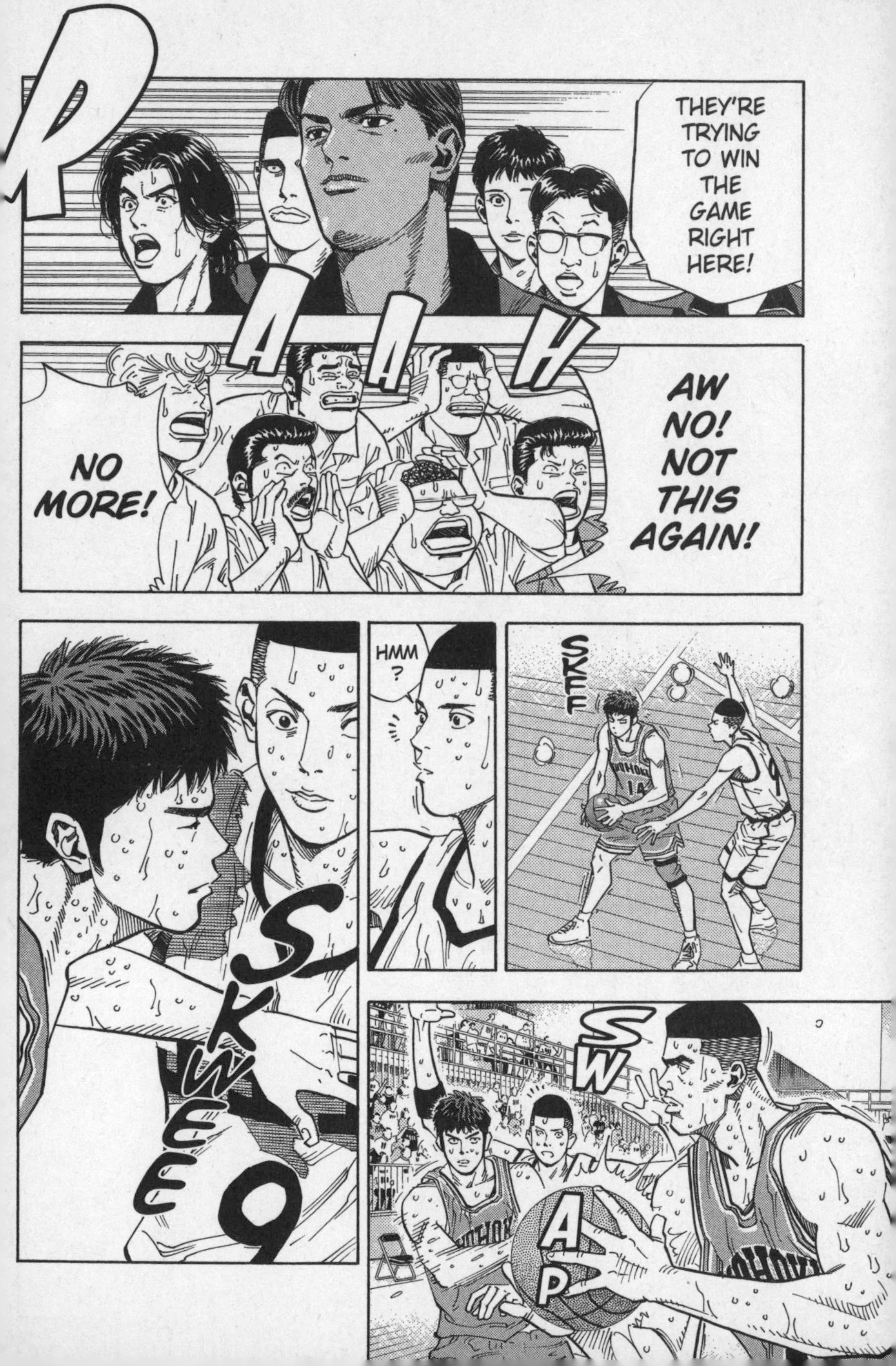
RAAAH
THEY'RE TRYING TO WIN THE GAME RIGHT HERE!
AW NO! NOT THIS AGAIN!
NO MORE!
SKFF
HMM ?
SWAP
SKWEEE

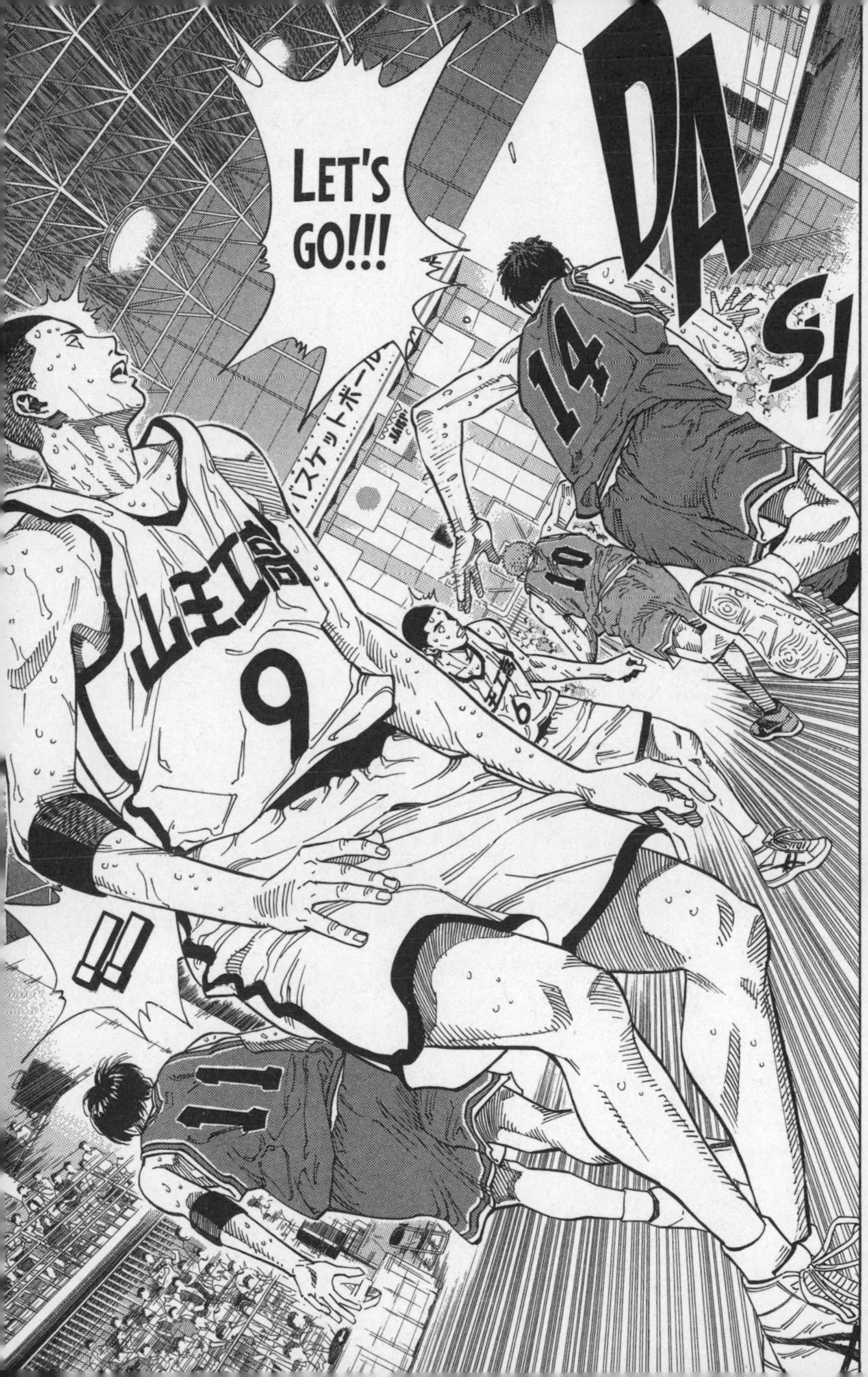
DASH
LET'S GO!!!
バスケットボール
!!

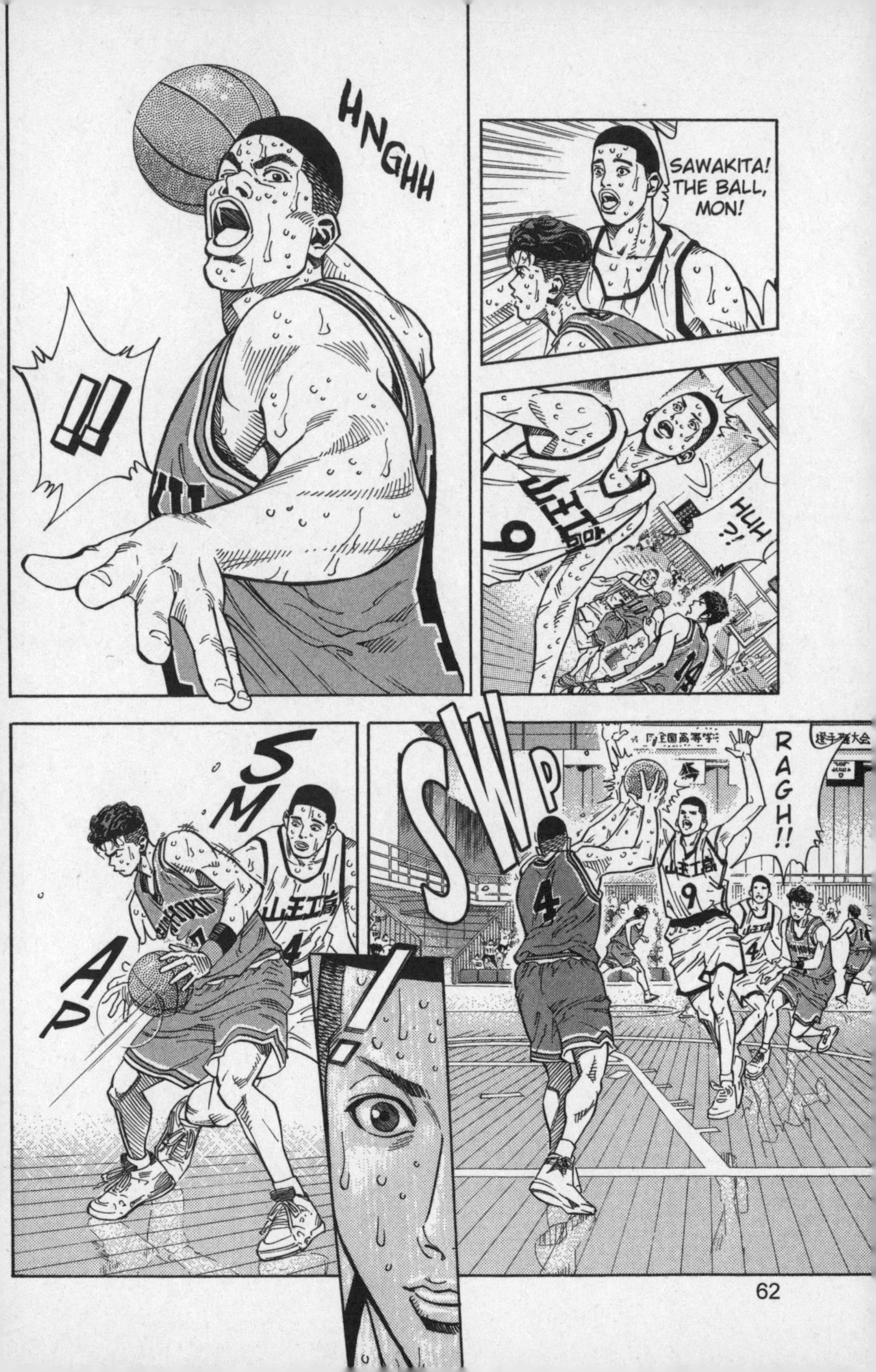
SAWAKITA! THE BALL, MON!
HUH ?!
HNGHH
!!
SWP
RAGH!!
!
SMAP

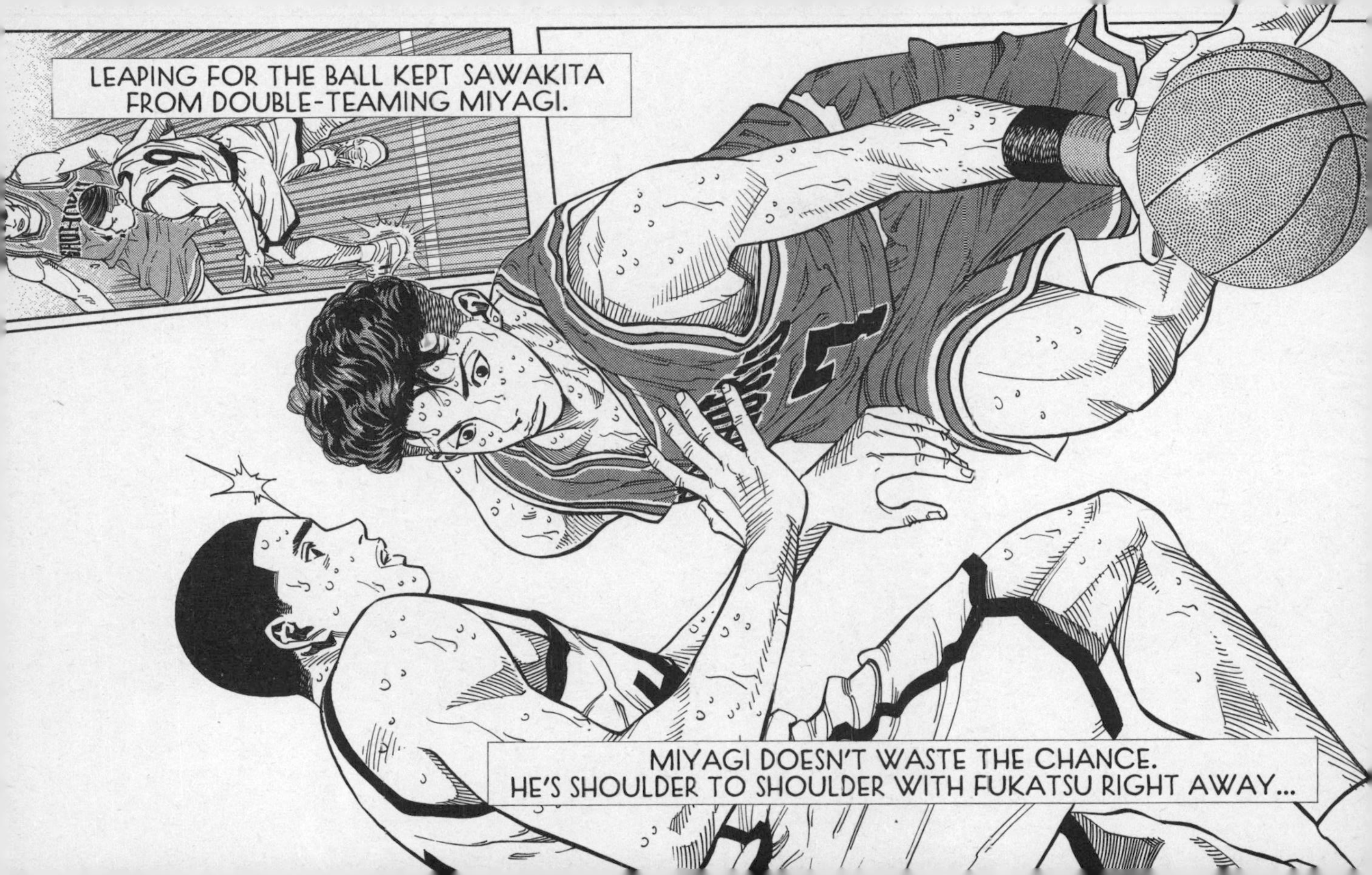
LEAPING FOR THE BALL KEPT SAWAKITA FROM DOUBLE-TEAMING MIYAGI.
MIYAGI DOESN'T WASTE THE CHANCE. HE'S SHOULDER TO SHOULDER WITH FUKATSU RIGHT AWAY...

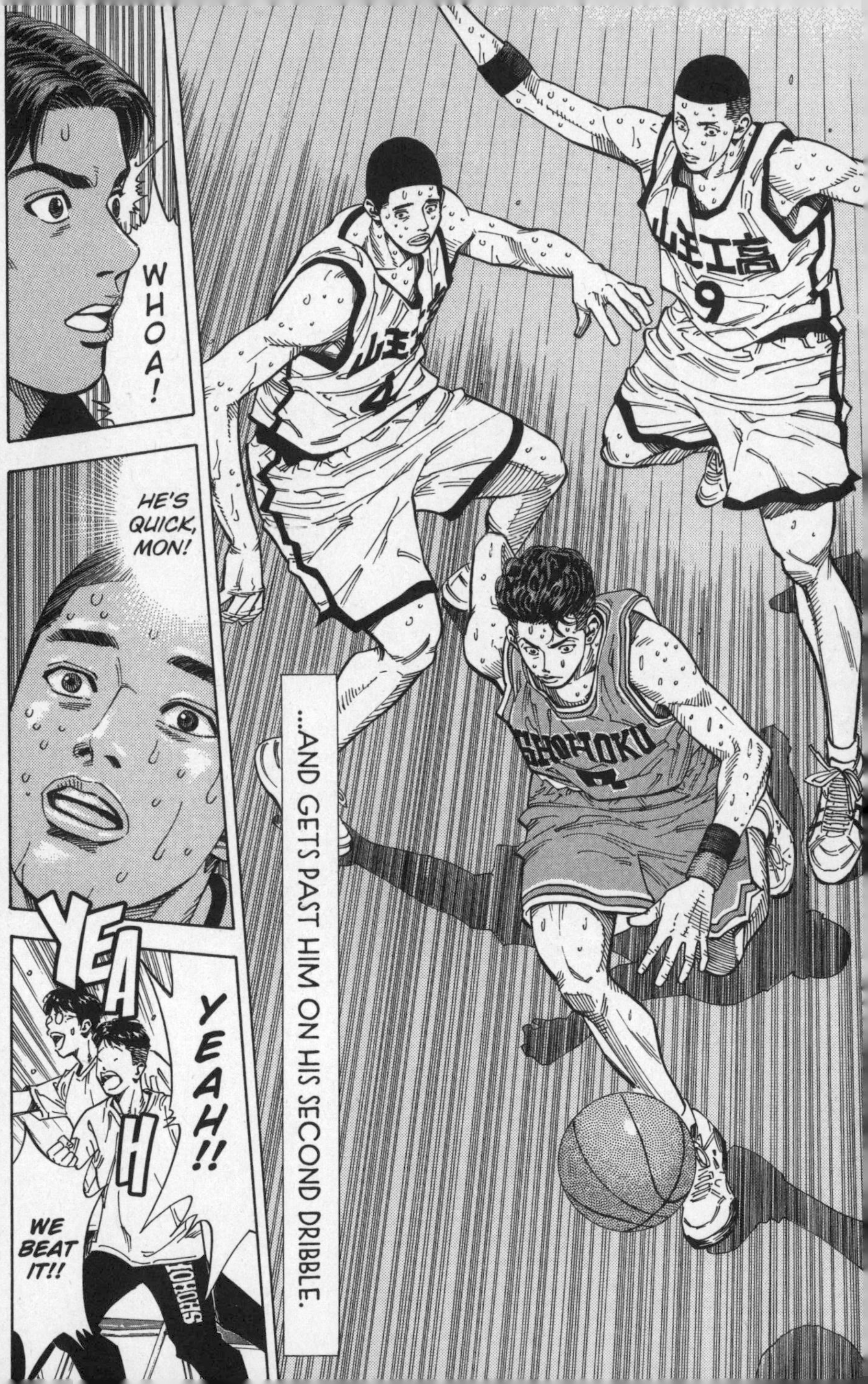
...AND GETS PAST HIM ON HIS SECOND DRIBBLE.
WHOA!
HE'S QUICK, MON!
YEAH!!
YEAH
WE BEAT IT!!

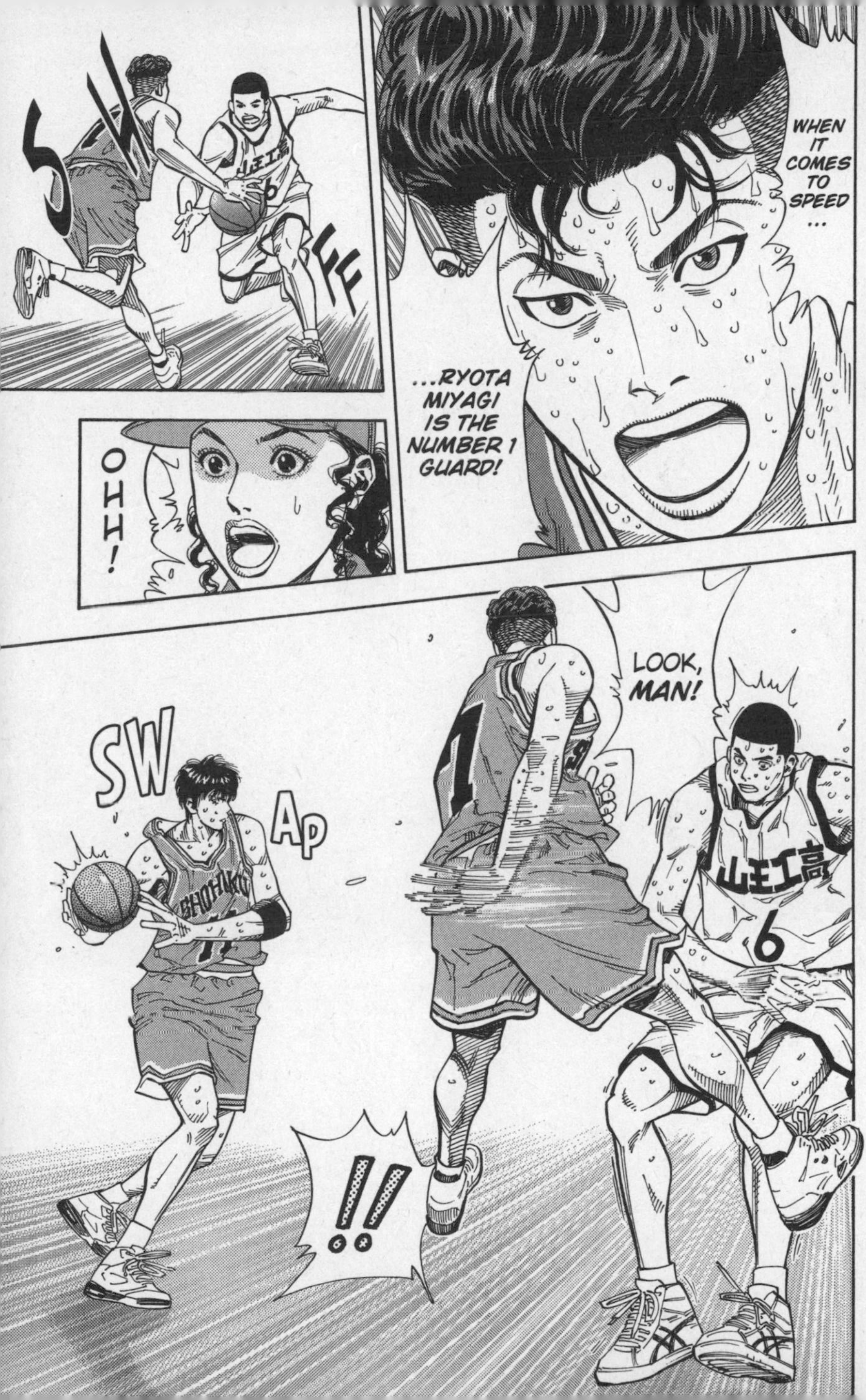
WHEN IT COMES TO SPEED ...
...RYOTA MIYAGI IS THE NUMBER 1 GUARD!
FF
OHH!
LOOK, MAN!
!!
SW
Ap

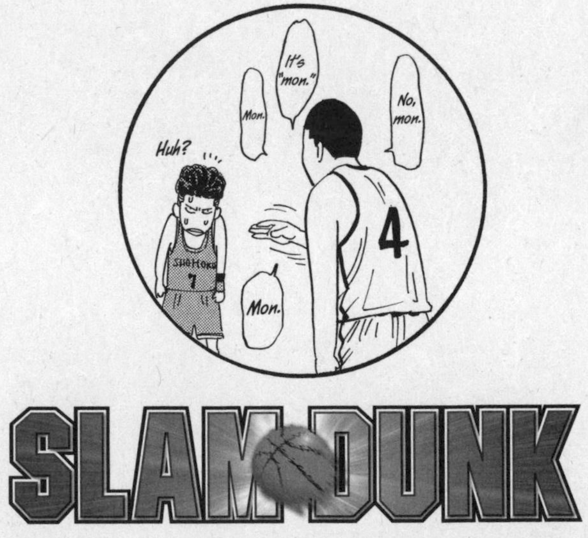
No, mon.
It's "mon."
Mon.
Huh?
Mon.

SLAM DUNK

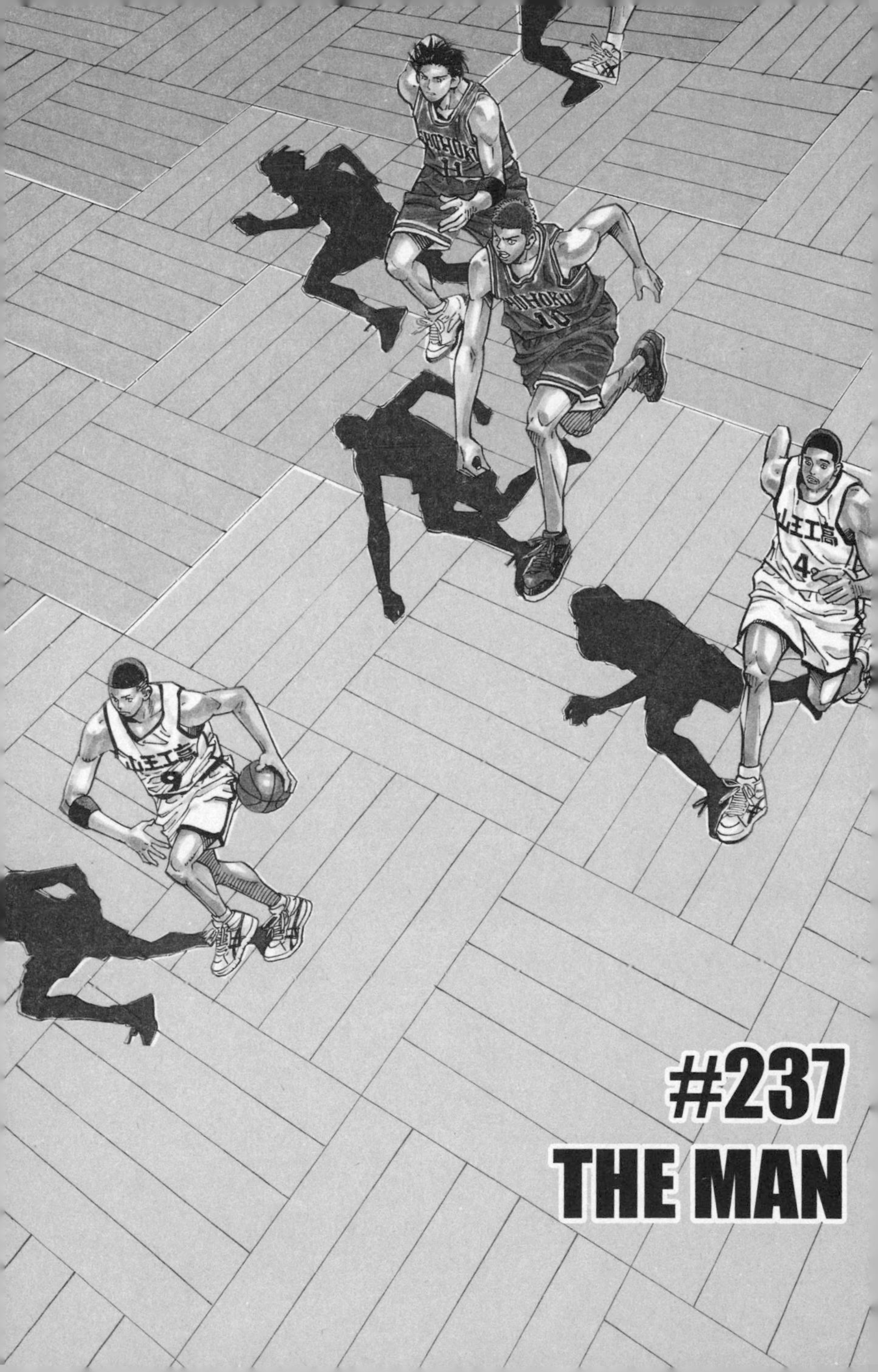

#237 THE MAN

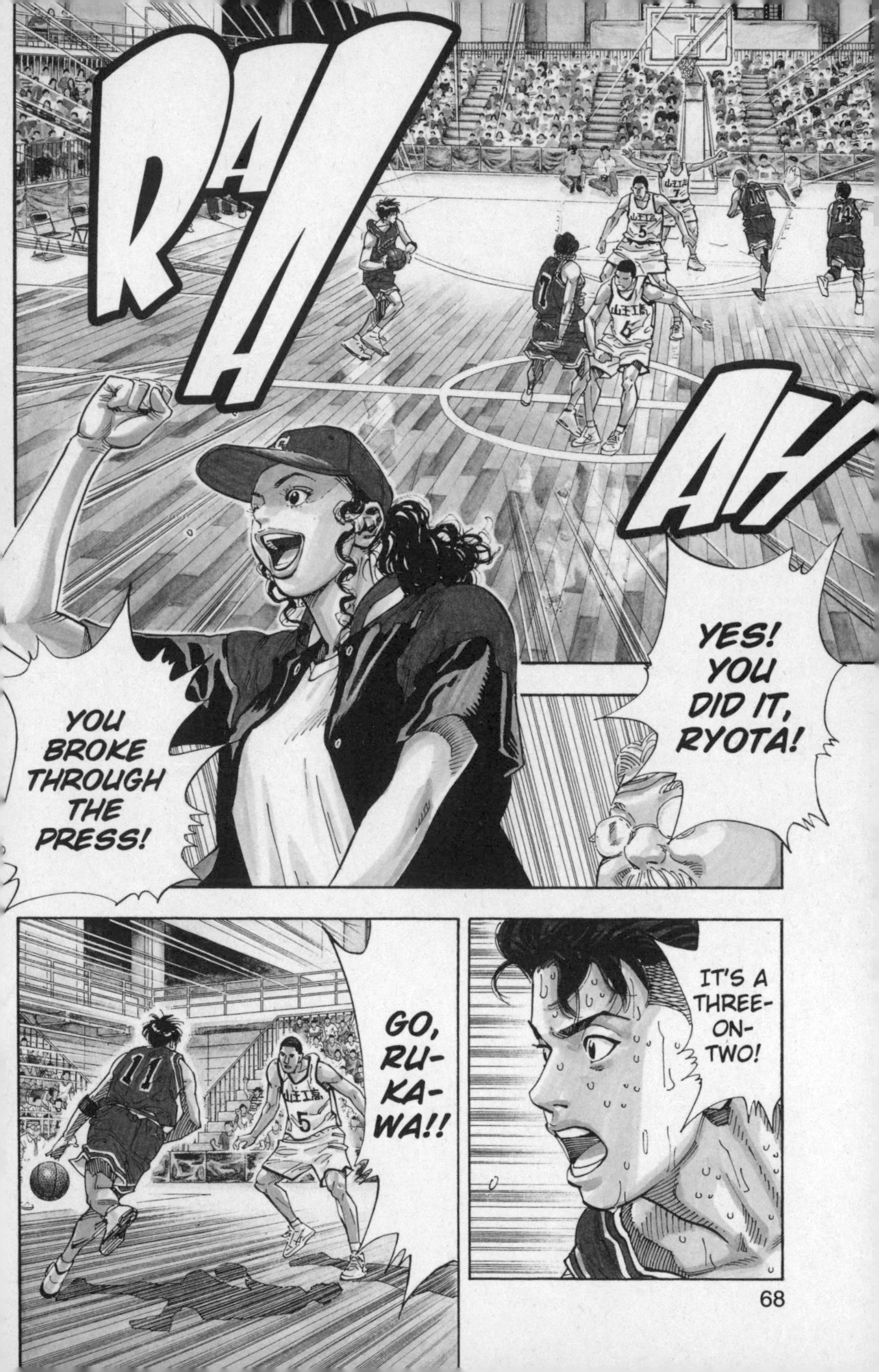
RAA
AH
YES! YOU DID IT, RYOTA!
YOU BROKE THROUGH THE PRESS!
IT'S A THREE-ON-TWO!
GO, RU-KA-WA!!

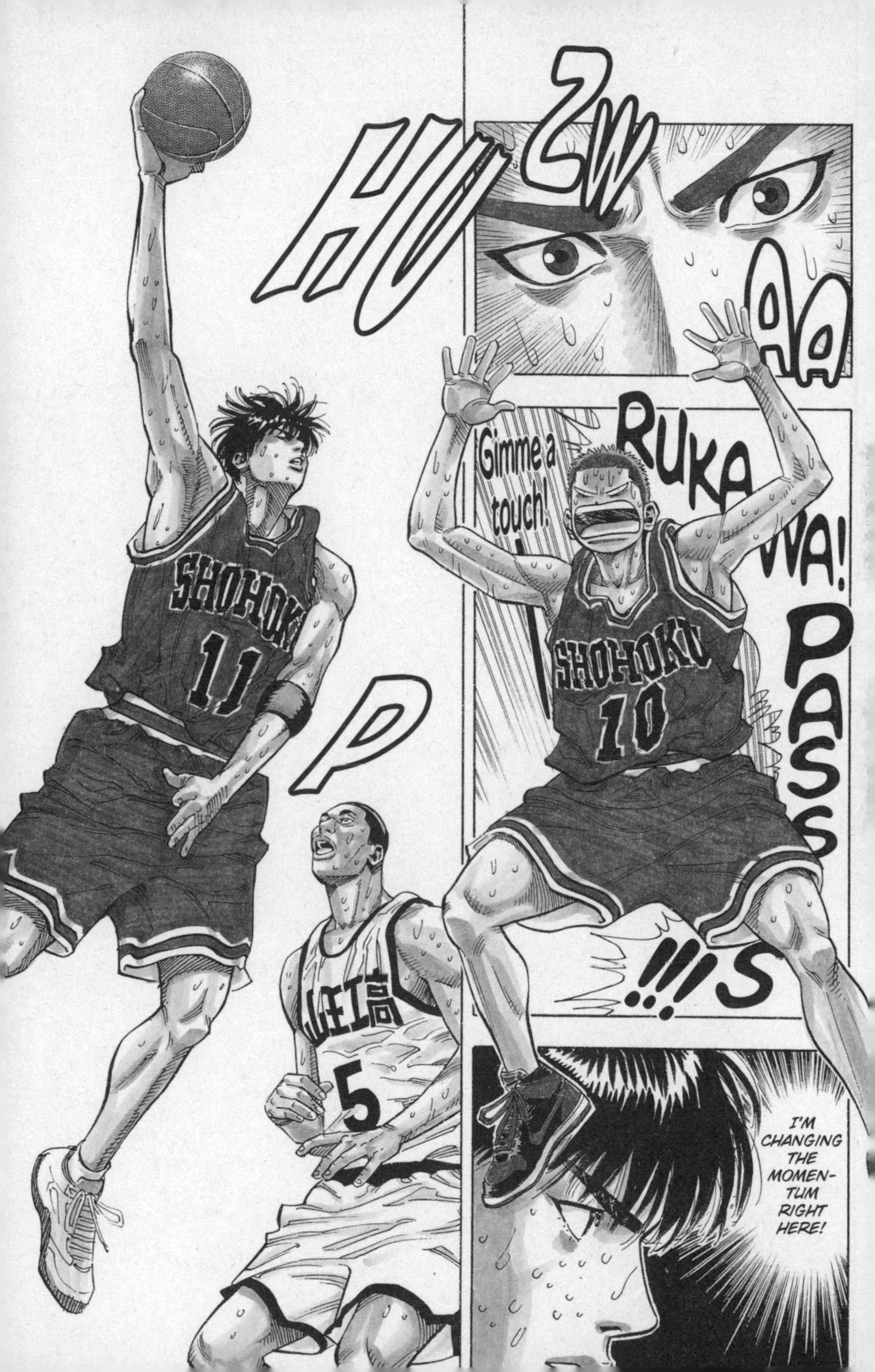
ZW
AA
RUKAWA!
Gimme a touch!
PASSS!!!
I'M CHANGING THE MOMENTUM RIGHT HERE!
HU
P

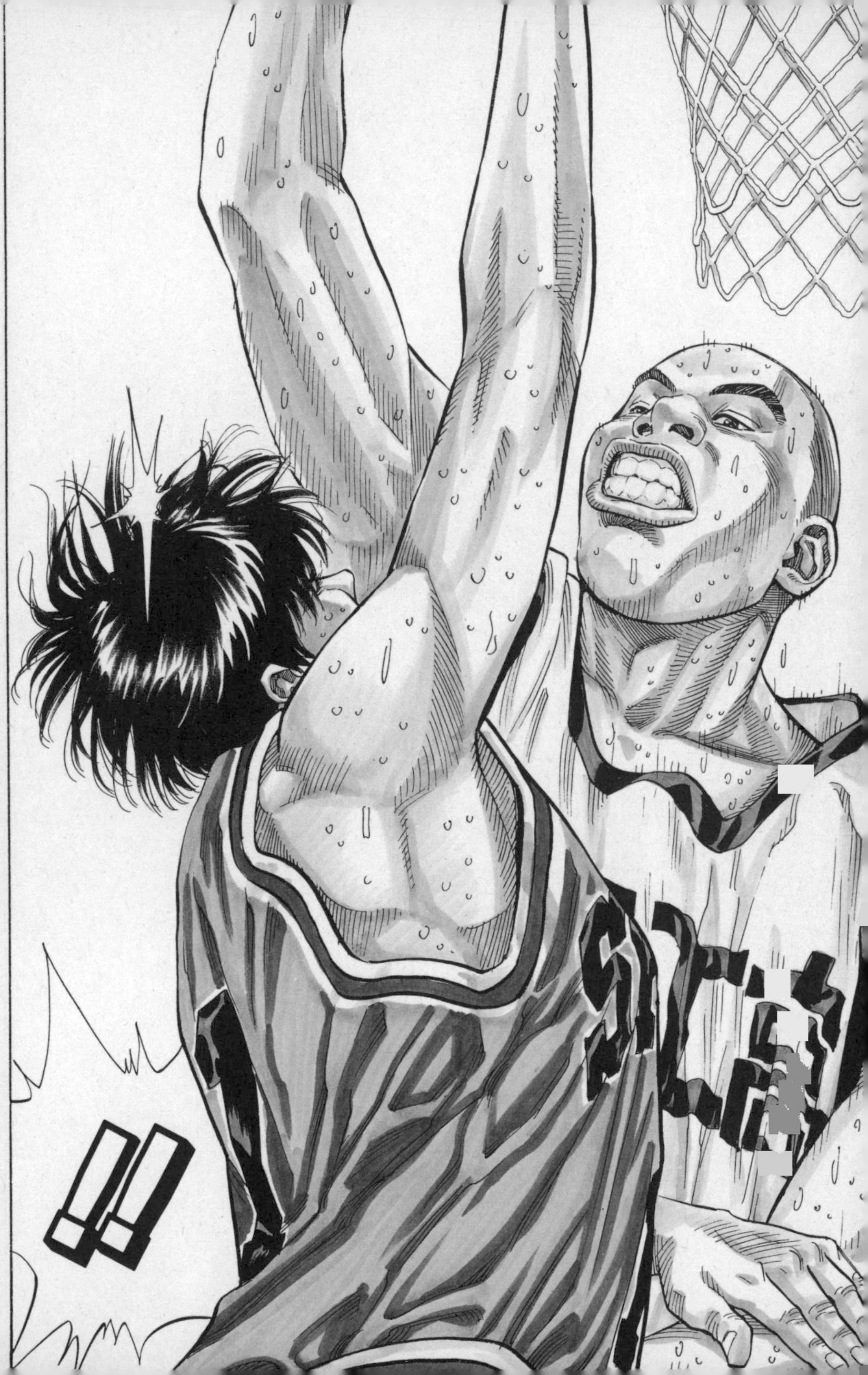
!!

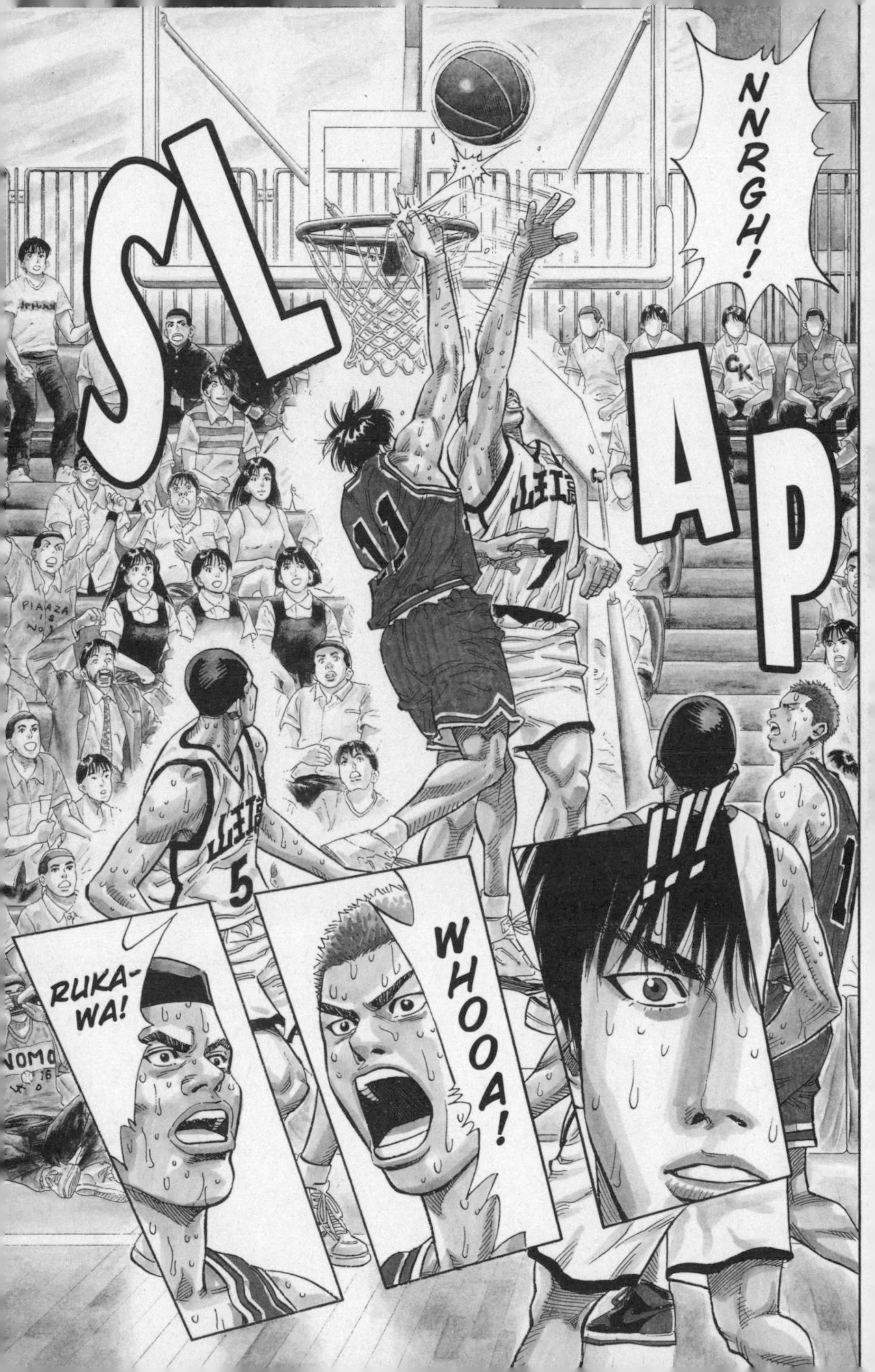
NNRGH!
SLAP
!!
WHOOA!
RUKA-
WA!

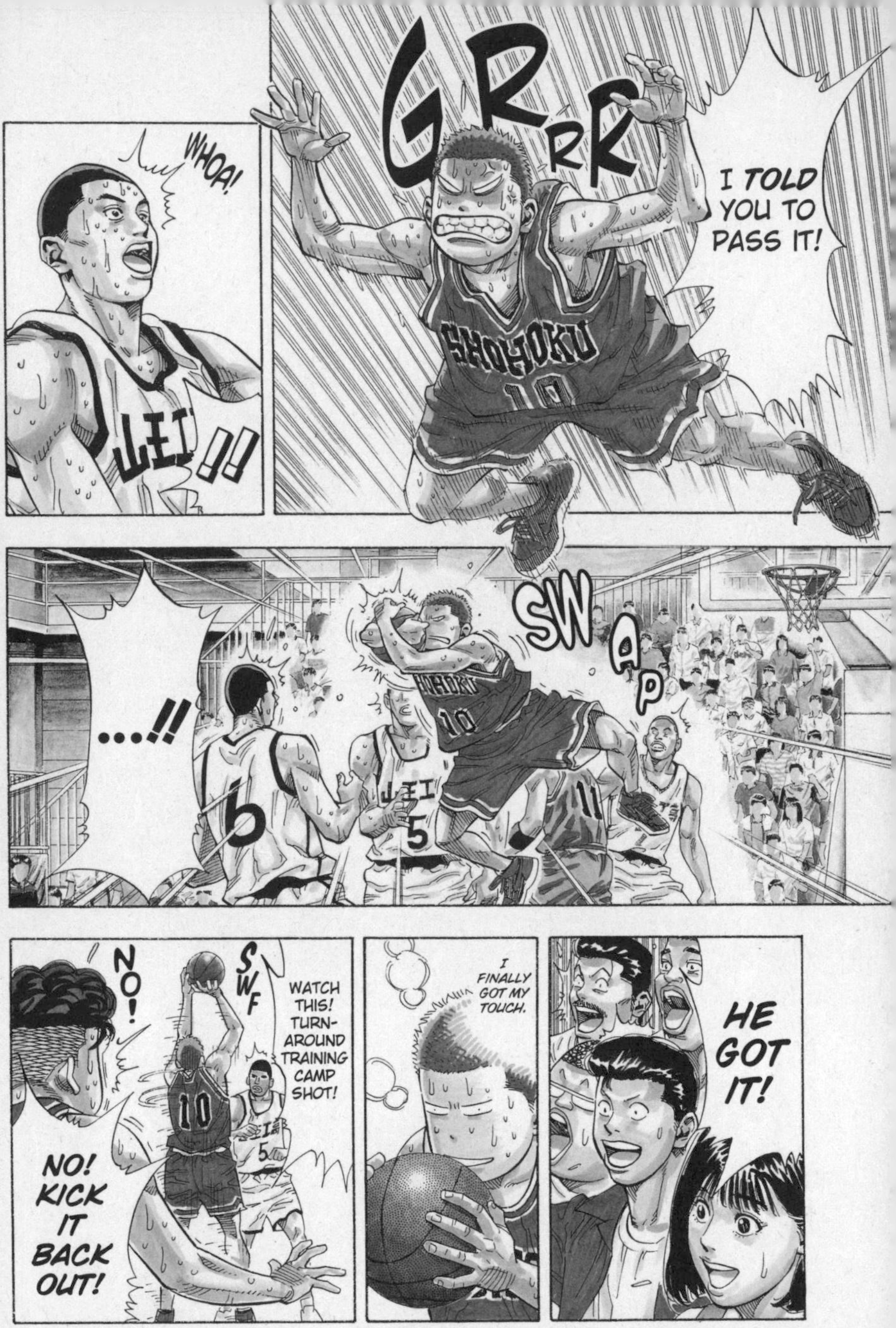
GRRR
I TOLD YOU TO PASS IT!
WHOA!
!!
SWAP
...!!
HE GOT IT!
I FINALLY GOT MY TOUCH.
SWF
WATCH THIS! TURN-AROUND TRAINING CAMP SHOT!
NO!
NO! KICK IT BACK OUT!

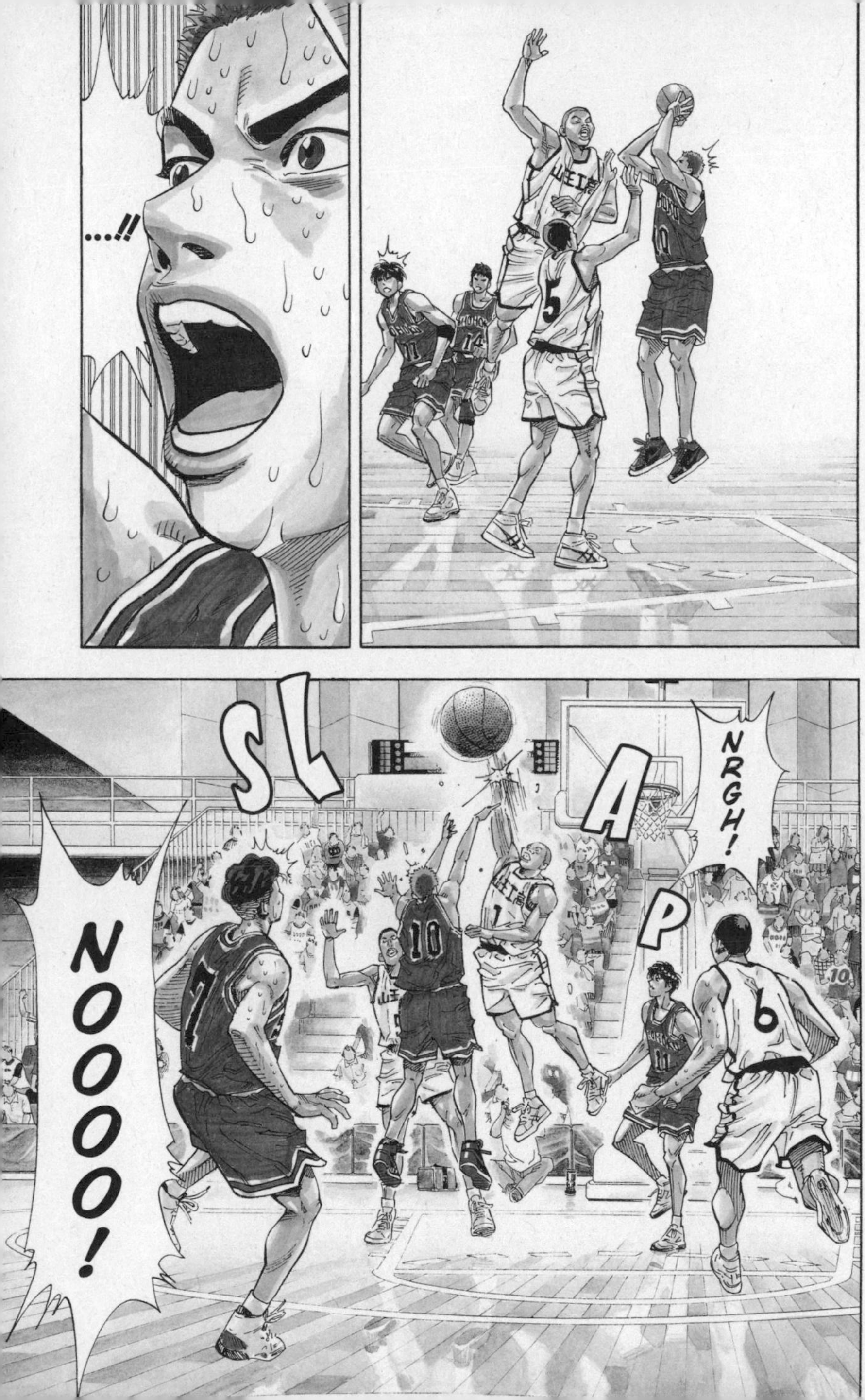
...!!
NRGH!
SLAP
NOOOO!

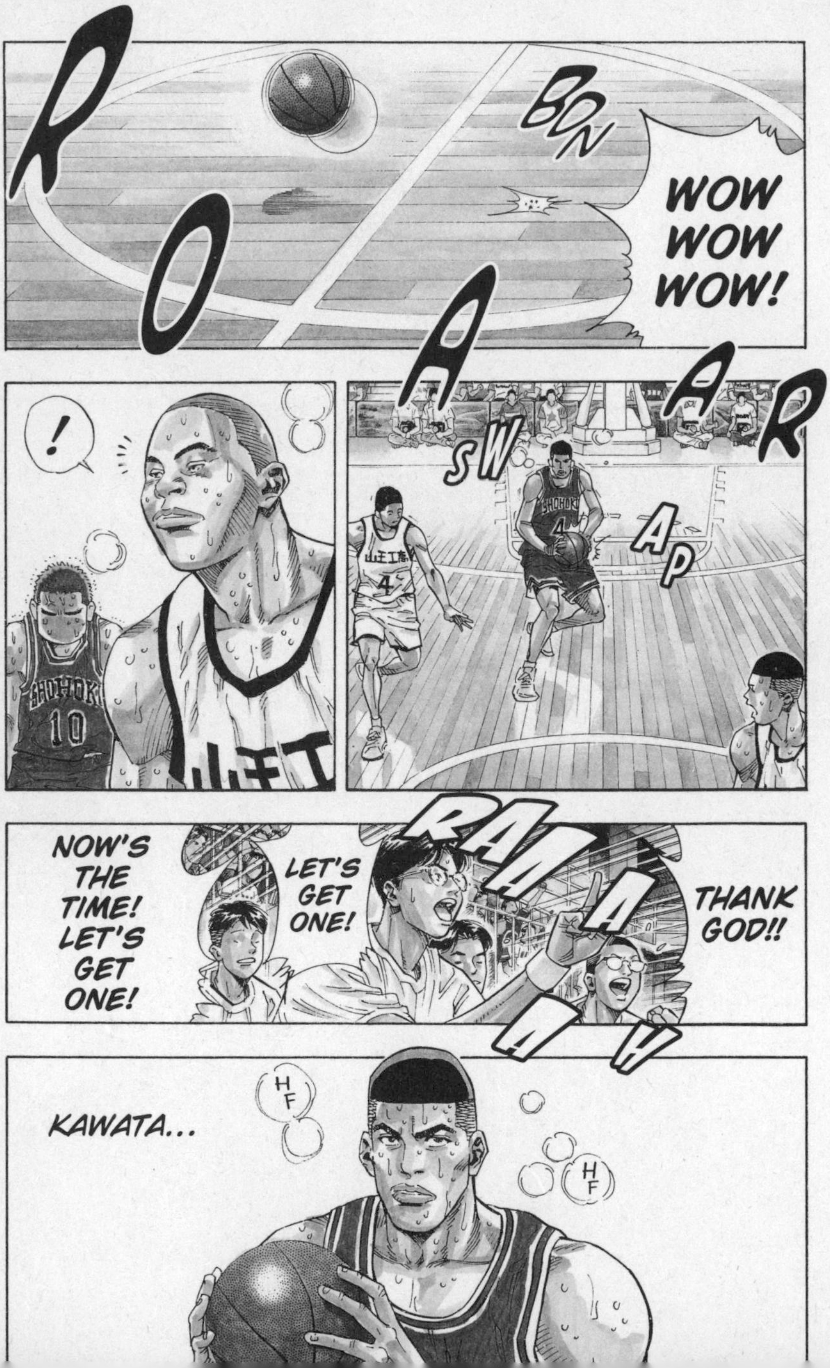
ROAAAR
BON
WOW WOW WOW!
SWAP
!
THANK GOD!!
LET'S GET ONE!
NOW'S THE TIME! LET'S GET ONE!
RAAAAAH
HF
HF
KAWATA...

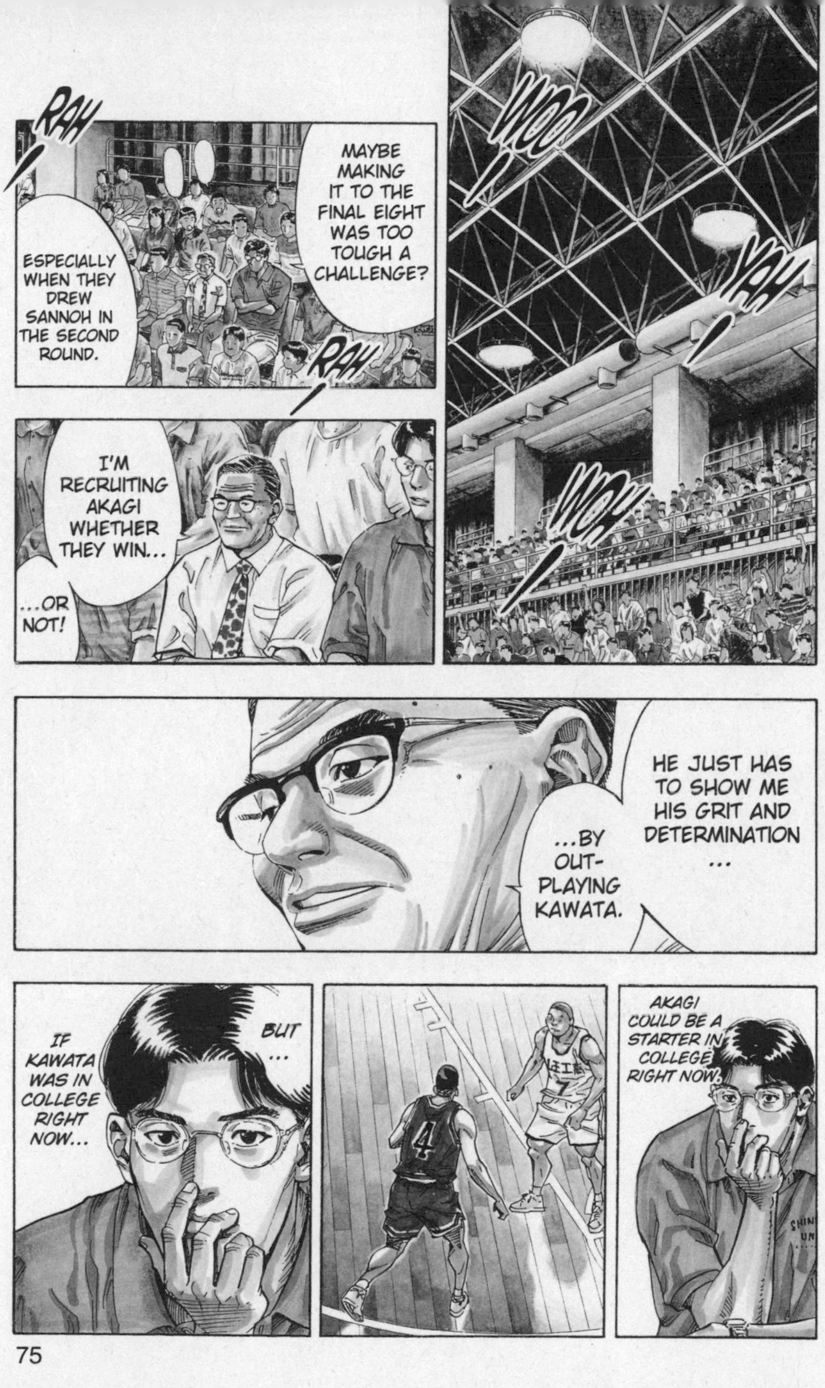
WOO
YAH
WAH
RAH
MAYBE MAKING IT TO THE FINAL EIGHT WAS TOO TOUGH A CHALLENGE?
ESPECIALLY WHEN THEY DREW SANNOH IN THE SECOND ROUND.
RAH
I'M RECRUITING AKAGI WHETHER THEY WIN...
...OR NOT!
HE JUST HAS TO SHOW ME HIS GRIT AND DETERMINATION...
...BY OUT-PLAYING KAWATA.
AKAGI COULD BE A STARTER IN COLLEGE RIGHT NOW.
BUT...
IF KAWATA WAS IN COLLEGE RIGHT NOW...

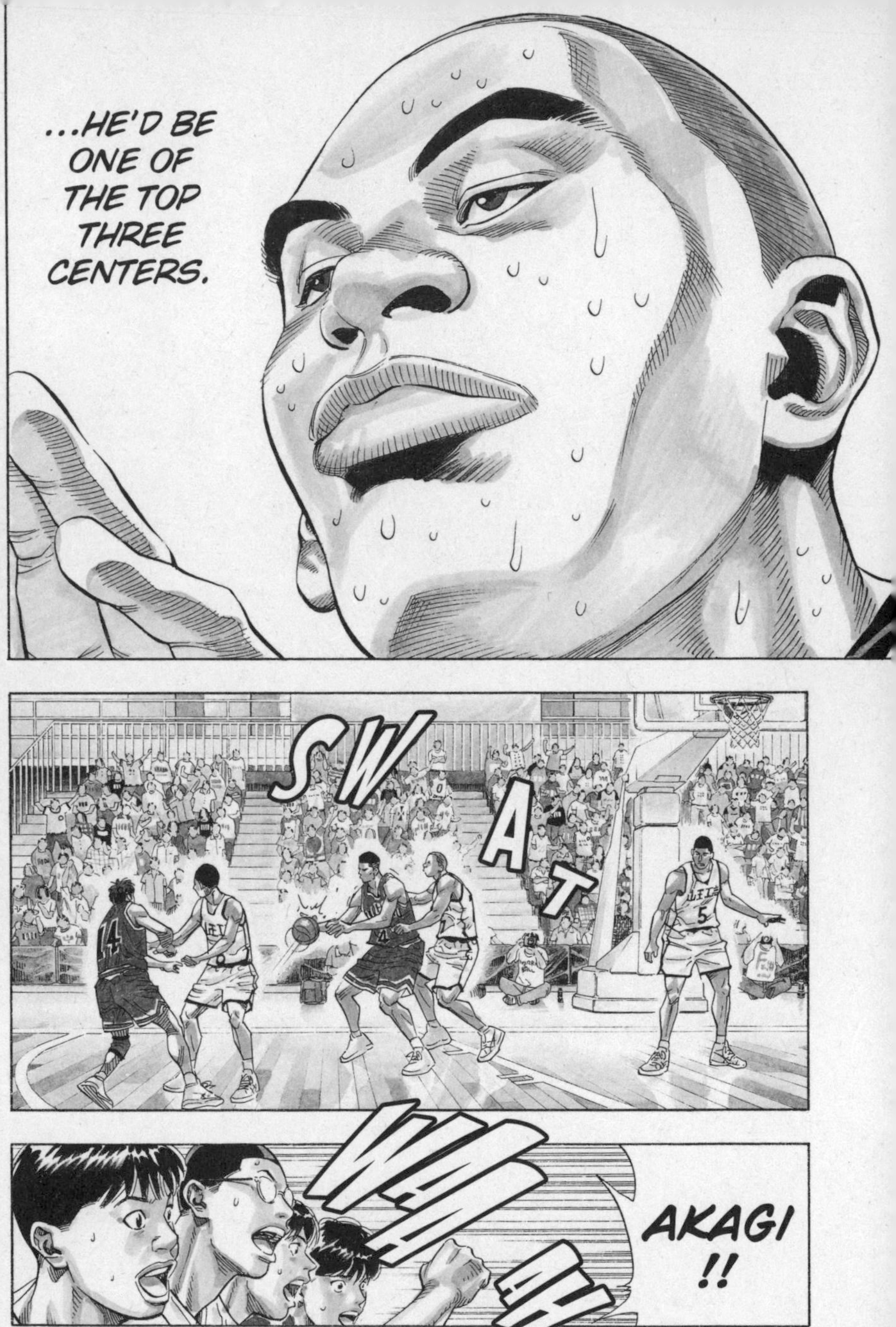
...HE'D BE ONE OF THE TOP THREE CENTERS.
SWAT
WAAAH
AKAGI !!

READ THIS WAY

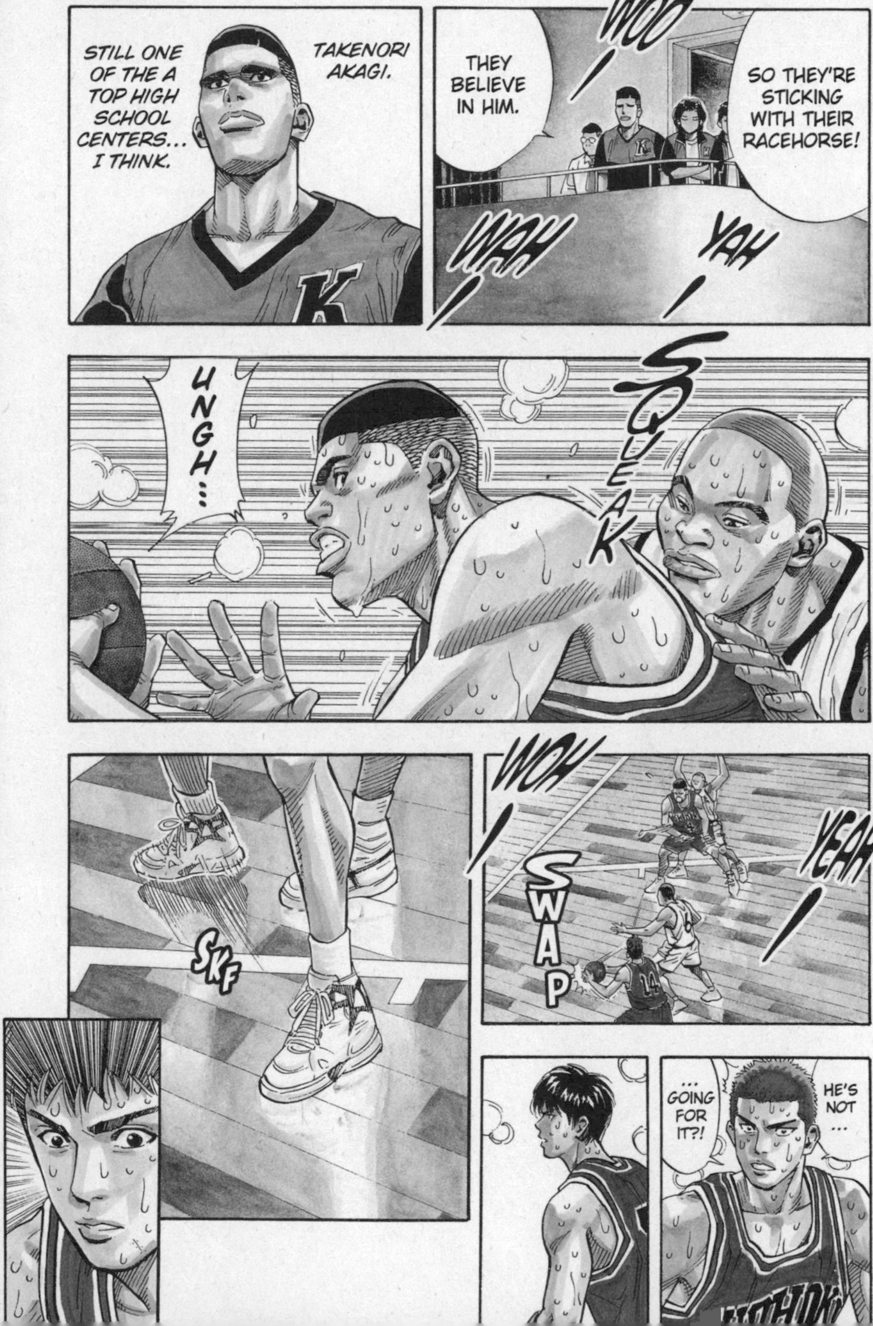
WOO
SO THEY'RE STICKING WITH THEIR RACEHORSE!
THEY BELIEVE IN HIM.
YAH
WAH
TAKENORI AKAGI.
STILL ONE OF THE A TOP HIGH SCHOOL CENTERS... I THINK.
SQUEAK
UNGH...
YEAH
WOH
SWAP
SKF
HE'S NOT ...
... GOING FOR IT?!

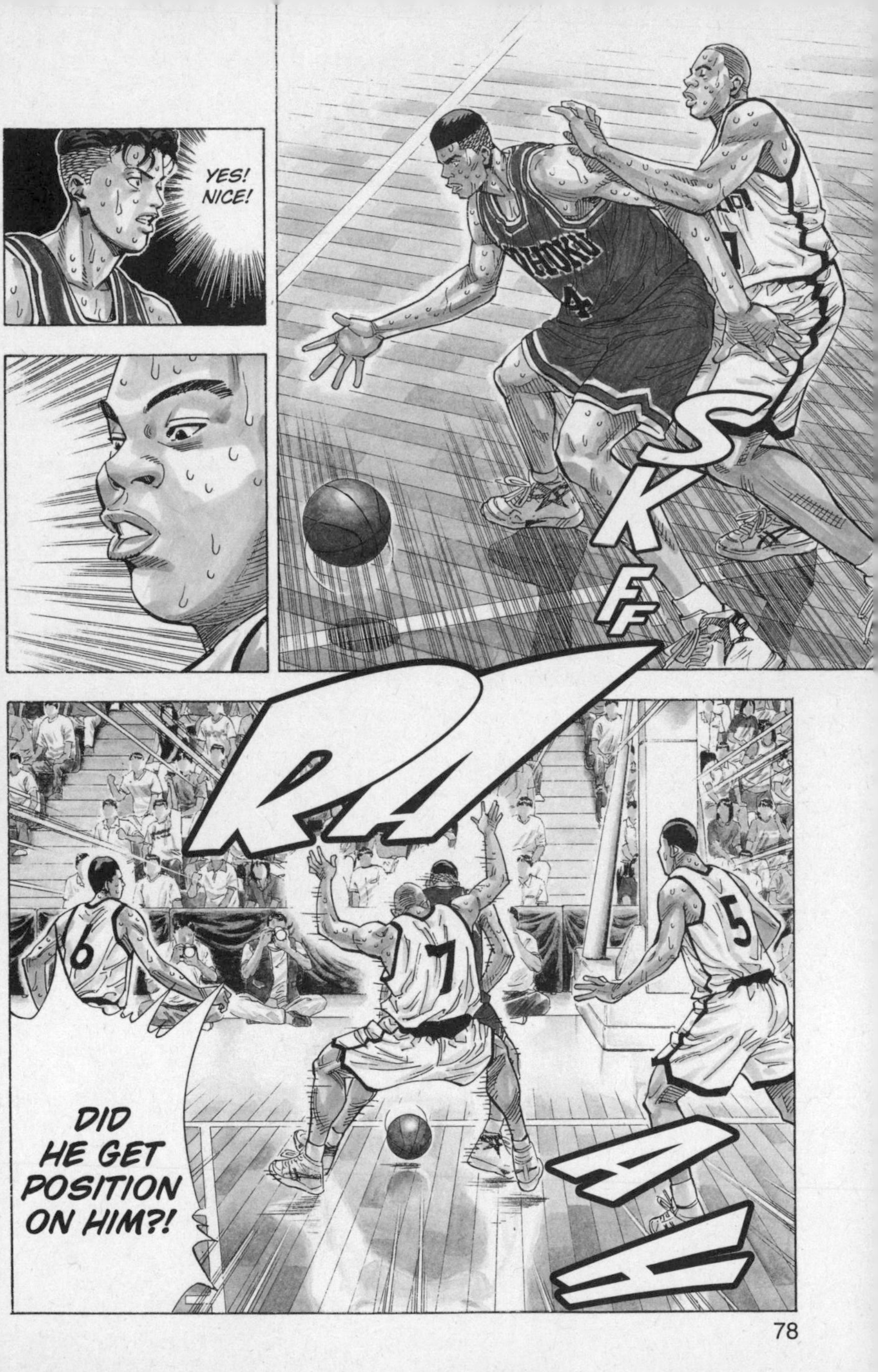
SKFF
YES! NICE!
RA
DID HE GET POSITION ON HIM?!
AA

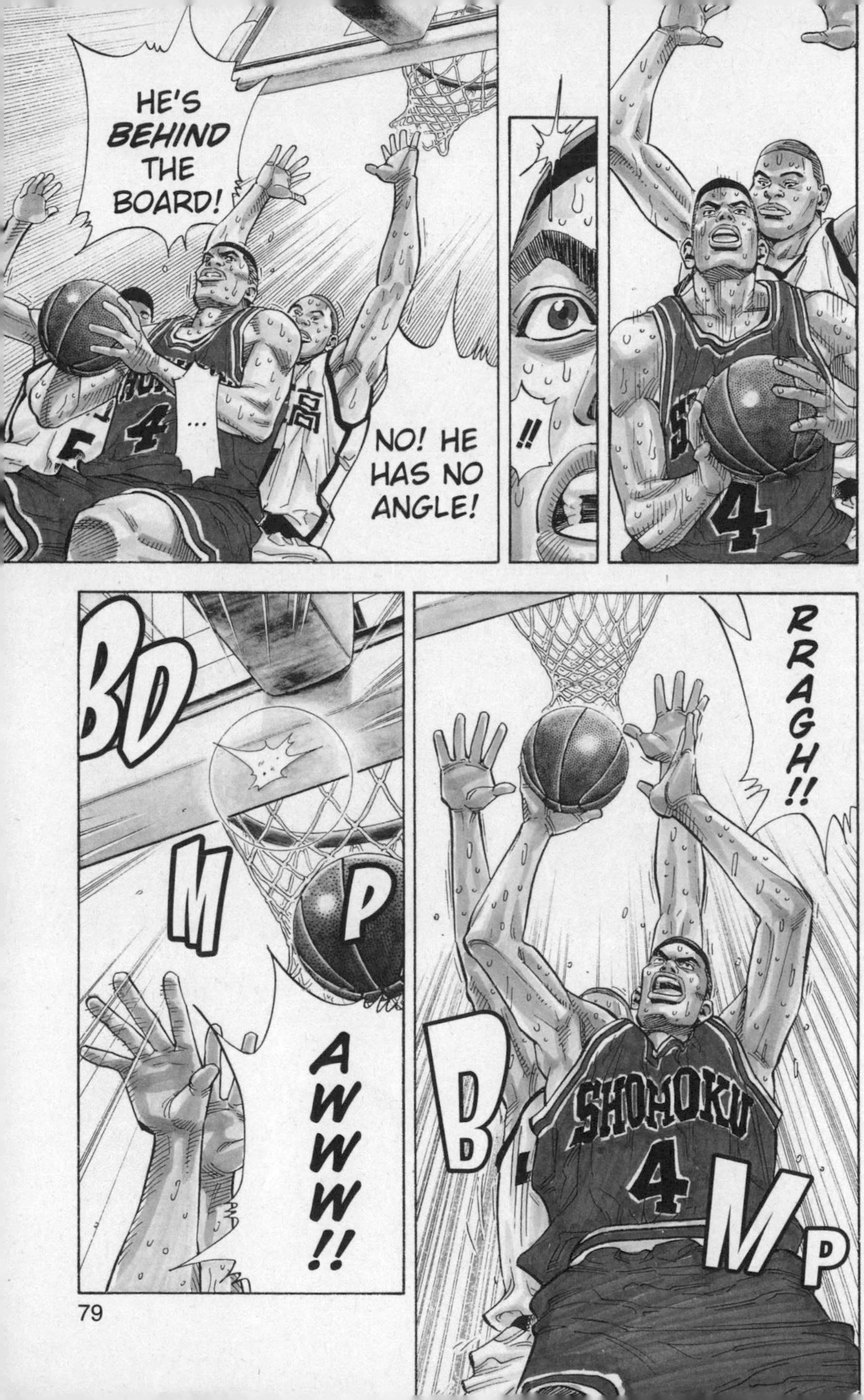
!!
HE'S BEHIND THE BOARD!
...
NO! HE HAS NO ANGLE!
RRAGH!!
BDMP
BDMP
AWWW!!

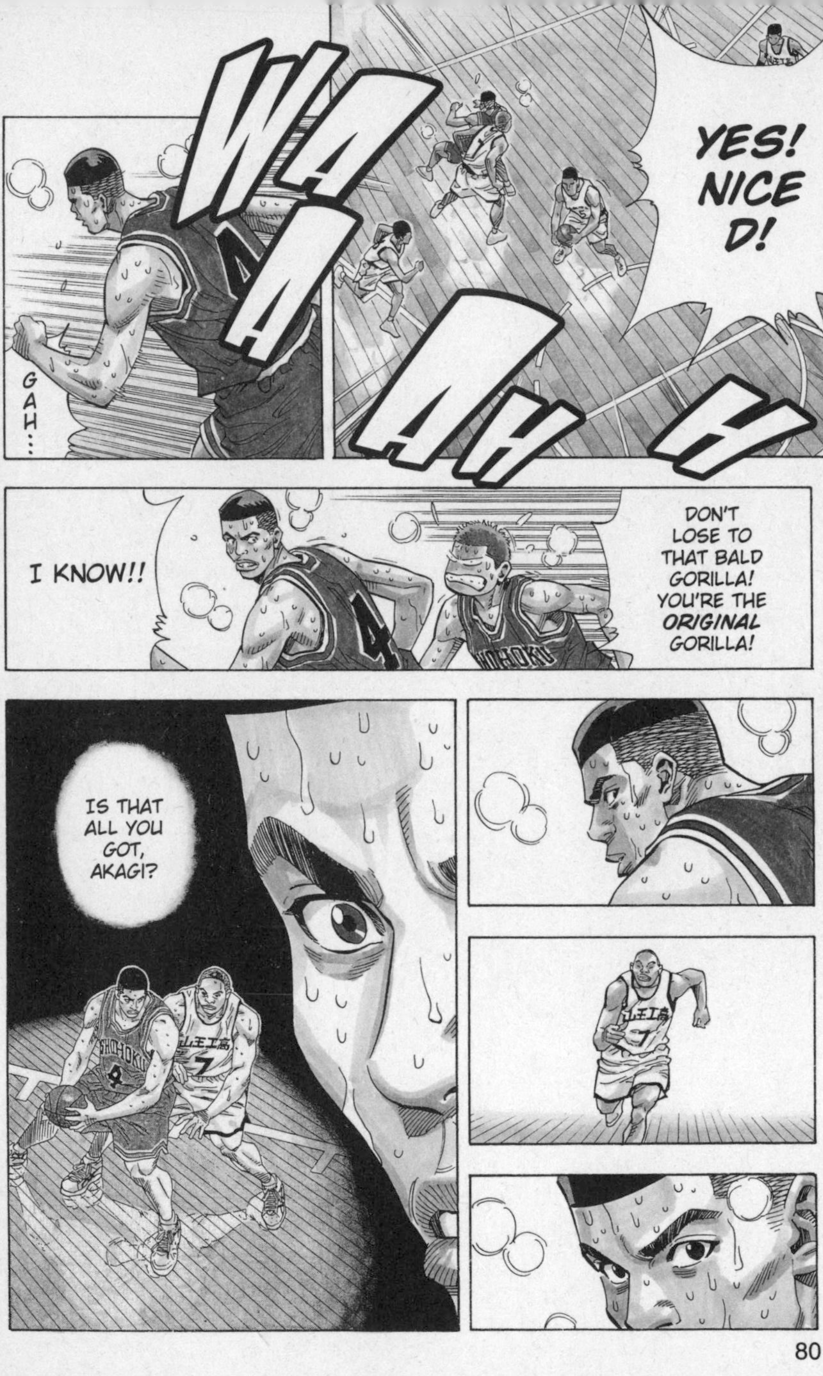
YES! NICE D!
WAAAAHH
GAH...
DON'T LOSE TO THAT BALD GORILLA! YOU'RE THE *ORIGINAL* GORILLA!
I KNOW!!
IS THAT ALL YOU GOT, AKAGI?

READ THIS WAY

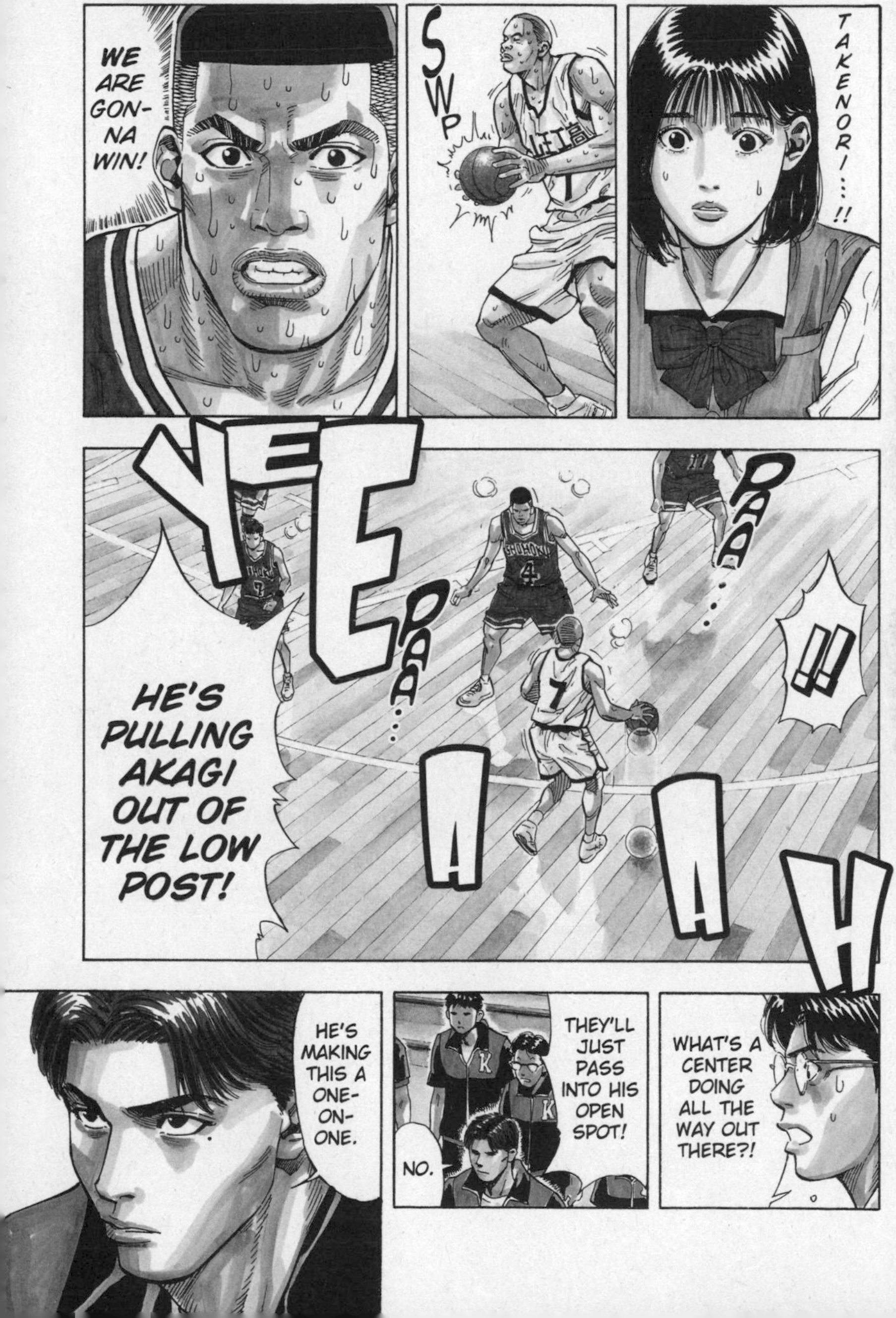
TAKENORI...!!
SWP
WE ARE GON-NA WIN!
DAA...
YEEAAAH
!!
DAA...
HE'S PULLING AKAGI OUT OF THE LOW POST!
WHAT'S A CENTER DOING ALL THE WAY OUT THERE?!
THEY'LL JUST PASS INTO HIS OPEN SPOT!
NO.
HE'S MAKING THIS A ONE-ON-ONE.

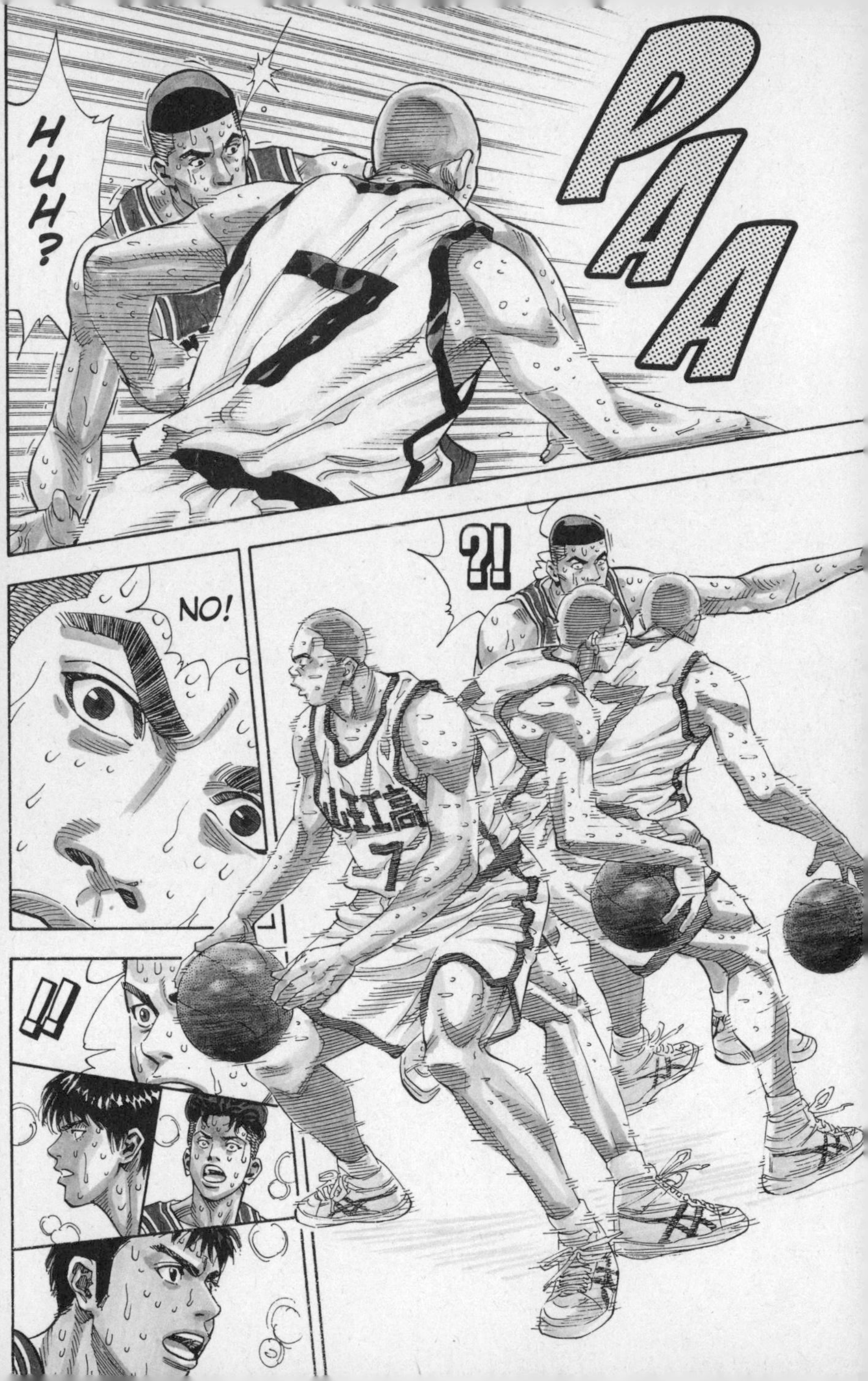
PAA
HUH?
?!
NO!
!!

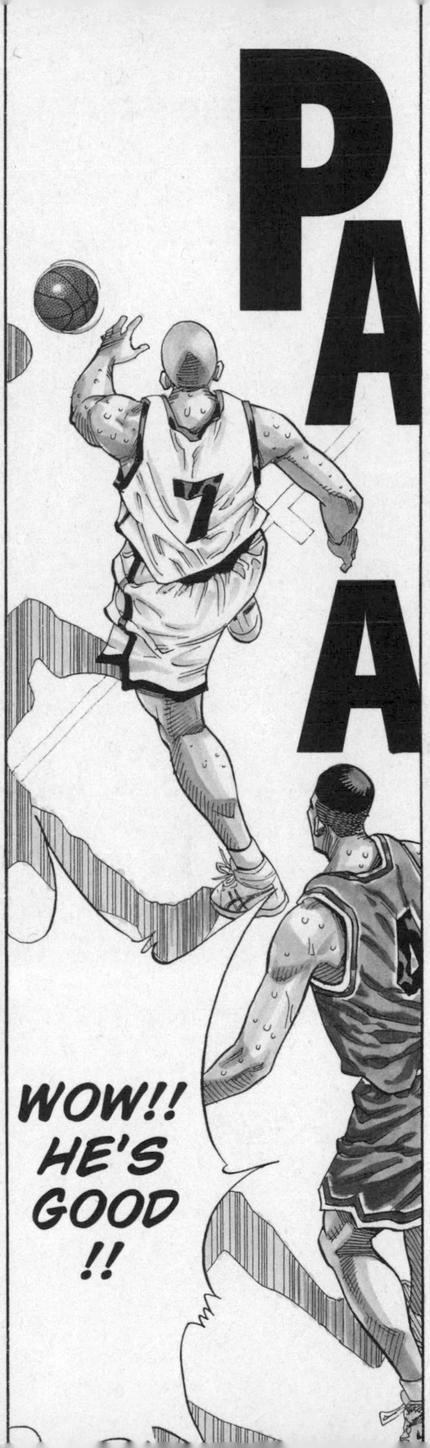
PAAA
WOW!! HE'S GOOD!!
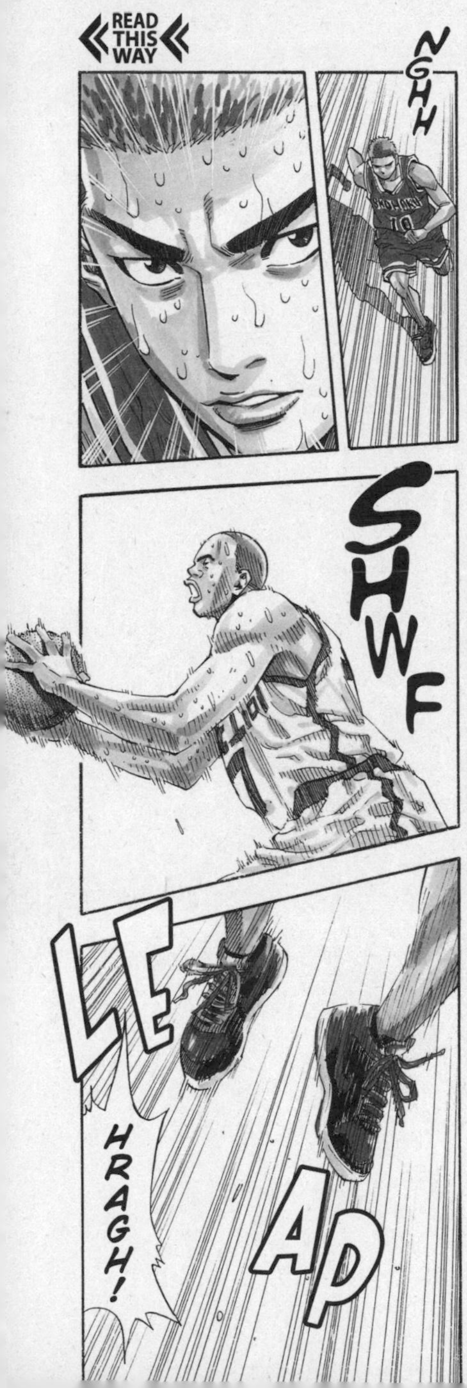
READ THIS WAY
NGHH
SHWF
LEAP
HRAGH!

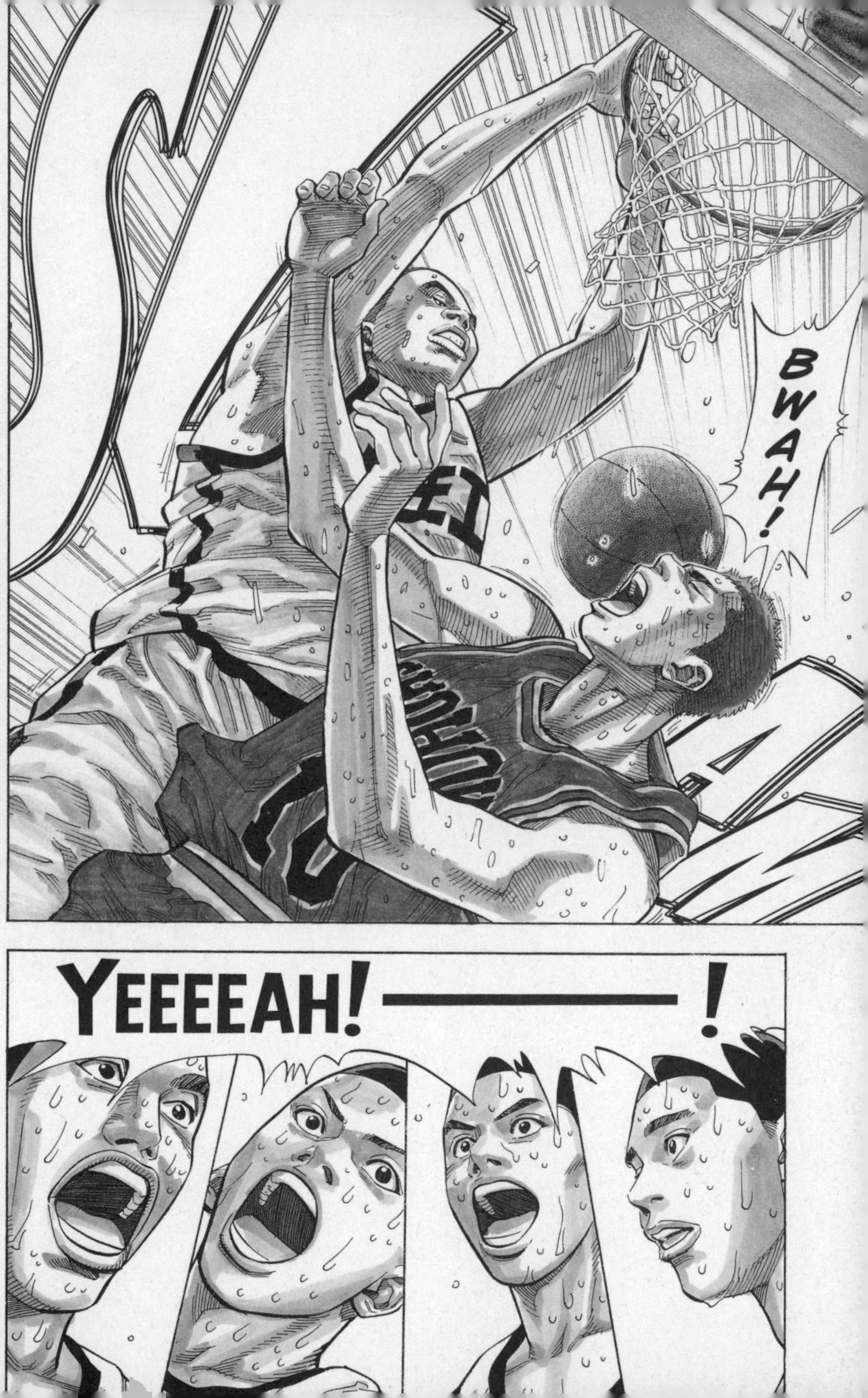
BWAH!
YEEEEAH! ——————— !

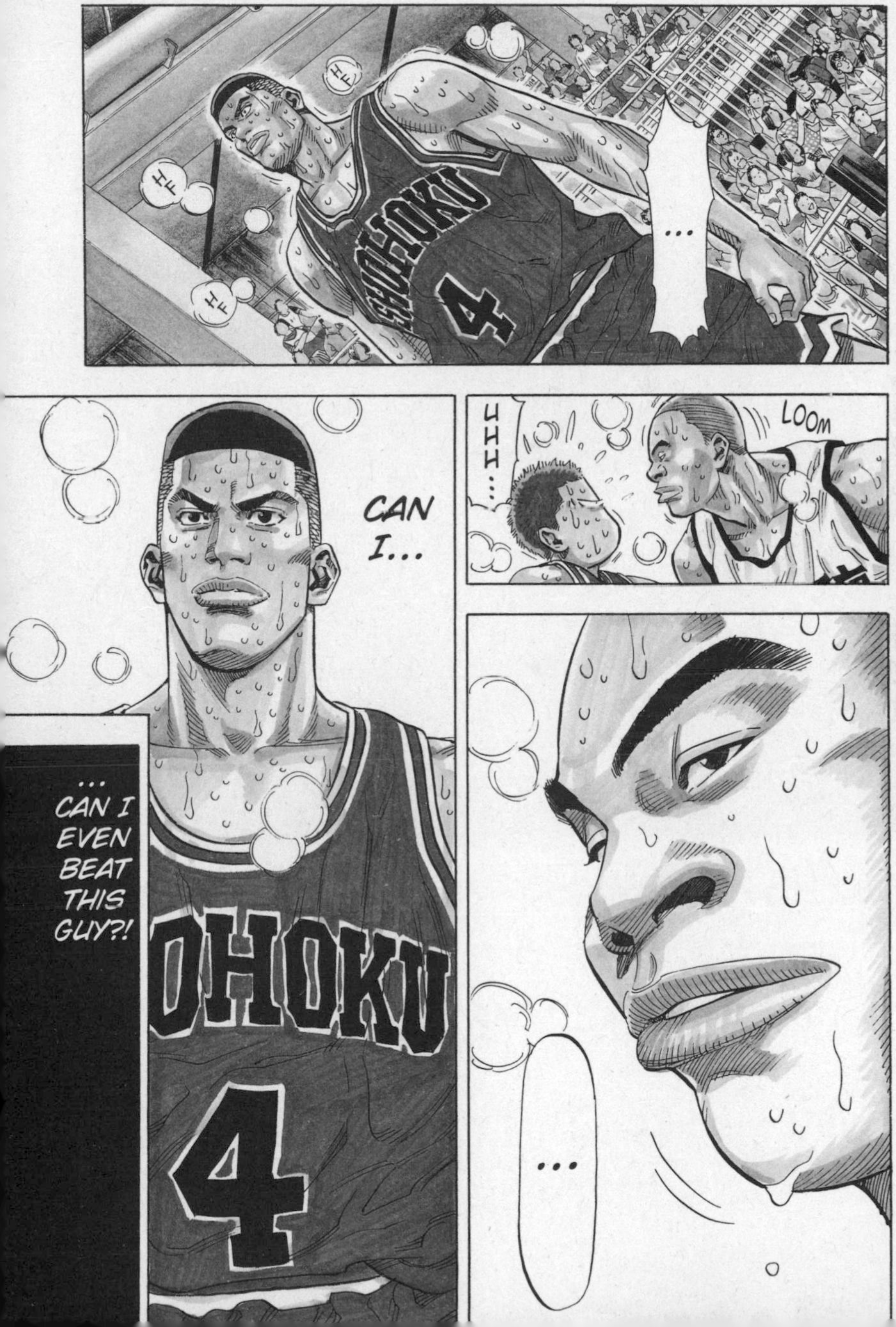
HF
HF
HF
...
UHH...
LOOM
...
CAN I...
... CAN I EVEN BEAT THIS GUY?!

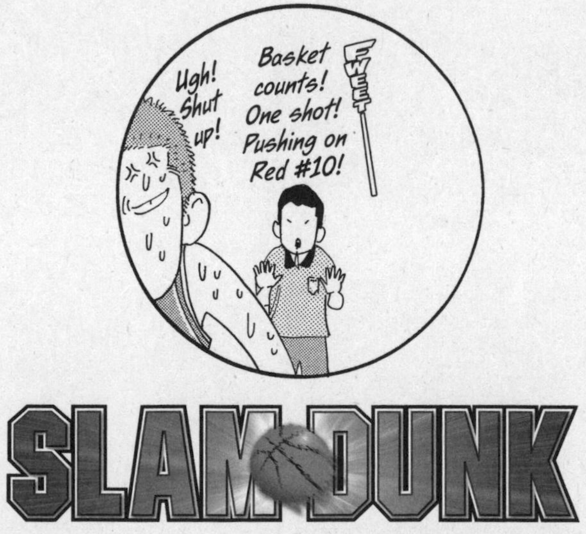
FWEET
Basket counts! One shot! Pushing on Red #10!
Ugh! Shut up!

SLAM DUNK

IN THE MIDDLE

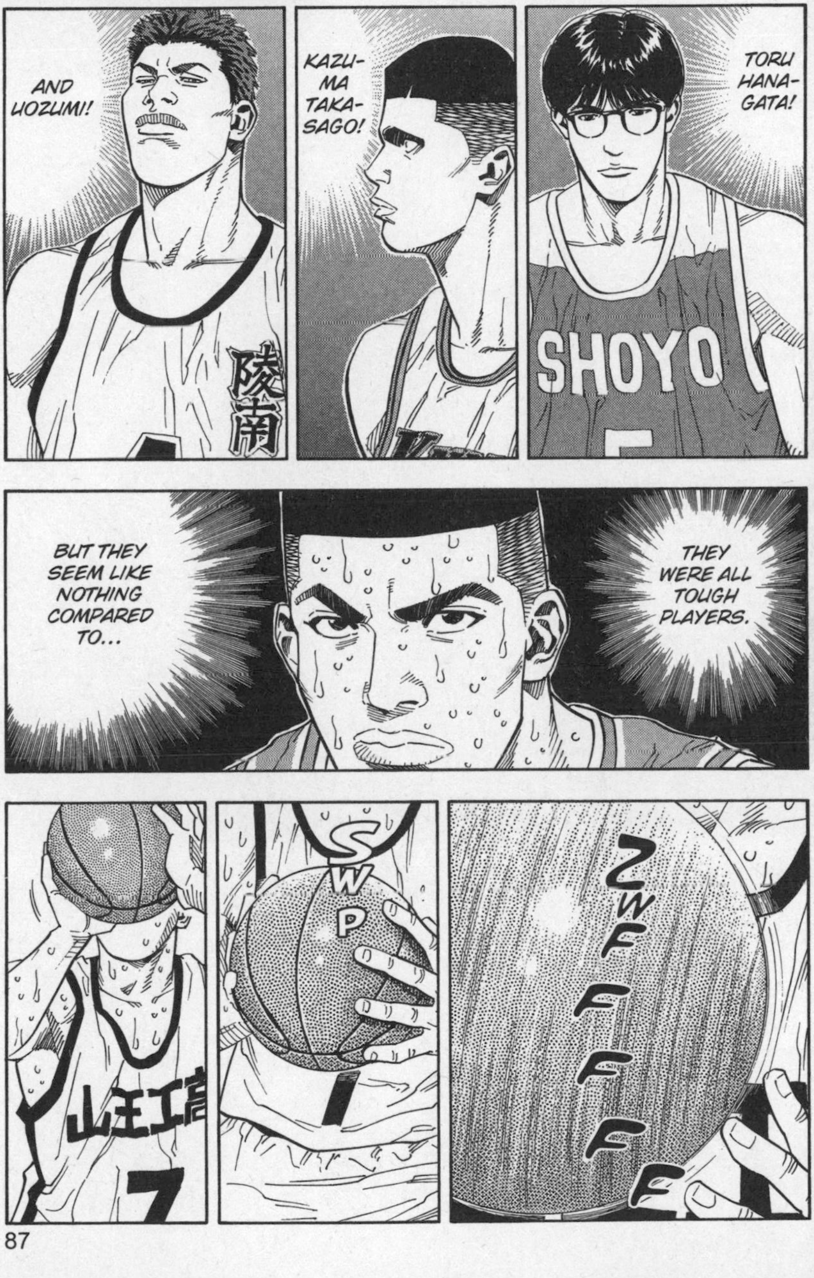
TORU HANAGATA!
SHOYO
KAZUMA TAKASAGO!
AND UOZUMI!
陵南
THEY WERE ALL TOUGH PLAYERS.
BUT THEY SEEM LIKE NOTHING COMPARED TO...
ZWFFFFFF
SWP
山王工

#238 IN THE MIDDLE

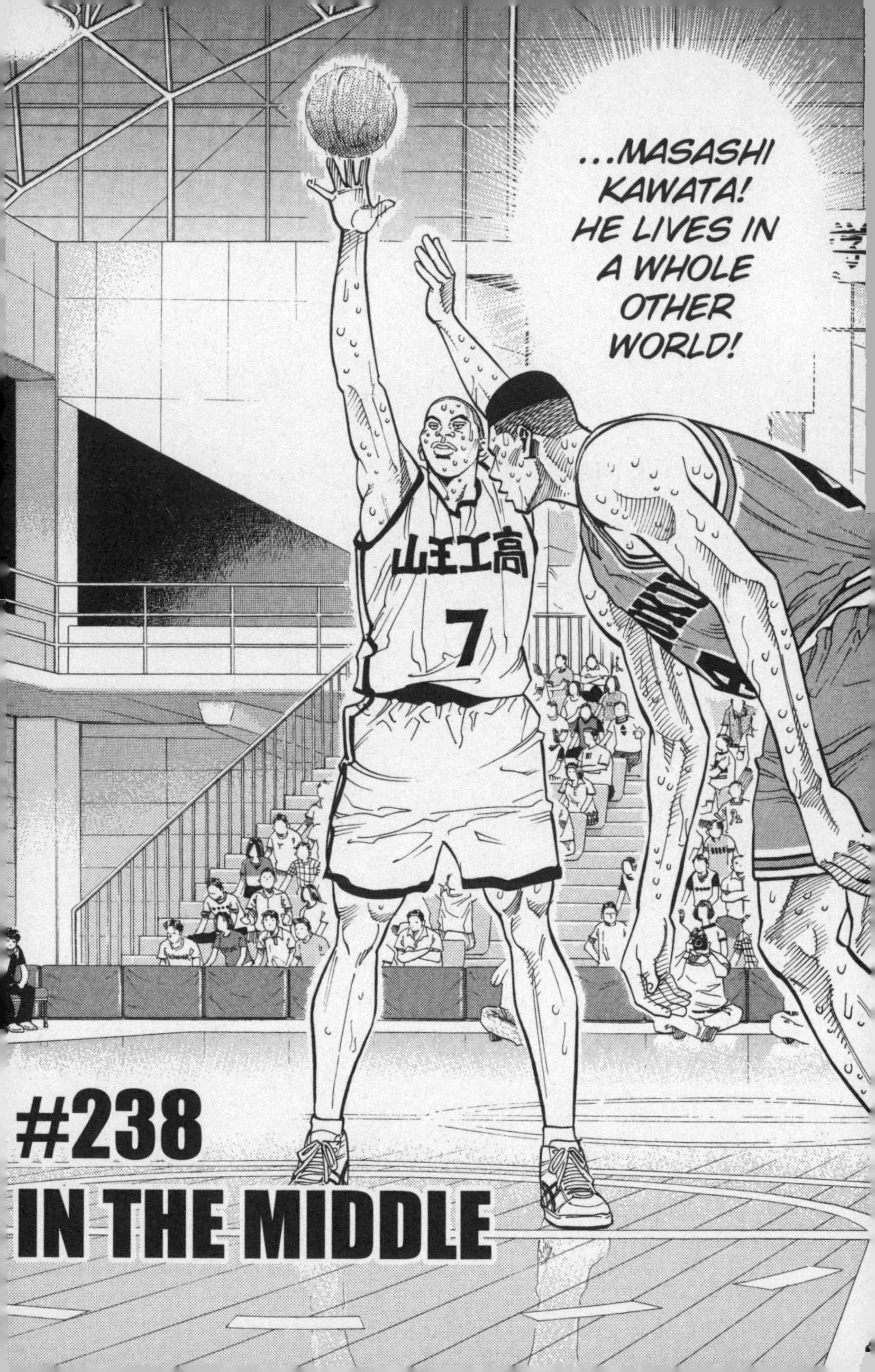
...MASASHI KAWATA! HE LIVES IN A WHOLE OTHER WORLD!
山王工高
7

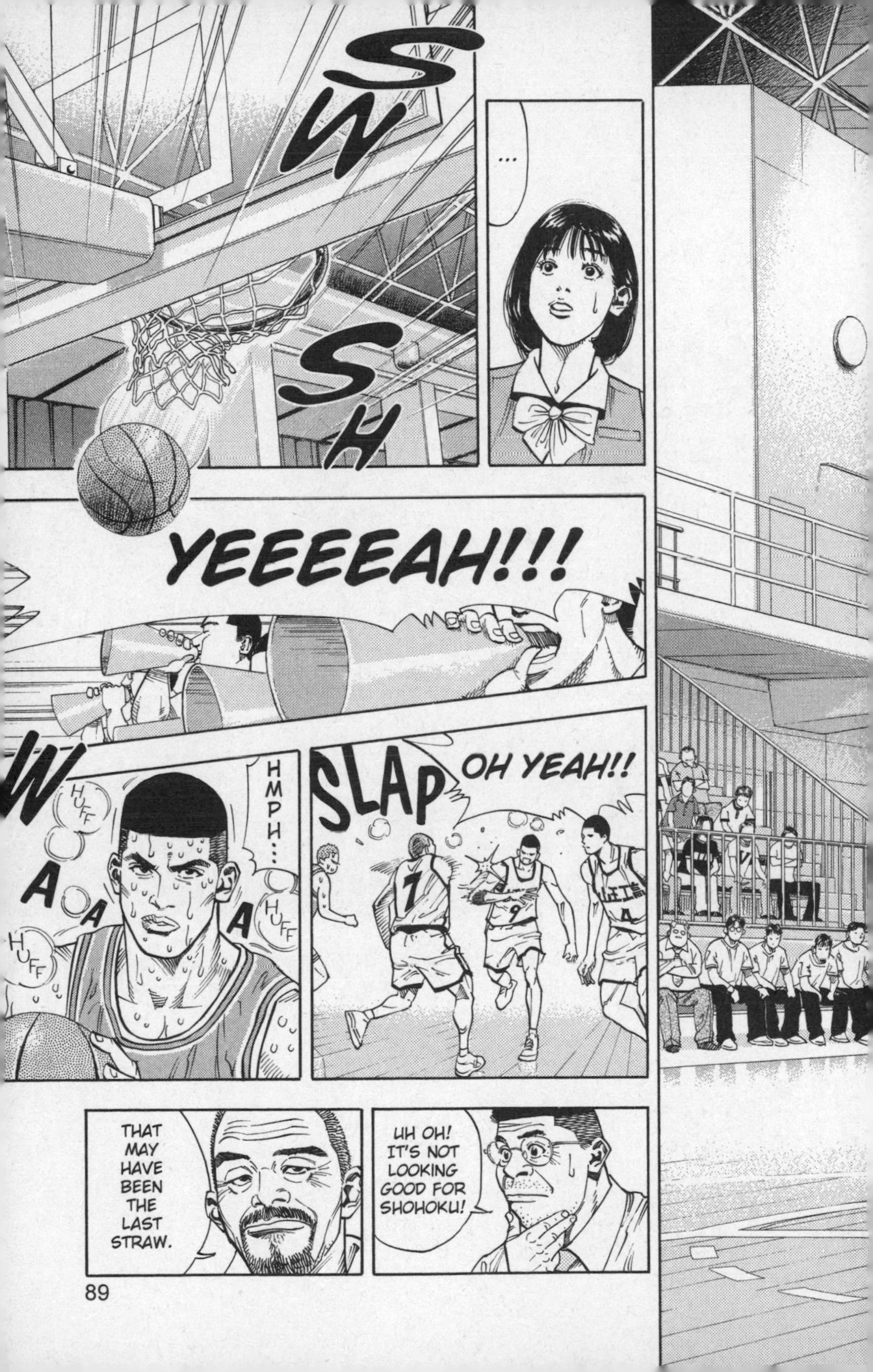
...
SWSH
YEEEEAH!!!
SLAP
OH YEAH!!
HMPH...
HUFF
HUFF
HUFF
WAAAA
UH OH! IT'S NOT LOOKING GOOD FOR SHOHOKU!
THAT MAY HAVE BEEN THE LAST STRAW.

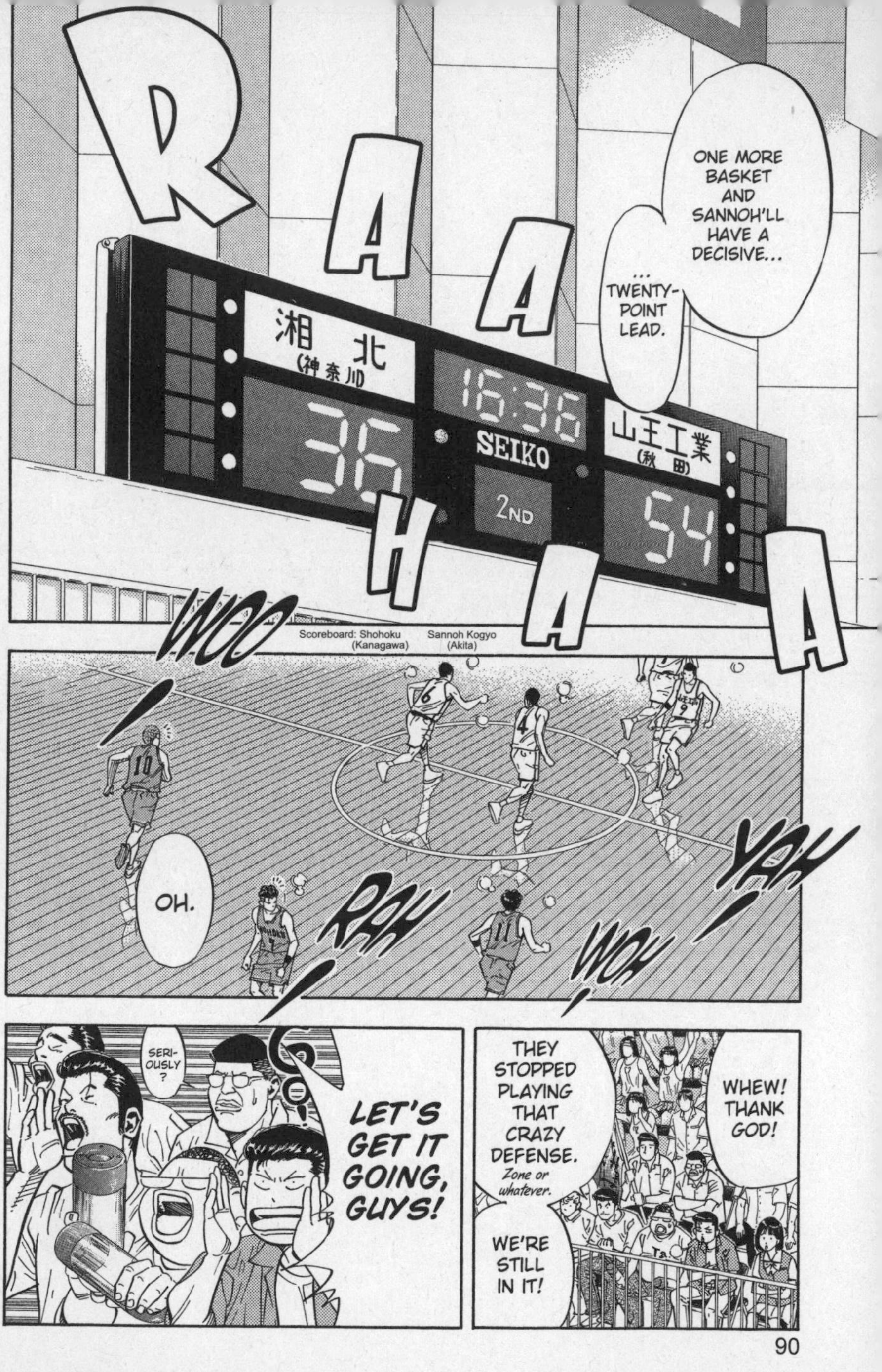
RAA
ONE MORE BASKET AND SANNOH'LL HAVE A DECISIVE...
...TWENTY-POINT LEAD.
湘北 (神奈川
16:36
SEIKO
山王工業 (秋田)
36
2ND
54
HAA
Scoreboard: Shohoku (Kanagawa) Sannoh Kogyo (Akita)
WOO!
YAH!
WOH!
RAH!
OH.
WHEW! THANK GOD!
THEY STOPPED PLAYING THAT CRAZY DEFENSE.
Zone or whatever.
WE'RE STILL IN IT!
LET'S GET IT GOING, GUYS!
SERI-OUSLY?

READ THIS WAY

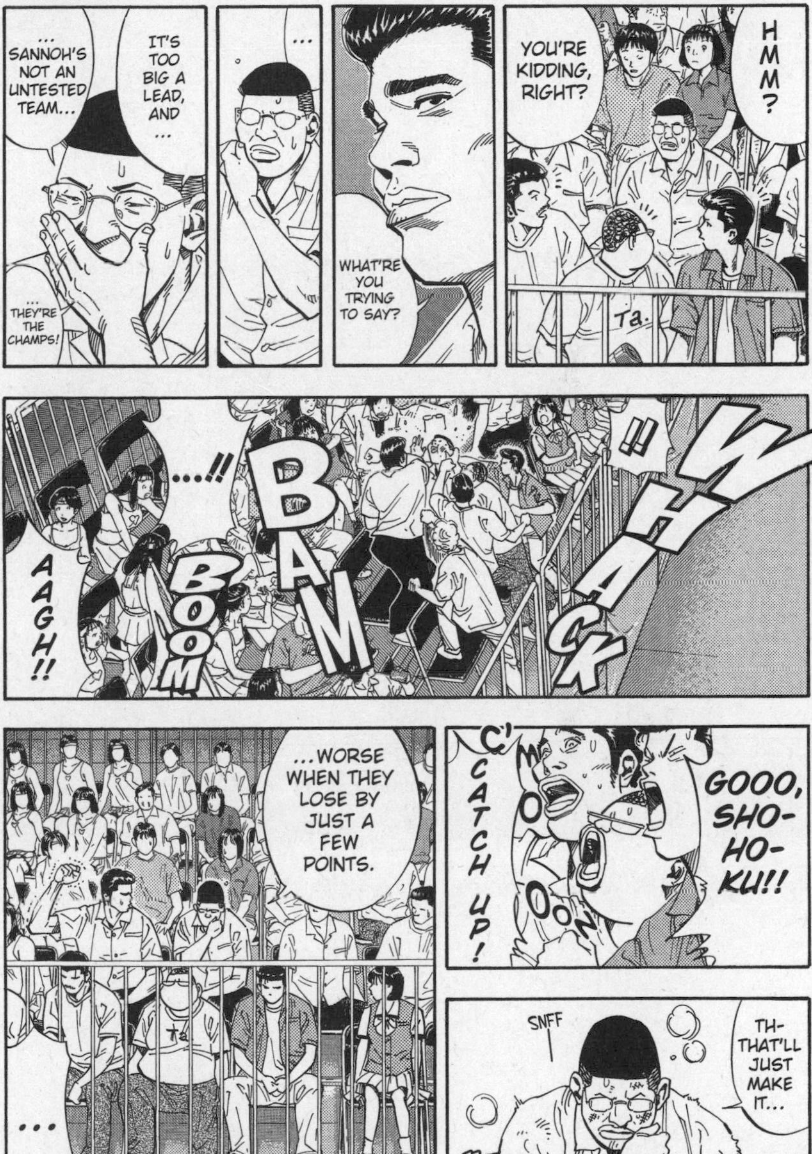
HMM?
YOU'RE KIDDING, RIGHT?
Ta.
WHAT'RE YOU TRYING TO SAY?
...
IT'S TOO BIG A LEAD, AND ...
...SANNOH'S NOT AN UNTESTED TEAM...
...THEY'RE THE CHAMPS!
WHACK
!!
BAM
BOOM
...!!
AAGH!!
GOOO, SHO-HO-KU!!
C'MOOOOON
CATCH UP!
TH-THAT'LL JUST MAKE IT...
SNFF
MUMBLE
...WORSE WHEN THEY LOSE BY JUST A FEW POINTS.
...

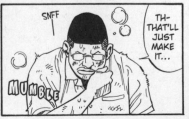

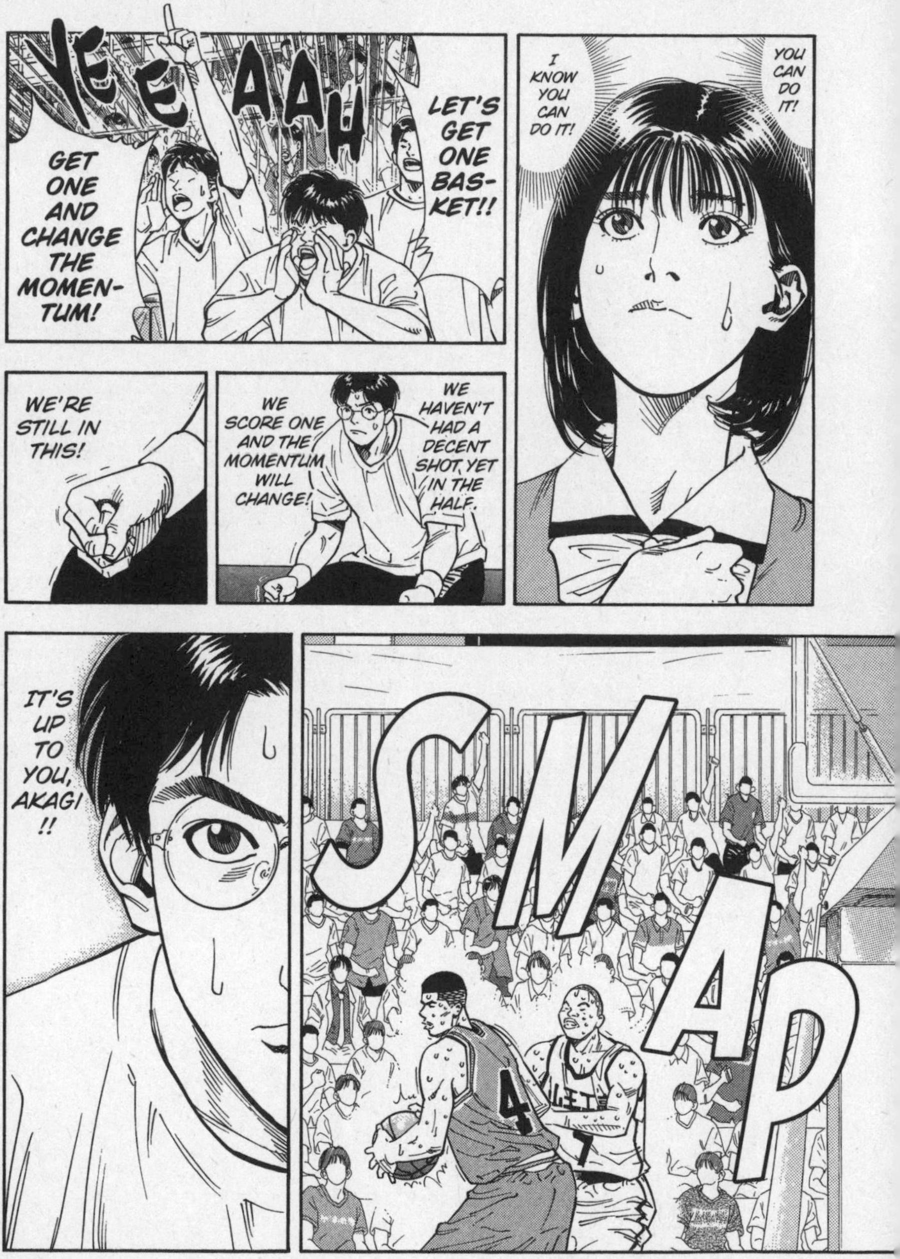
YOU CAN DO IT!
I KNOW YOU CAN DO IT!
YEEAAH
LET'S GET ONE BAS-KET!!
GET ONE AND CHANGE THE MOMEN-TUM!
WE HAVEN'T HAD A DECENT SHOT YET IN THE HALF.
WE SCORE ONE AND THE MOMENTUM WILL CHANGE!
WE'RE STILL IN THIS!
SMAP
IT'S UP TO YOU, AKAGI !!

READ THIS WAY

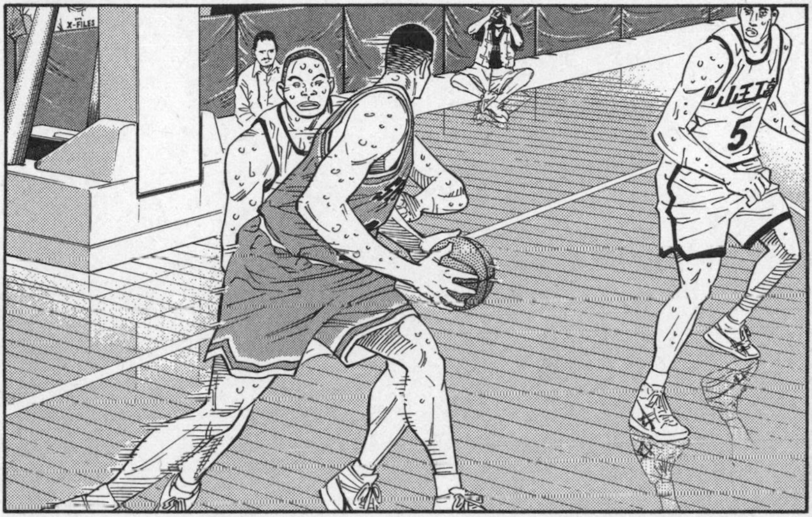
山王工高

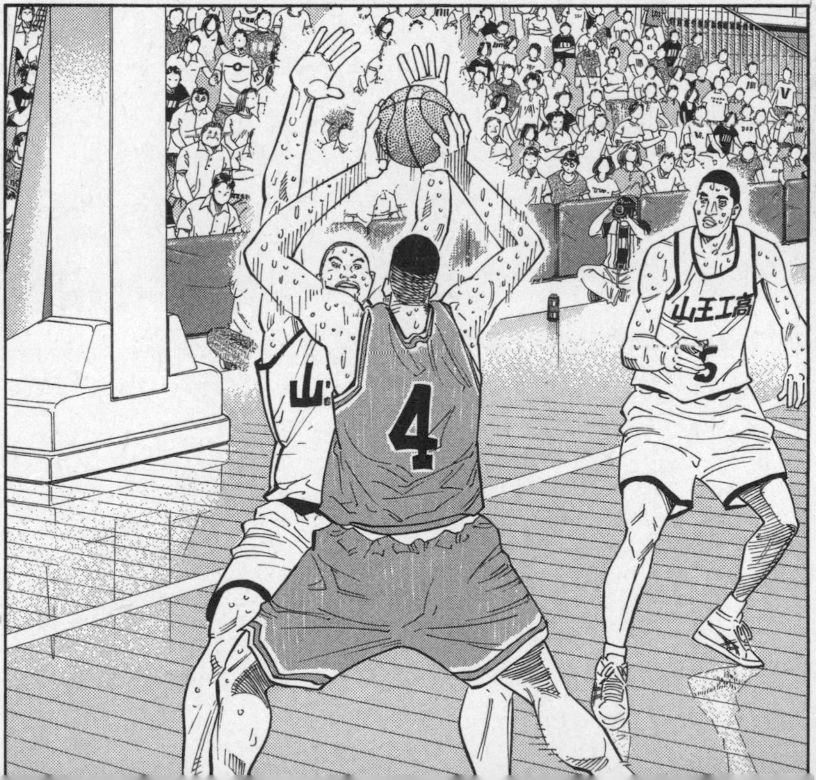
山王工高

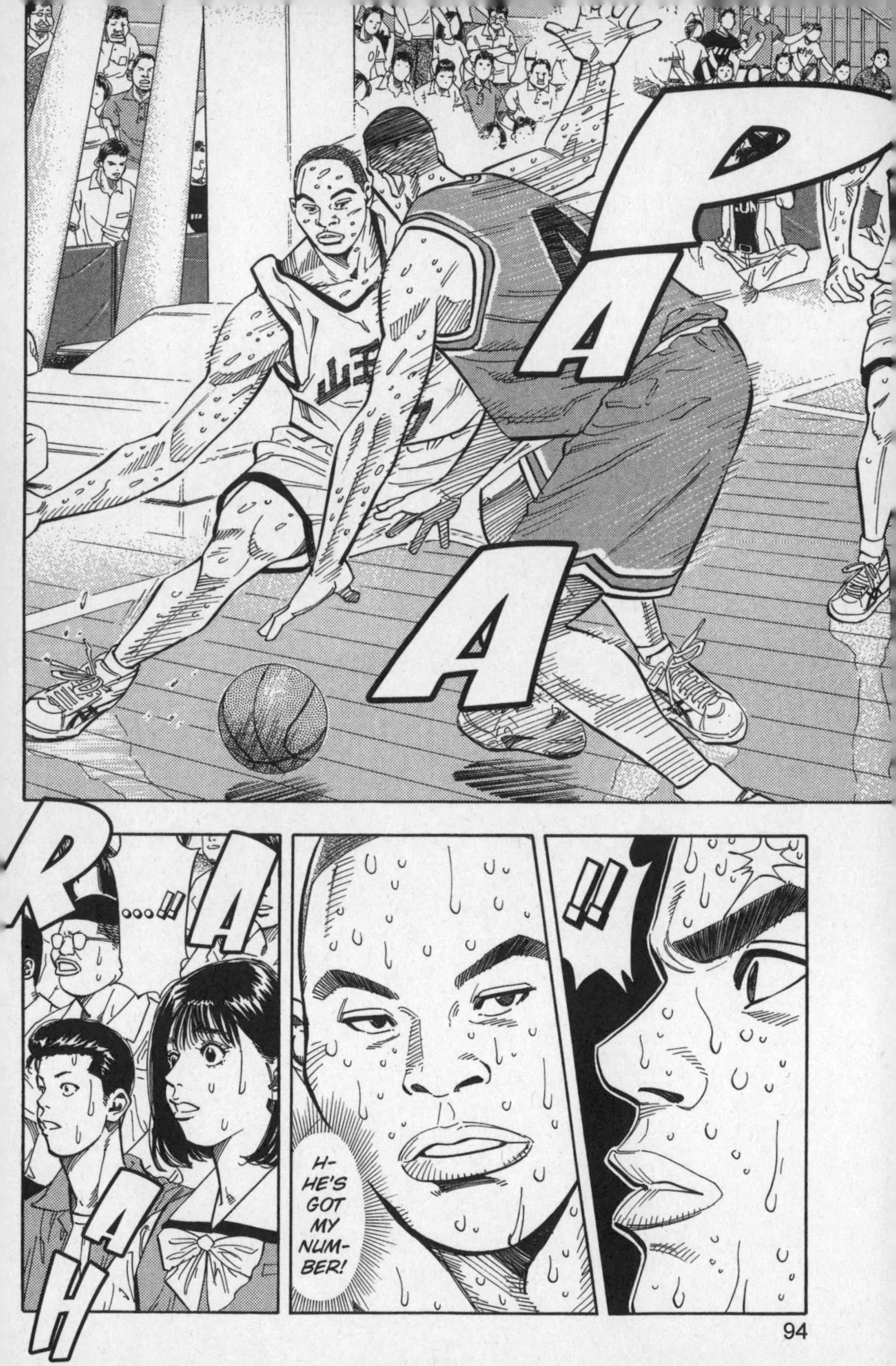
PAA
!!
H-HE'S GOT MY NUMBER!
P...!!
AAH

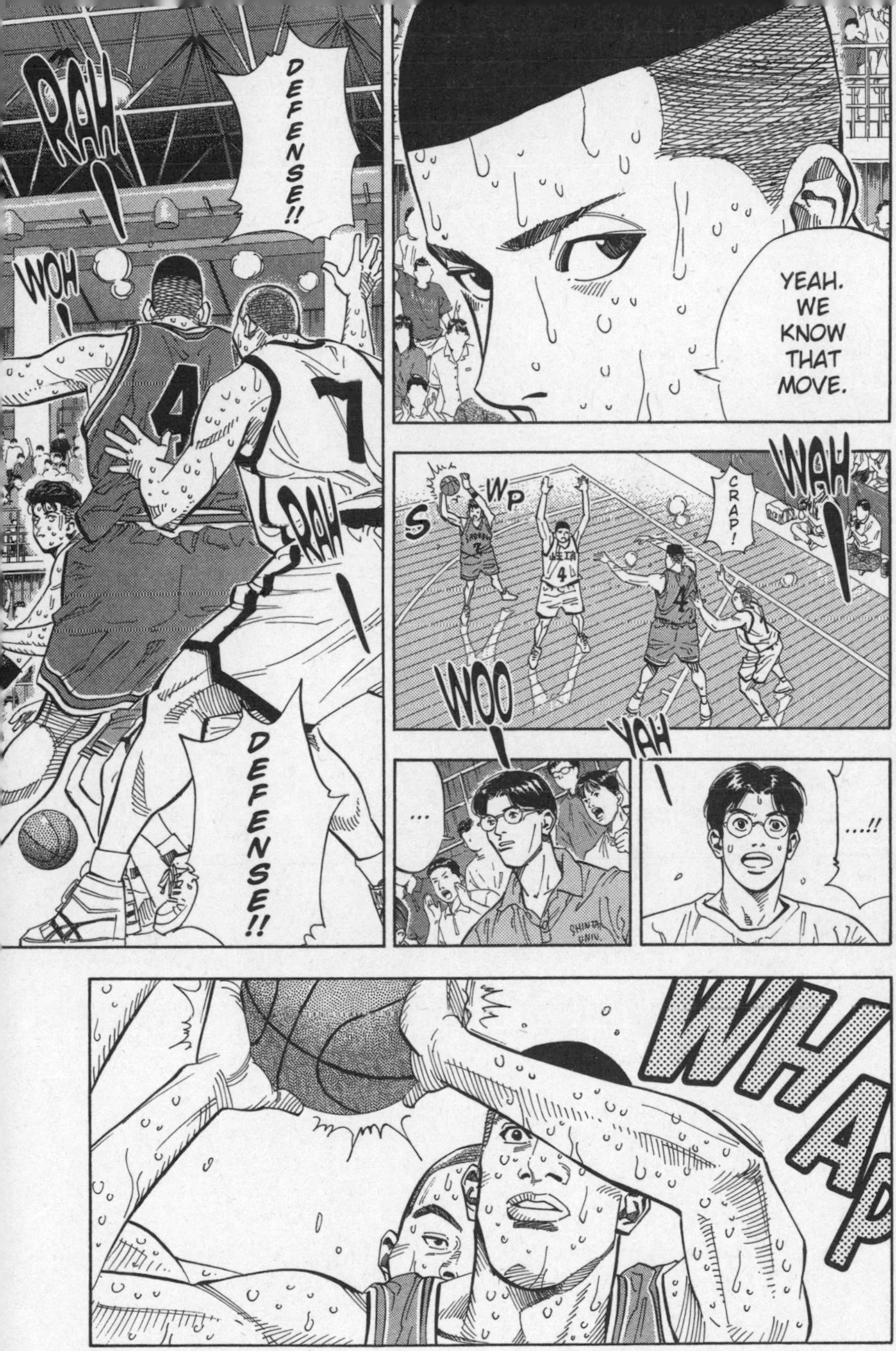
YEAH. WE KNOW THAT MOVE.
WAH!
CRAP!
S
WP
WOO!
YAH!
...!!
...
RAH!
DEFENSE!!
WOH!
RAH!
DEFENSE!!
WHAP

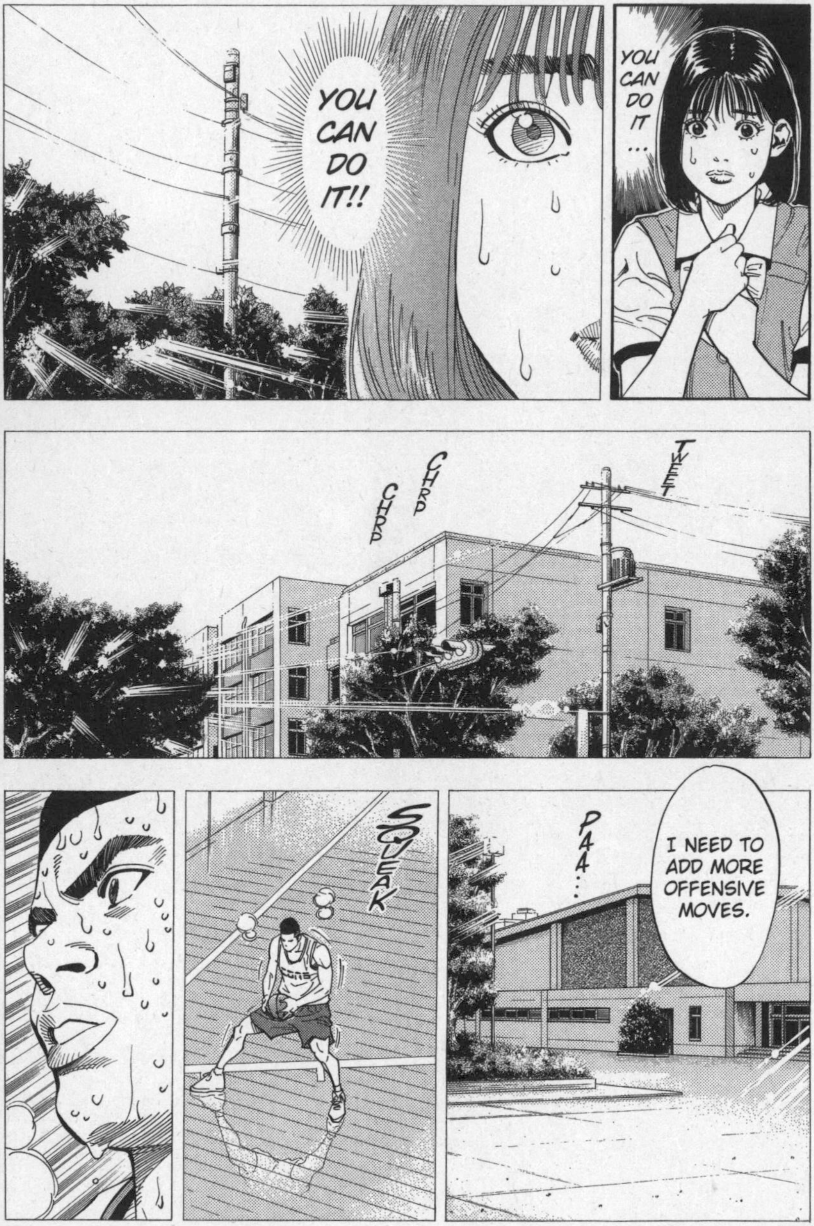
YOU CAN DO IT ...
YOU CAN DO IT!!
TWEET
CHRP CHRP
I NEED TO ADD MORE OFFENSIVE MOVES.
PAA...
SQUEAK

READ THIS WAY

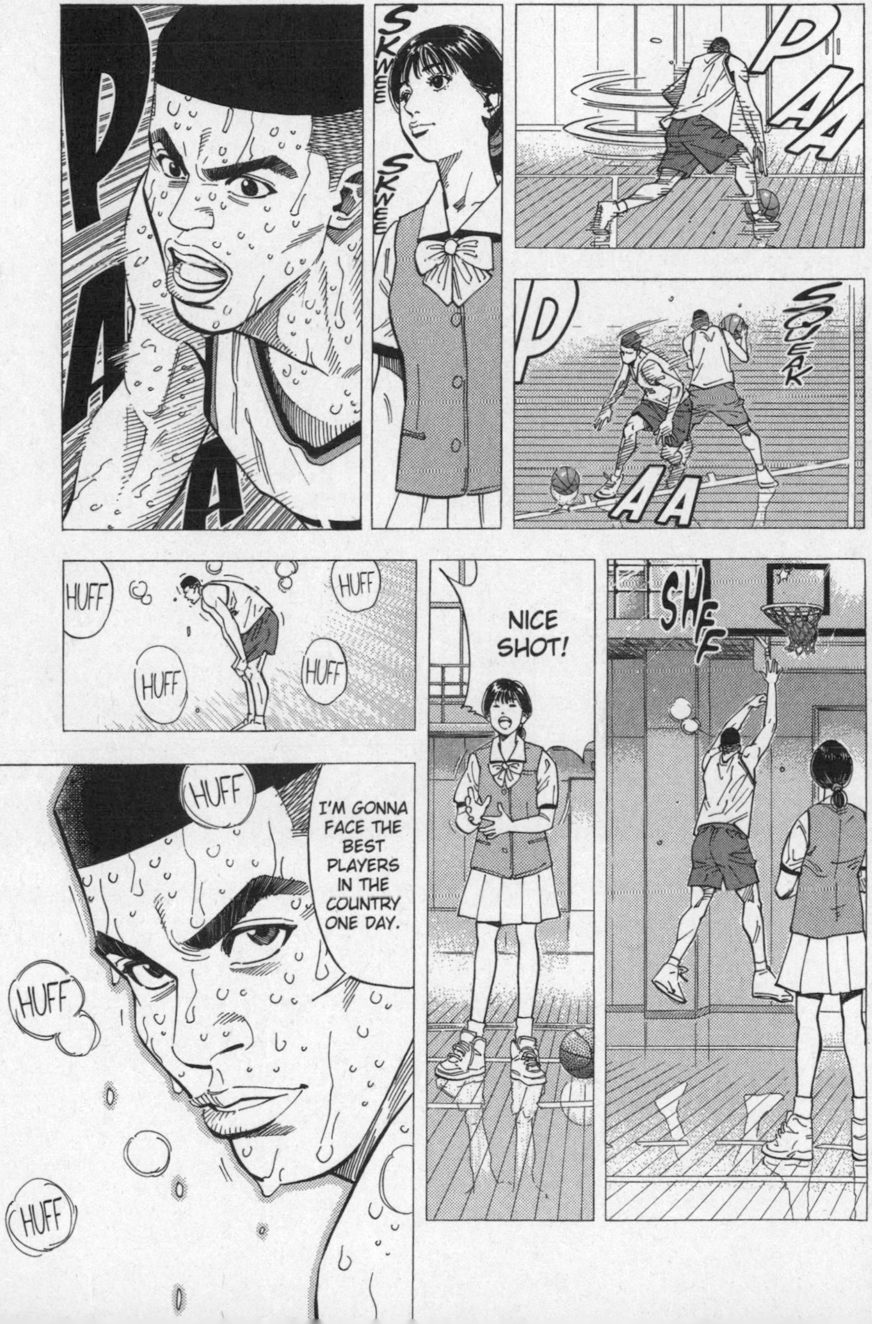
PAA
P
SQUEEK
AA
SKWEE
SKWEE
PAA
SHFF
NICE SHOT!
HUFF
HUFF
HUFF
HUFF
HUFF
I'M GONNA FACE THE BEST PLAYERS IN THE COUNTRY ONE DAY.
HUFF
HUFF

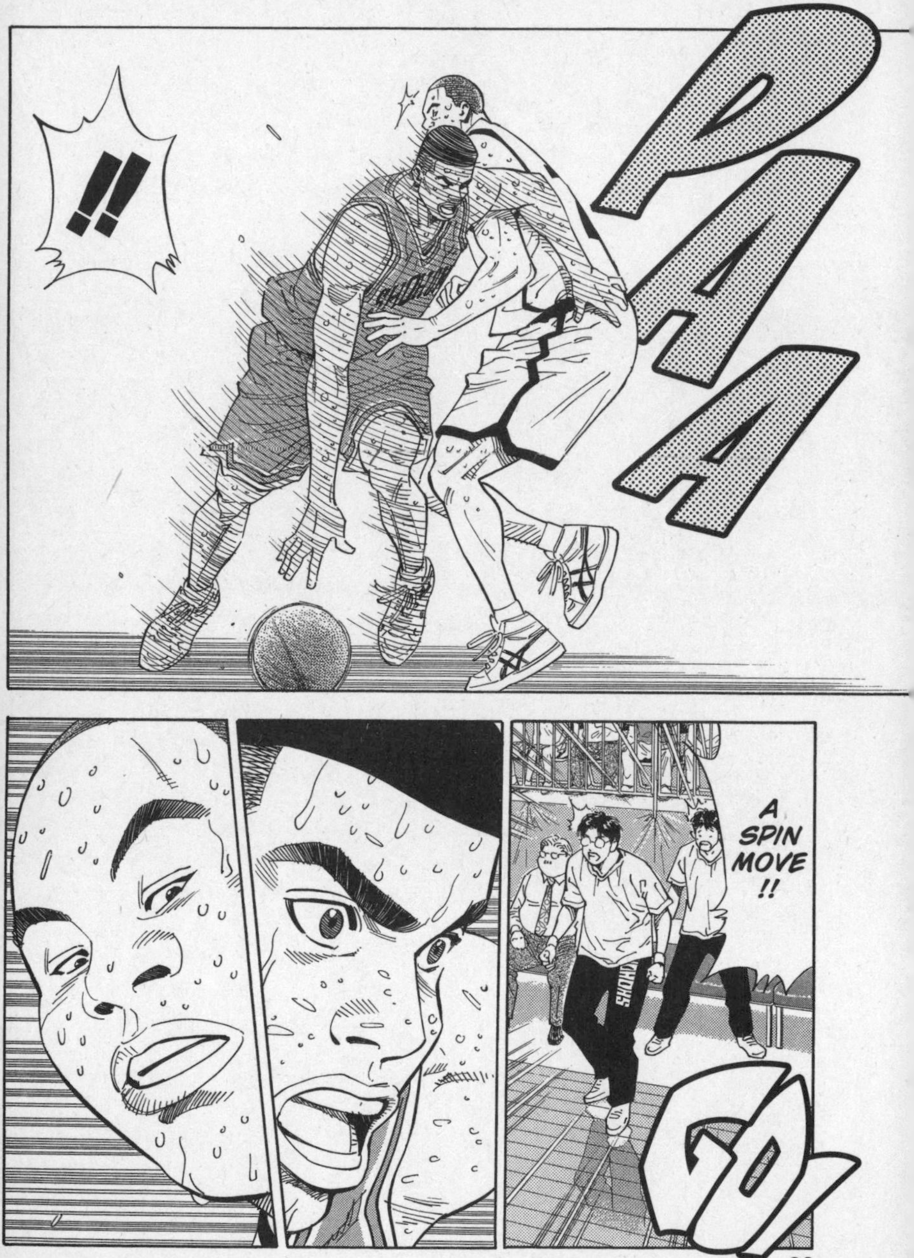
PAA
!!
A SPIN MOVE !!
GO!

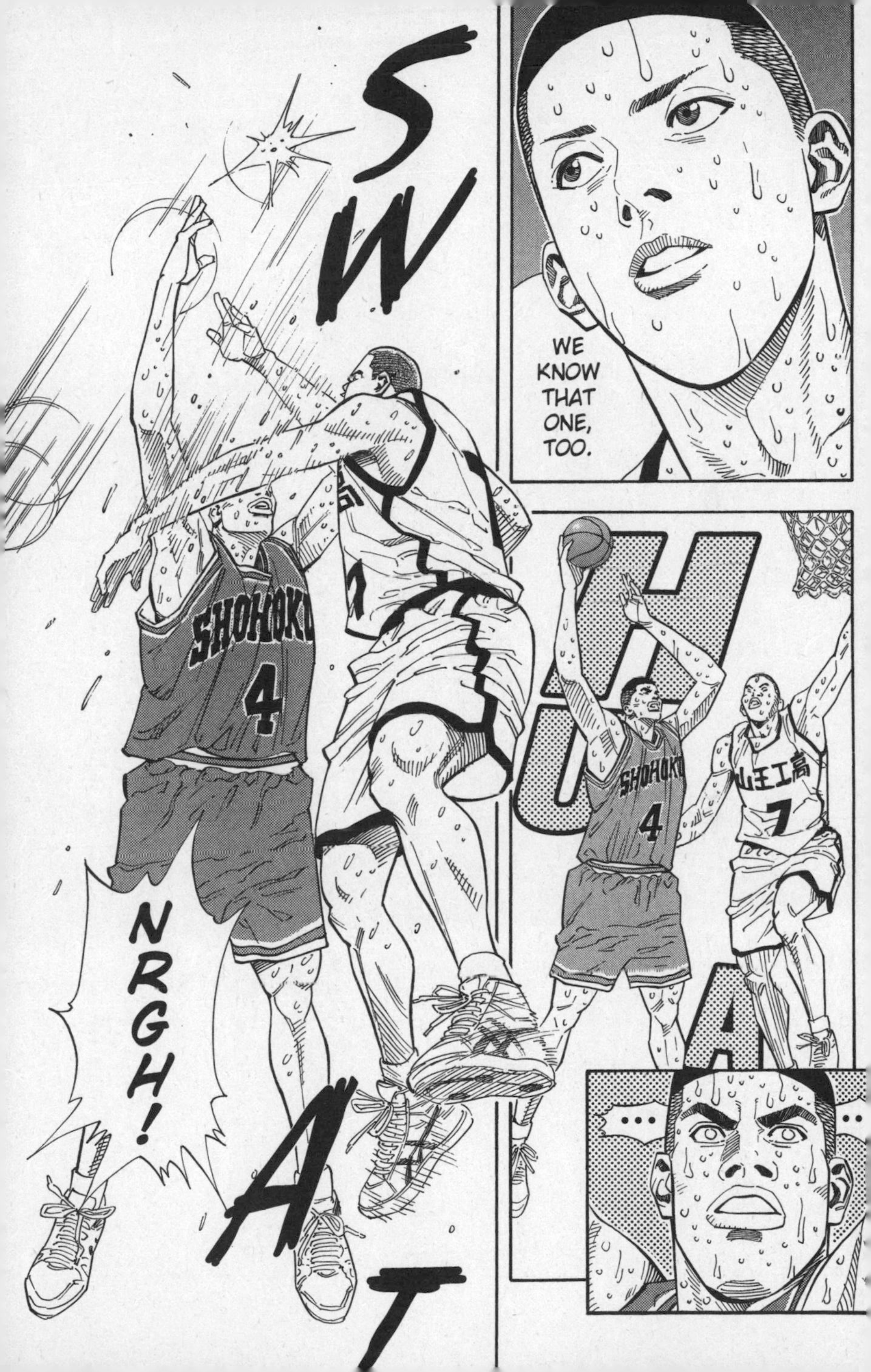
WE KNOW THAT ONE, TOO.
...
...
SWAT
NRGH!

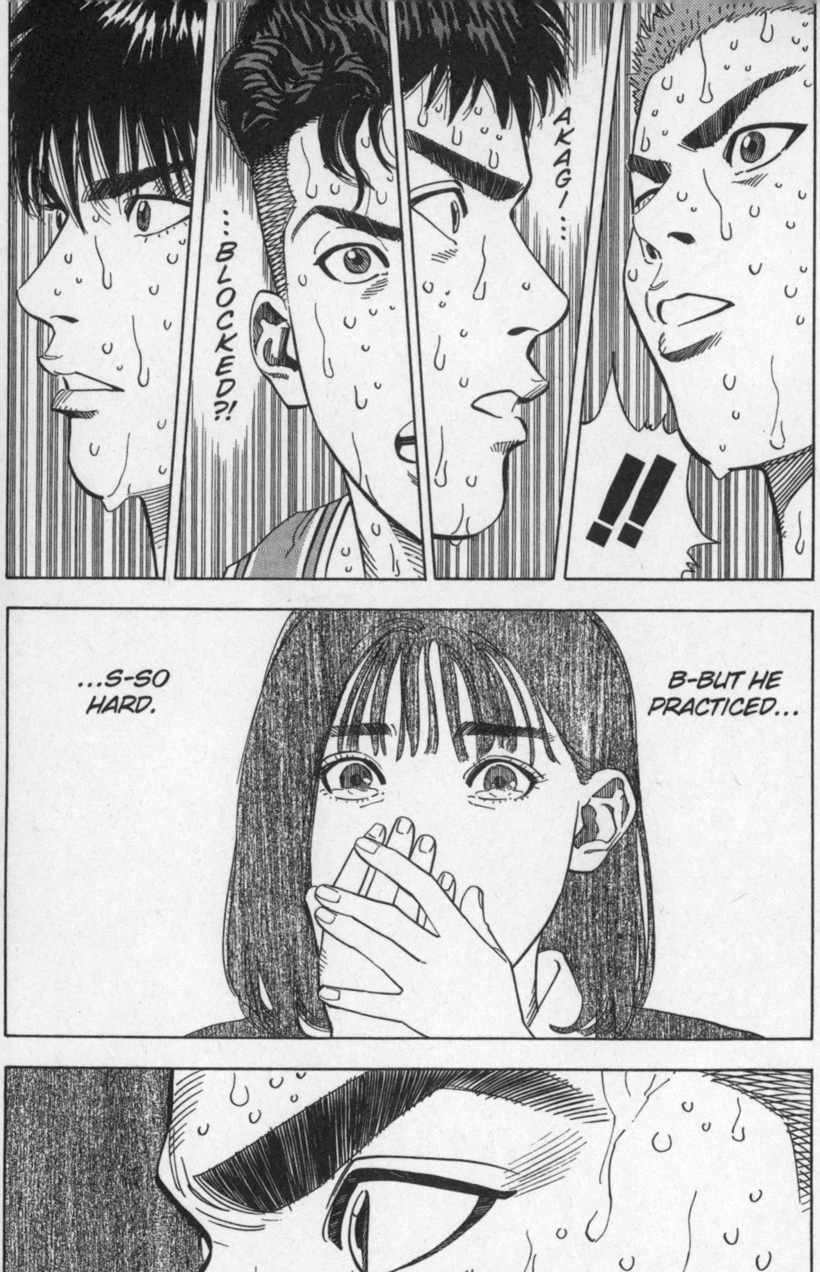
!!
AKAGI...
...BLOCKED?!
B-BUT HE PRACTICED...
...S-SO HARD.

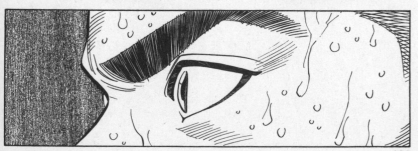

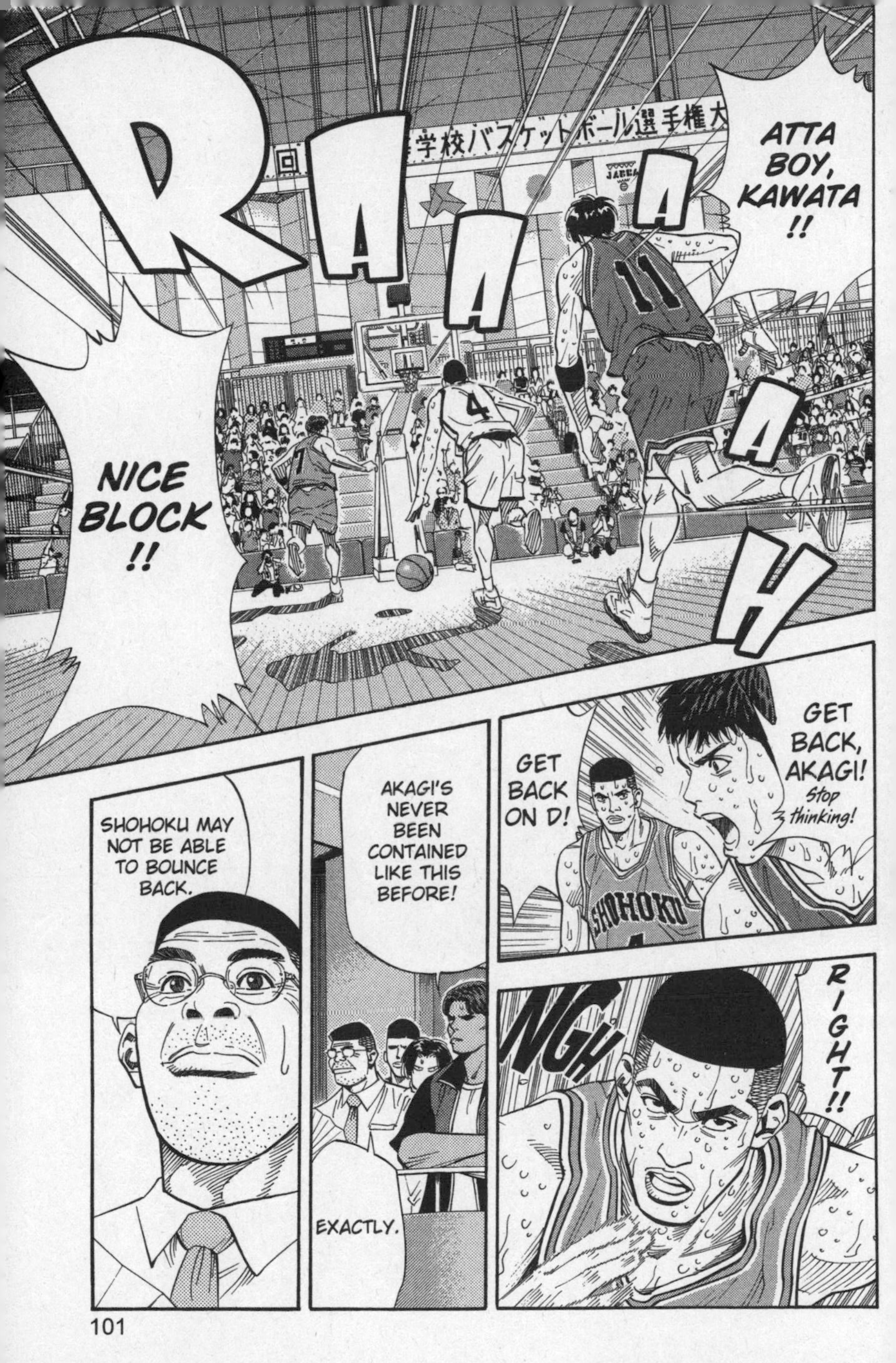
ATTA BOY, KAWATA!!
RAAAAAH
学校バスケットボール選手権大
NICE BLOCK!!
GET BACK, AKAGI! Stop thinking!
GET BACK ON D!
RIGHT!!
NGH
AKAGI'S NEVER BEEN CONTAINED LIKE THIS BEFORE!
EXACTLY.
SHOHOKU MAY NOT BE ABLE TO BOUNCE BACK.

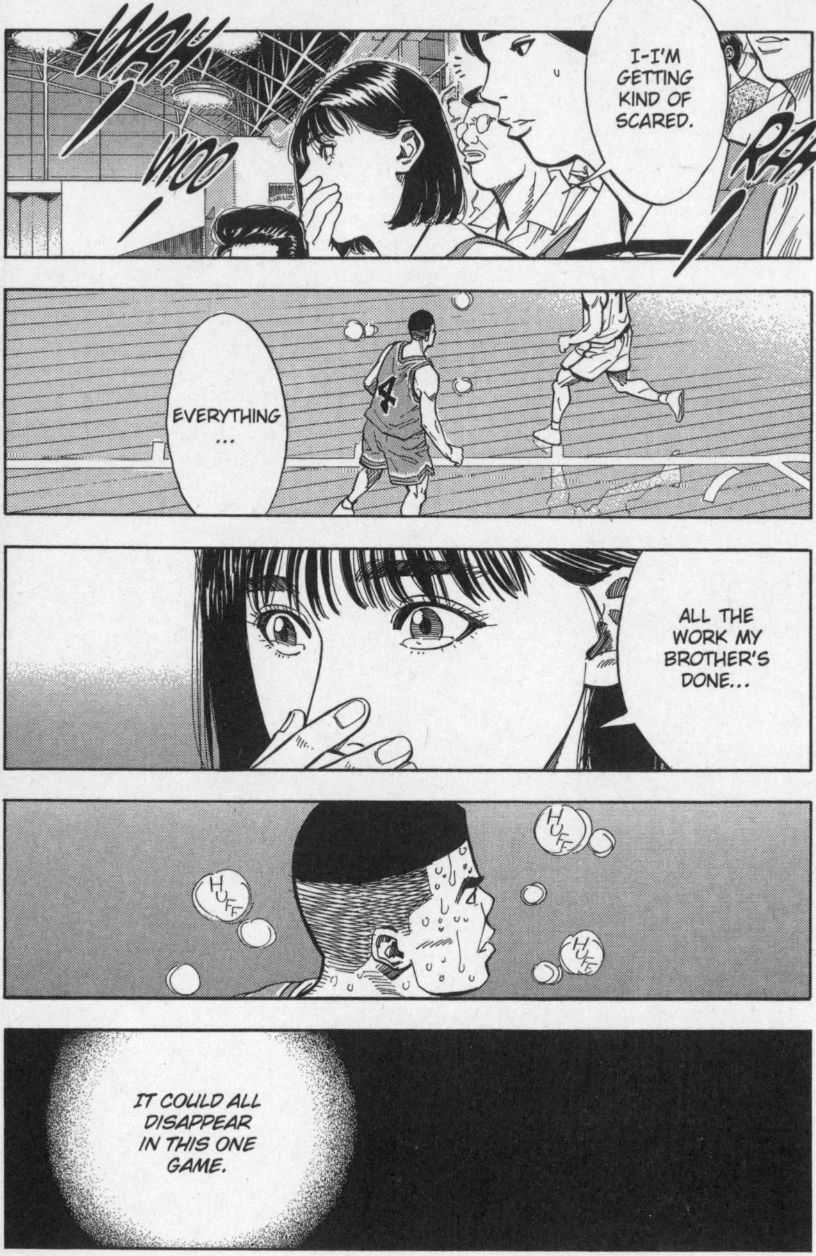
RAH
I-I'M GETTING KIND OF SCARED.
WAH
WOO
EVERYTHING ...
ALL THE WORK MY BROTHER'S DONE...
HUFF
HUFF
HUFF
IT COULD ALL DISAPPEAR IN THIS ONE GAME.

READ THIS WAY

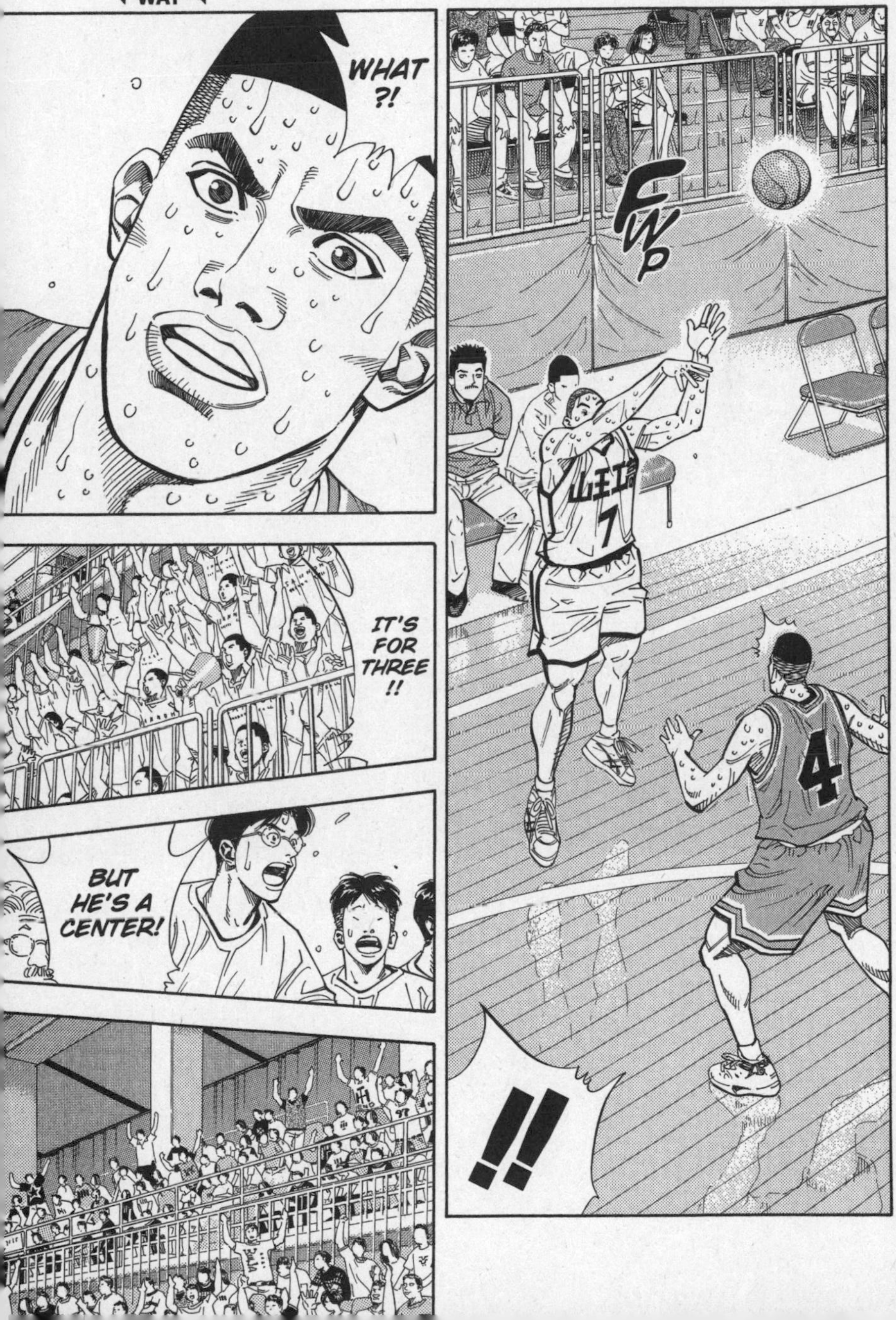
FWP
!!
WHAT ?!
IT'S FOR THREE !!
BUT HE'S A CENTER!

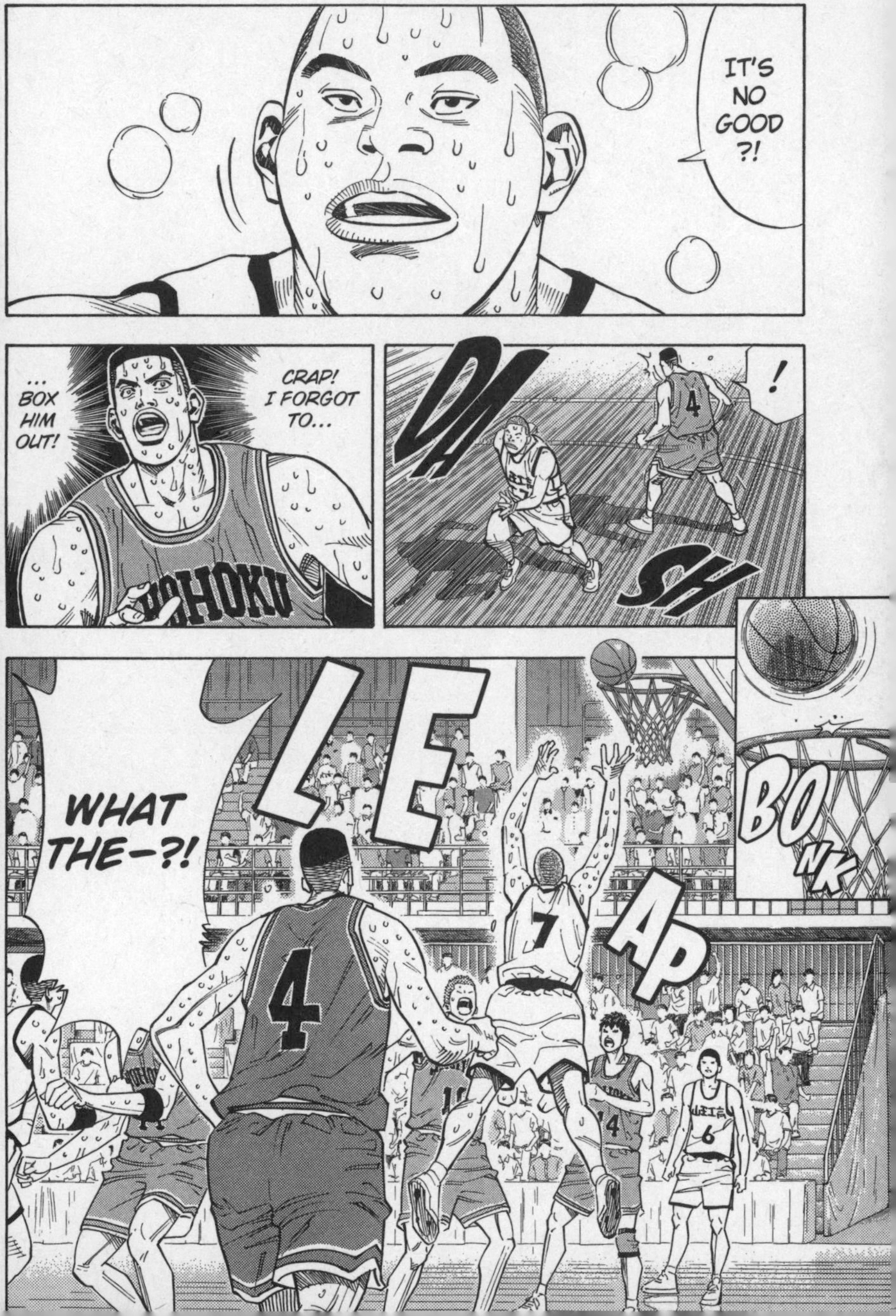
IT'S NO GOOD ?!
!
DA
SH
CRAP! I FORGOT TO...
... BOX HIM OUT!
BONK
LEAP
WHAT THE-?!

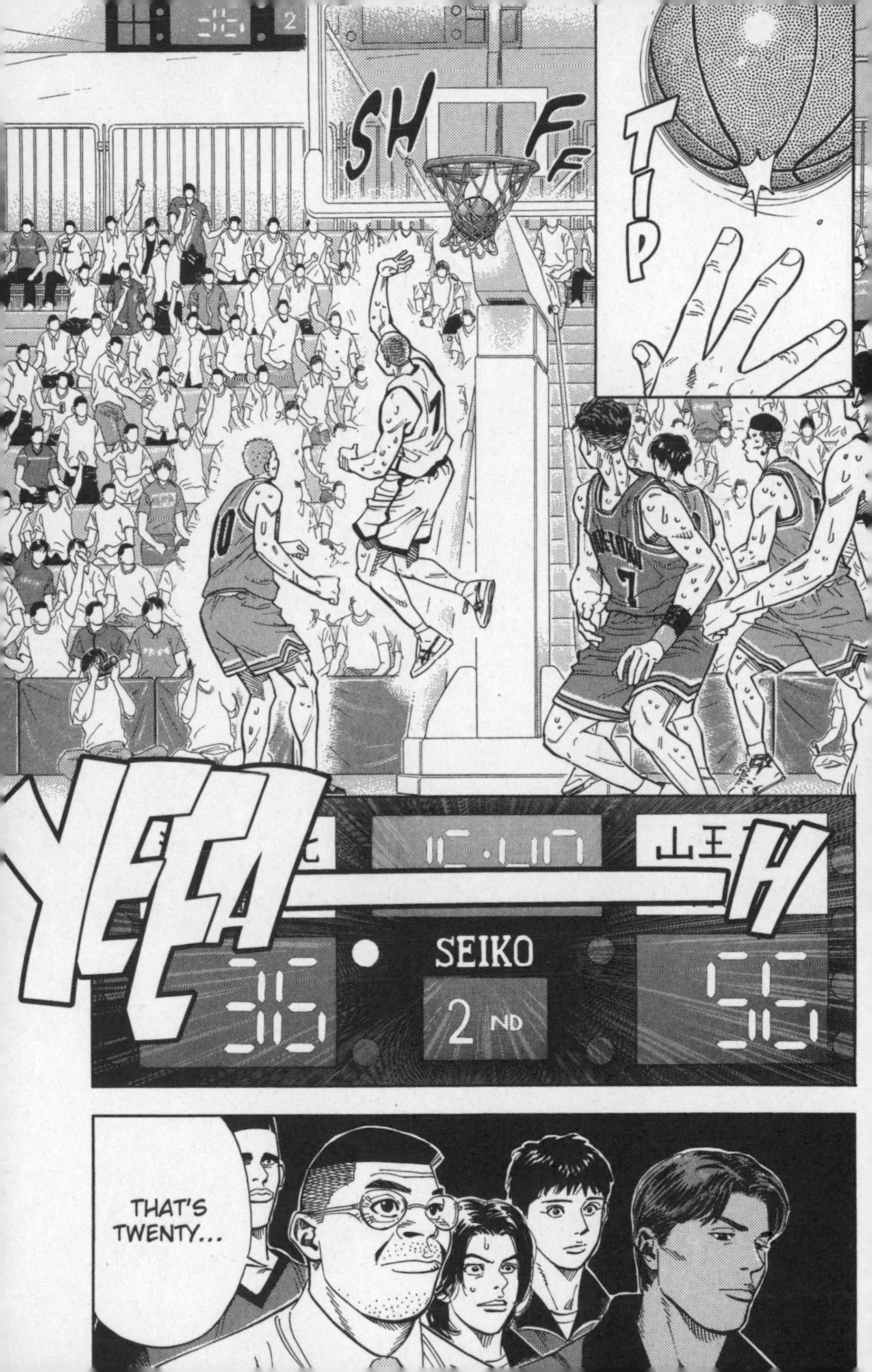
TIP
SHFF
YEEAH
SEIKO
2 ND
THAT'S TWENTY...

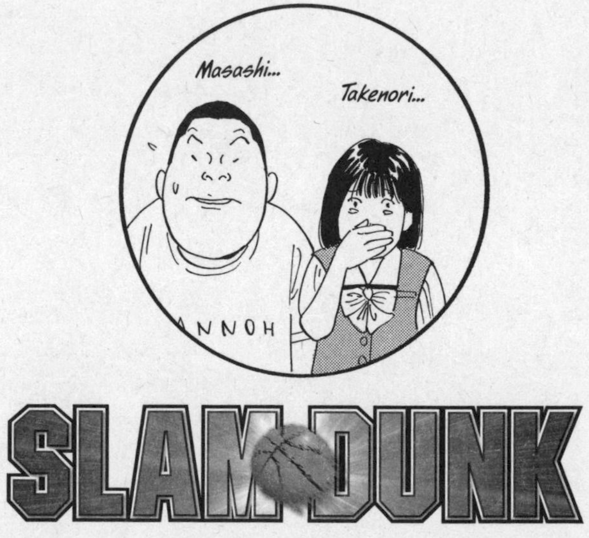
Masashi...
Takenori...
ANNOH

SLAM DUNK

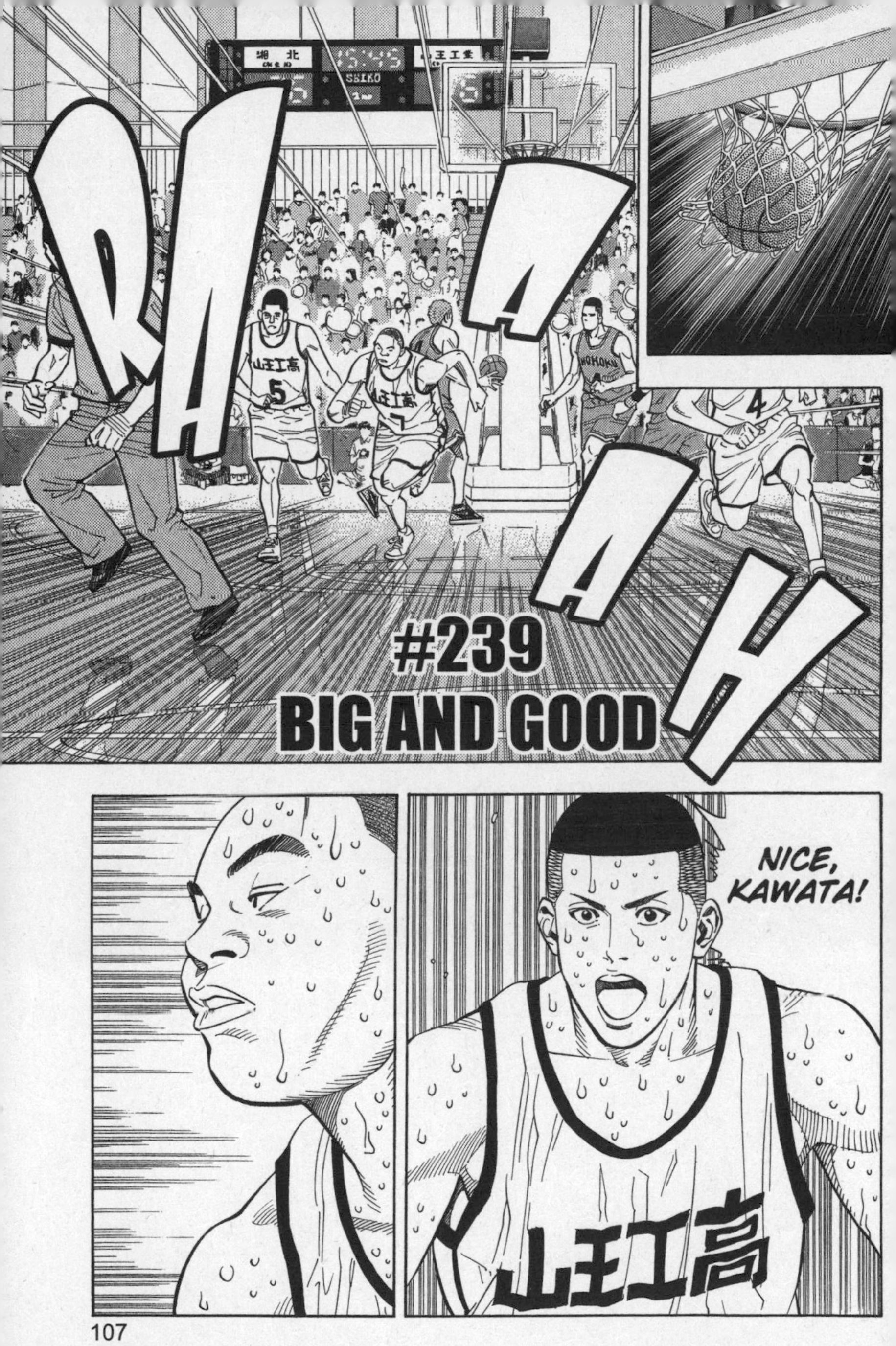
RAAAH
#239
BIG AND GOOD
NICE, KAWATA!

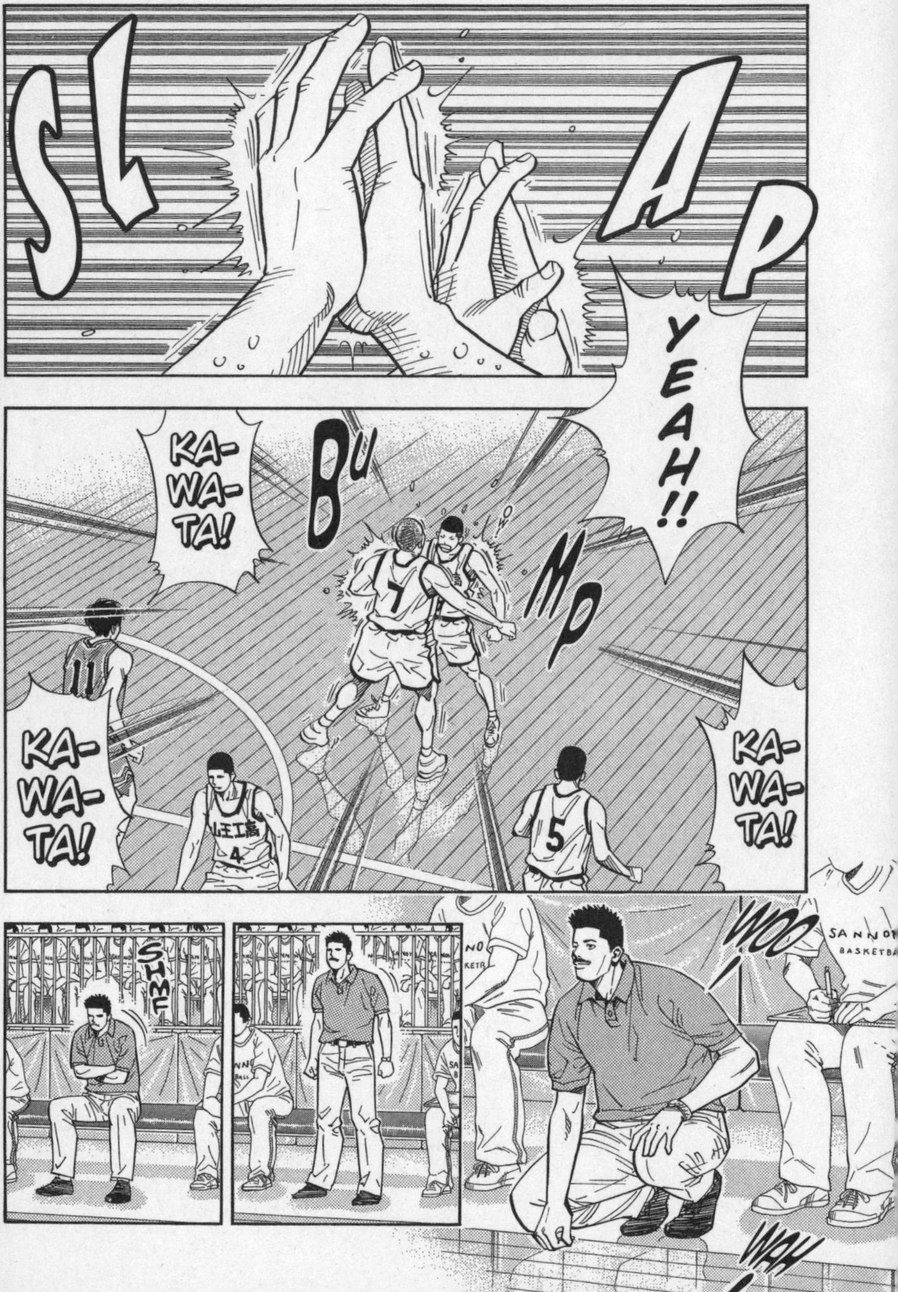
SLAP
YEAH!!
BUMP
KA-WA-TA!
KA-WA-TA!
KA-WA-TA!
WOO! WAH!
SHMF

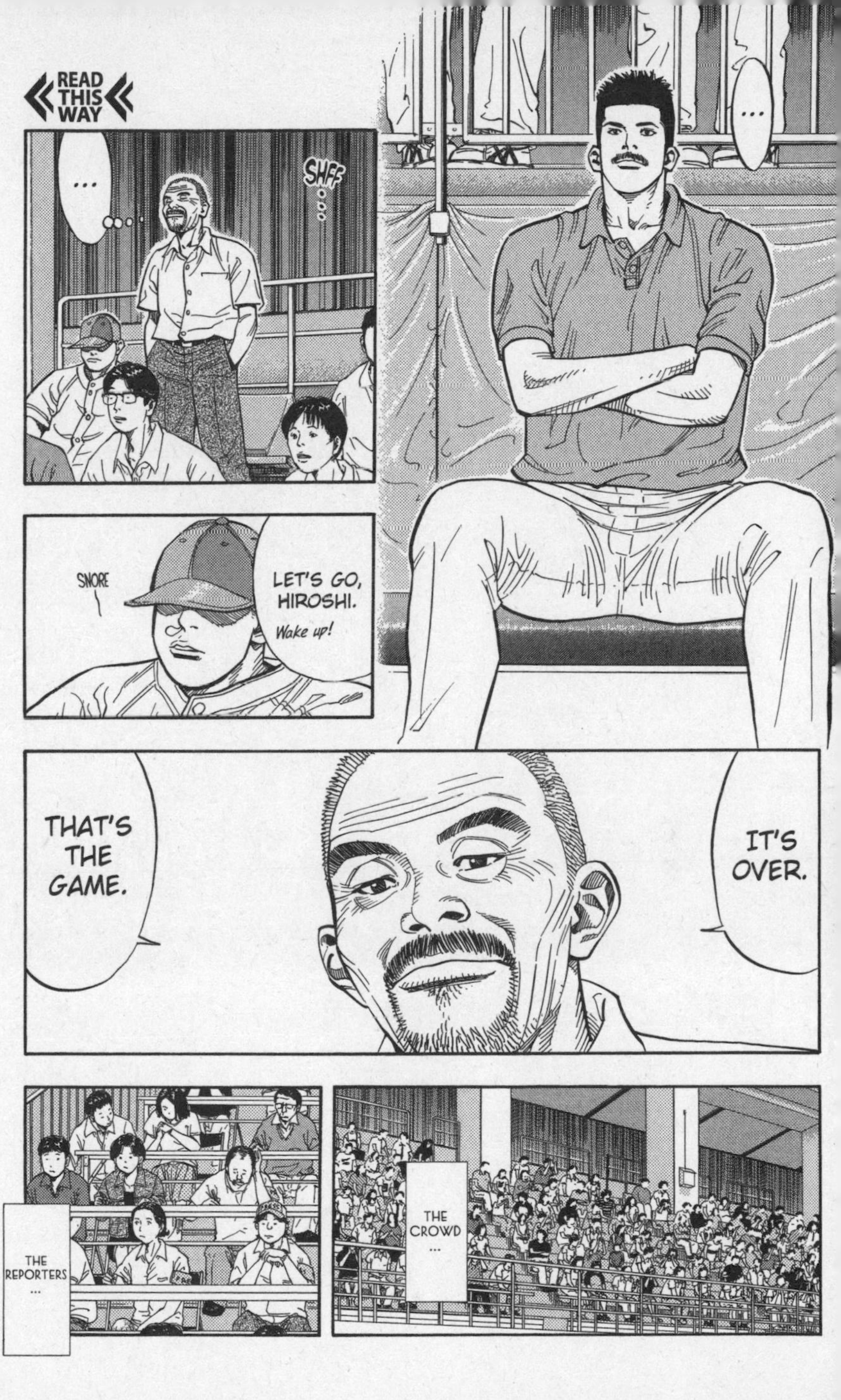
READ THIS WAY
...
...
SHFF
LET'S GO, HIROSHI.
Wake up!
SNORE
IT'S OVER.
THAT'S THE GAME.
THE CROWD ...
THE REPORTERS ...

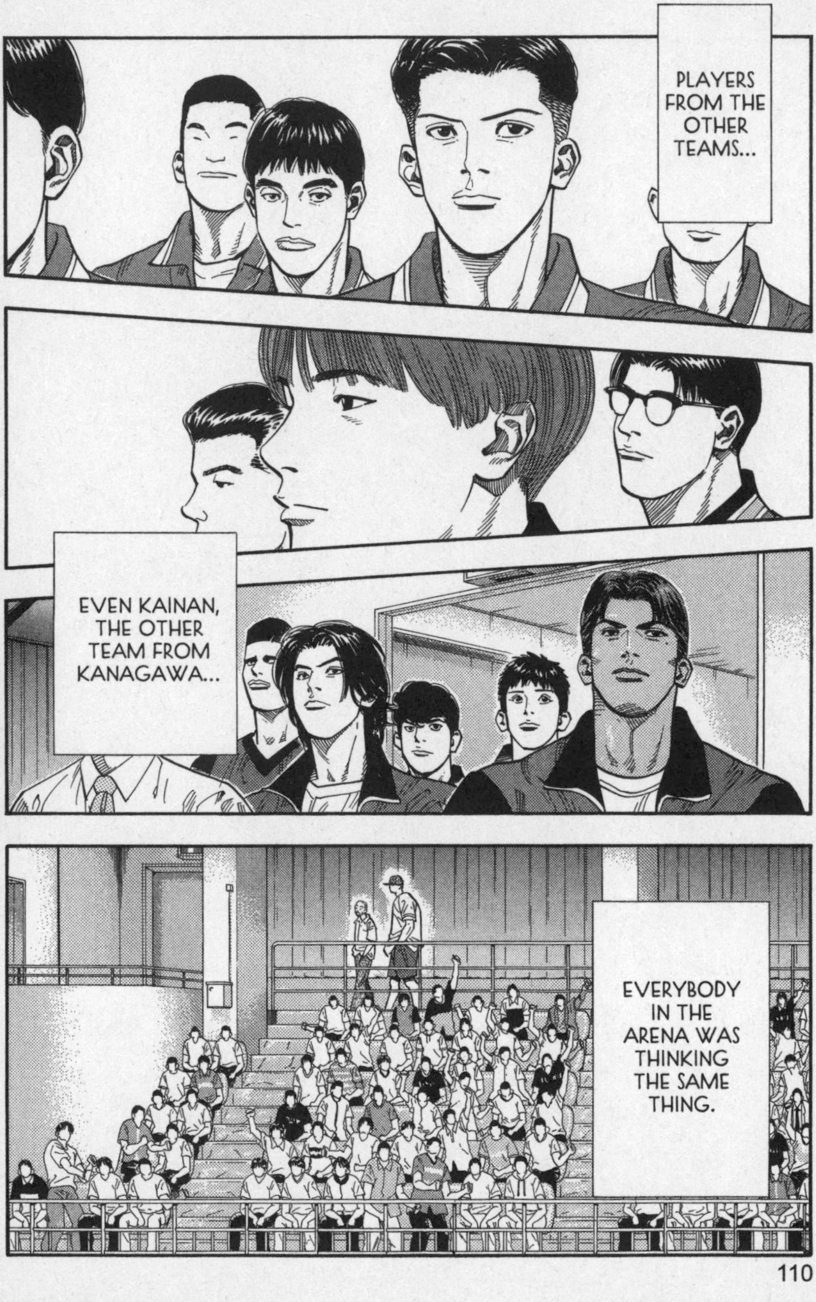
PLAYERS FROM THE OTHER TEAMS...
EVEN KAINAN, THE OTHER TEAM FROM KANAGAWA...
EVERYBODY IN THE ARENA WAS THINKING THE SAME THING.

READ THIS WAY

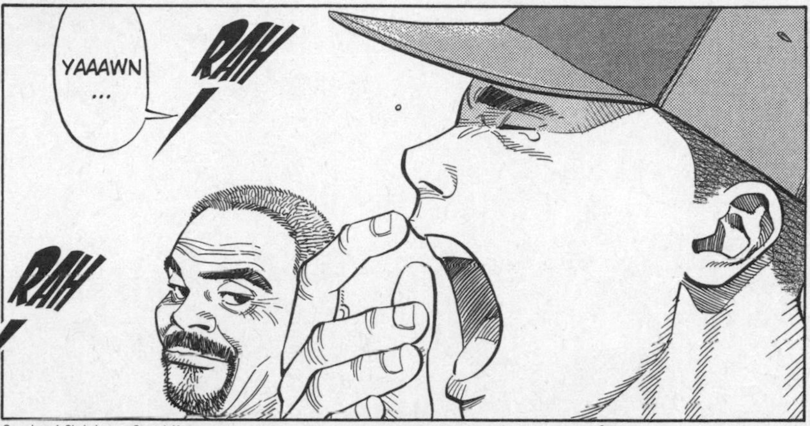
RAH
YAAAWN ...
RAH

Scoreboard: Shohoku (Kanagawa) Sannoh Kogyo (Akita)

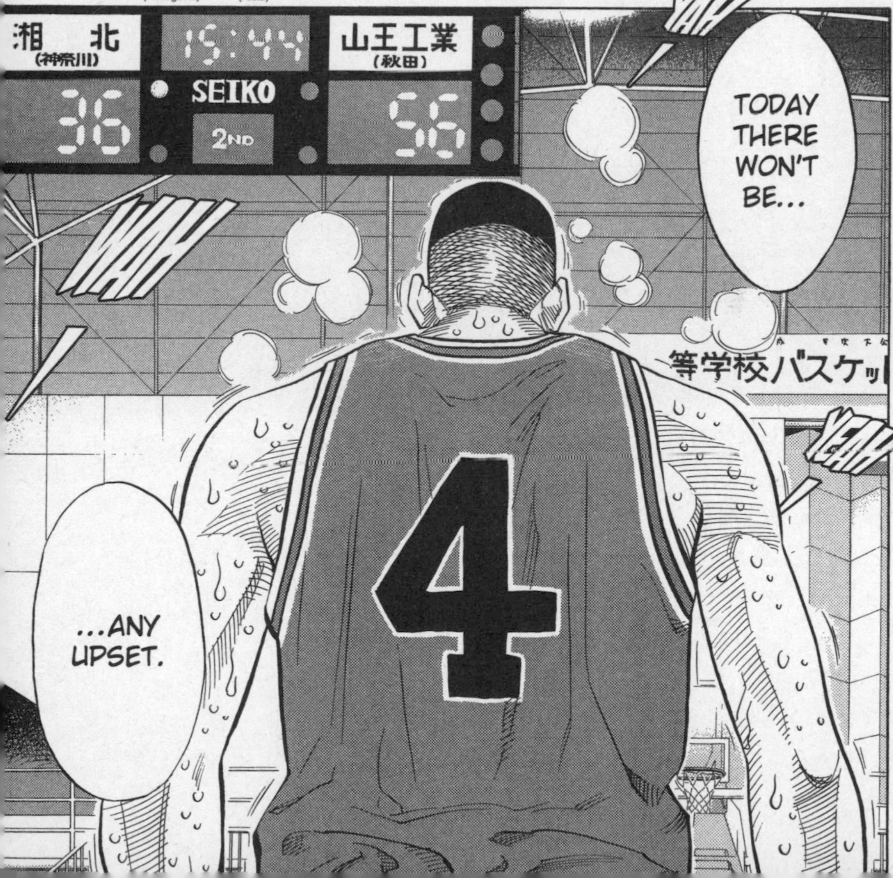
YAH
TODAY THERE WON'T BE...
湘北 (神奈川)
15:44
山王工業 (秋田)
36
SEIKO
2ND
56
WAH
等学校バスケッ
YEAH
...ANY UPSET.

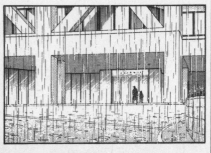

GEEZ.

IT'S POURING.

HOW CAN YOU GET LOST GOING TO THE STADIUM?!

GASP

HU

GASP

GASP

SHOHO

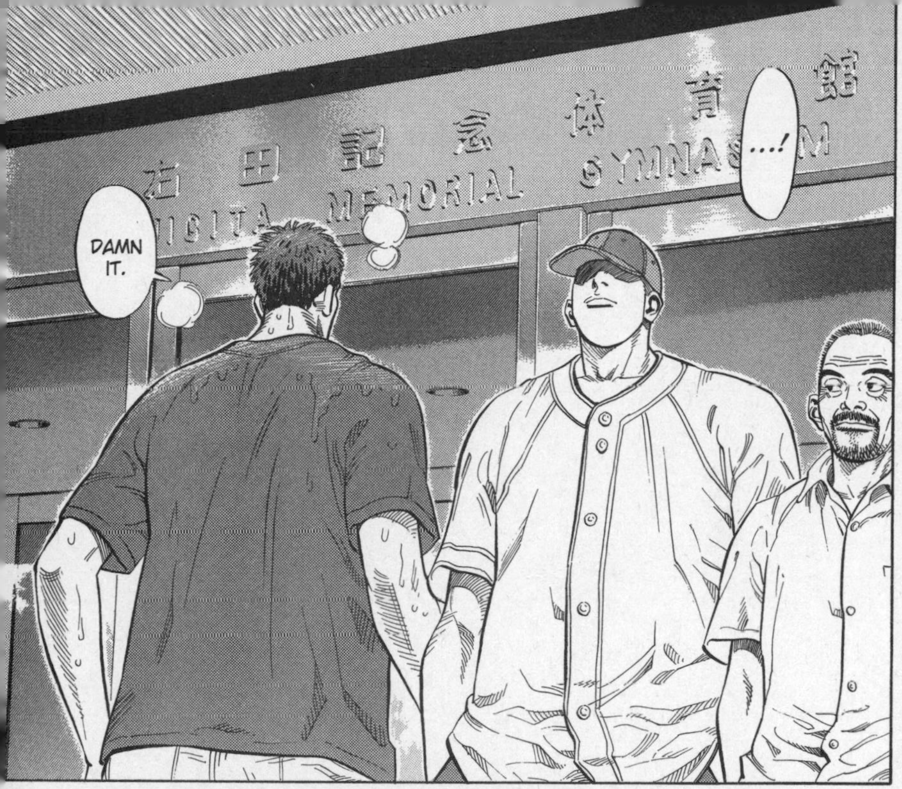
...!
DAMN IT.

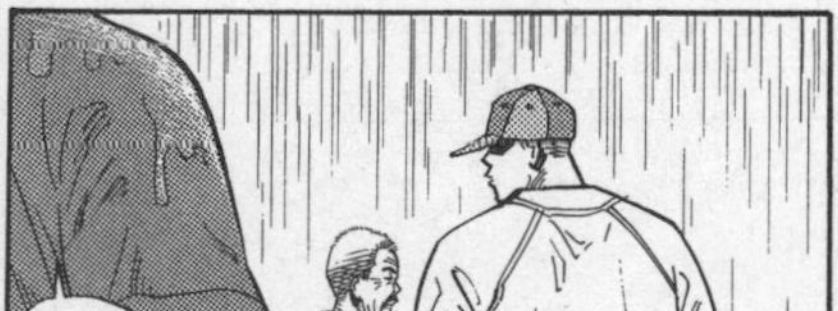
THEY BETTER STILL BE PLAYING.

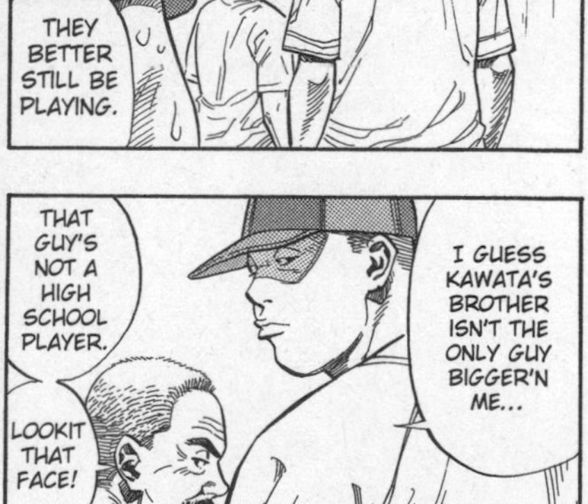
I GUESS KAWATA'S BROTHER ISN'T THE ONLY GUY BIGGER'N ME...
THAT GUY'S NOT A HIGH SCHOOL PLAYER.
LOOKIT THAT FACE!

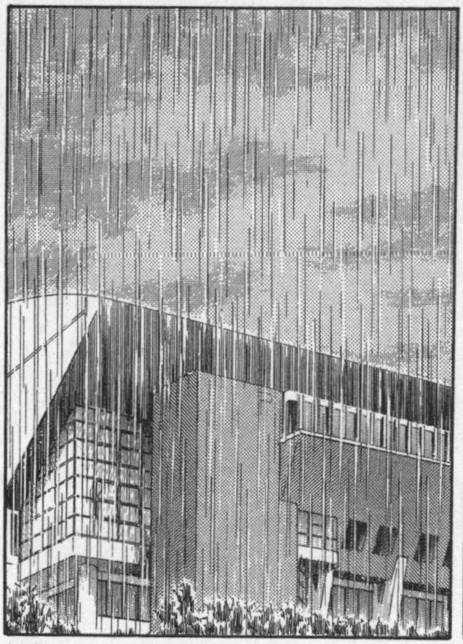

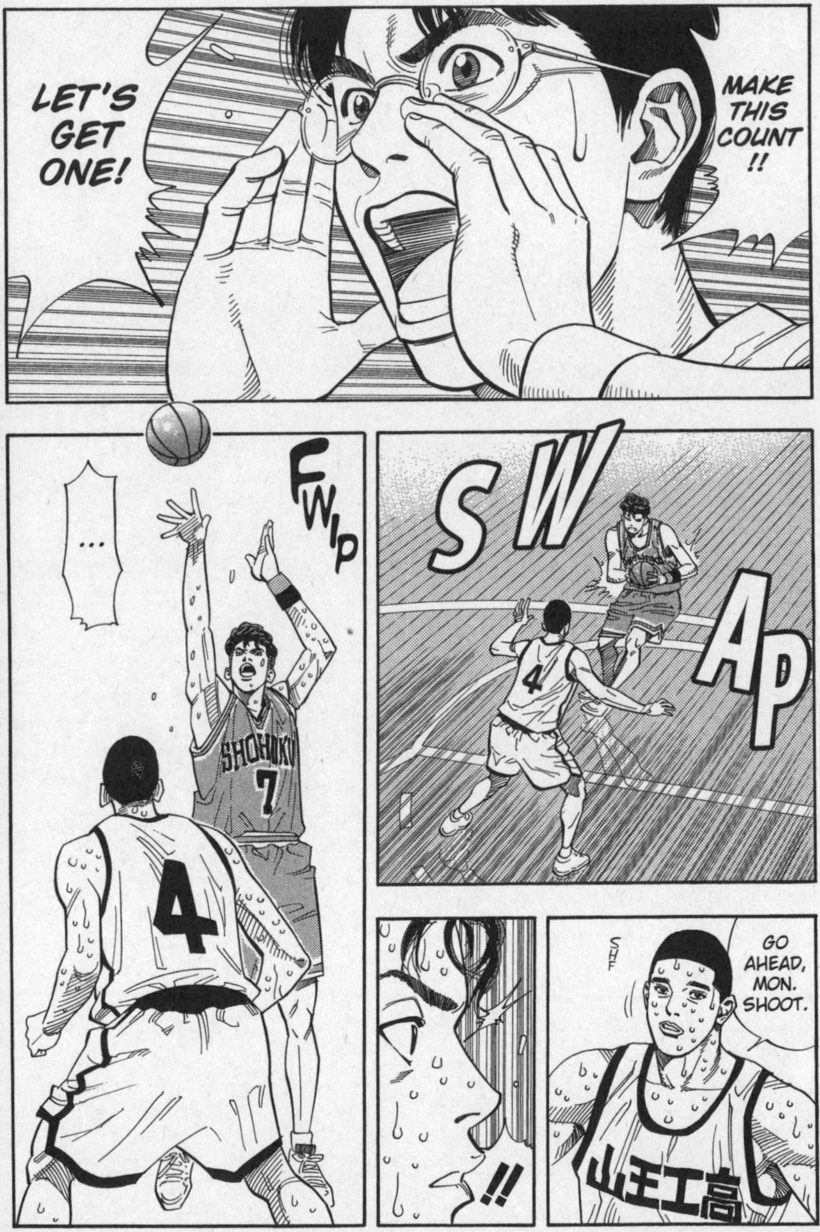
MAKE THIS COUNT !!
LET'S GET ONE!
SWAP
SHF
GO AHEAD, MON. SHOOT.
!!
FWIP
...

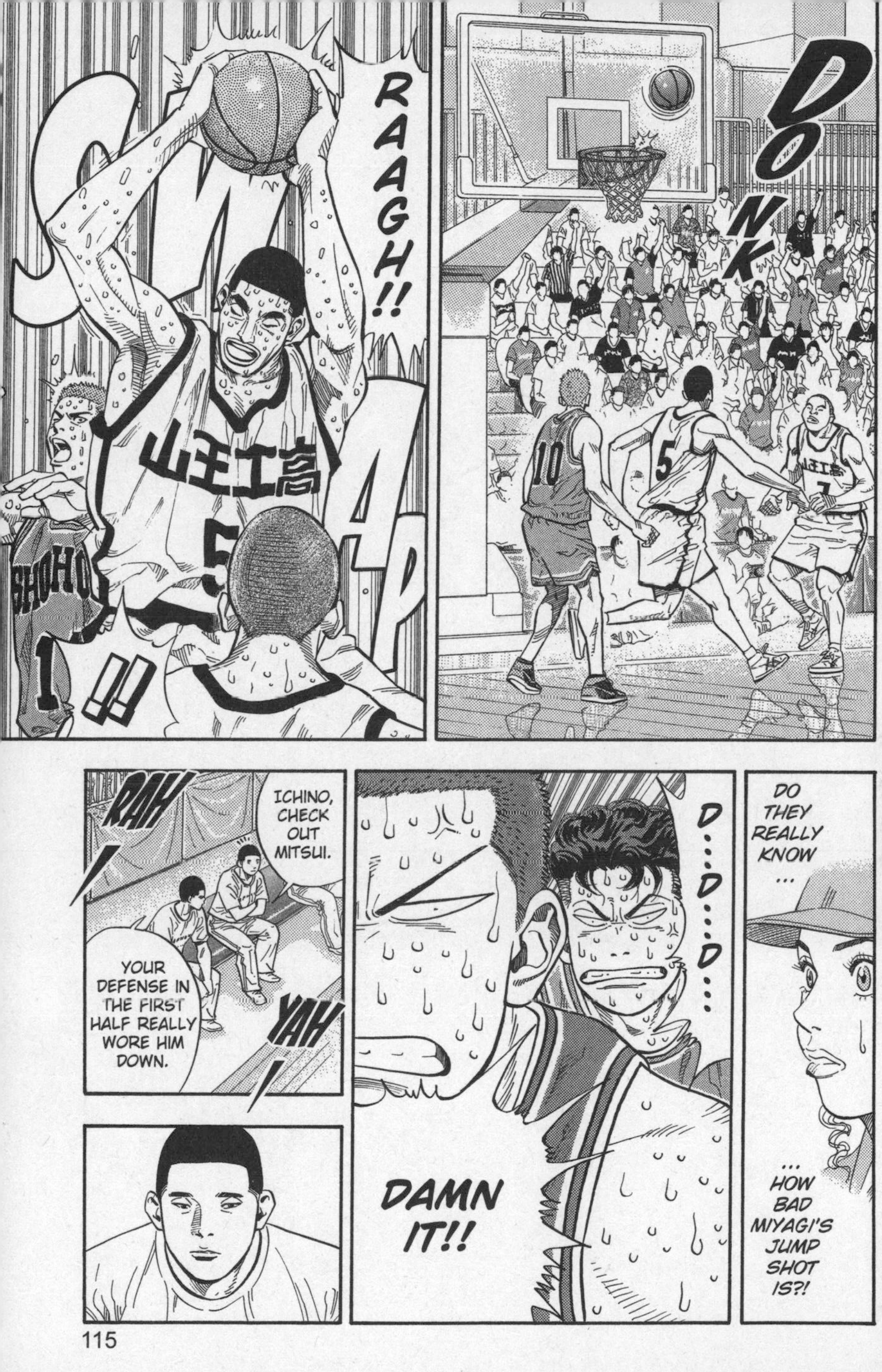
DONK
RAAGH!!
!!
DO THEY REALLY KNOW ...
... HOW BAD MIYAGI'S JUMP SHOT IS?!
D...D...D...
DAMN IT!!
RAH
ICHINO, CHECK OUT MITSUI.
YOUR DEFENSE IN THE FIRST HALF REALLY WORE HIM DOWN.
YAH

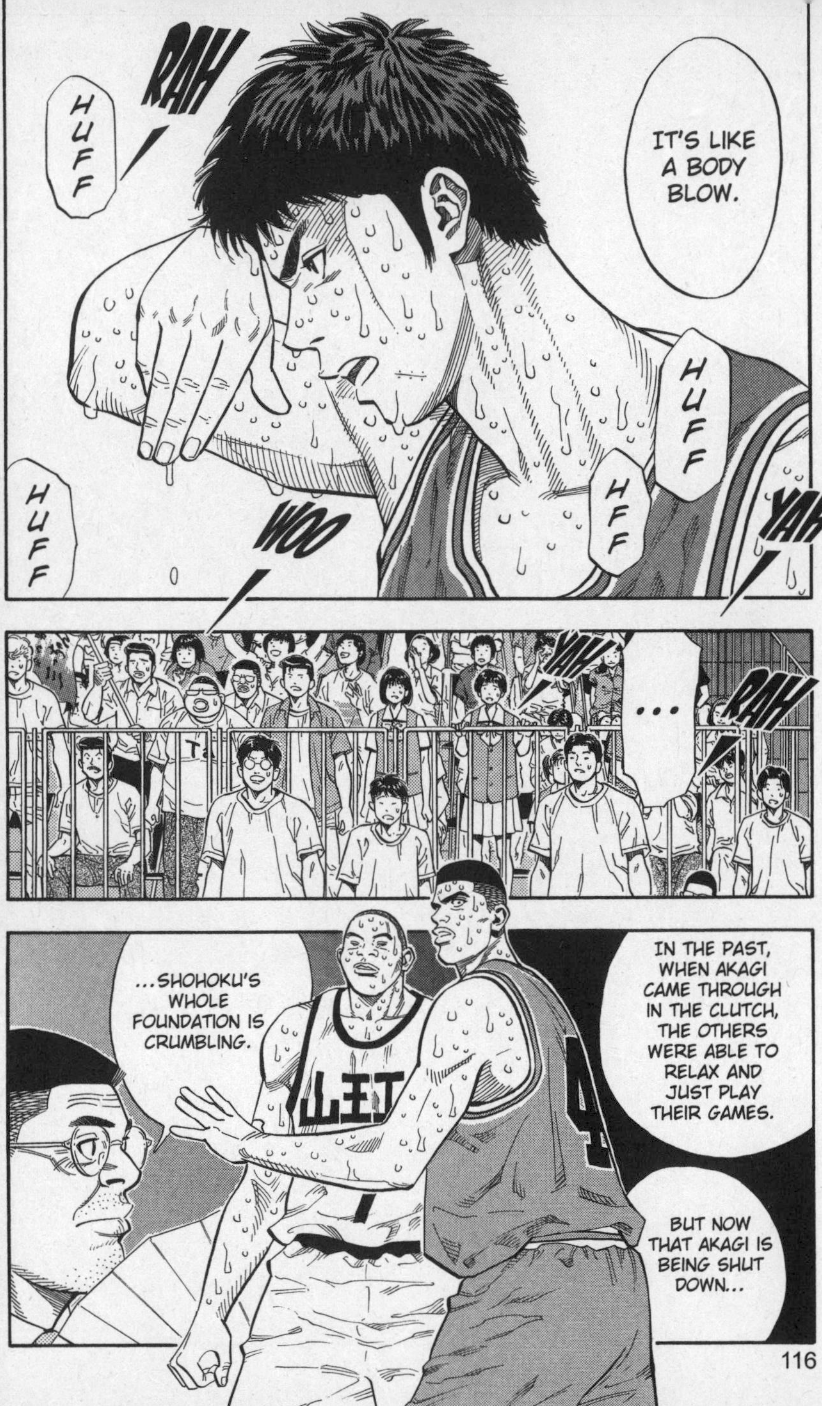
IT'S LIKE A BODY BLOW.
HUFF
HFF
YAH
RAH
HUFF
WOO
HUFF
RAH
YAH
...
IN THE PAST, WHEN AKAGI CAME THROUGH IN THE CLUTCH, THE OTHERS WERE ABLE TO RELAX AND JUST PLAY THEIR GAMES.
BUT NOW THAT AKAGI IS BEING SHUT DOWN...
...SHOHOKU'S WHOLE FOUNDATION IS CRUMBLING.

READ THIS WAY

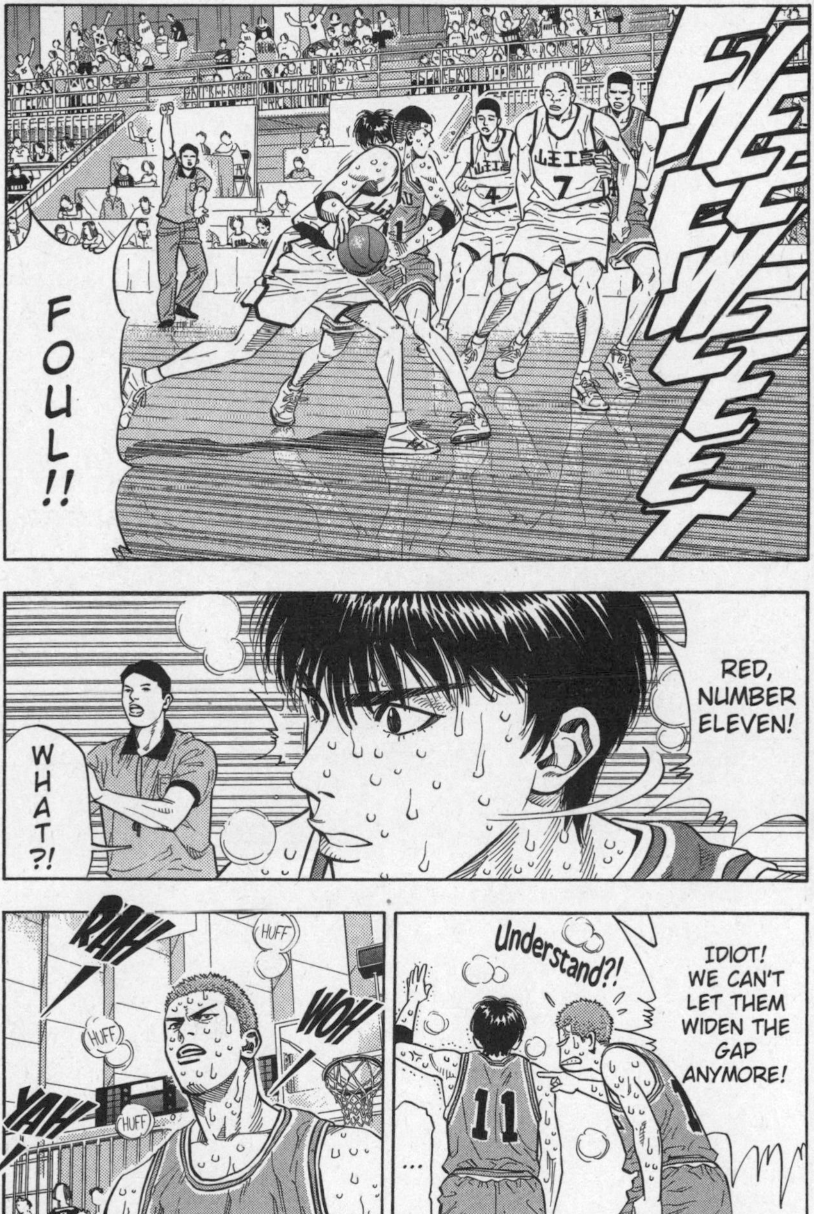
FWEEEEET
FOUL!!
RED, NUMBER ELEVEN!
WHAT?!
IDIOT! WE CAN'T LET THEM WIDEN THE GAP ANYMORE!
Understand?!
...
RAH
WOH
YAH
HUFF
HUFF
HUFF

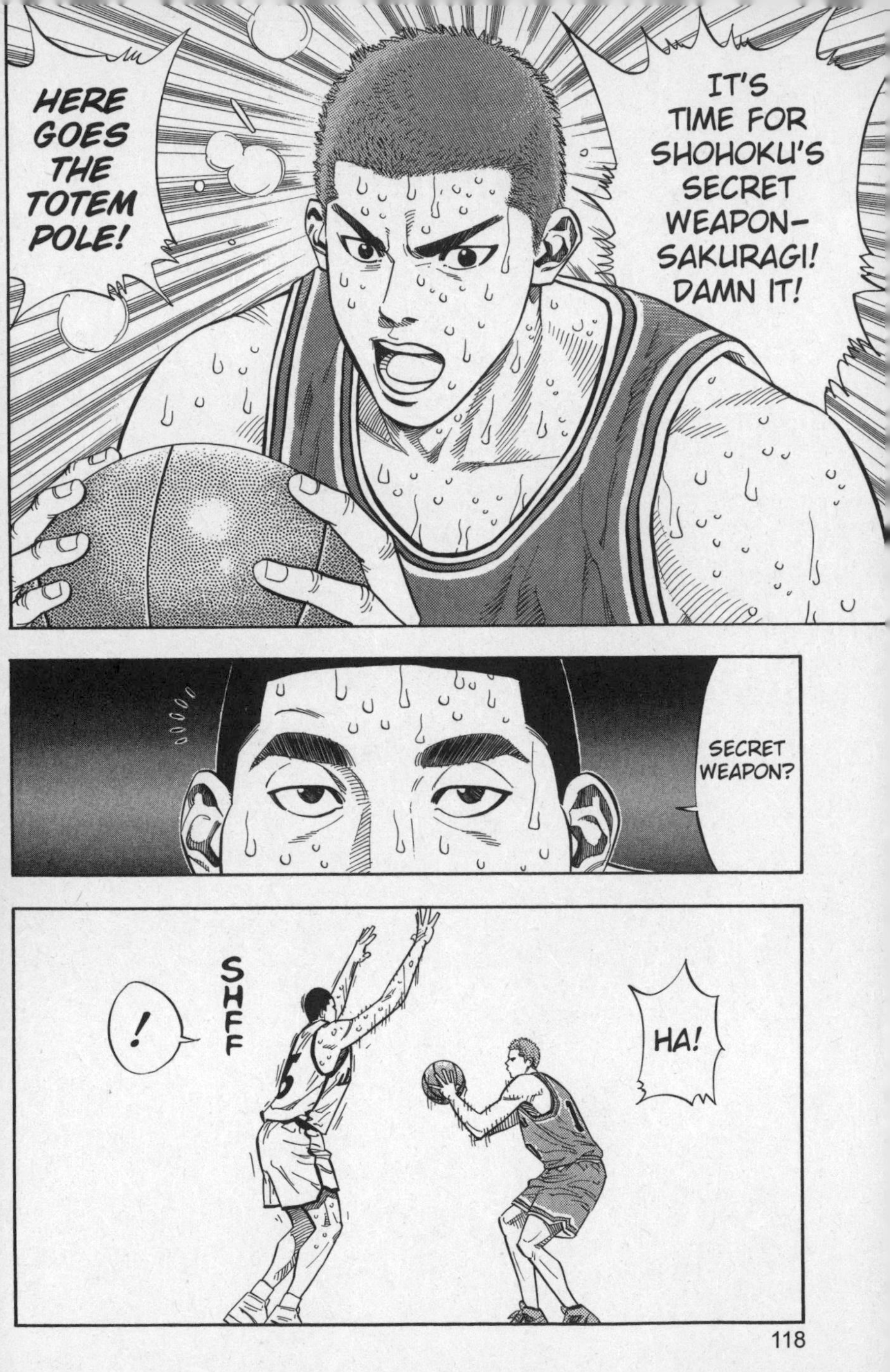
IT'S TIME FOR SHOHOKU'S SECRET WEAPON-SAKURAGI! DAMN IT!
HERE GOES THE TOTEM POLE!
SECRET WEAPON?
HA!
SHFF
!

READ THIS WAY

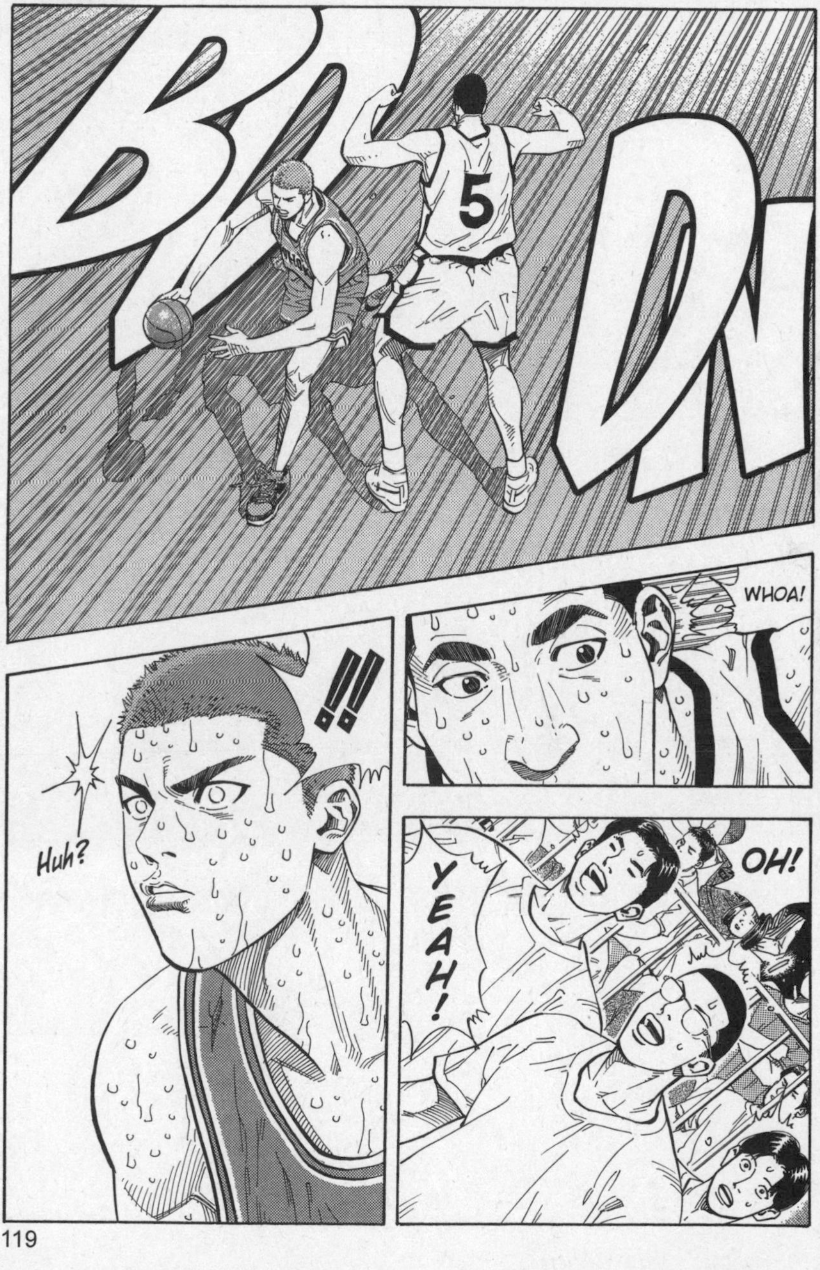

WHOA!
OH!
YEAH!
!!!
Huh?

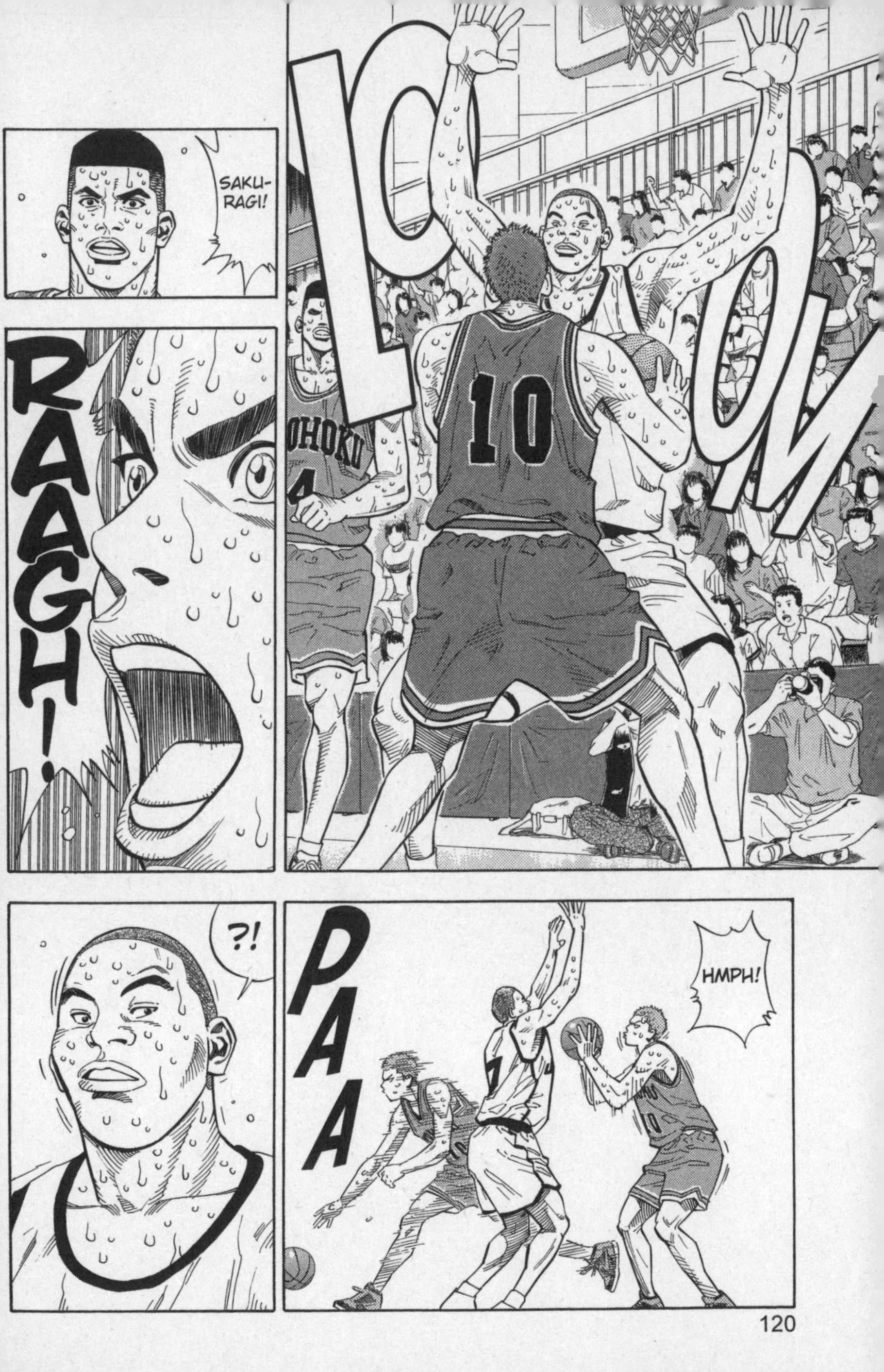
SAKU-
RAGI!
RAAGH!
PAAA
HMPH!
?!

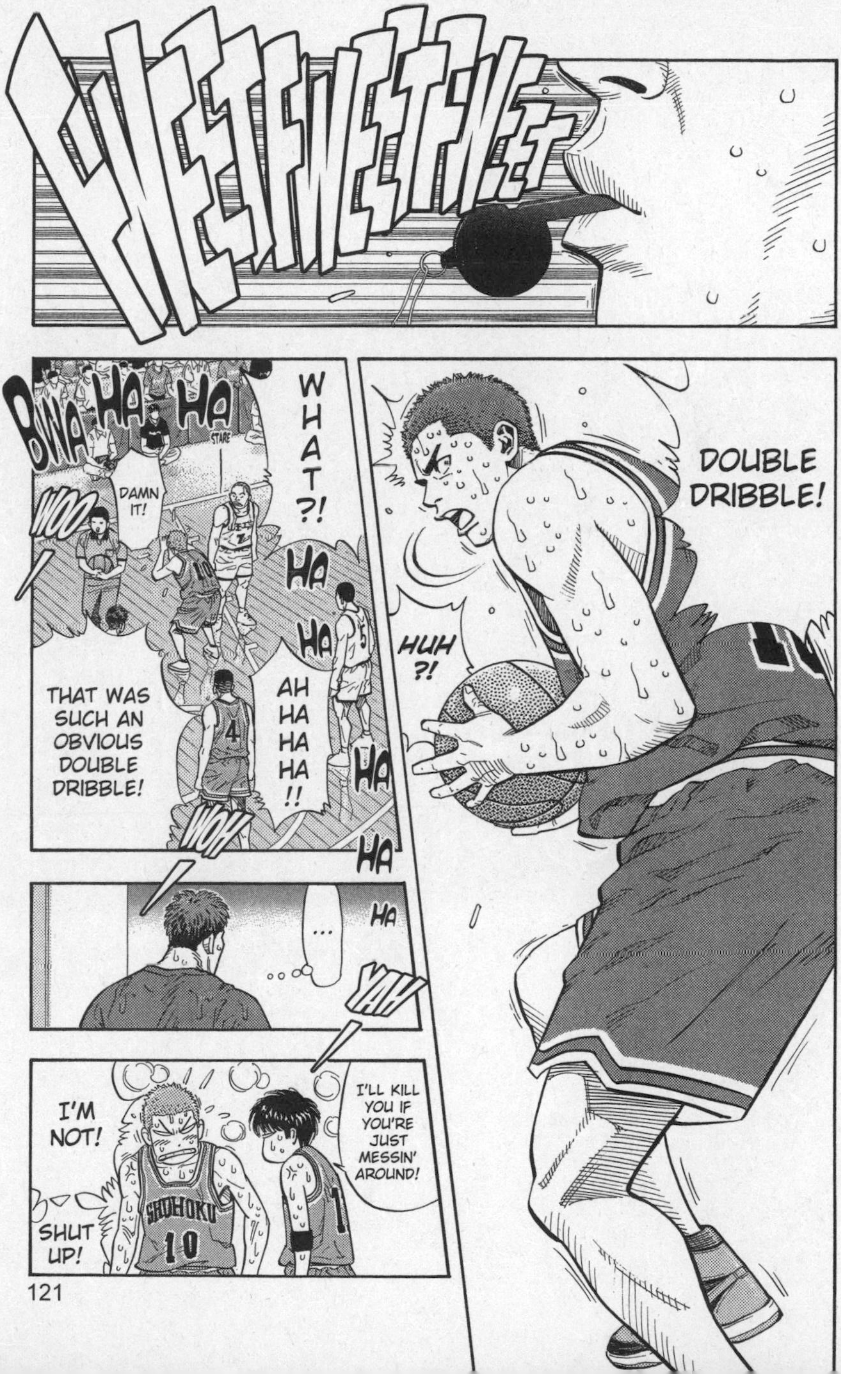
DOUBLE DRIBBLE!
HUH?!
WHAT?!
BWA HA HA
STARE
DAMN IT!
WOO
HA HA
AH HA HA HA!!
THAT WAS SUCH AN OBVIOUS DOUBLE DRIBBLE!
WOH
HA HA HA
...
YAH
I'LL KILL YOU IF YOU'RE JUST MESSIN' AROUND!
I'M NOT!
SHUT UP!
SHOHOKU 10

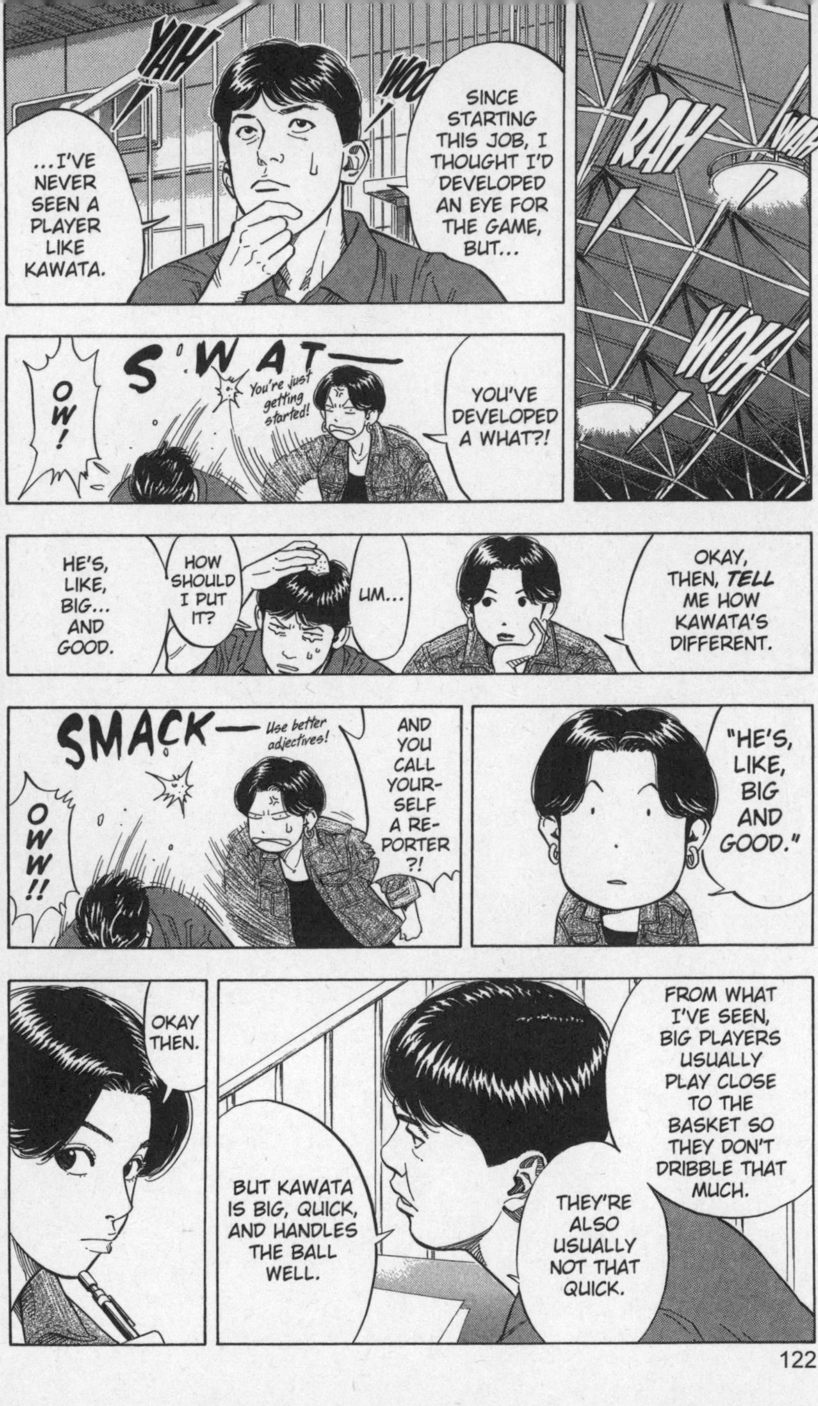
RAH
WAH
WOH
WOO
YAH
SINCE STARTING THIS JOB, I THOUGHT I'D DEVELOPED AN EYE FOR THE GAME, BUT...
...I'VE NEVER SEEN A PLAYER LIKE KAWATA.
YOU'VE DEVELOPED A WHAT?!
SWAT—
You're just getting started!
OW!
OKAY, THEN, TELL ME HOW KAWATA'S DIFFERENT.
UM...
HOW SHOULD I PUT IT?
HE'S, LIKE, BIG... AND GOOD.
"HE'S, LIKE, BIG AND GOOD."
AND YOU CALL YOURSELF A REPORTER?!
SMACK—
Use better adjectives!
OWW!!
FROM WHAT I'VE SEEN, BIG PLAYERS USUALLY PLAY CLOSE TO THE BASKET SO THEY DON'T DRIBBLE THAT MUCH.
THEY'RE ALSO USUALLY NOT THAT QUICK.
BUT KAWATA IS BIG, QUICK, AND HANDLES THE BALL WELL.
OKAY THEN.

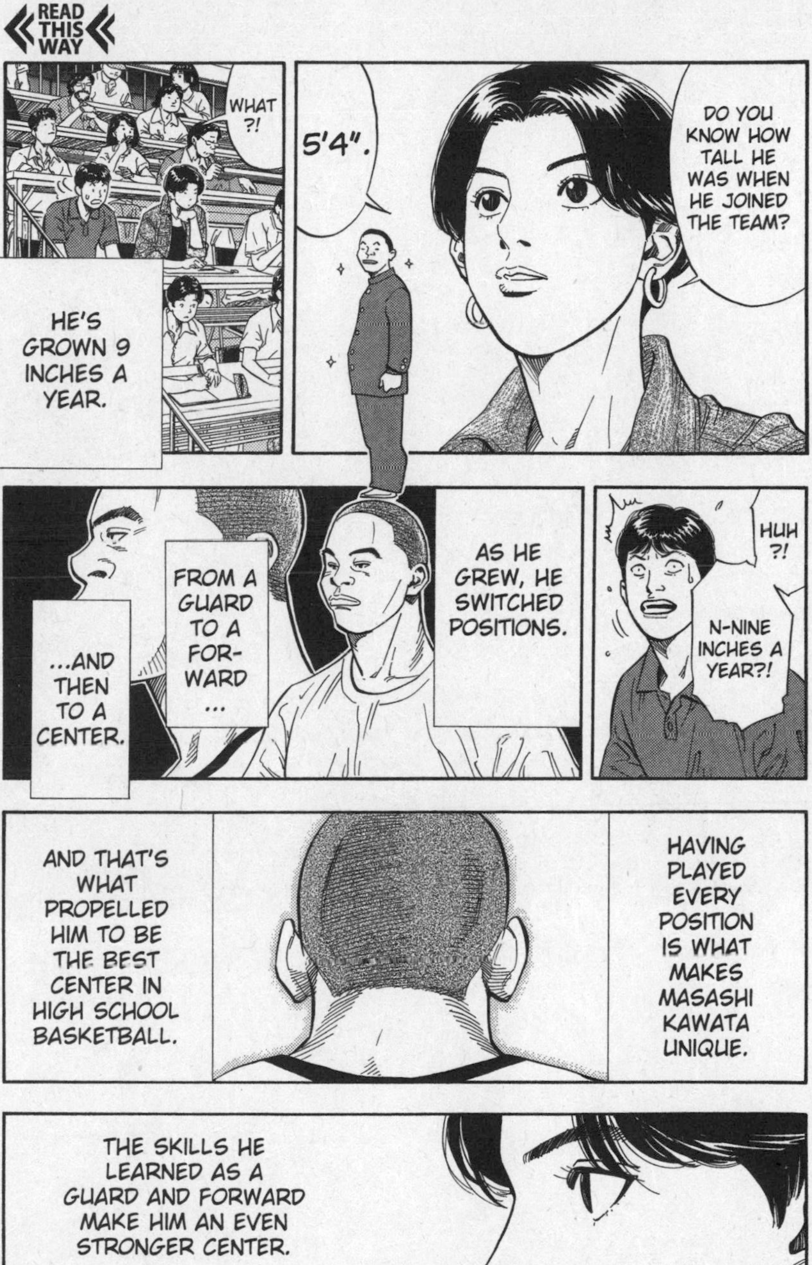
READ THIS WAY
DO YOU KNOW HOW TALL HE WAS WHEN HE JOINED THE TEAM?
5'4".
WHAT ?!
HE'S GROWN 9 INCHES A YEAR.
HUH ?!
N-NINE INCHES A YEAR?!
AS HE GREW, HE SWITCHED POSITIONS.
FROM A GUARD TO A FOR-WARD ...
...AND THEN TO A CENTER.
HAVING PLAYED EVERY POSITION IS WHAT MAKES MASASHI KAWATA UNIQUE.
AND THAT'S WHAT PROPELLED HIM TO BE THE BEST CENTER IN HIGH SCHOOL BASKETBALL.
THE SKILLS HE LEARNED AS A GUARD AND FORWARD MAKE HIM AN EVEN STRONGER CENTER.

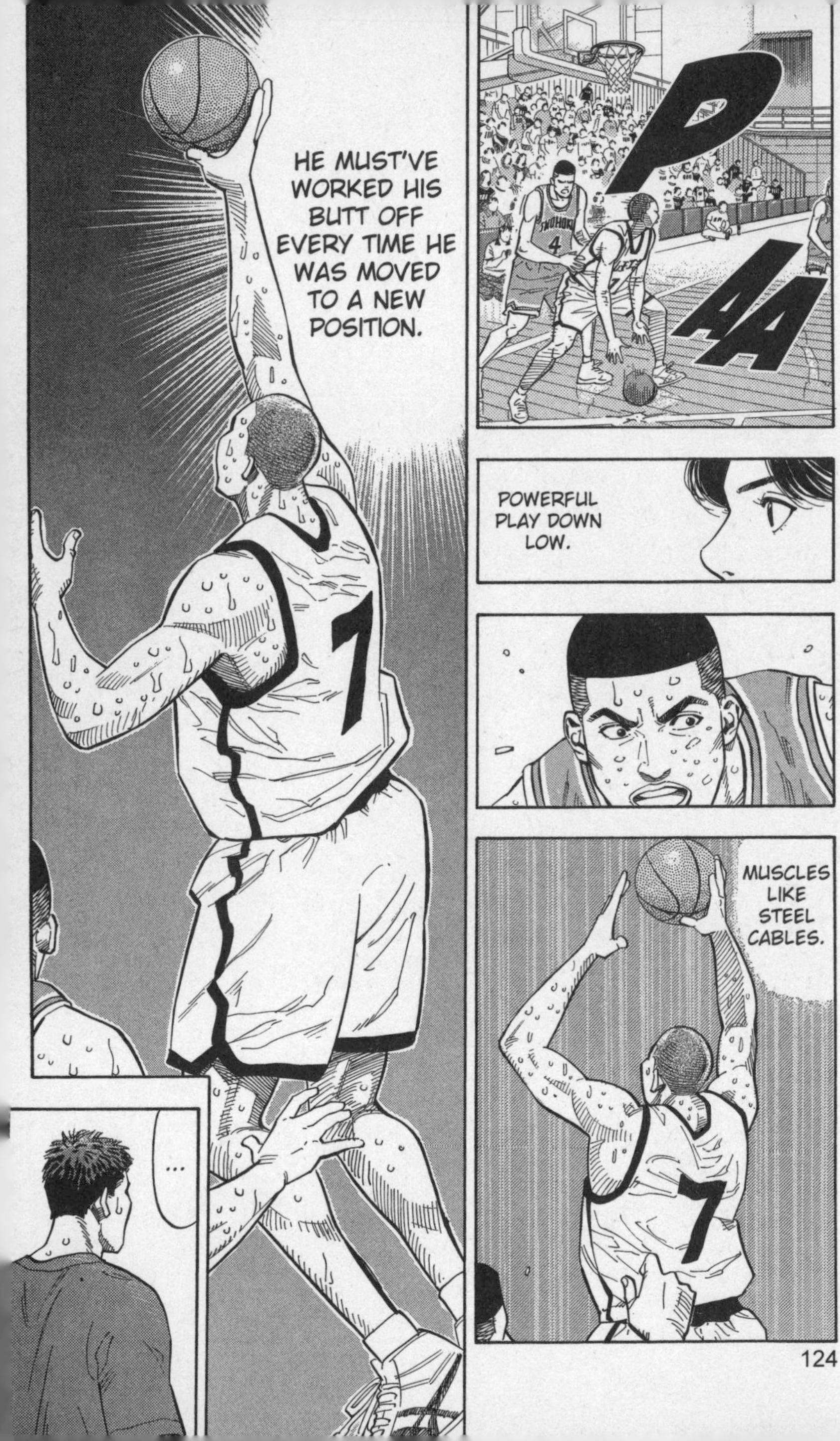
PAA
POWERFUL PLAY DOWN LOW.
MUSCLES LIKE STEEL CABLES.
HE MUST'VE WORKED HIS BUTT OFF EVERY TIME HE WAS MOVED TO A NEW POSITION.
...

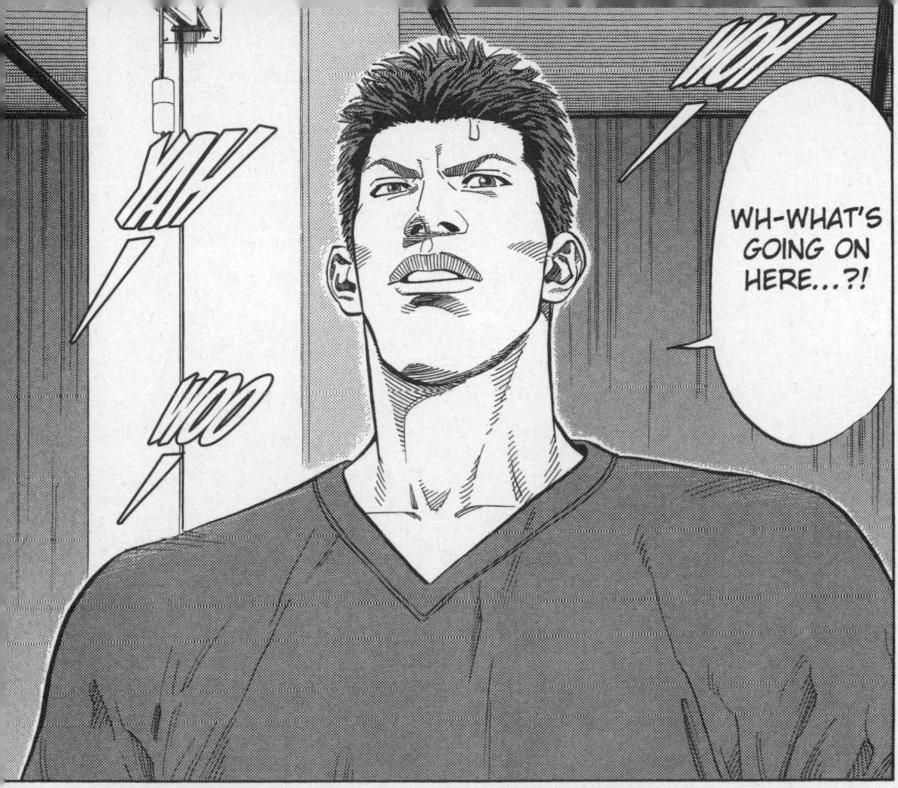
WOH!
WH-WHAT'S GOING ON HERE...?!
YAH!
WOO

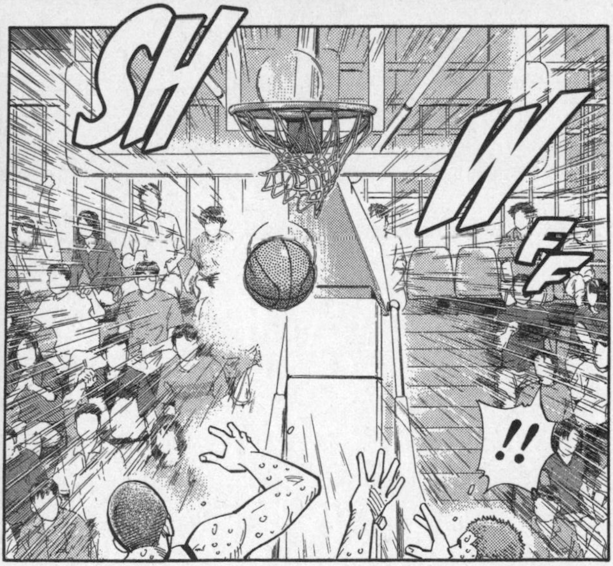
SH
W
FF
!!

SHOHOKU IS FORCED TO TAKE THEIR LAST TIMEOUT.

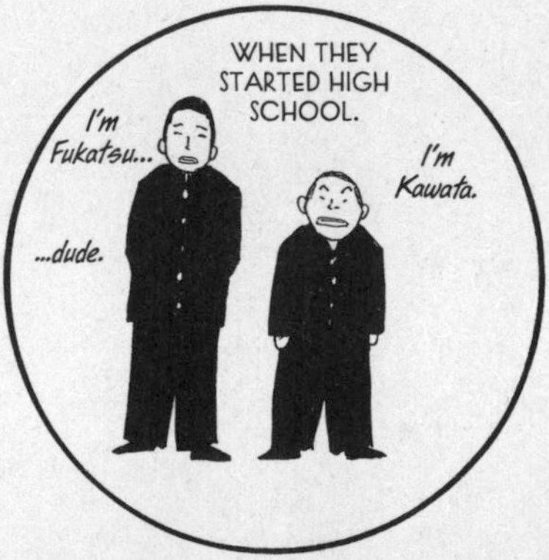
WHEN THEY STARTED HIGH SCHOOL.
I'm Kawata.
I'm Fukatsu...
...dude.

SLAM DUNK

UNCOOL SHOHOKU

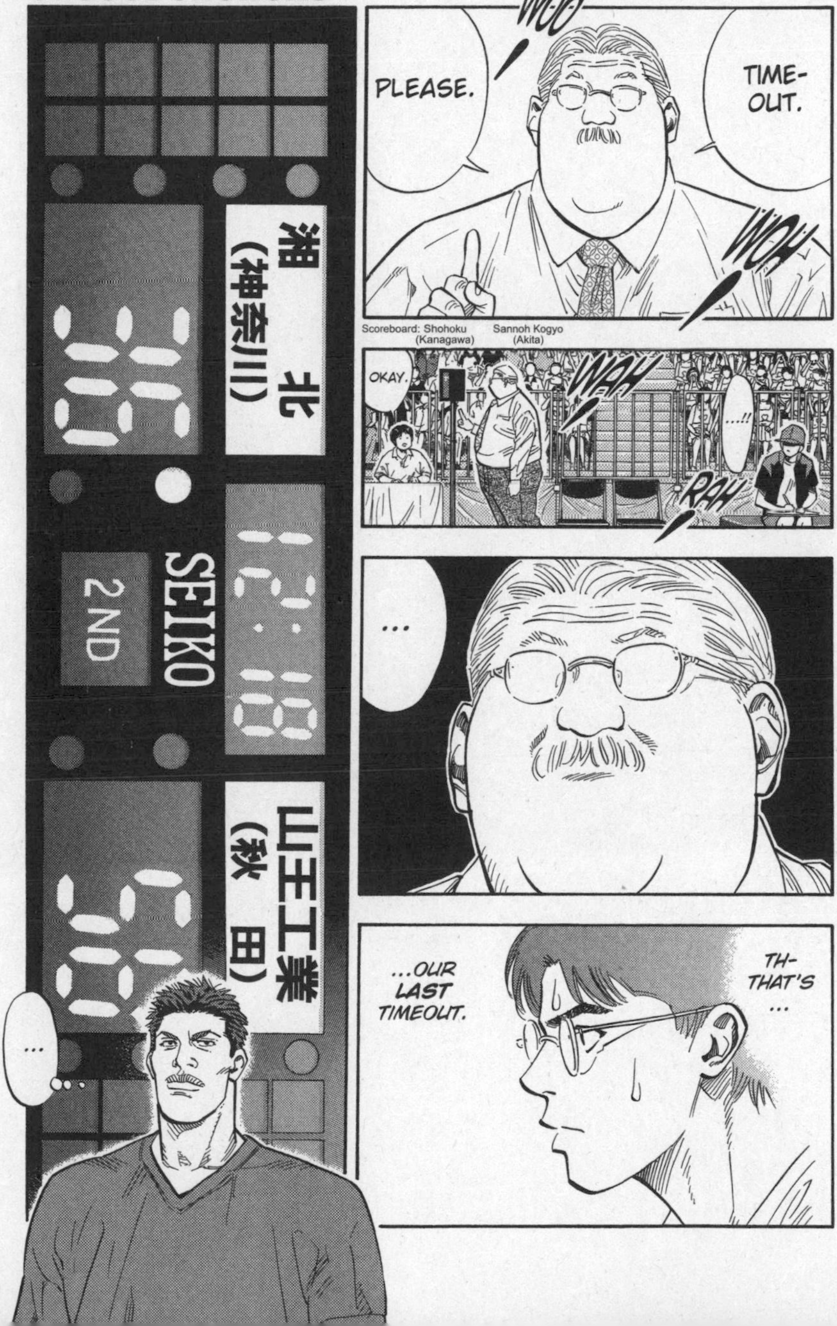
TIME-OUT.
PLEASE.
WOO
WOH
Scoreboard: Shohoku (Kanagawa) Sannoh Kogyo (Akita)
...!!
OKAY.
WAH
RAH
...
TH-THAT'S ...
...OUR LAST TIMEOUT.
湘北 (神奈川)
SEIKO
2ND
山王工業 (秋田)
...

#240 UNCOOL SHOHOKU

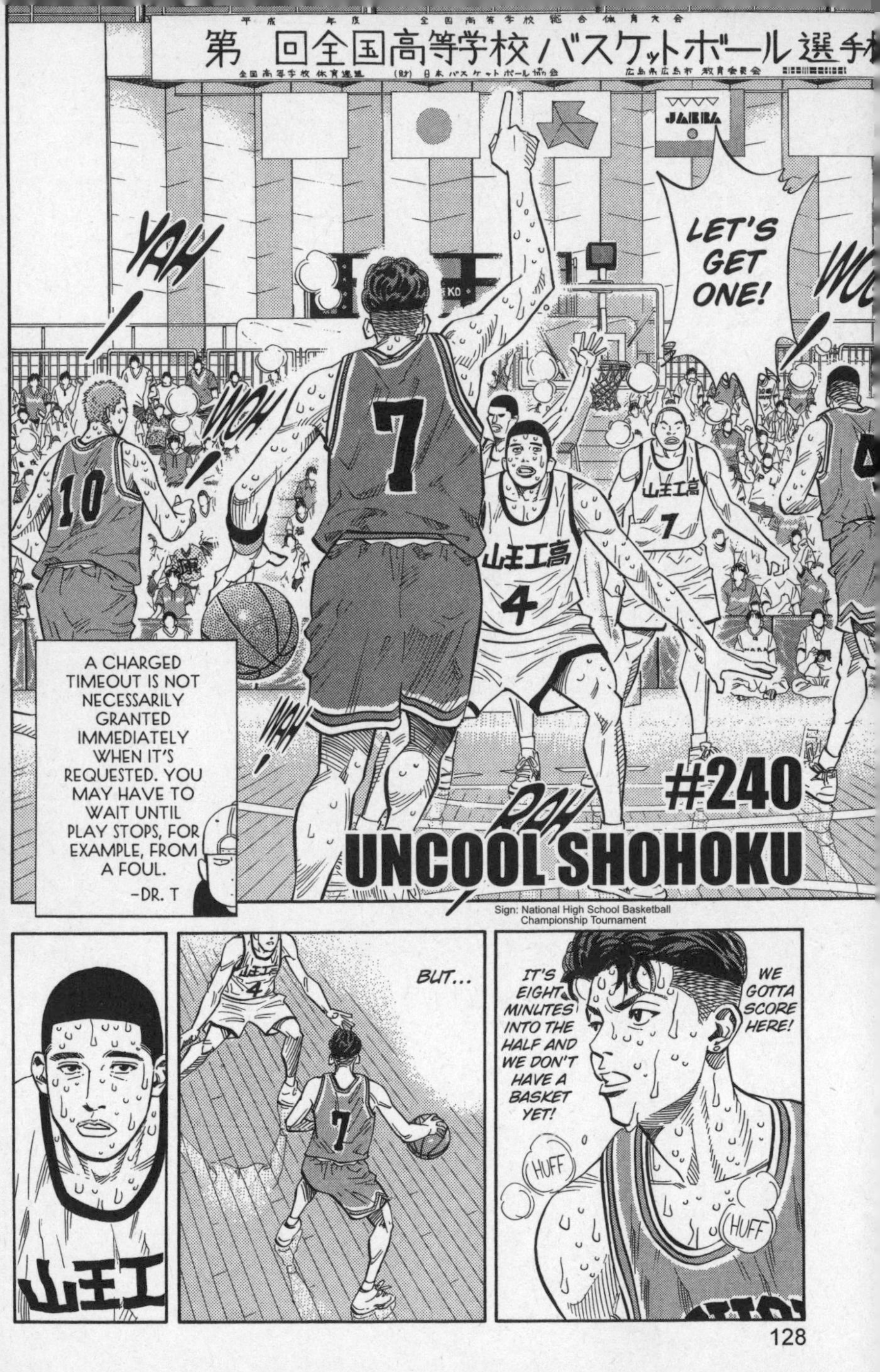
第　回全国高等学校バスケットボール選手権
JABBA
LET'S GET ONE!
WOO
YAH!
WOH!
YAH!
POH
#240
UNCOOL SHOHOKU
A CHARGED TIMEOUT IS NOT NECESSARILY GRANTED IMMEDIATELY WHEN IT'S REQUESTED. YOU MAY HAVE TO WAIT UNTIL PLAY STOPS, FOR EXAMPLE, FROM A FOUL.
–DR. T
WE GOTTA SCORE HERE!
IT'S EIGHT MINUTES INTO THE HALF AND WE DON'T HAVE A BASKET YET!
HUFF
HUFF
BUT...

Sign: National High School Basketball Championship Tournament

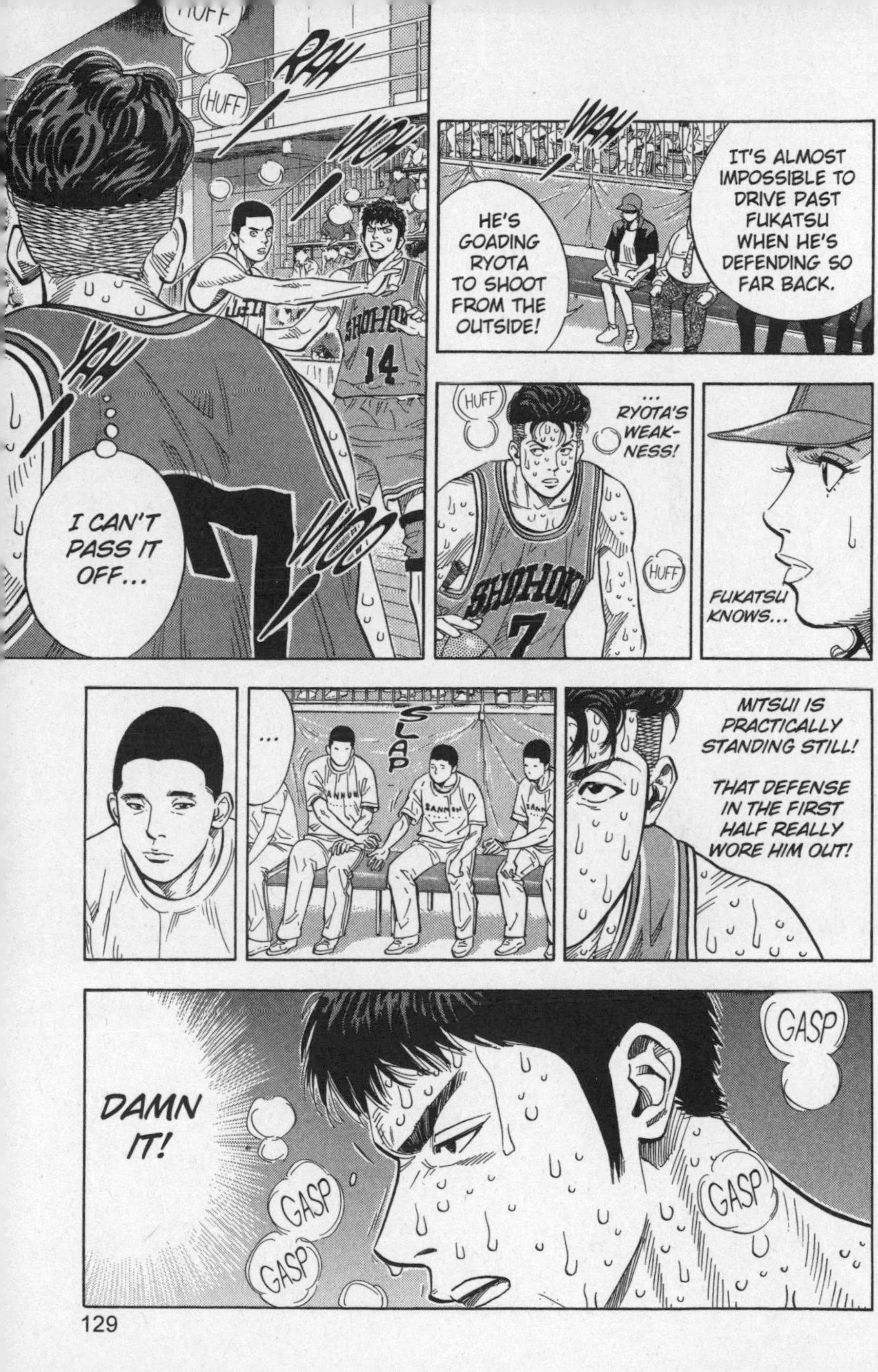
WAH
IT'S ALMOST IMPOSSIBLE TO DRIVE PAST FUKATSU WHEN HE'S DEFENDING SO FAR BACK.
HE'S GOADING RYOTA TO SHOOT FROM THE OUTSIDE!
FUKATSU KNOWS...
HUFF
... RYOTA'S WEAKNESS!
HUFF
HUFF
RAH
HUFF
WOH
YAH
I CAN'T PASS IT OFF...
WOO
MITSUI IS PRACTICALLY STANDING STILL!
THAT DEFENSE IN THE FIRST HALF REALLY WORE HIM OUT!
...
SLAP
GASP
DAMN IT!
GASP
GASP
GASP

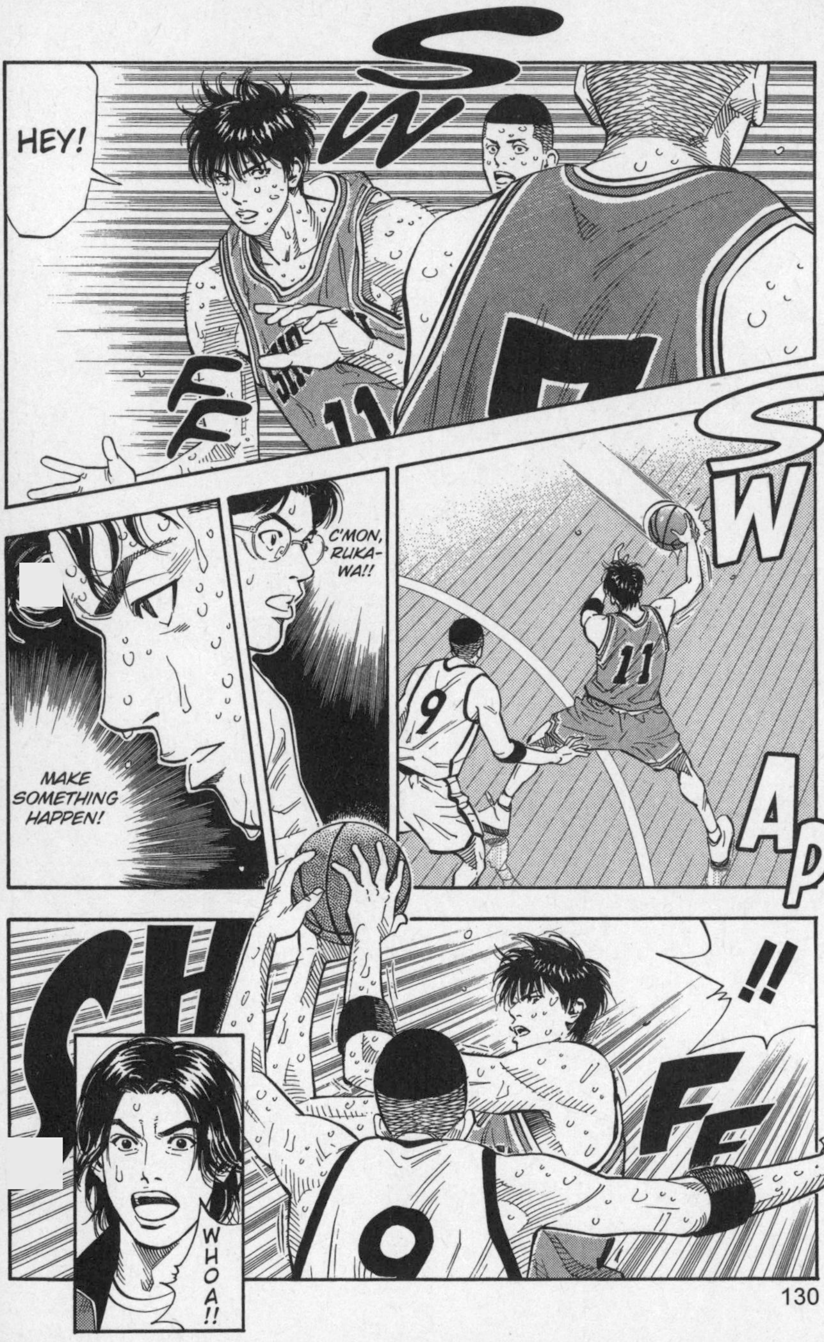
SW
HEY!
FF
SW
AP
C'MON, RUKAWA!!
MAKE SOMETHING HAPPEN!
!!
FF
CH
WHOA!!

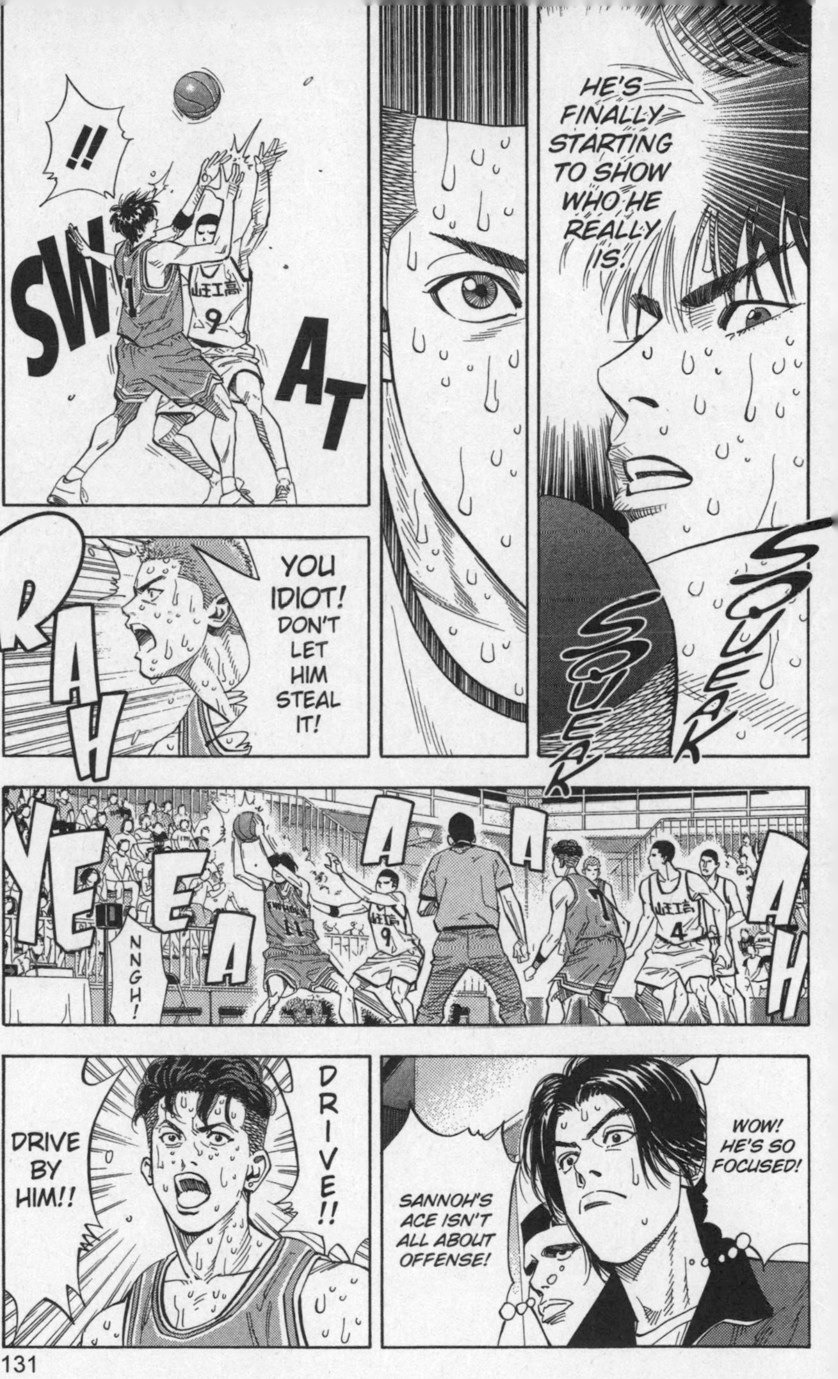
HE'S FINALLY STARTING TO SHOW WHO HE REALLY IS!
SQUEAK
SQUEAK
!!
SWAT
YOU IDIOT! DON'T LET HIM STEAL IT!
RAAH
YEEAAAAH
NNGH!
WOW! HE'S SO FOCUSED!
SANNOH'S ACE ISN'T ALL ABOUT OFFENSE!
DRIVE!!
DRIVE BY HIM!!

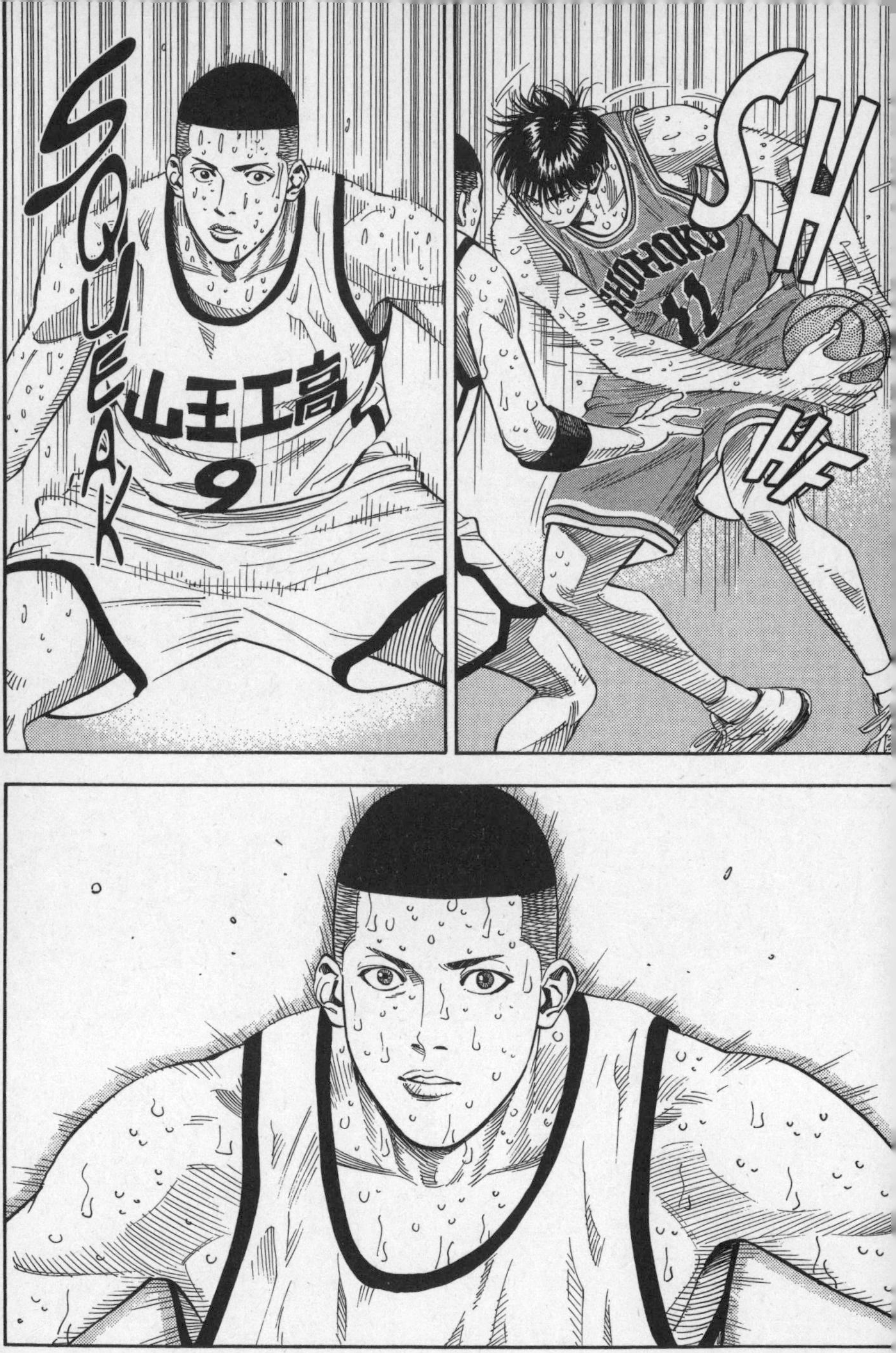
SH
HF
SQUEAK

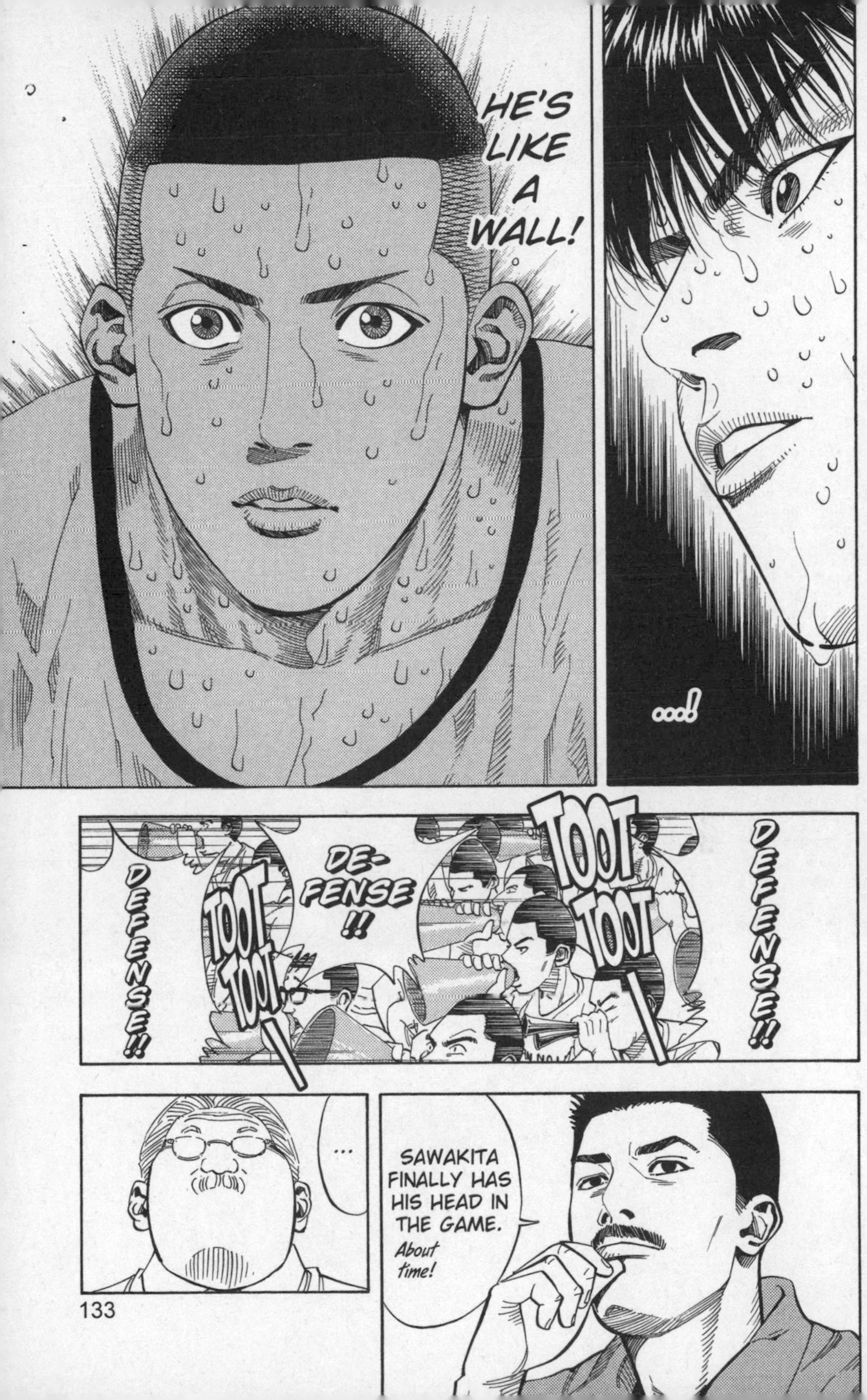
...!
HE'S LIKE A WALL!
DEFENSE!!
TOOT TOOT
DE-FENSE!!
TOOT TOOT
DEFENSE!!
SAWAKITA FINALLY HAS HIS HEAD IN THE GAME.
About time!
...

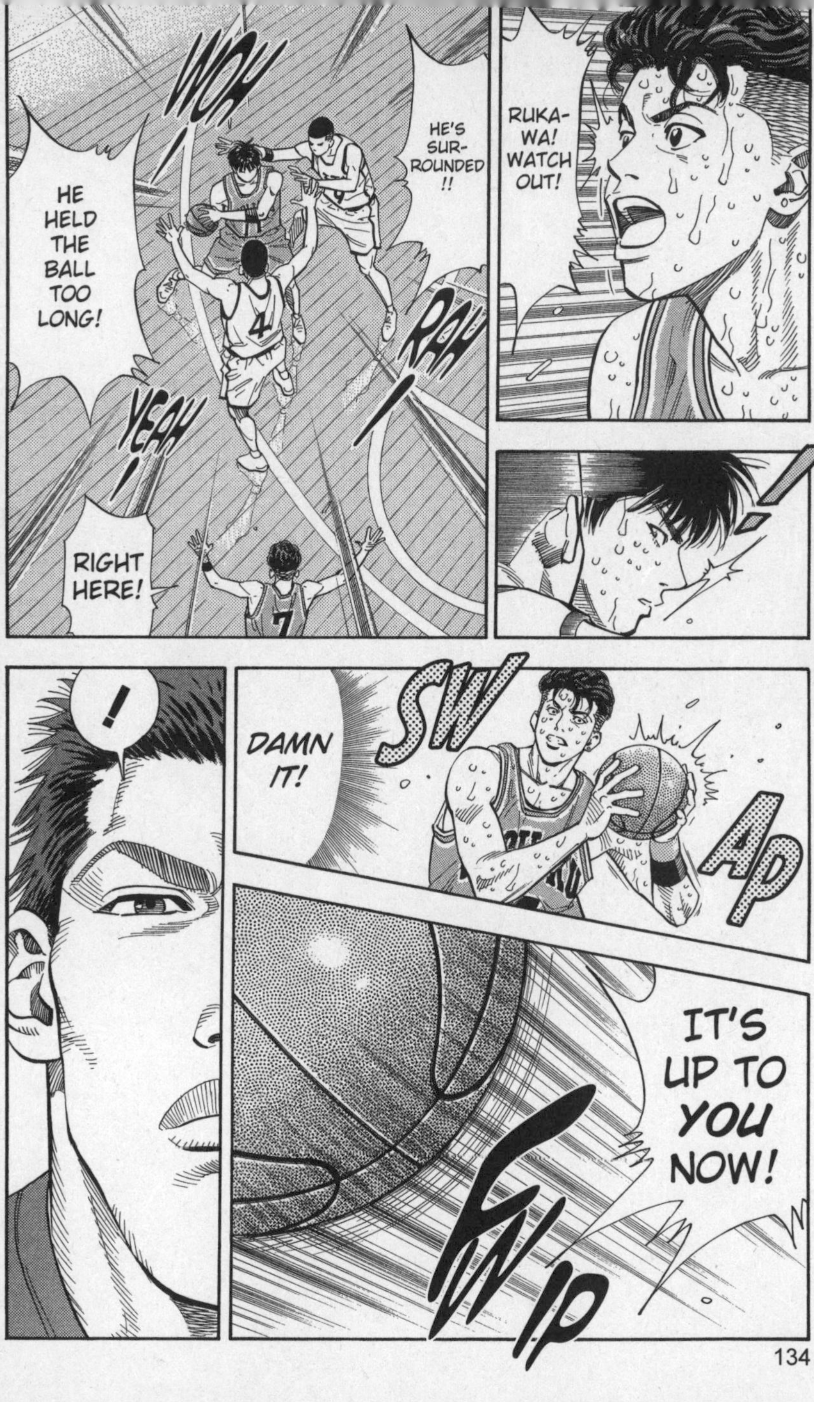
RUKA-WA! WATCH OUT!
!
HE'S SUR-ROUNDED !!
WOH
HE HELD THE BALL TOO LONG!
RAH
YEAH
RIGHT HERE!
DAMN IT!
SWAP
IT'S UP TO YOU NOW!
WHIP
!

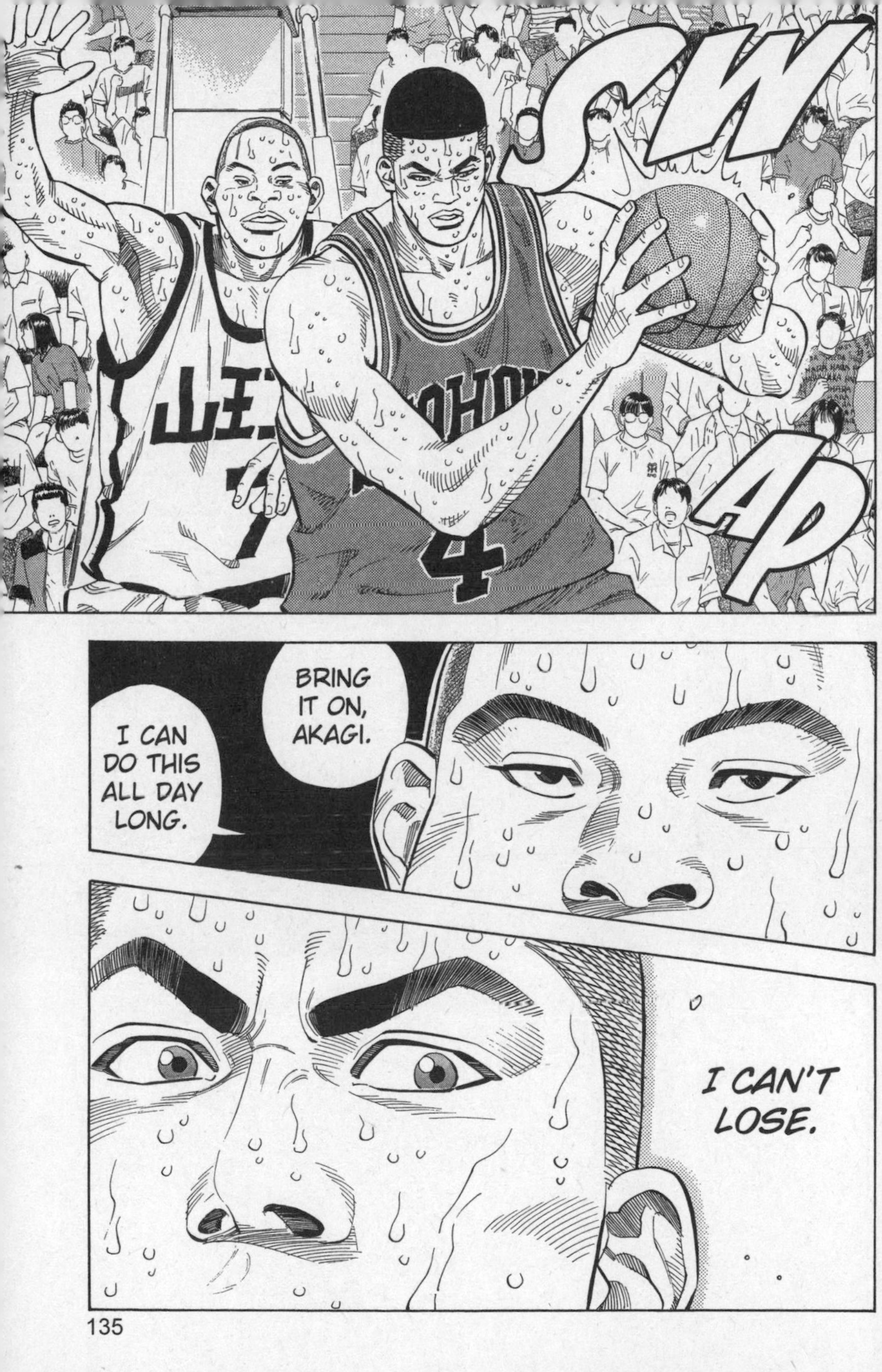
SWAP
BRING IT ON, AKAGI.
I CAN DO THIS ALL DAY LONG.
I CAN'T LOSE.

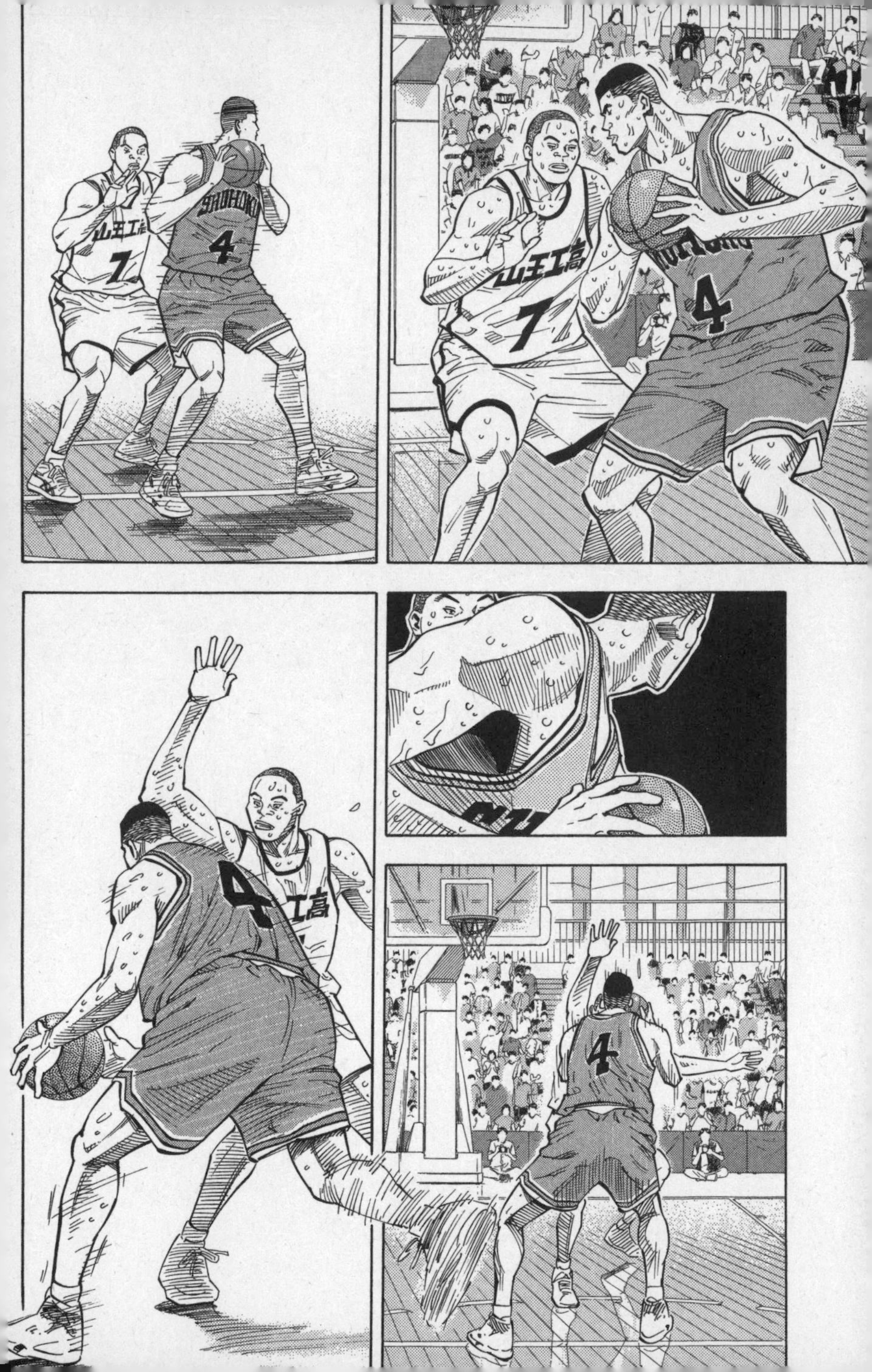
山王工高
SHOHOKU

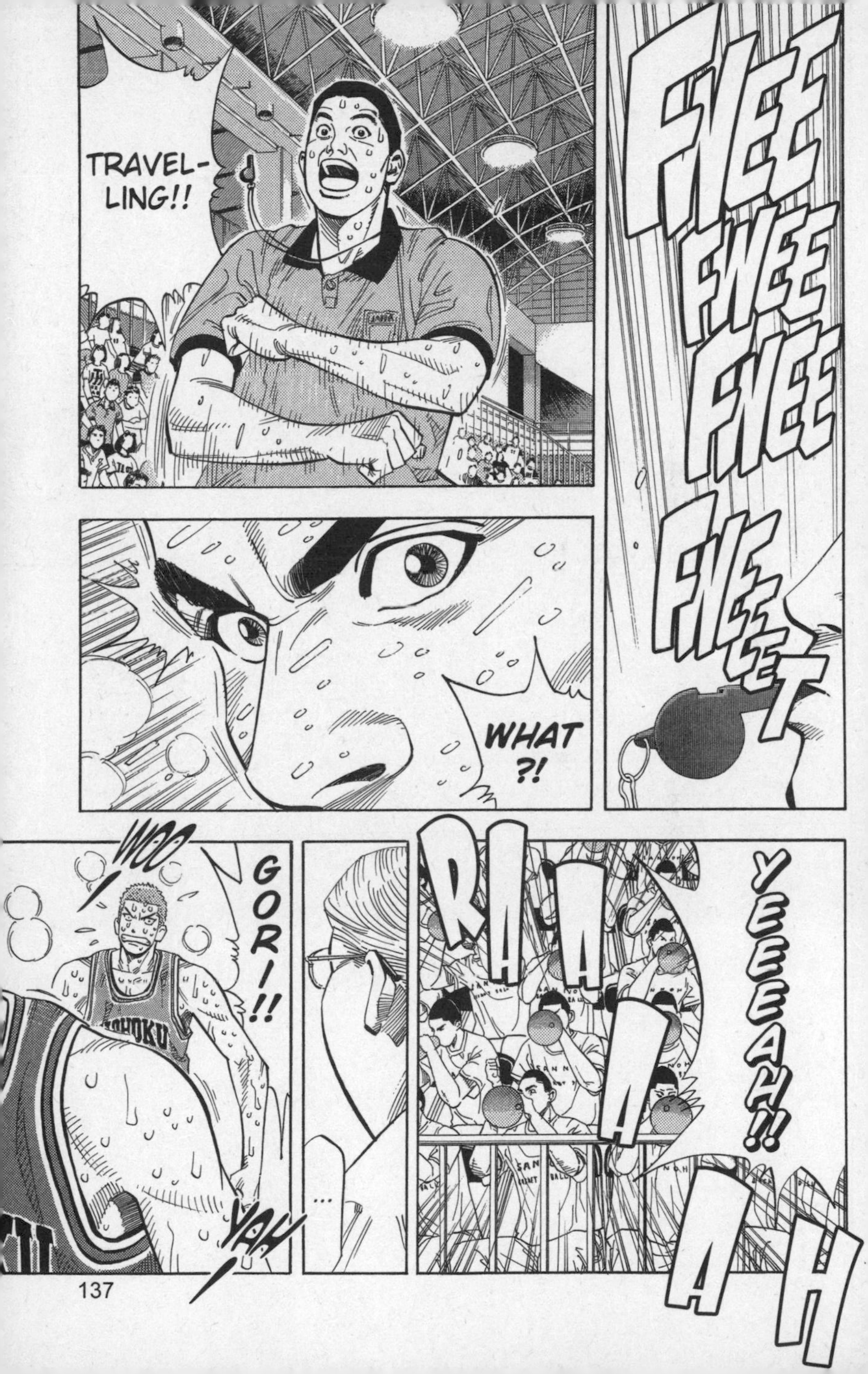
FWEE
FWEE
FWEE
FWEEEET
TRAVEL-
LING!!
WHAT
?!
YEEEAAH!!
RAAAAAAH
...
WOO!
GORI!!
YAH!

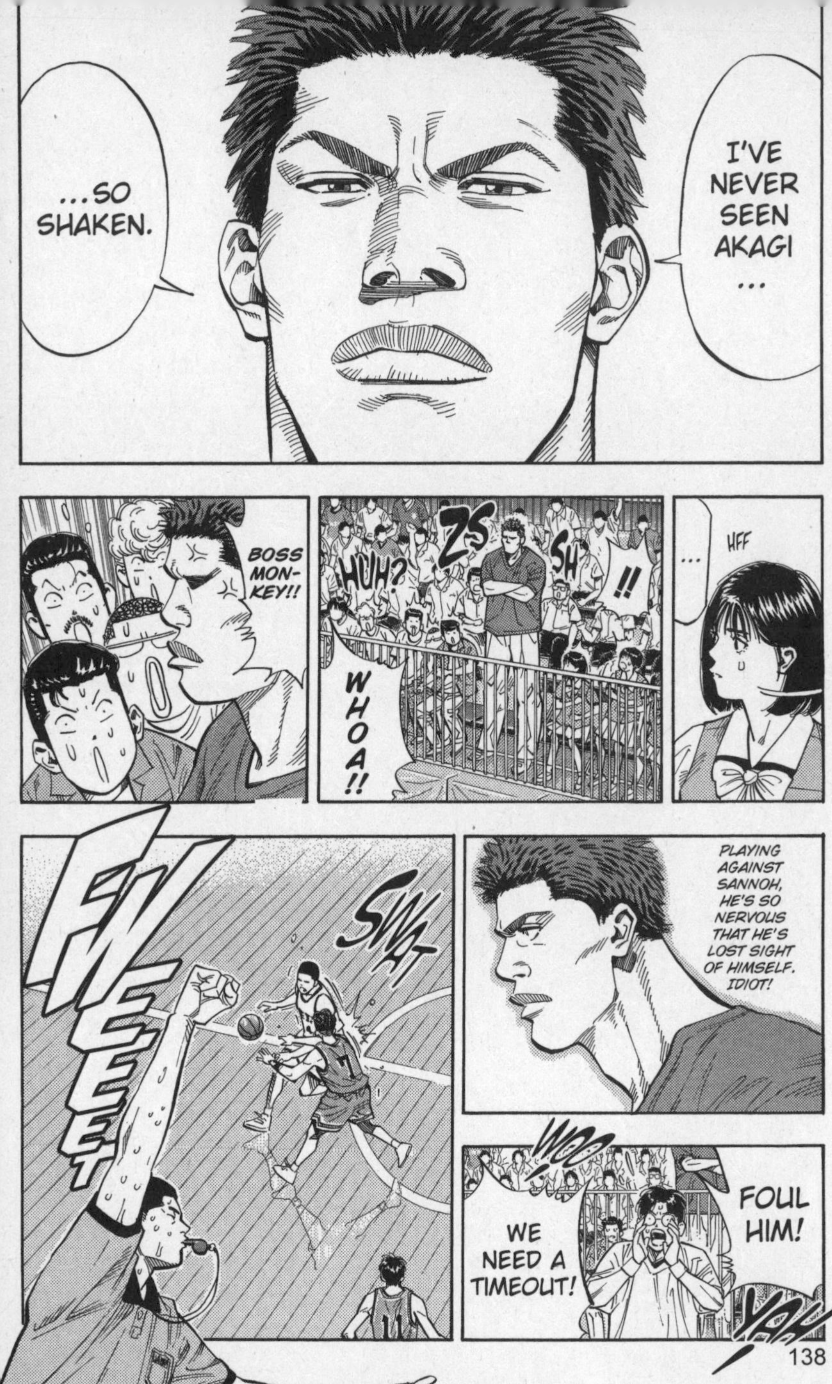
I'VE NEVER SEEN AKAGI ...
...SO SHAKEN.
...
HFF
ZS
SH
!!
HUH?
WHOA!!
BOSS MONKEY!!
PLAYING AGAINST SANNOH, HE'S SO NERVOUS THAT HE'S LOST SIGHT OF HIMSELF. IDIOT!
WOO
FOUL HIM!
WE NEED A TIMEOUT!
YAH
SWAT
FWEEEET

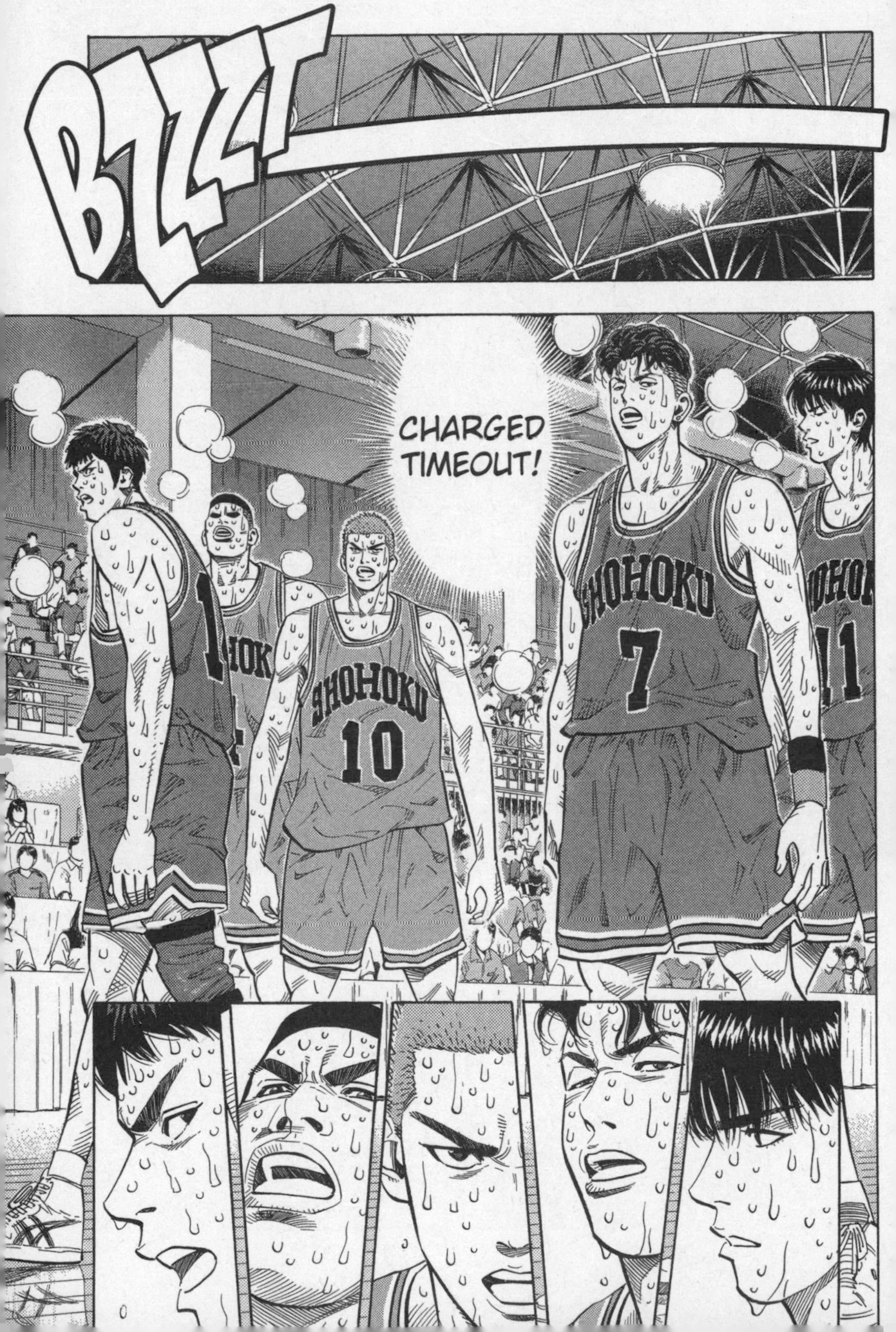
BZZZT
CHARGED TIMEOUT!
SHOHOKU
7
SHOHOKU
10
11
1
4

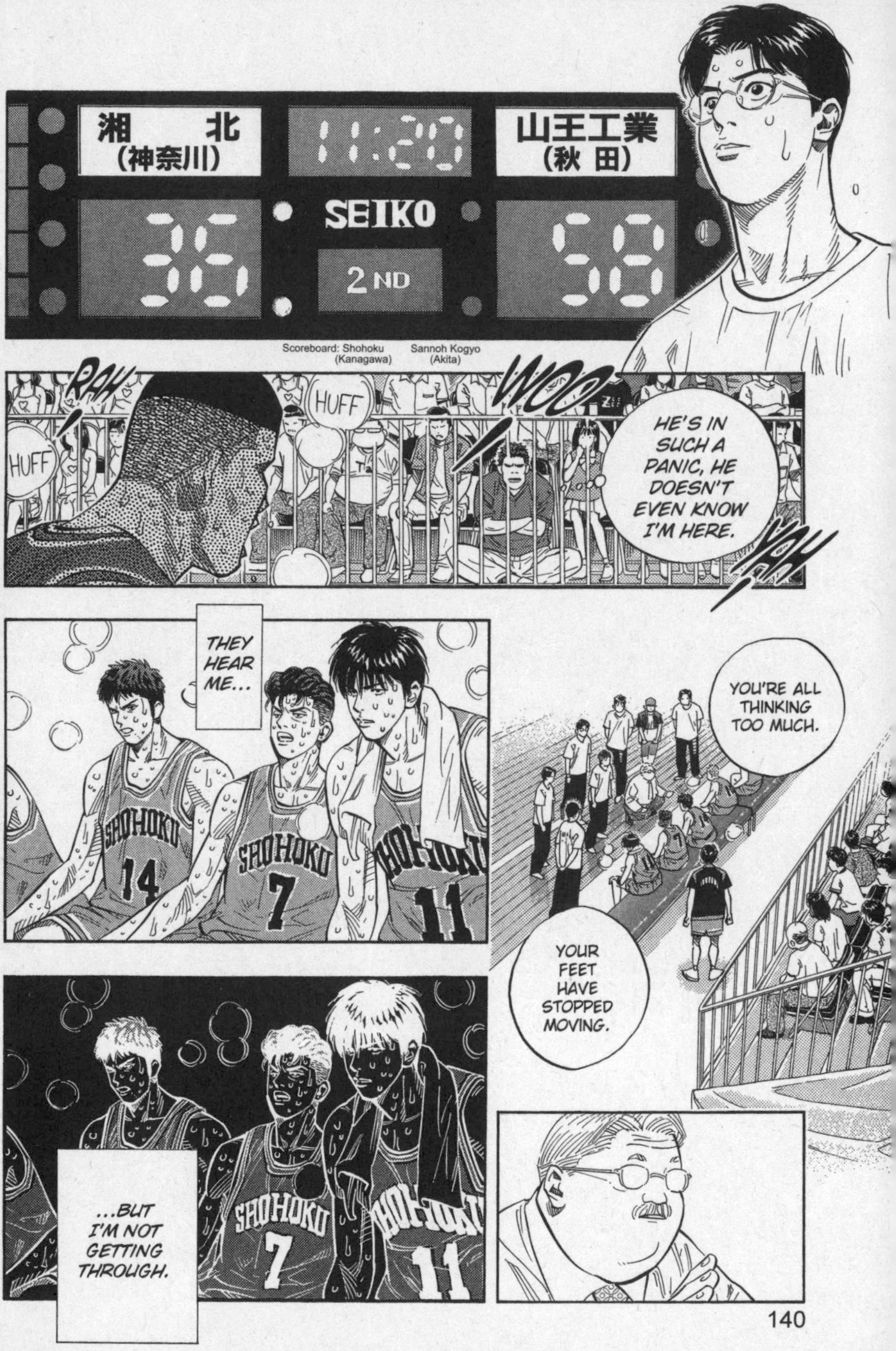
湘北
(神奈川)
11:20
山王工業
(秋田)
SEIKO
36
58
2ND
Scoreboard: Shohoku (Kanagawa) Sannoh Kogyo (Akita)
YAH
HE'S IN SUCH A PANIC, HE DOESN'T EVEN KNOW I'M HERE.
WOO
HUFF
RAH
HUFF
YOU'RE ALL THINKING TOO MUCH.
YOUR FEET HAVE STOPPED MOVING.
THEY HEAR ME...
...BUT I'M NOT GETTING THROUGH.

READ THIS WAY

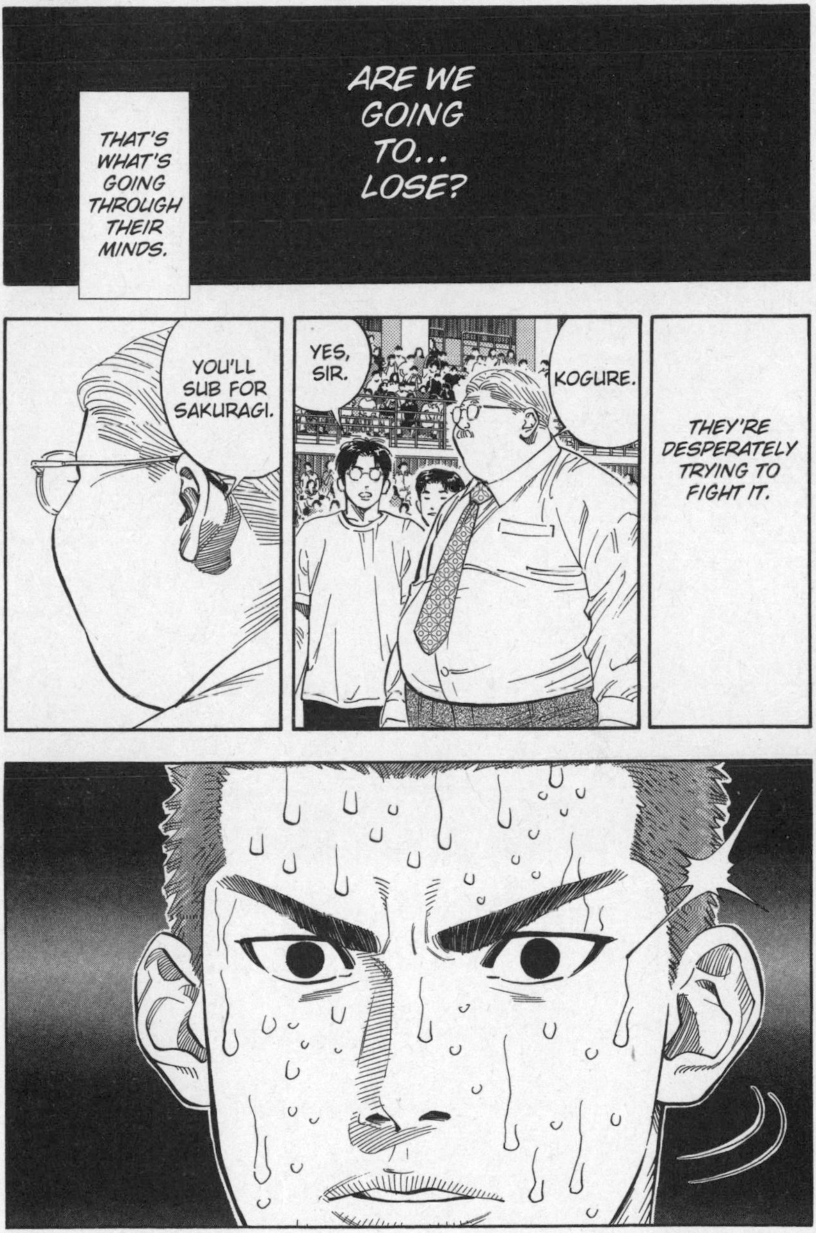
ARE WE GOING TO... LOSE?
THAT'S WHAT'S GOING THROUGH THEIR MINDS.
THEY'RE DESPERATELY TRYING TO FIGHT IT.
KOGURE.
YES, SIR.
YOU'LL SUB FOR SAKURAGI.

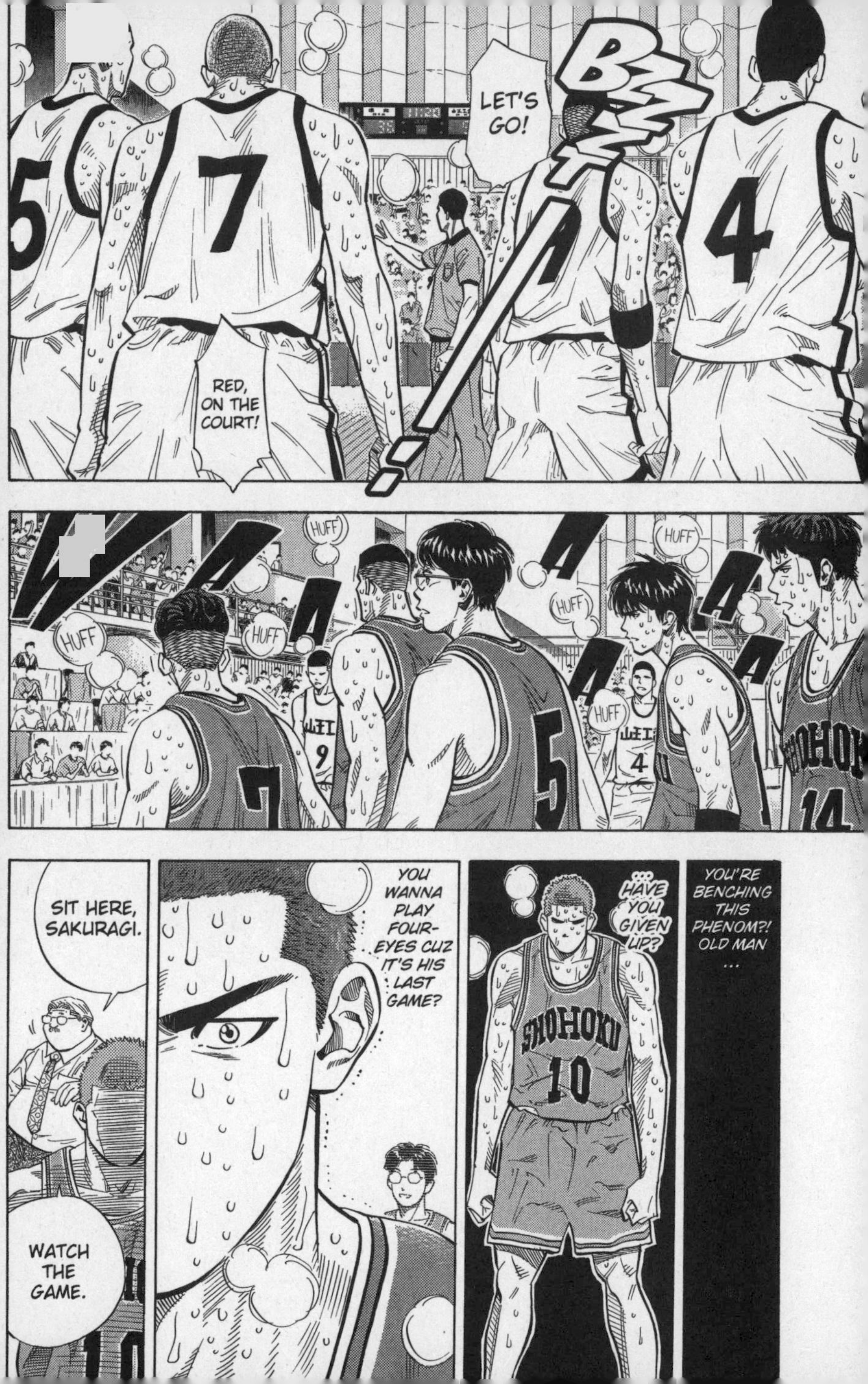
LET'S GO!
RED, ON THE COURT!
HUFF
HUFF
HUFF
HUFF
HUFF
YOU'RE BENCHING THIS PHENOM?! OLD MAN ...
...HAVE YOU GIVEN UP?
YOU WANNA PLAY FOUR-EYES CUZ IT'S HIS LAST GAME?
SIT HERE, SAKURAGI.
WATCH THE GAME.

READ THIS WAY

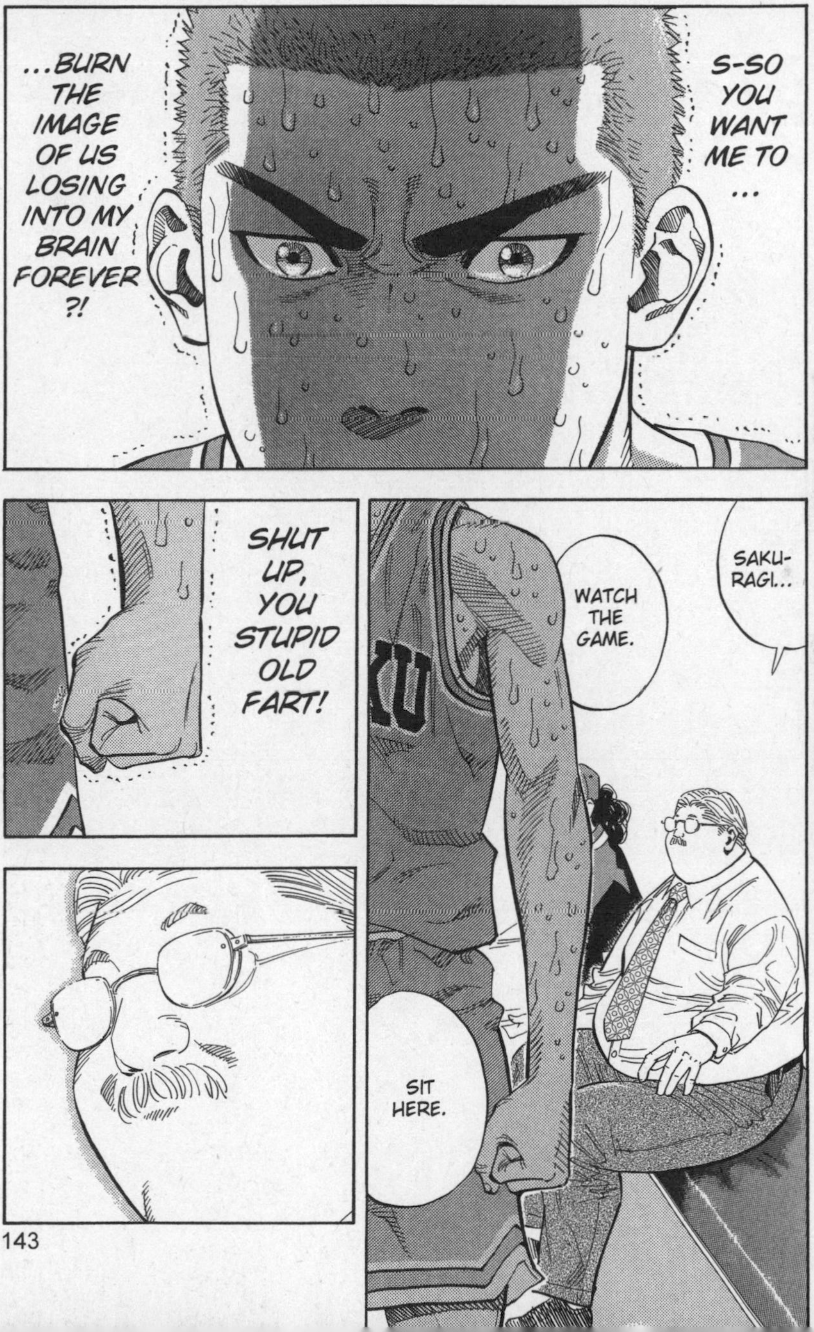
S-SO YOU WANT ME TO ...
...BURN THE IMAGE OF US LOSING INTO MY BRAIN FOREVER ?!
SAKU-RAGI...
WATCH THE GAME.
SIT HERE.
SHUT UP, YOU STUPID OLD FART!

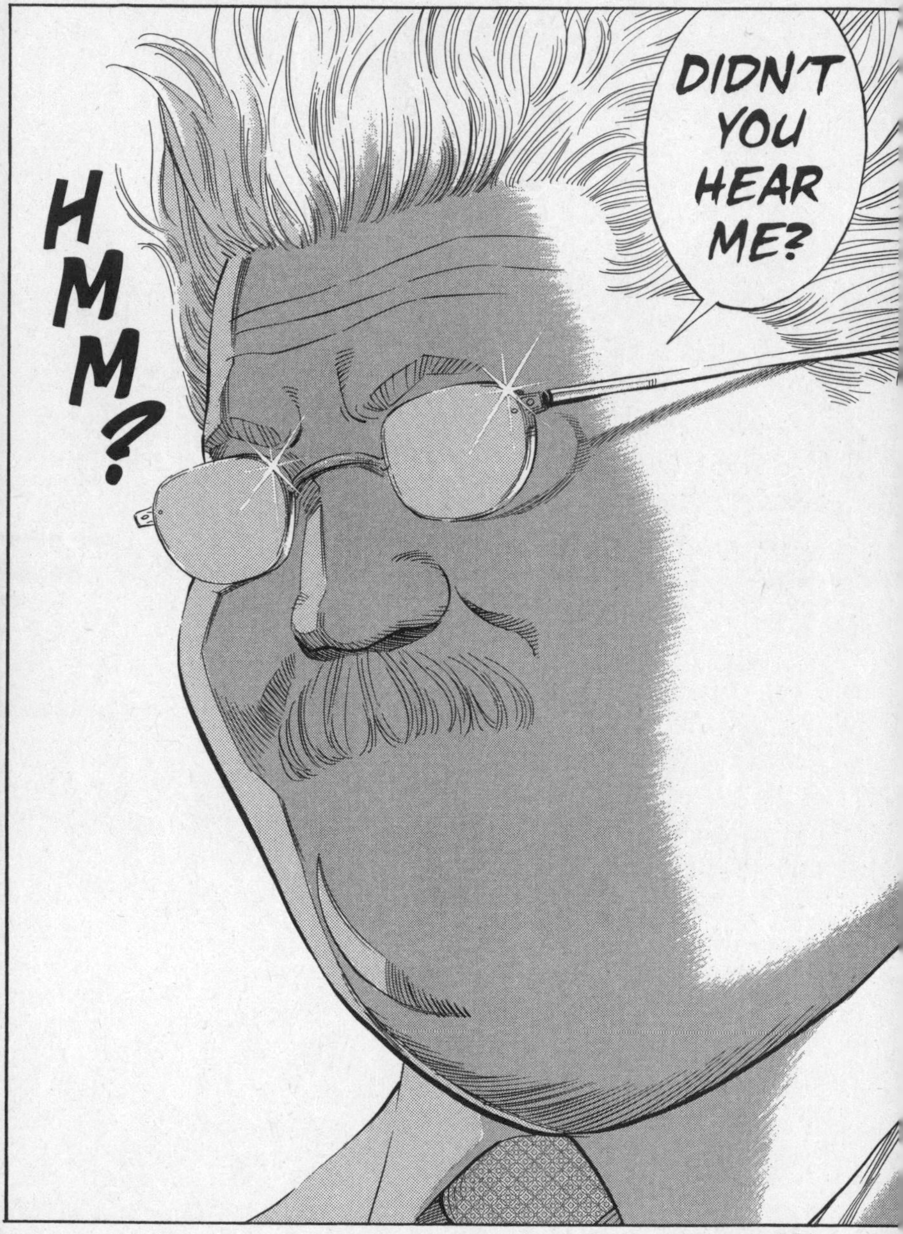
DIDN'T YOU HEAR ME?
HMM?

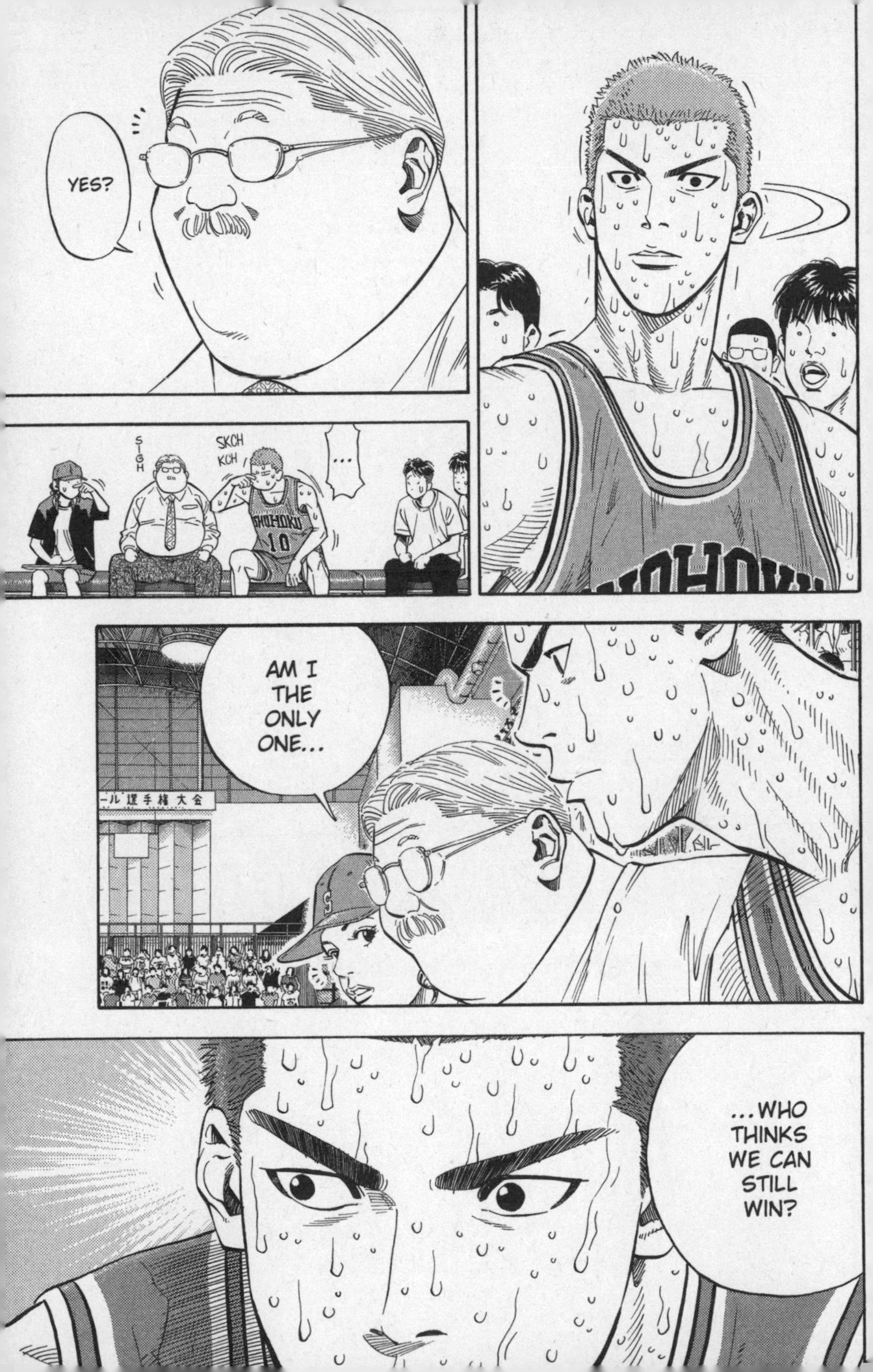
YES?
...
SKCH KCH
SIGH
AM I THE ONLY ONE...
ール選手権大会
...WHO THINKS WE CAN STILL WIN?

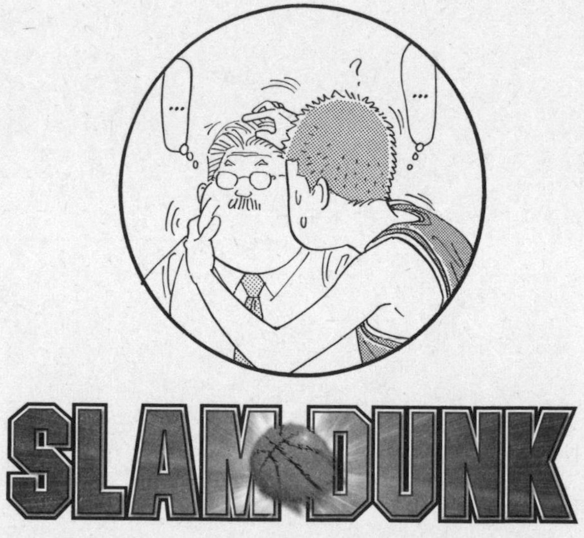
...
?
...

SLAM DUNK

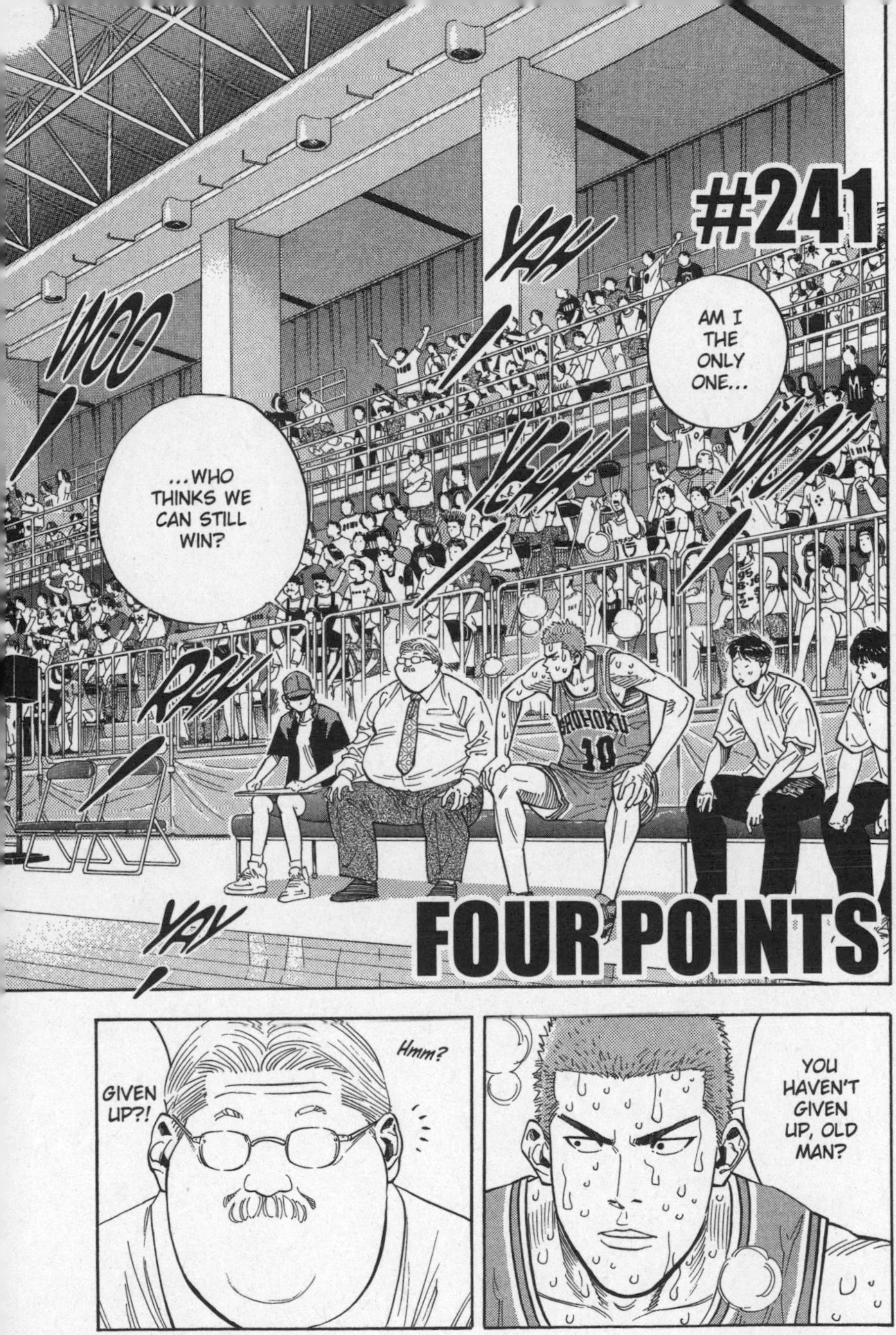

#241
YAH!
AM I THE ONLY ONE...
WAH!
YEAH!
WOO!
...WHO THINKS WE CAN STILL WIN?
RAH!
FOUR POINTS
YAY!
YOU HAVEN'T GIVEN UP, OLD MAN?
Hmm?
GIVEN UP?!

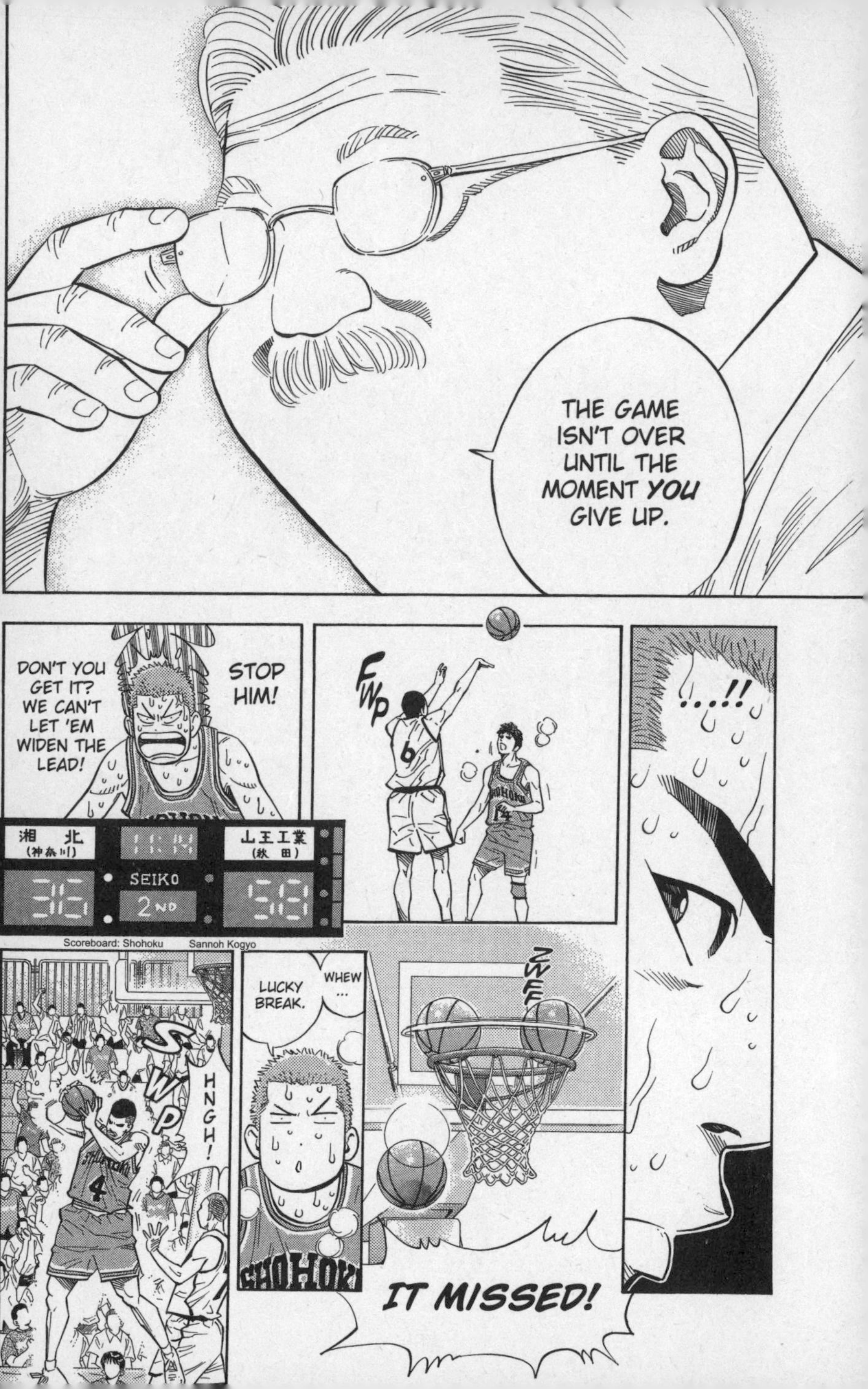
THE GAME ISN'T OVER UNTIL THE MOMENT YOU GIVE UP.
...!!
FWP
STOP HIM!
DON'T YOU GET IT? WE CAN'T LET 'EM WIDEN THE LEAD!
湘北 (神奈川)
11:14
山王工業 (秋田)
SEIKO
2ND
Scoreboard: Shohoku Sannoh Kogyo
ZWFF
WHEW...
LUCKY BREAK.
IT MISSED!
SWP
HNGH!

READ THIS WAY

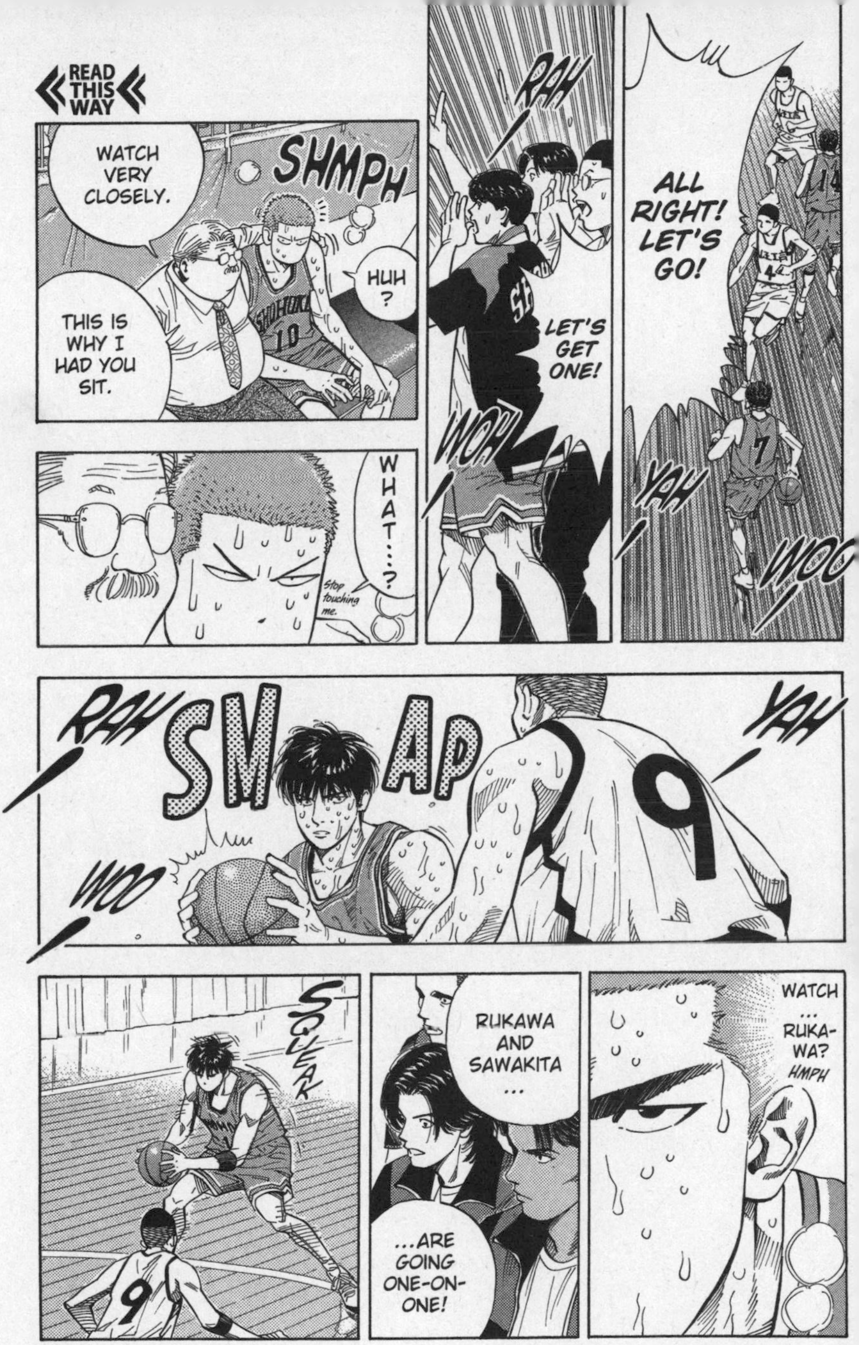

ALL RIGHT! LET'S GO!
YAH
WOO
RAH
LET'S GET ONE!
WOH
WATCH VERY CLOSELY.
SHMPH
HUH?
THIS IS WHY I HAD YOU SIT.
WHAT...?
Stop touching me.
YAH
SMAP
RAH
WOO
WATCH... RUKAWA?
HMPH
RUKAWA AND SAWAKITA...
...ARE GOING ONE-ON-ONE!
SQUEAK

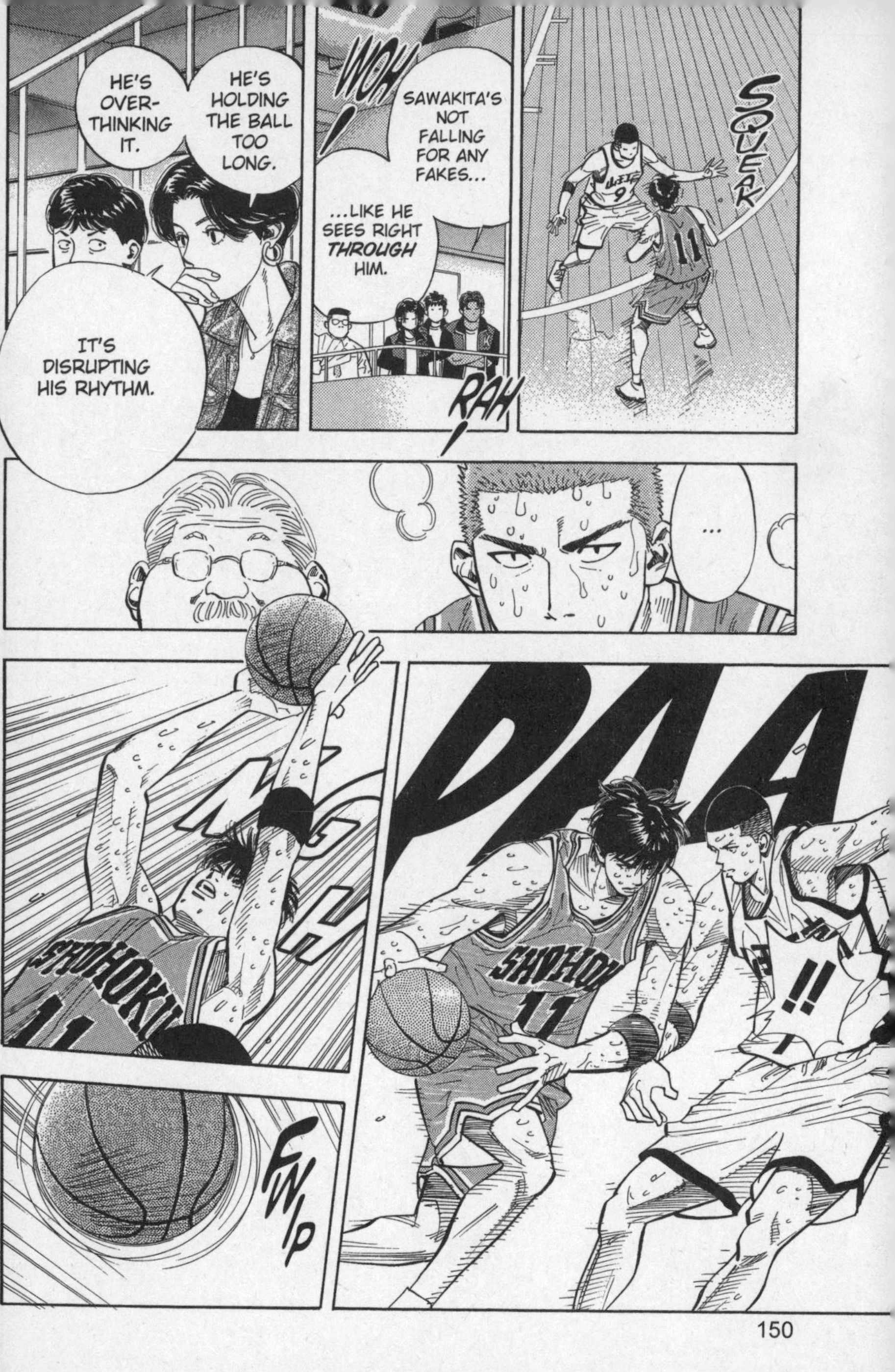
SQUEEK
WOH!
SAWAKITA'S NOT FALLING FOR ANY FAKES...
...LIKE HE SEES RIGHT *THROUGH* HIM.
RAH!
HE'S HOLDING THE BALL TOO LONG.
HE'S OVER-THINKING IT.
IT'S DISRUPTING HIS RHYTHM.
...
PAA
!!
FWIP

READ THIS WAY

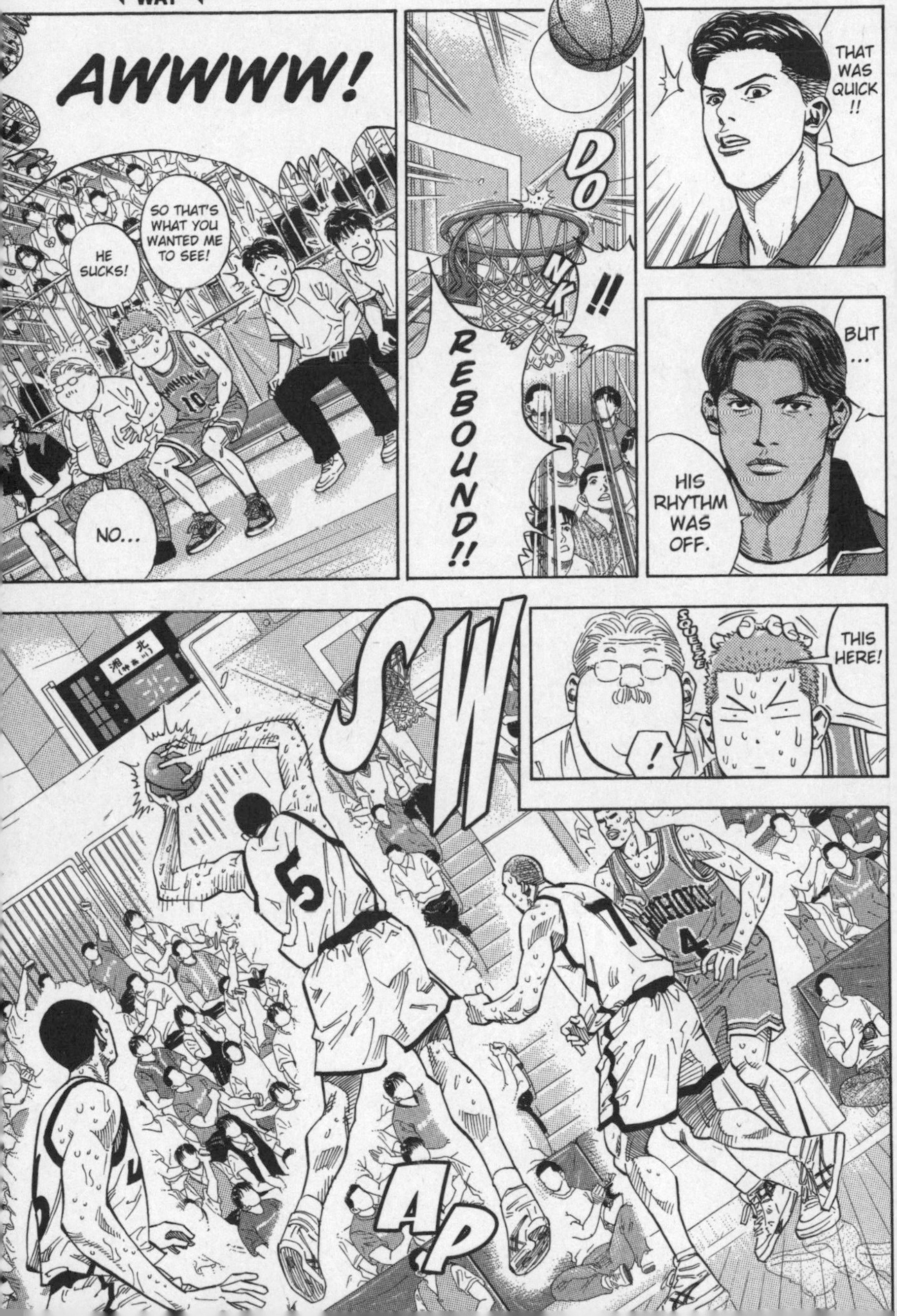
THAT WAS QUICK!!
BUT ...
HIS RHYTHM WAS OFF.
DONK!!
REBOUND!!
AWWWW!
SO THAT'S WHAT YOU WANTED ME TO SEE!
HE SUCKS!
NO...
THIS HERE!
SQUEEZE
!
湘北
SW
AP

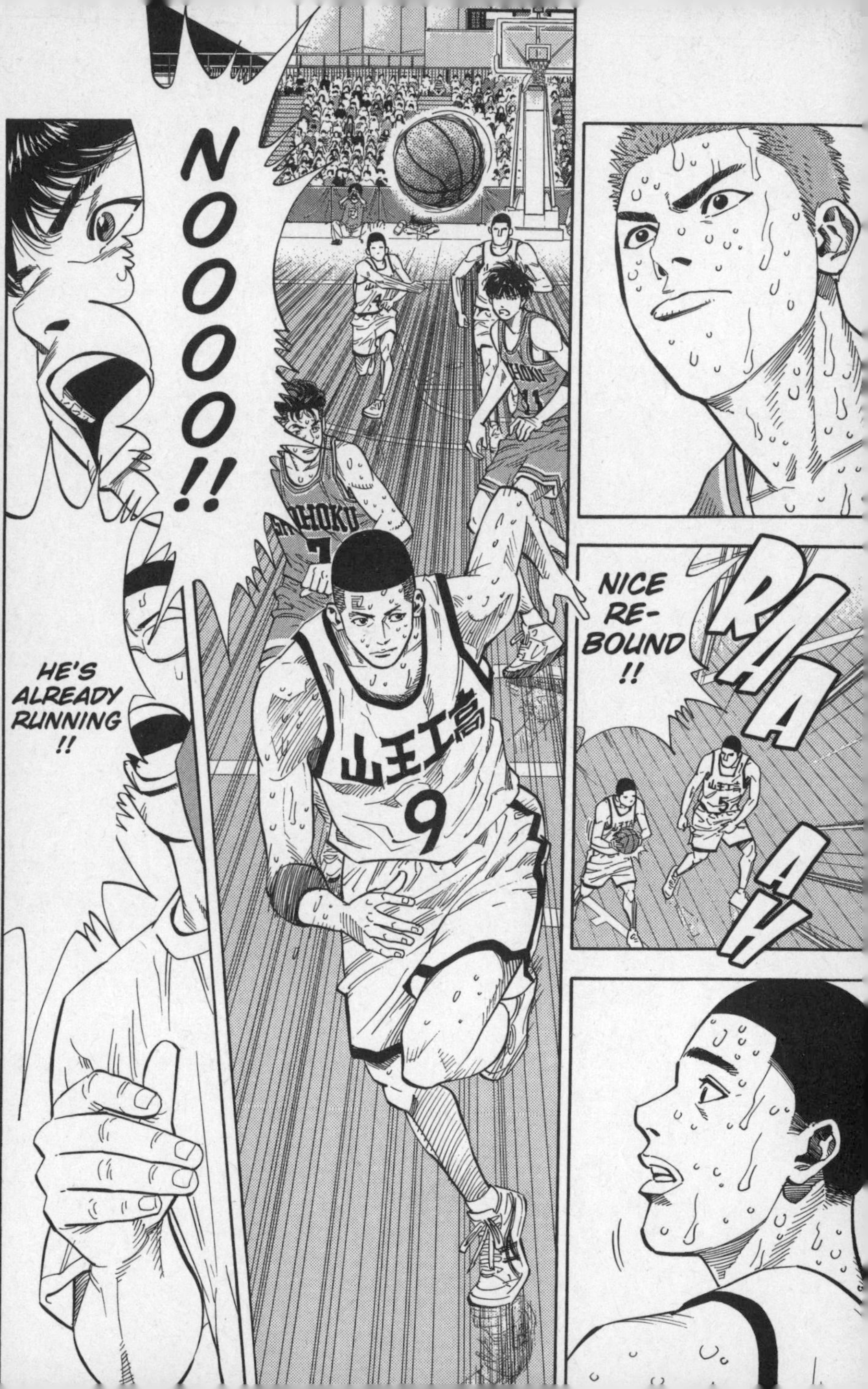
NICE RE-BOUND!!
RAAAH
NOOOO!!
HE'S ALREADY RUNNING!!

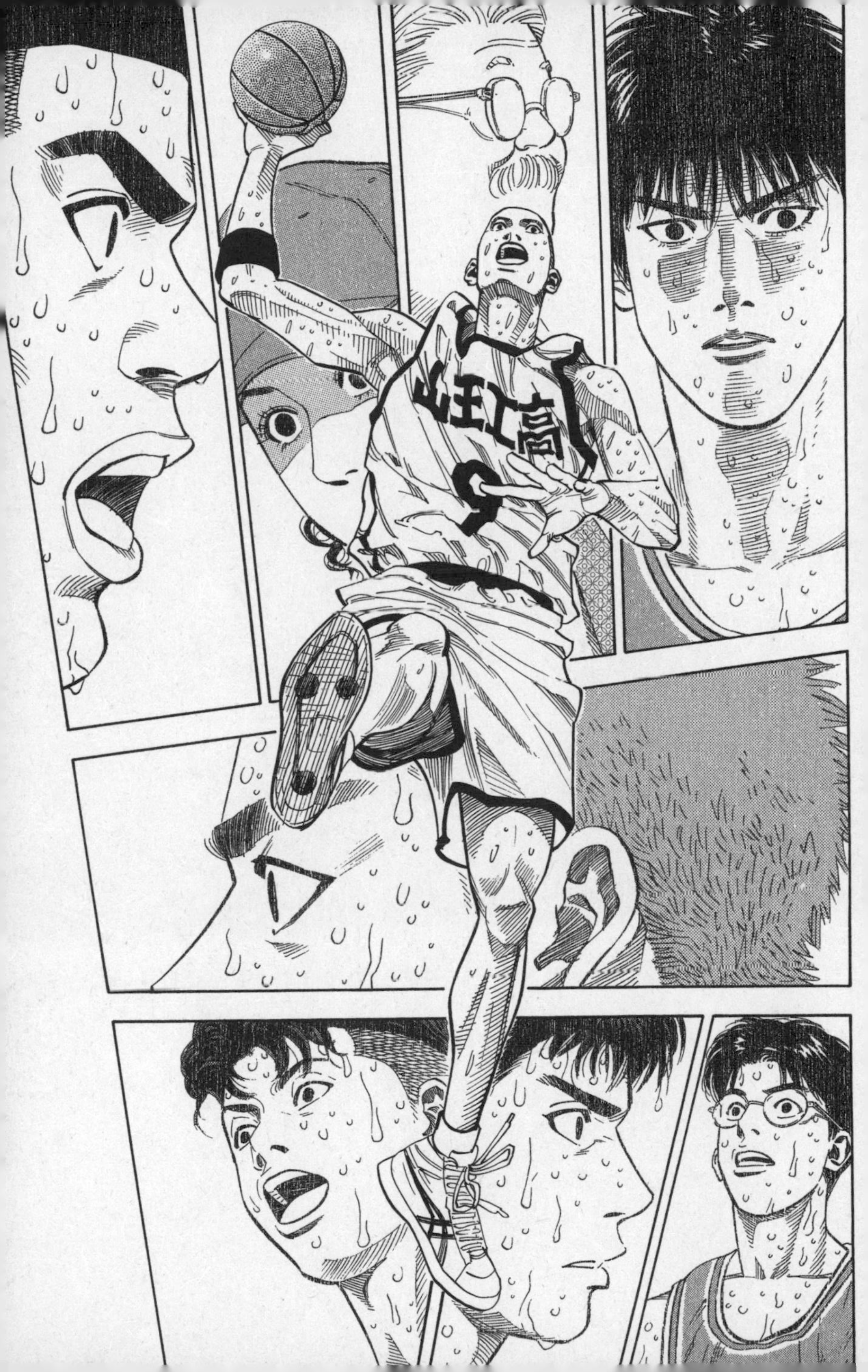
山王工高

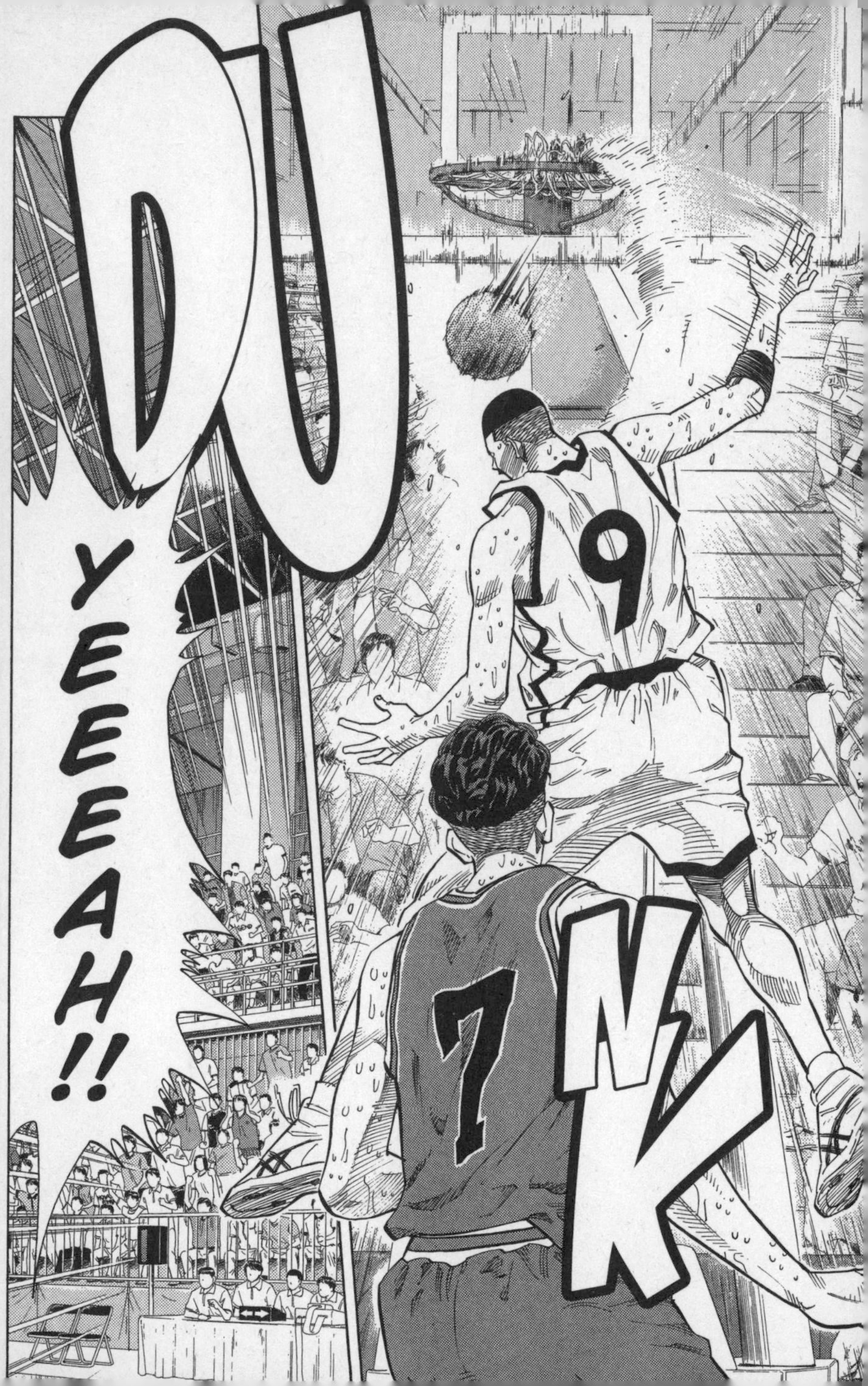
DUNK
YEEEAH!!

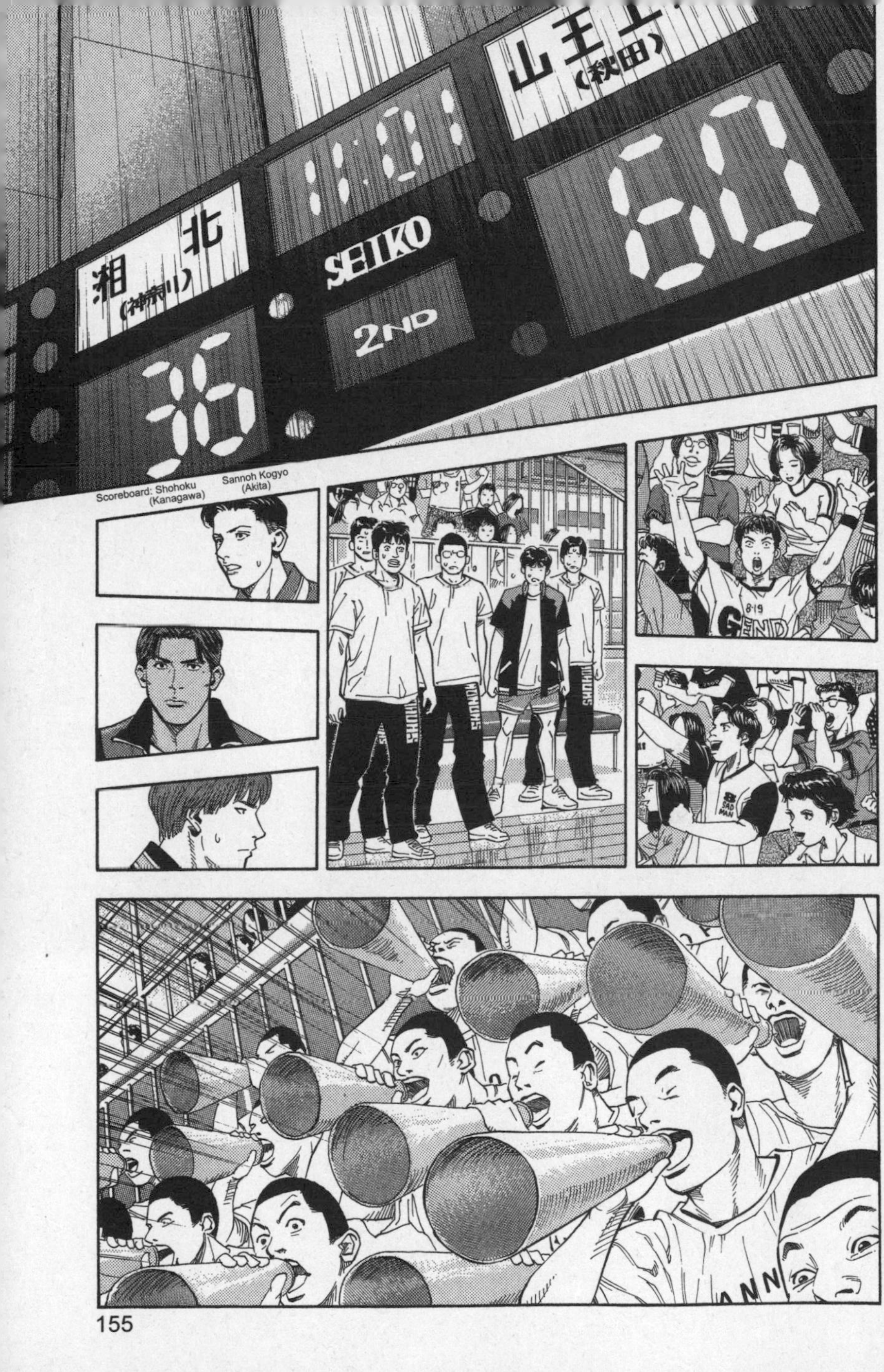
湘北 (神奈川)
山王工 (秋田)
SEIKO
2ND
Scoreboard: Shohoku (Kanagawa) Sannoh Kogyo (Akita)

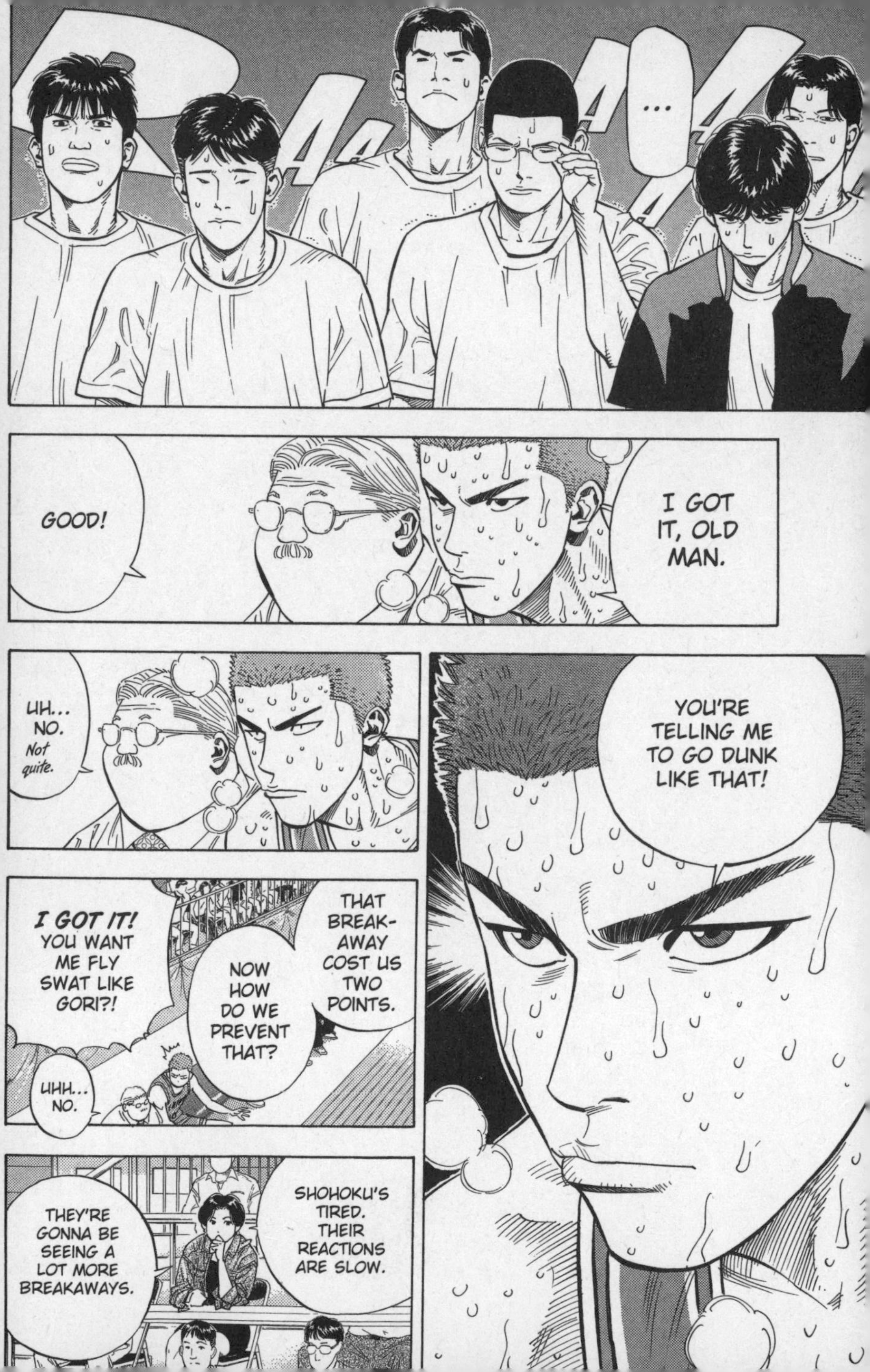
...
I GOT IT, OLD MAN.
GOOD!
YOU'RE TELLING ME TO GO DUNK LIKE THAT!
UH... NO. *Not quite.*
THAT BREAK-AWAY COST US TWO POINTS.
NOW HOW DO WE PREVENT THAT?
I GOT IT! YOU WANT ME FLY SWAT LIKE GORI?!
UHH... NO.
SHOHOKU'S TIRED. THEIR REACTIONS ARE SLOW.
THEY'RE GONNA BE SEEING A LOT MORE BREAKAWAYS.

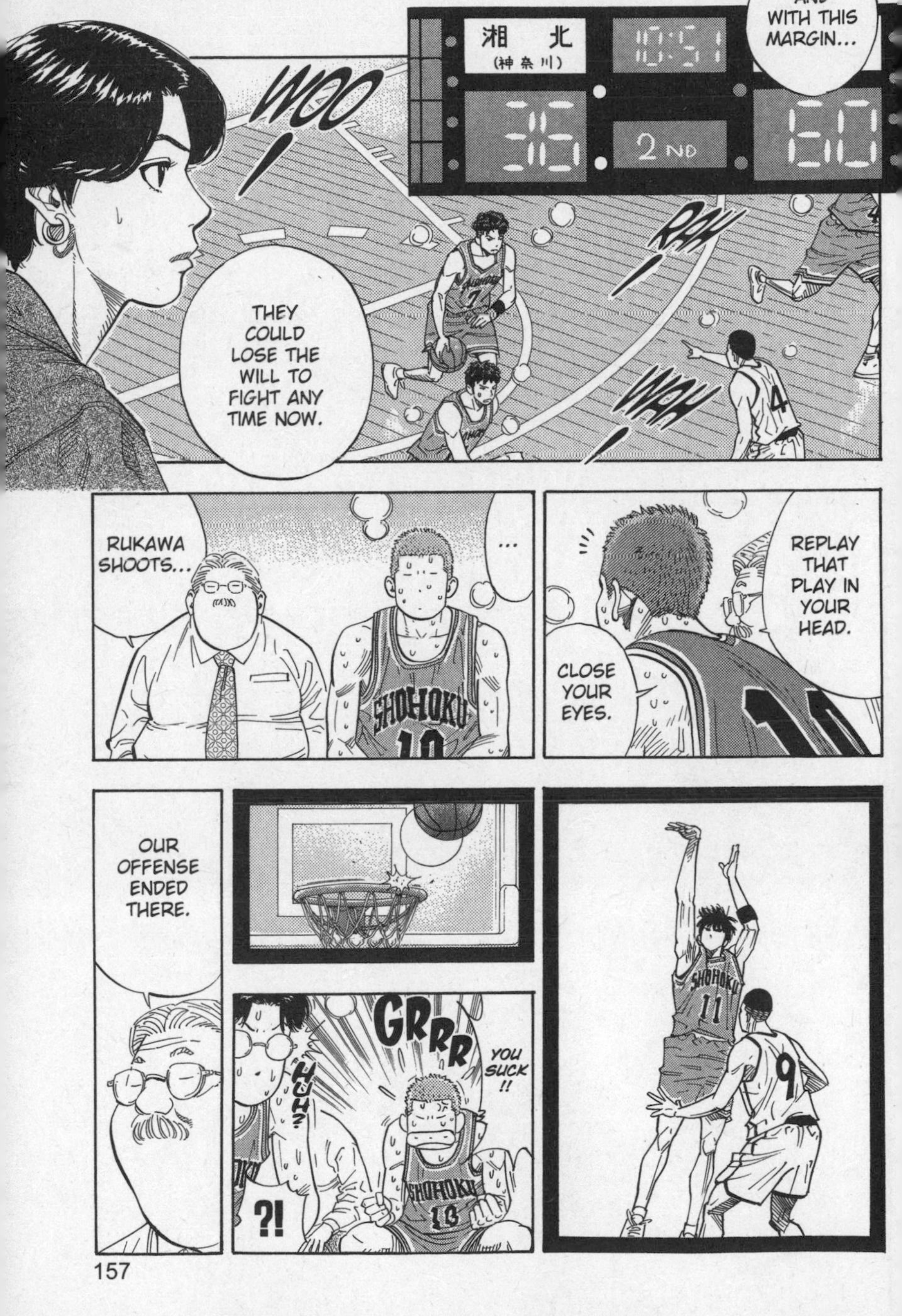

AND WITH THIS MARGIN...
湘北
(神奈川)
2ND
WOO
RAH
THEY COULD LOSE THE WILL TO FIGHT ANY TIME NOW.
WAH
REPLAY THAT PLAY IN YOUR HEAD.
CLOSE YOUR EYES.
...
RUKAWA SHOOTS...
GRRR
YOU SUCK!!
HUH?
?!
OUR OFFENSE ENDED THERE.

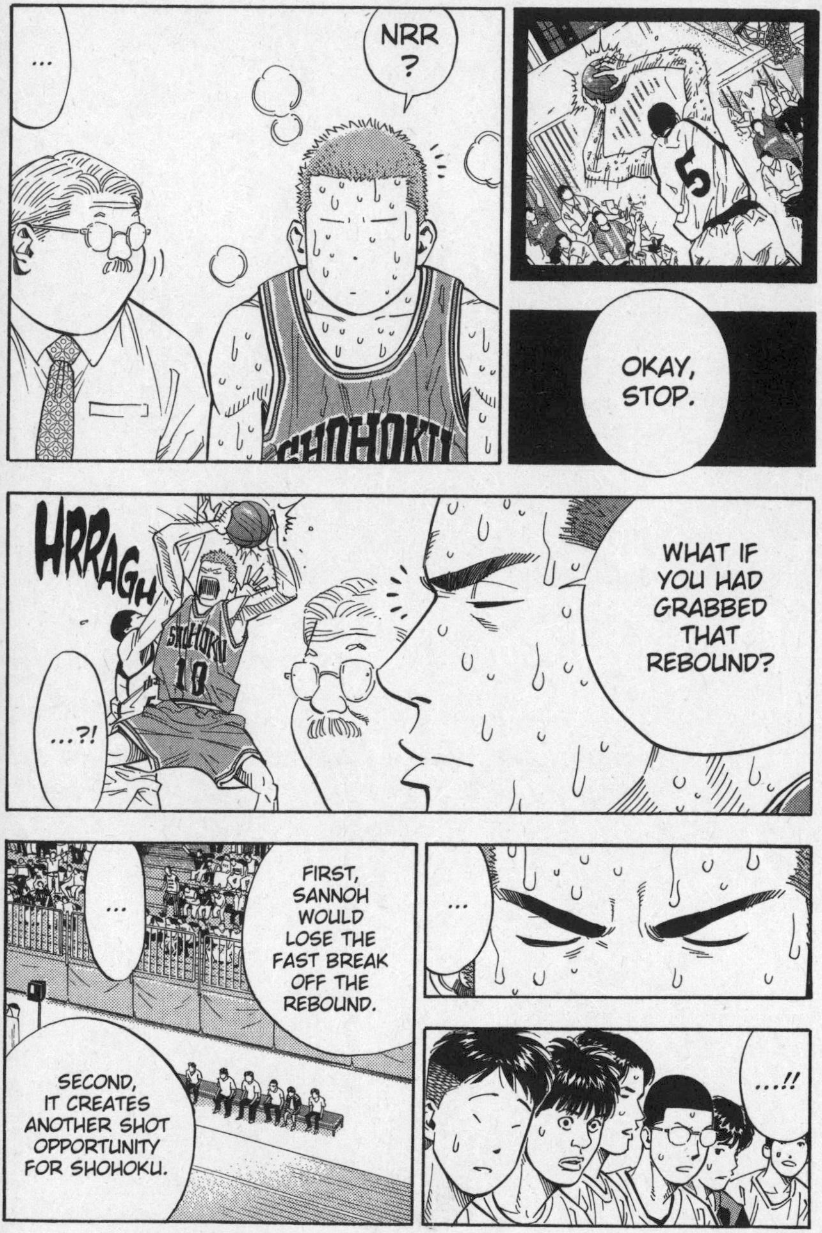
OKAY, STOP.
NRR ?
...
WHAT IF YOU HAD GRABBED THAT REBOUND?
HRRAGH
...?!
...
...!!
FIRST, SANNOH WOULD LOSE THE FAST BREAK OFF THE REBOUND.
...
SECOND, IT CREATES ANOTHER SHOT OPPORTUNITY FOR SHOHOKU.

IN OTHER WORDS, THE TWO-POINT LOSS TURNS INTO...

...A CHANCE FOR A TWO-POINT GAIN.

DO YOU UNDERSTAND, SAKURAGI?

EVERY OFFENSIVE REBOUND YOU GET...

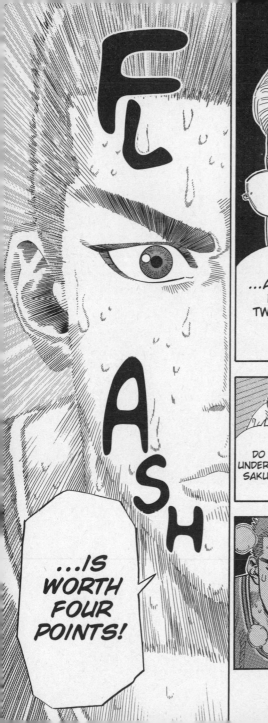

...IS WORTH FOUR POINTS!

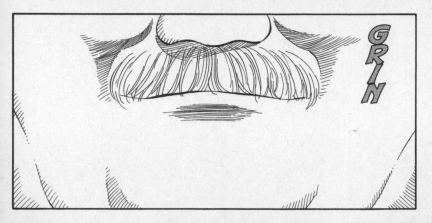

GRIN
第
IF YOU CAN DO THAT, YOU'LL BE THE TRUMP CARD THAT GETS US BACK IN THE GAME!
...!!
STICK BALL, STICK BALL, STICK BALL ...
NNNNGH!!
SHHF

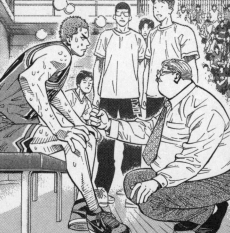

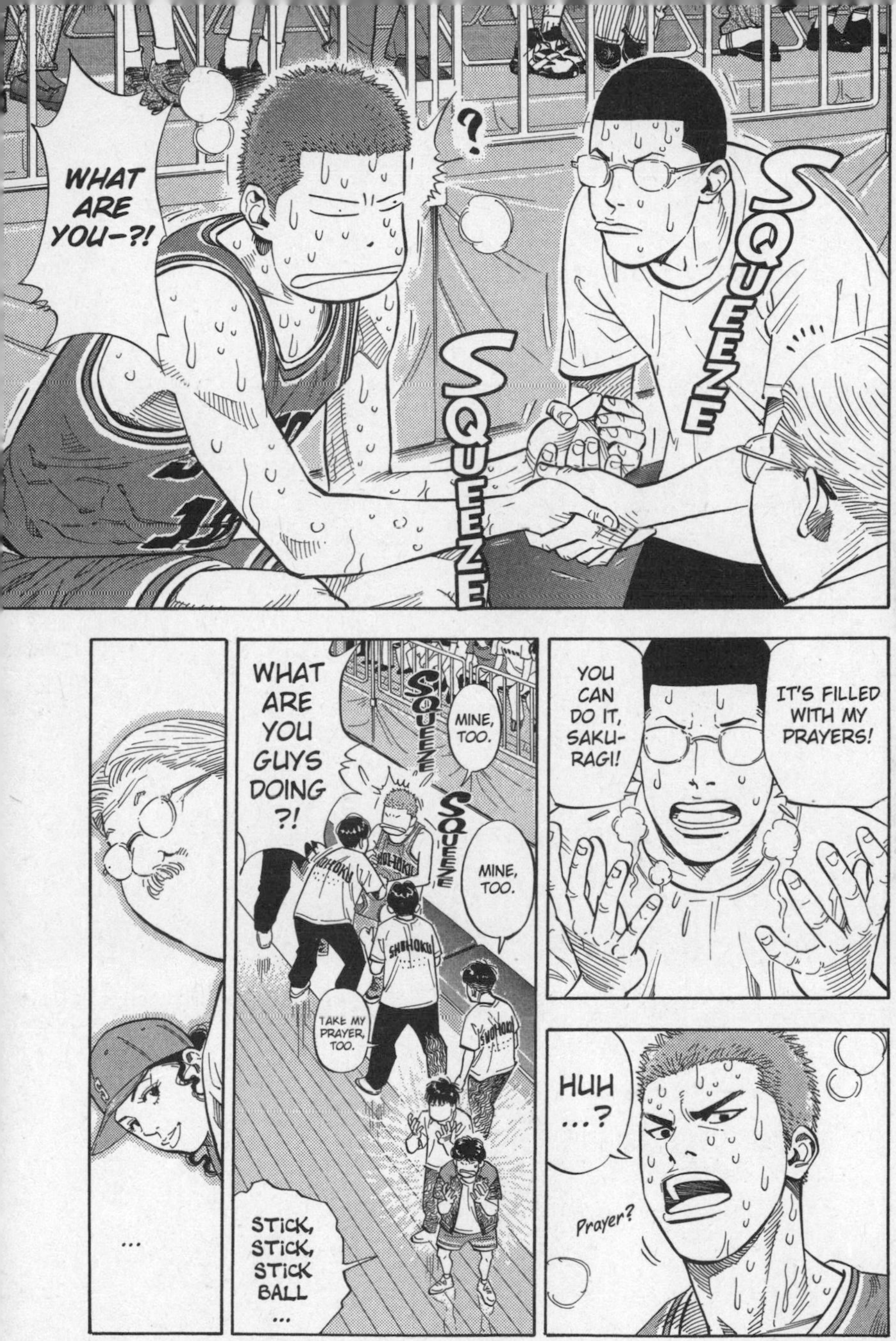
SQUEEZE
?
WHAT ARE YOU-?!
SQUEEZE
IT'S FILLED WITH MY PRAYERS!
YOU CAN DO IT, SAKU-RAGI!
HUH ...?
Prayer?
SQUEEZE
MINE, TOO.
WHAT ARE YOU GUYS DOING ?!
SQUEEZE
MINE, TOO.
TAKE MY PRAYER, TOO.
STICK, STICK, STICK BALL ...
...

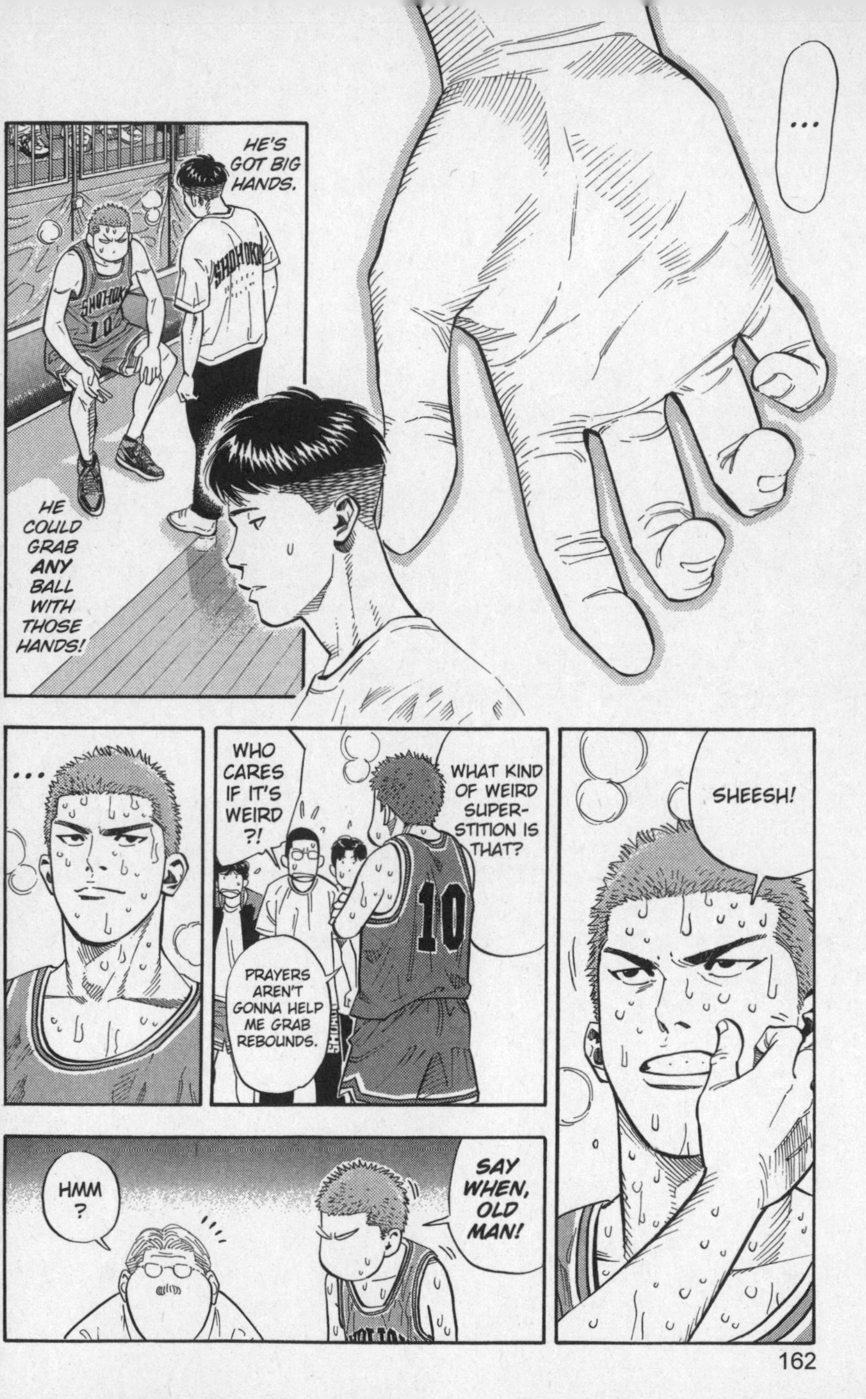
...
HE'S GOT BIG HANDS.
HE COULD GRAB ANY BALL WITH THOSE HANDS!
SHEESH!
WHAT KIND OF WEIRD SUPERSTITION IS THAT?
WHO CARES IF IT'S WEIRD?!
PRAYERS AREN'T GONNA HELP ME GRAB REBOUNDS.
...
SAY WHEN, OLD MAN!
HMM?

READ THIS WAY

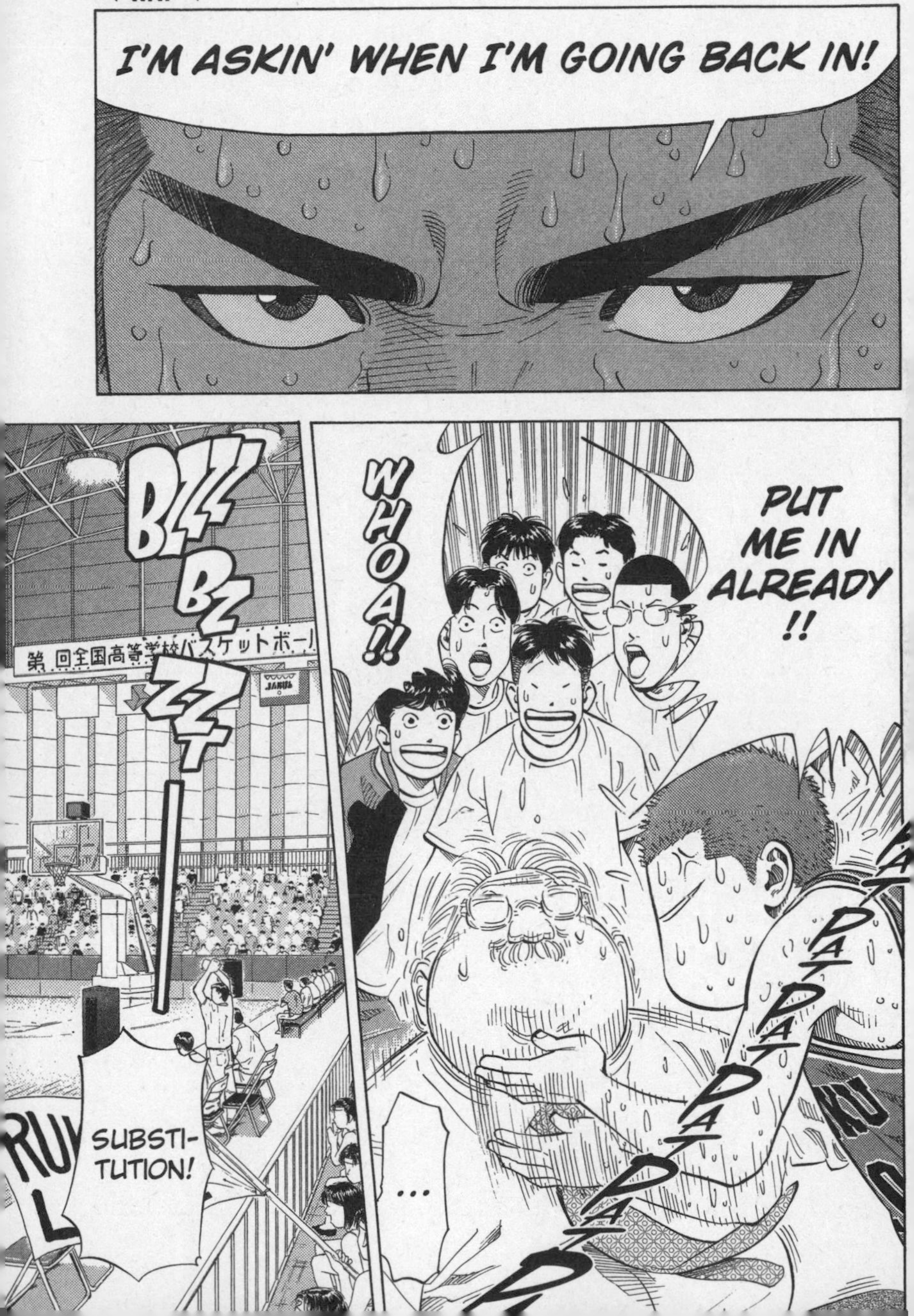
I'M ASKIN' WHEN I'M GOING BACK IN!
PUT ME IN ALREADY !!
WHOA!!
...
PAT DAT DAT DAT DAT
BZZ BZ ZZT
第 回全国高等学校バスケットボー
SUBSTI-TUTION!

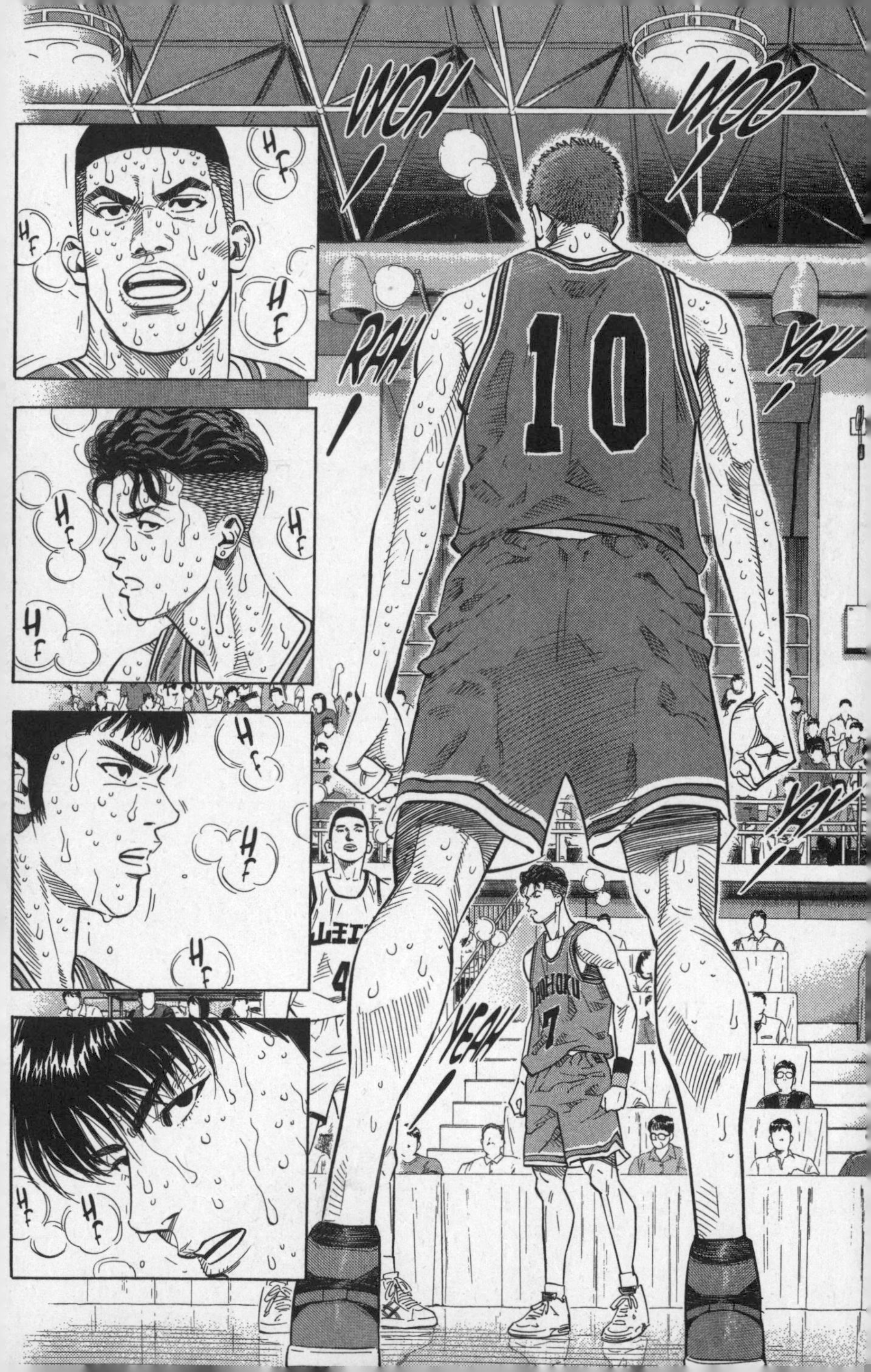
WOO!
WOH!
YAH!
RAH!
YAH!
YEAH!
HF HF HF
HF HF HF
HF HF HF
HF HF

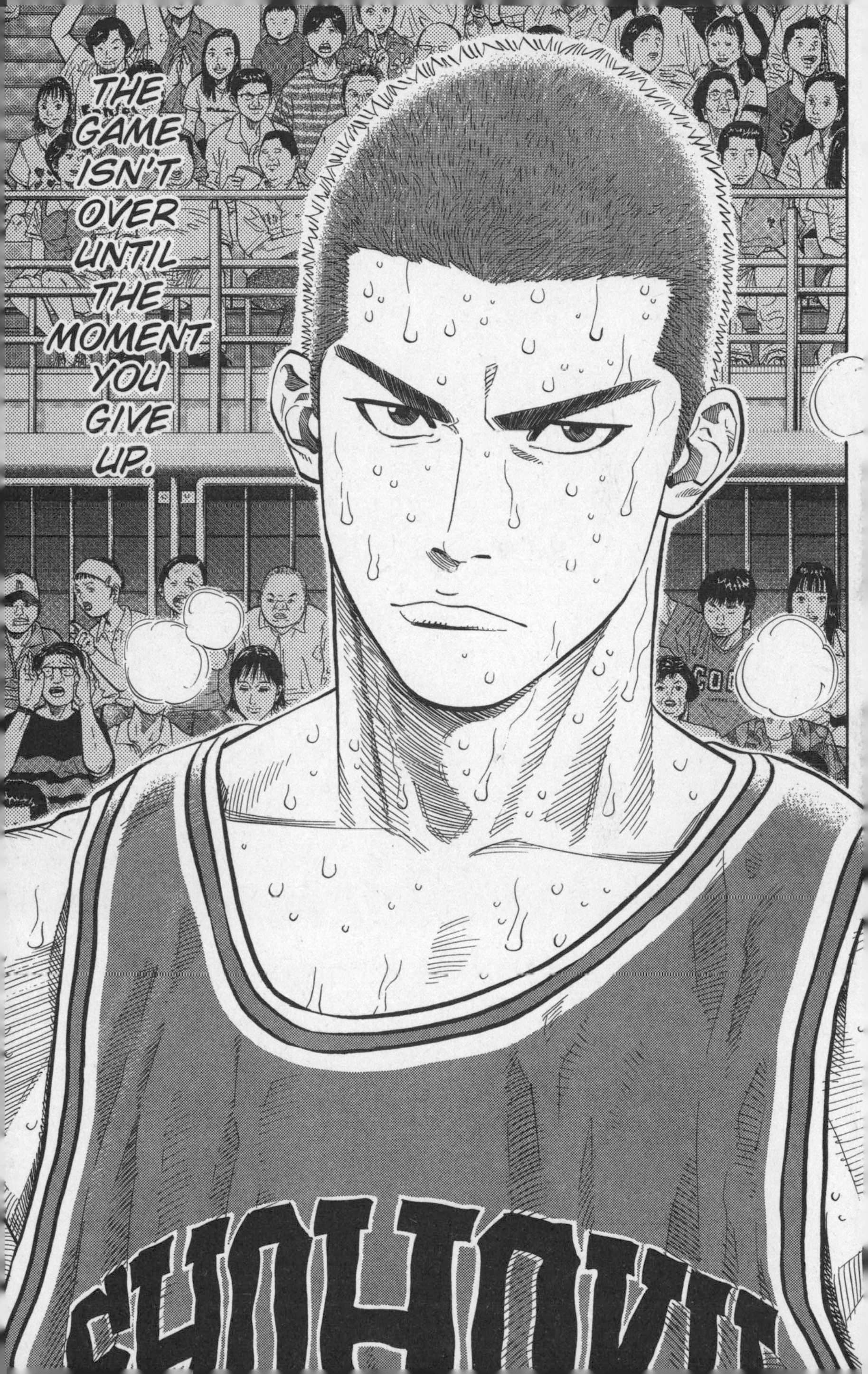
THE GAME ISN'T OVER UNTIL THE MOMENT YOU GIVE UP.

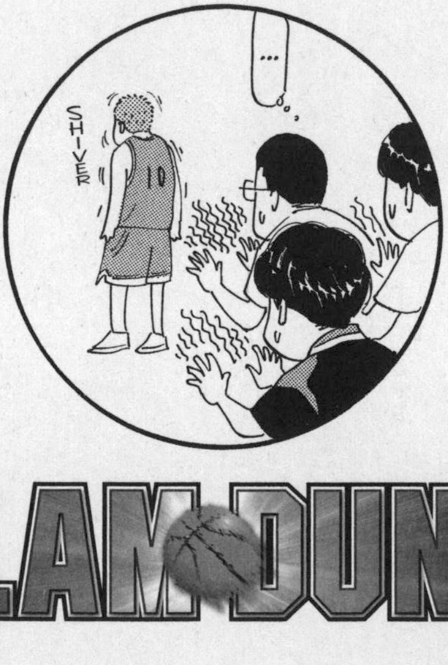
...
SHIVER

SLAM DUNK

THE TRUMP CARD ARRIVES

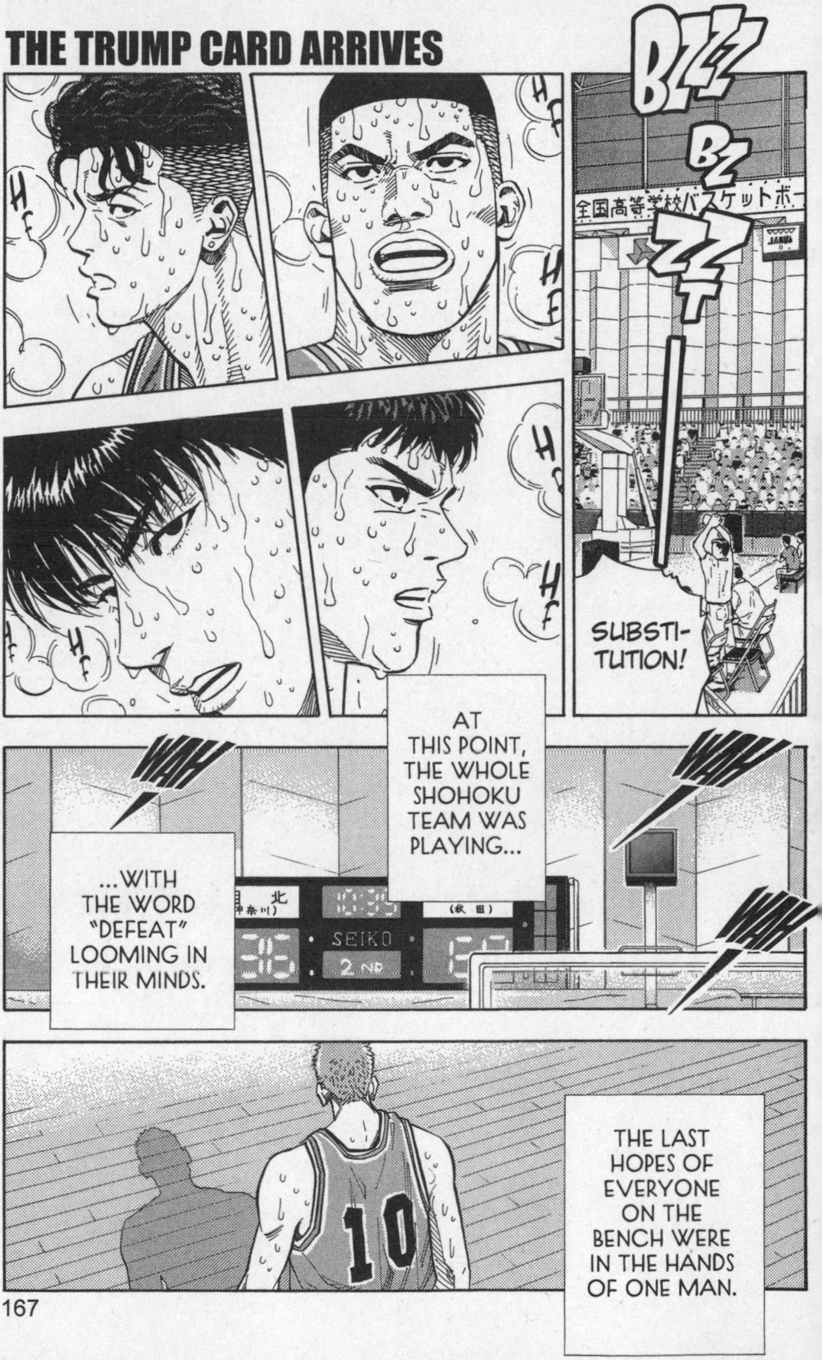

BZZZ
BZ
全国高等学校バスケットボー
ZZZT
SUBSTI-TUTION!
HF
HF
HF
HF
HF
HF
HF
HF
WAH
WAH
WAH
AT THIS POINT, THE WHOLE SHOHOKU TEAM WAS PLAYING...
...WITH THE WORD "DEFEAT" LOOMING IN THEIR MINDS.
SEIKO
THE LAST HOPES OF EVERYONE ON THE BENCH WERE IN THE HANDS OF ONE MAN.

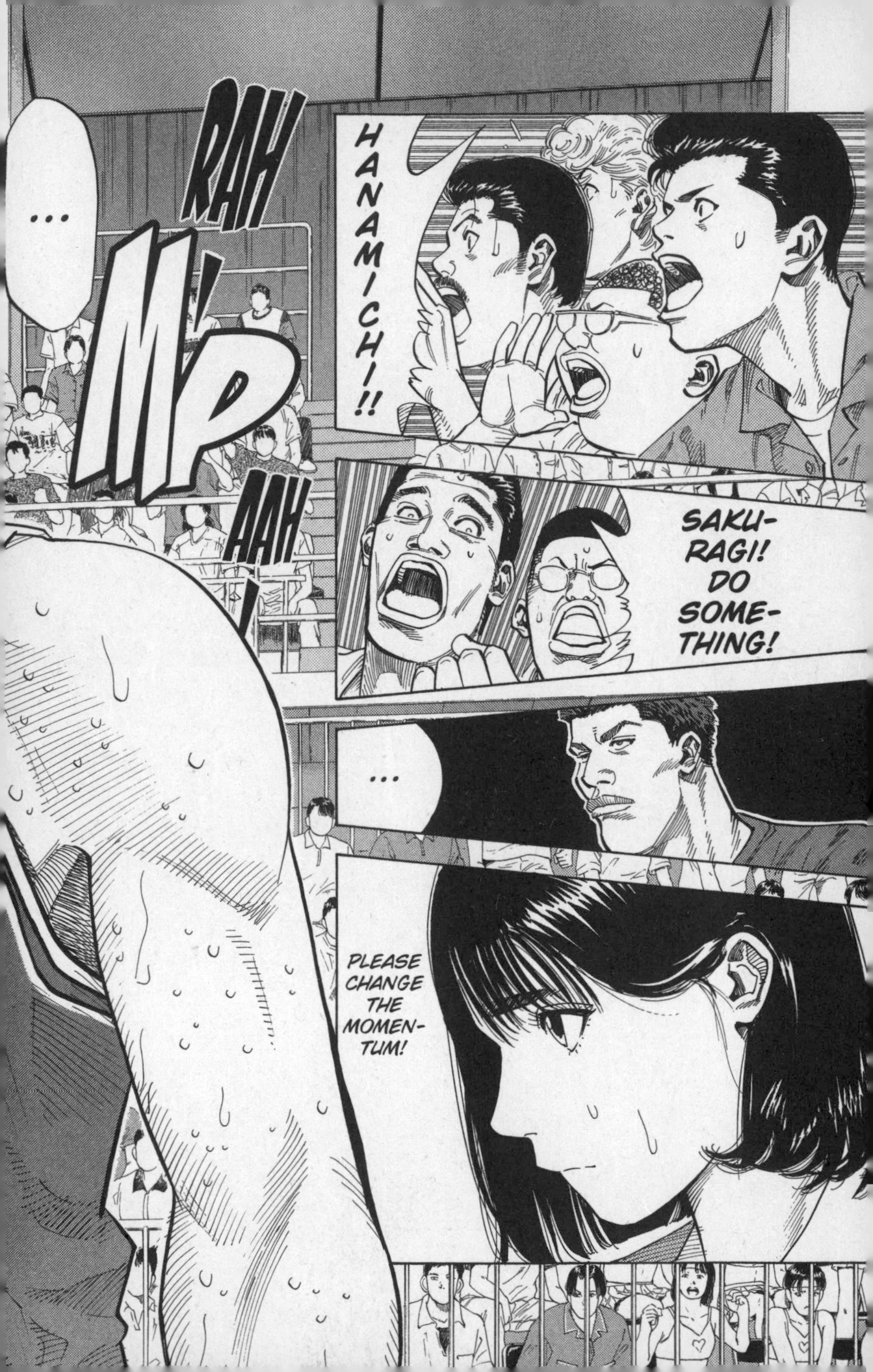
HANAMICHI!!
SAKURAGI! DO SOMETHING!
...
PLEASE CHANGE THE MOMENTUM!
...
RAH
M'P
AAH

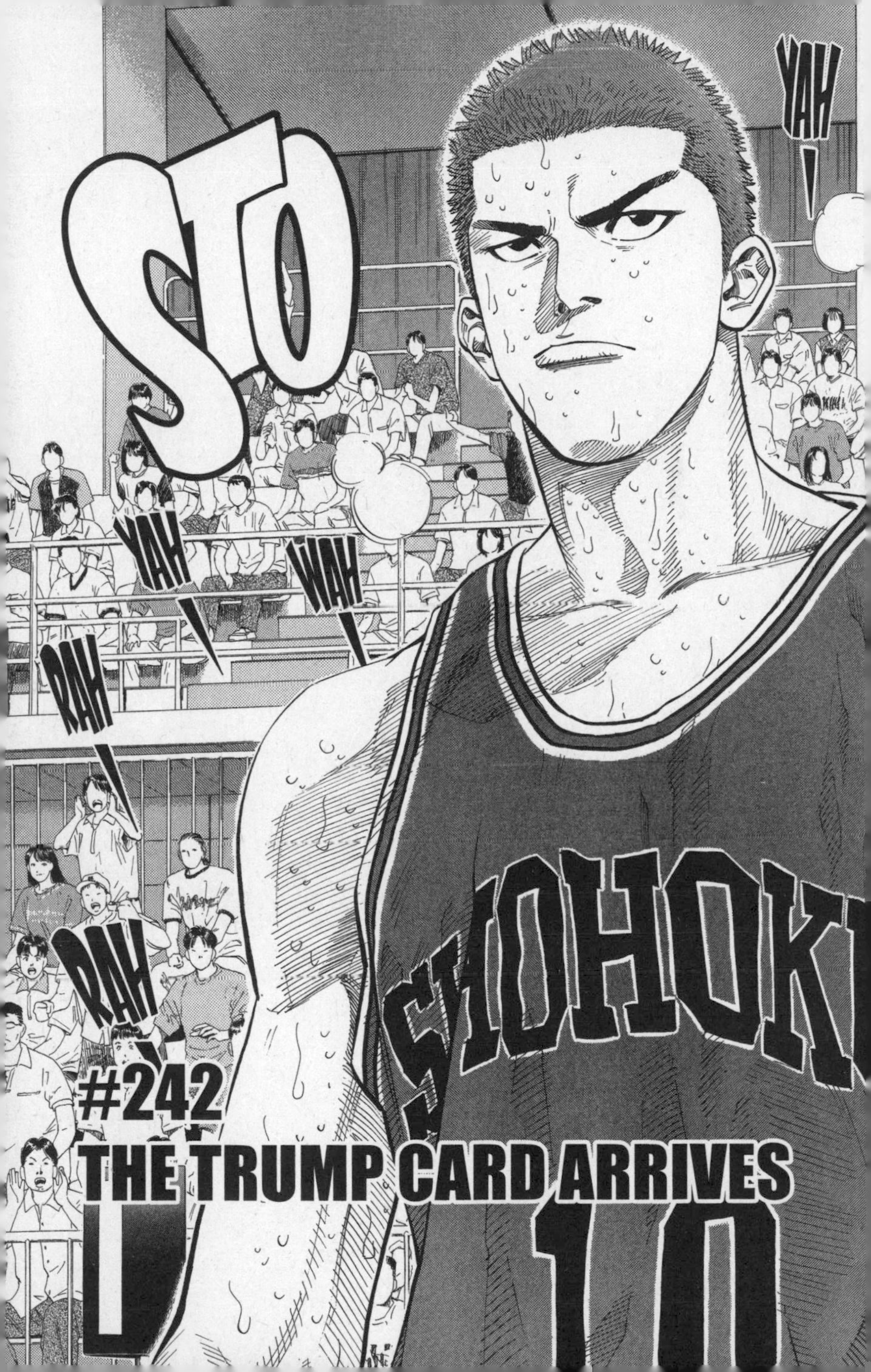
YAH!
SHO
WAH!
YAH!
RAH!
RAH!
#242
THE TRUMP CARD ARRIVES

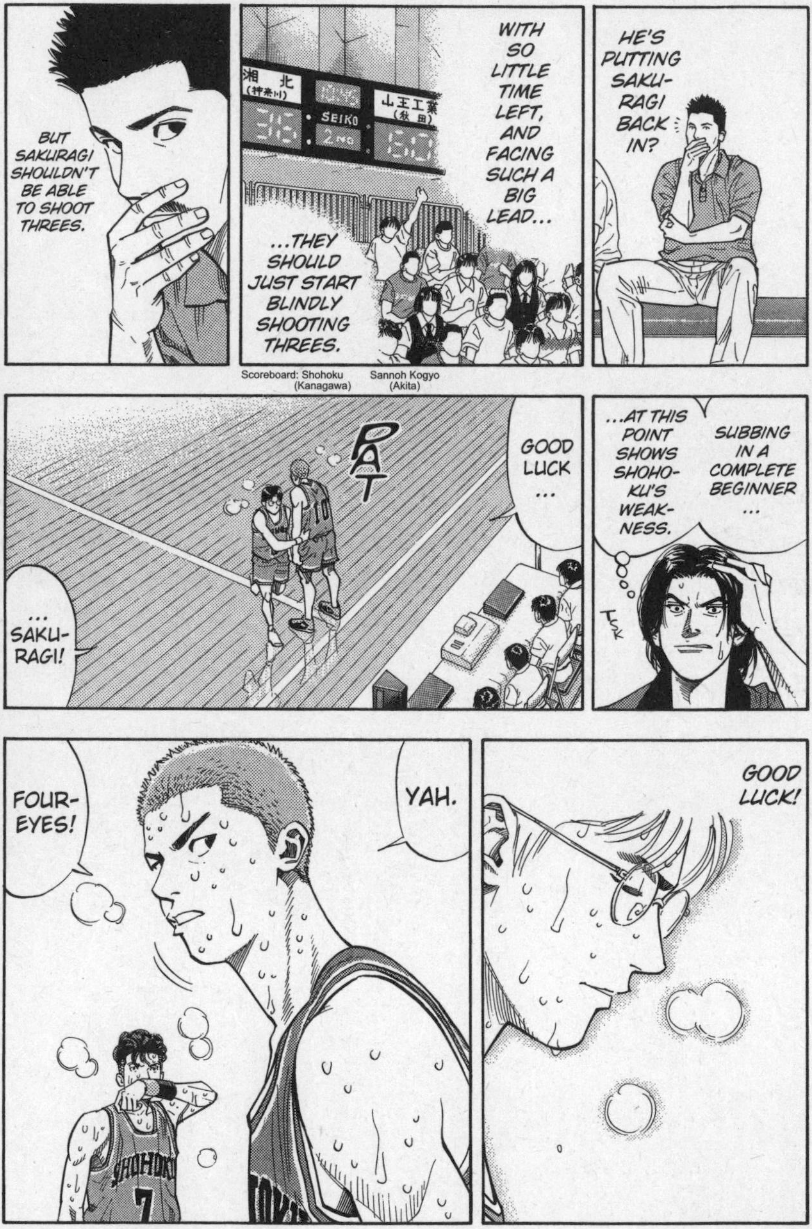
HE'S PUTTING SAKURAGI BACK IN?
WITH SO LITTLE TIME LEFT, AND FACING SUCH A BIG LEAD...
...THEY SHOULD JUST START BLINDLY SHOOTING THREES.
BUT SAKURAGI SHOULDN'T BE ABLE TO SHOOT THREES.
SUBBING IN A COMPLETE BEGINNER ...
...AT THIS POINT SHOWS SHOHOKU'S WEAKNESS.
TSK
GOOD LUCK ...
PAT
... SAKURAGI!
GOOD LUCK!
YAH.
FOUR-EYES!
Scoreboard: Shohoku (Kanagawa) Sannoh Kogyo (Akita)

READ THIS WAY

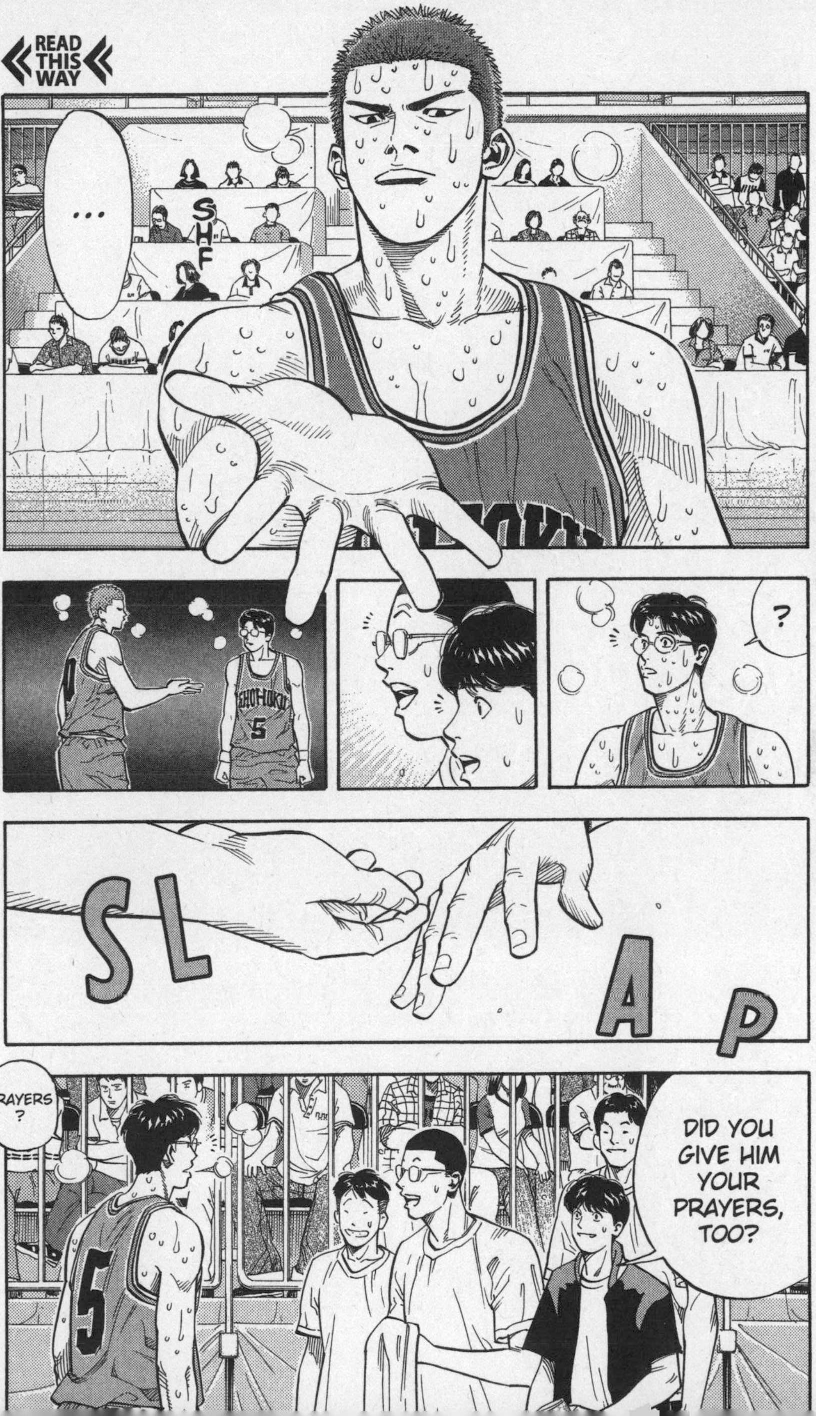
...
SHF
?
SLAP
DID YOU GIVE HIM YOUR PRAYERS, TOO?
PRAYERS ?

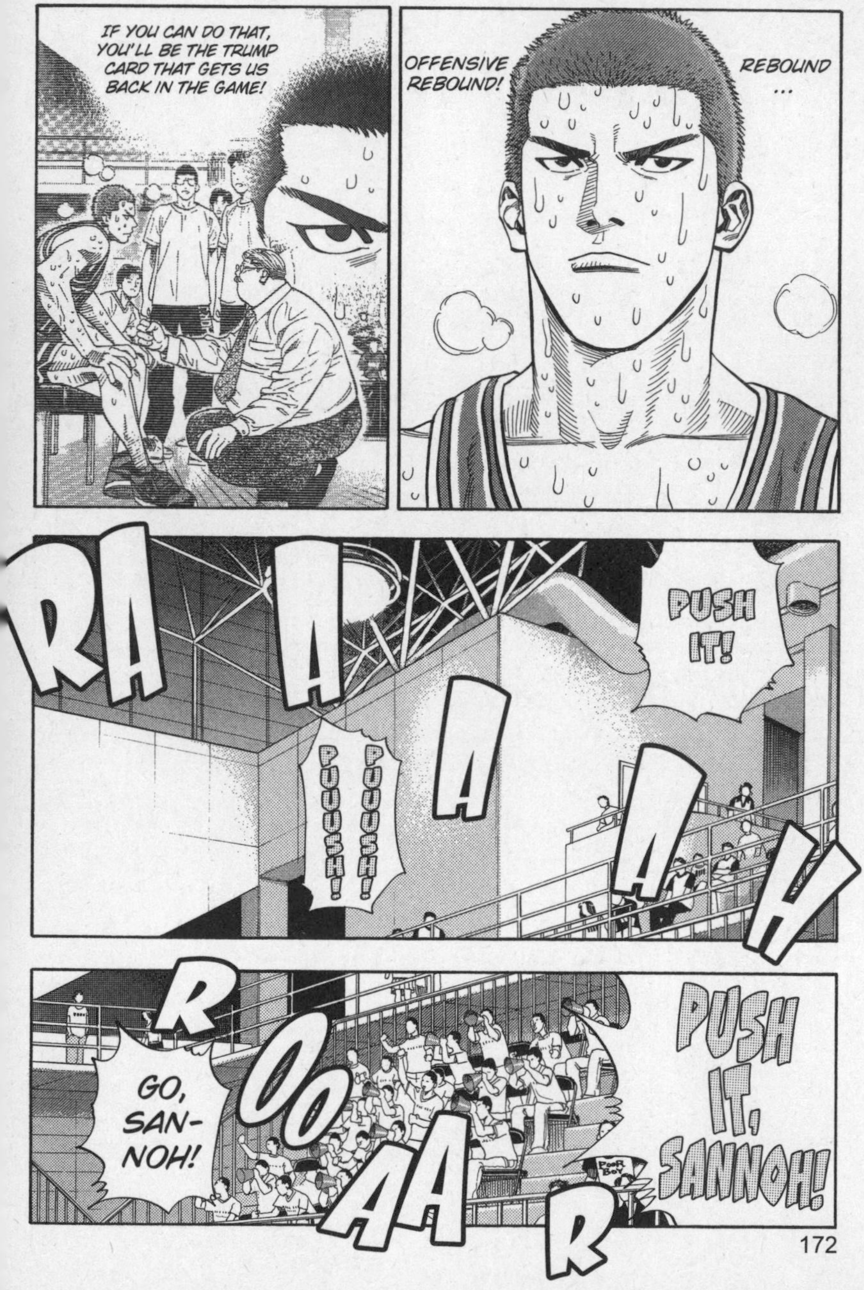
REBOUND ...
OFFENSIVE REBOUND!
IF YOU CAN DO THAT, YOU'LL BE THE TRUMP CARD THAT GETS US BACK IN THE GAME!
PUSH IT!
RAAAAH
PUUUUSH! PUUUUSH!
PUSH IT, SANNOH!
ROOAAAR
GO, SAN-NOH!
POOR BOY

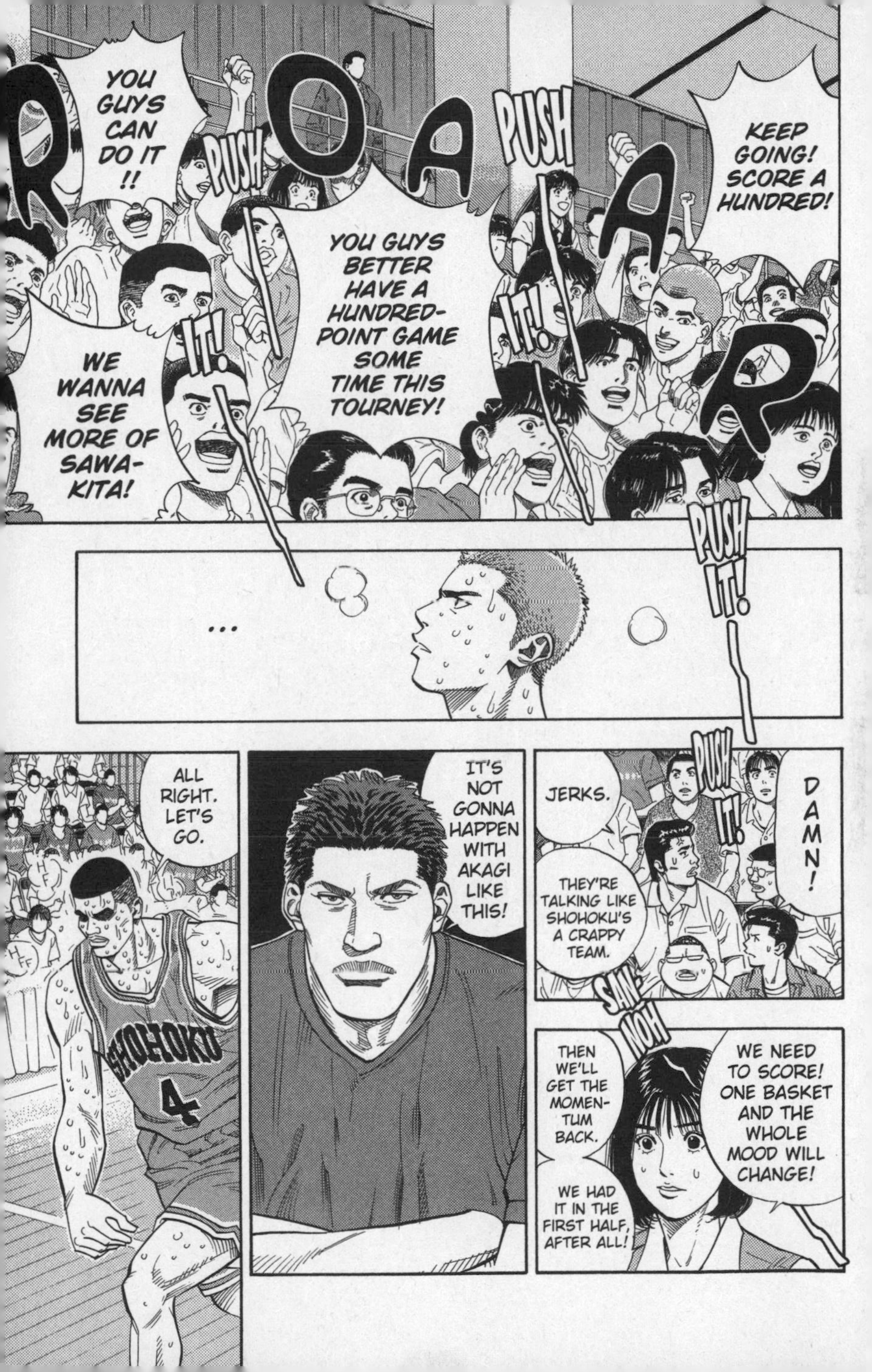
KEEP GOING! SCORE A HUNDRED!
ROAAR
PUSH IT!
PUSH IT!
YOU GUYS BETTER HAVE A HUNDRED-POINT GAME SOME TIME THIS TOURNEY!
YOU GUYS CAN DO IT !!
WE WANNA SEE MORE OF SAWA-KITA!
PUSH IT!
...
DAMN!
JERKS.
PUSH IT!
THEY'RE TALKING LIKE SHOHOKU'S A CRAPPY TEAM.
SAN-NOH
WE NEED TO SCORE! ONE BASKET AND THE WHOLE MOOD WILL CHANGE!
THEN WE'LL GET THE MOMEN-TUM BACK.
WE HAD IT IN THE FIRST HALF, AFTER ALL!
IT'S NOT GONNA HAPPEN WITH AKAGI LIKE THIS!
ALL RIGHT. LET'S GO.
HFF
HFF
SHOHOKU
4

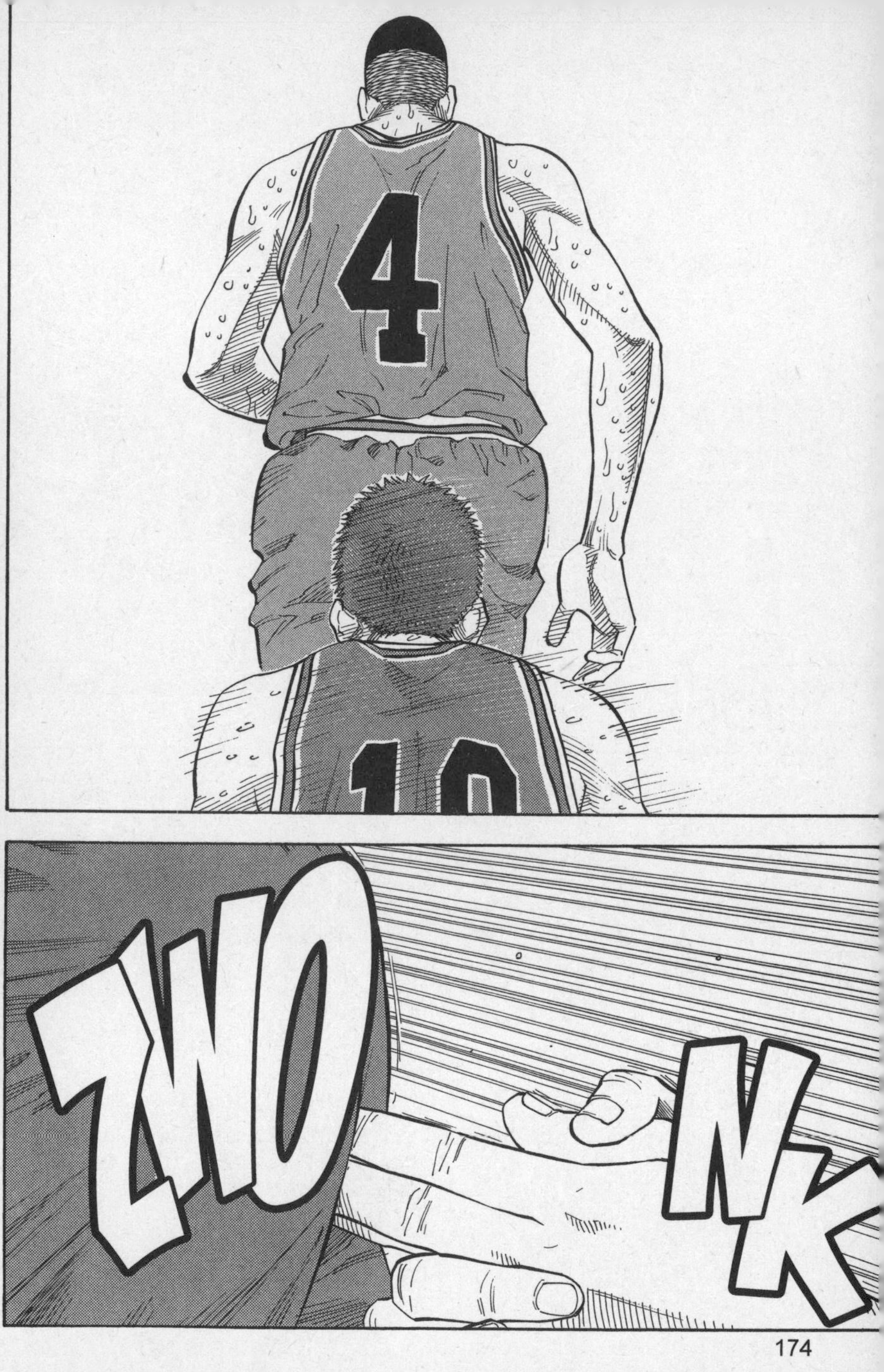
ZWONK

READ THIS WAY

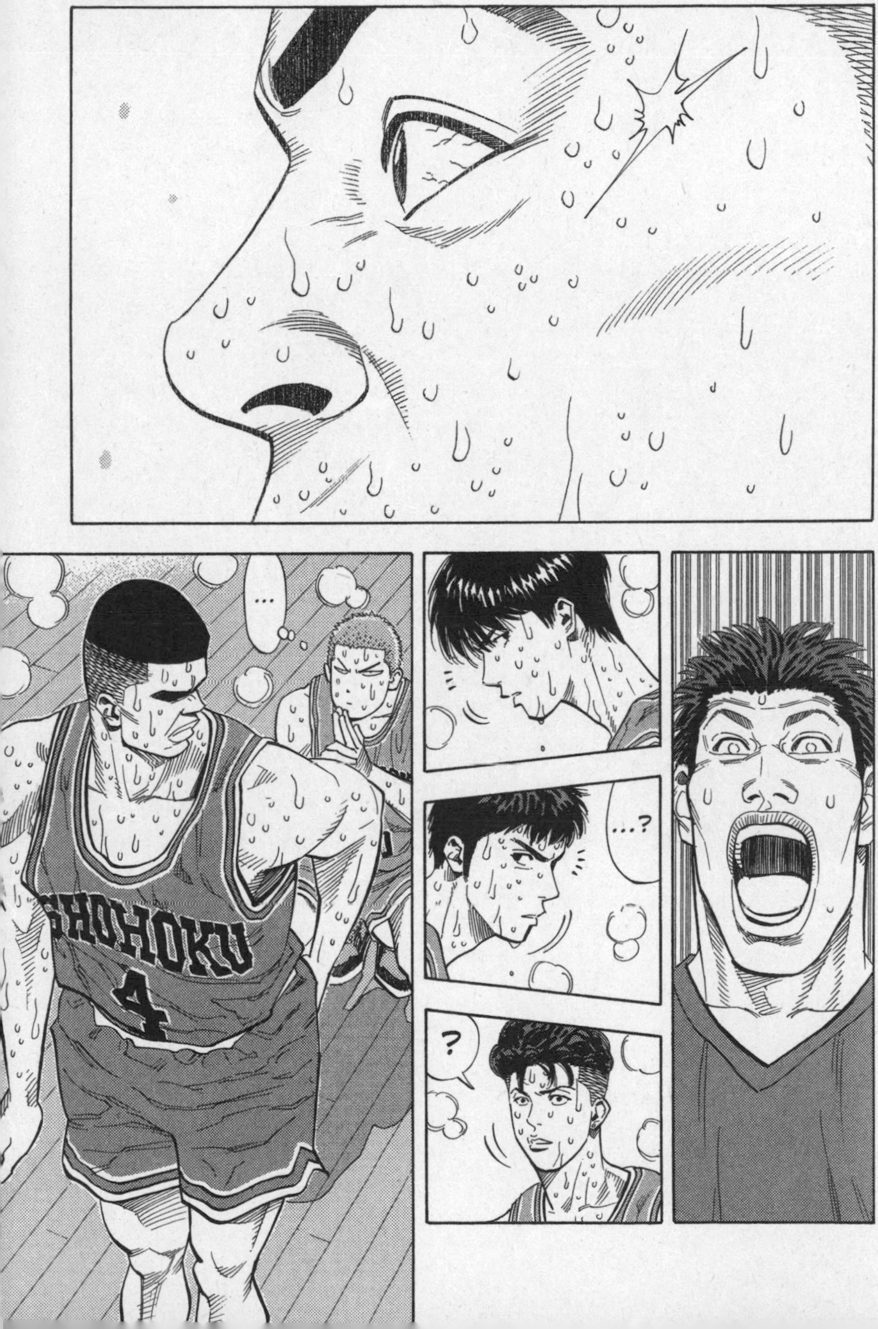
...?
?
...

...
SAKURAGI KNEW IT INSTINCTIVELY.
SMIRK
QUIVER
QUIVER
WHY ARE YOU SCREWING AROUND AT A TIME LIKE THIS ?!
...
B
OK
!!
WHOOOA
WHAT'S GOING ON?!
HUH
H-HE POKED HIM IN THE BUTT!
GASP
I SAW IT!
WHA
...
EHH
WOH
WHAT HAPPENED ?!

READ THIS WAY

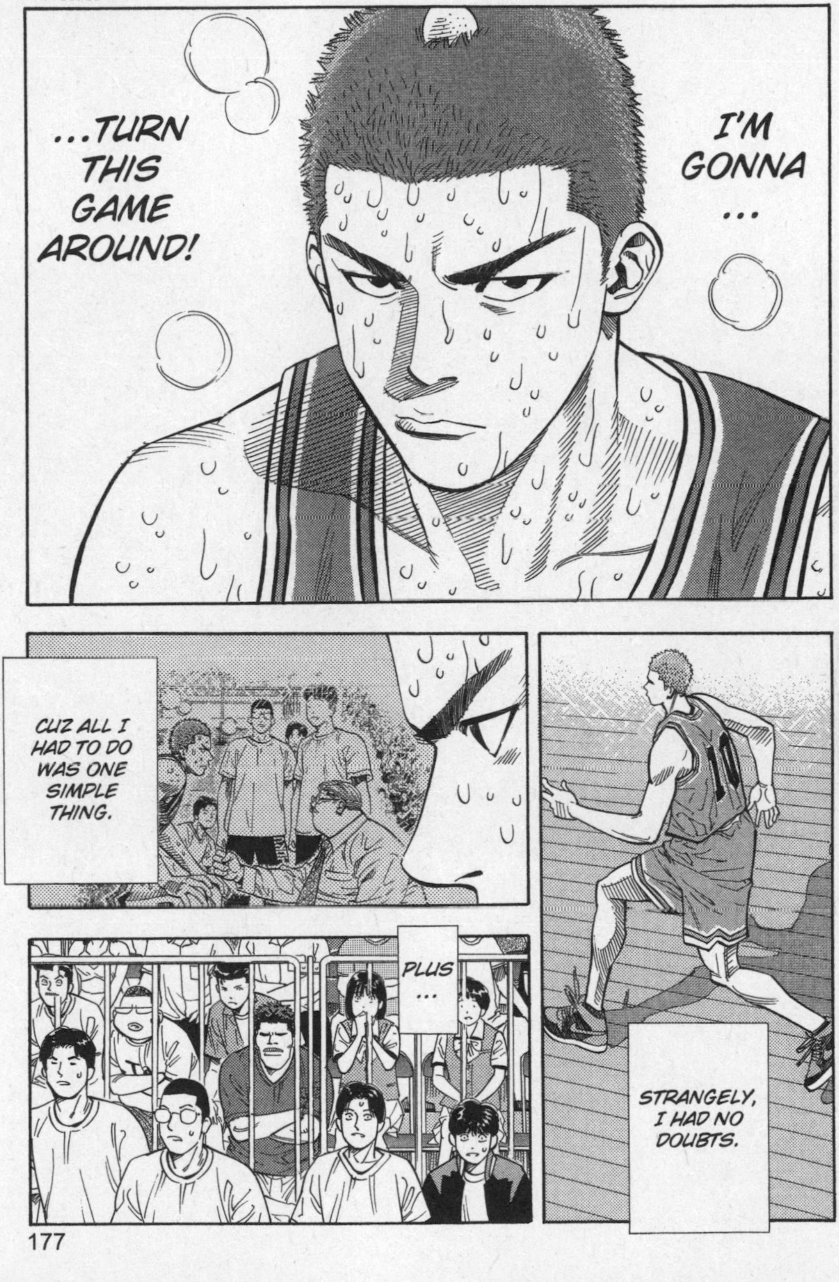

I'M GONNA ...
...TURN THIS GAME AROUND!
STRANGELY, I HAD NO DOUBTS.
CUZ ALL I HAD TO DO WAS ONE SIMPLE THING.
PLUS ...

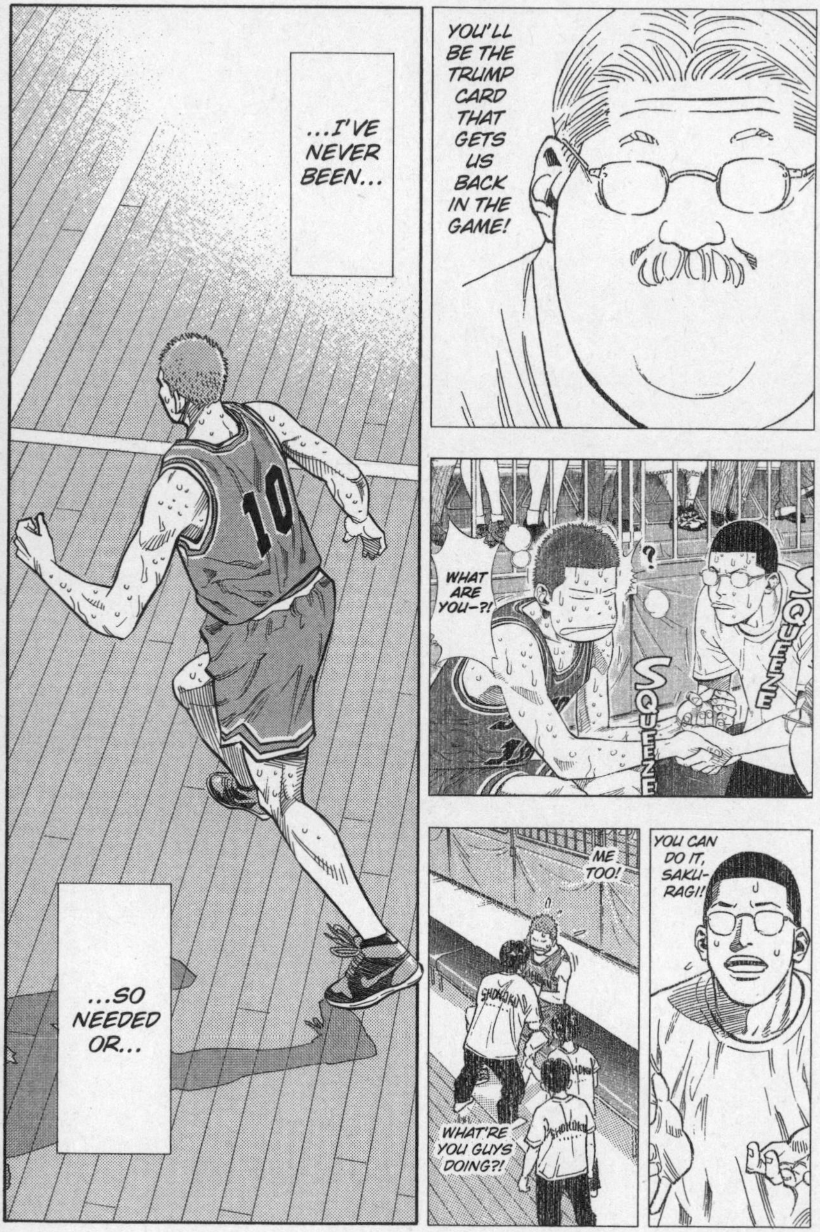
YOU'LL BE THE TRUMP CARD THAT GETS US BACK IN THE GAME!
WHAT ARE YOU-?!
?
SQUEEZE
SQUEEZE
YOU CAN DO IT, SAKURAGI!!
ME TOO!
WHAT'RE YOU GUYS DOING?!
...I'VE NEVER BEEN...
...SO NEEDED OR...

READ THIS WAY

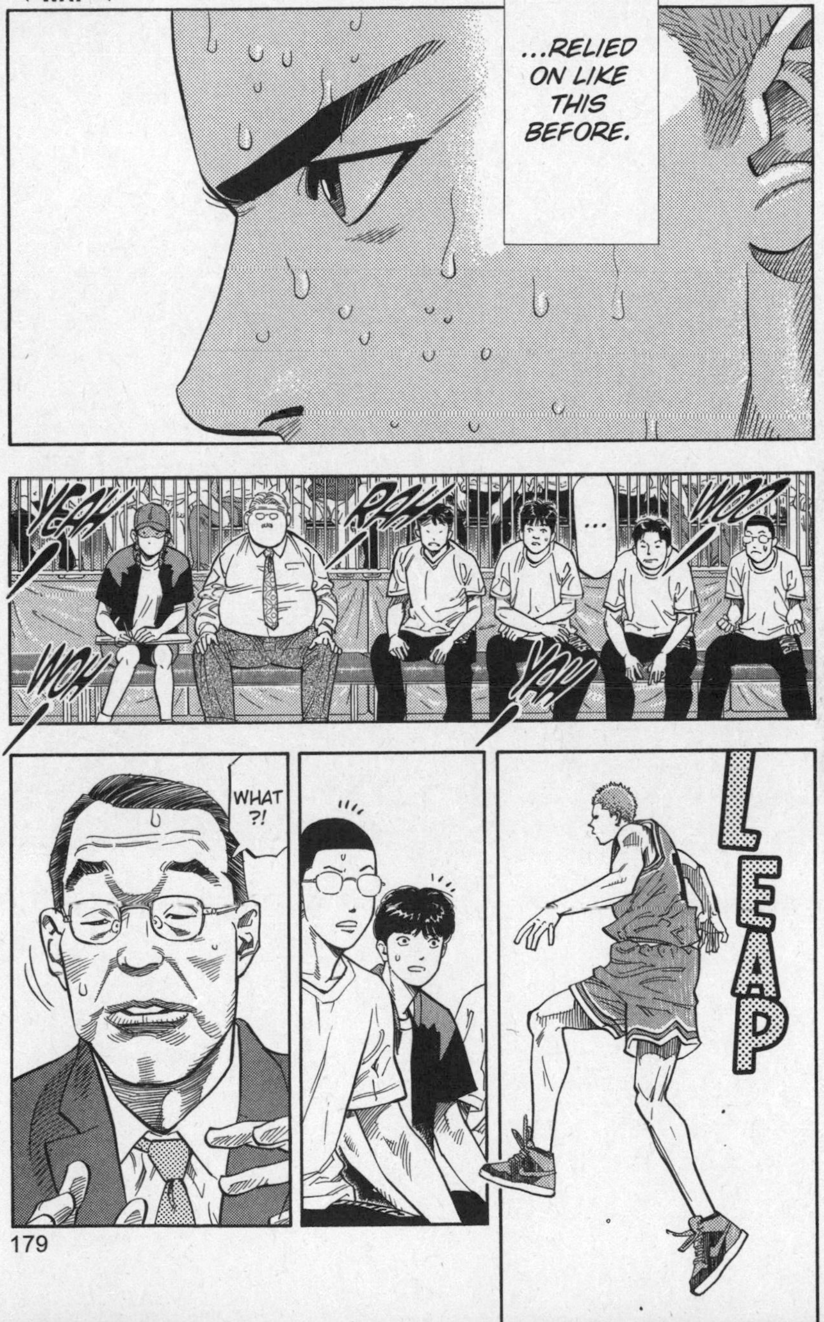
...RELIED ON LIKE THIS BEFORE.
WOO
...
RAH
YEAH
YAH
WOH
LEAP
WHAT ?!

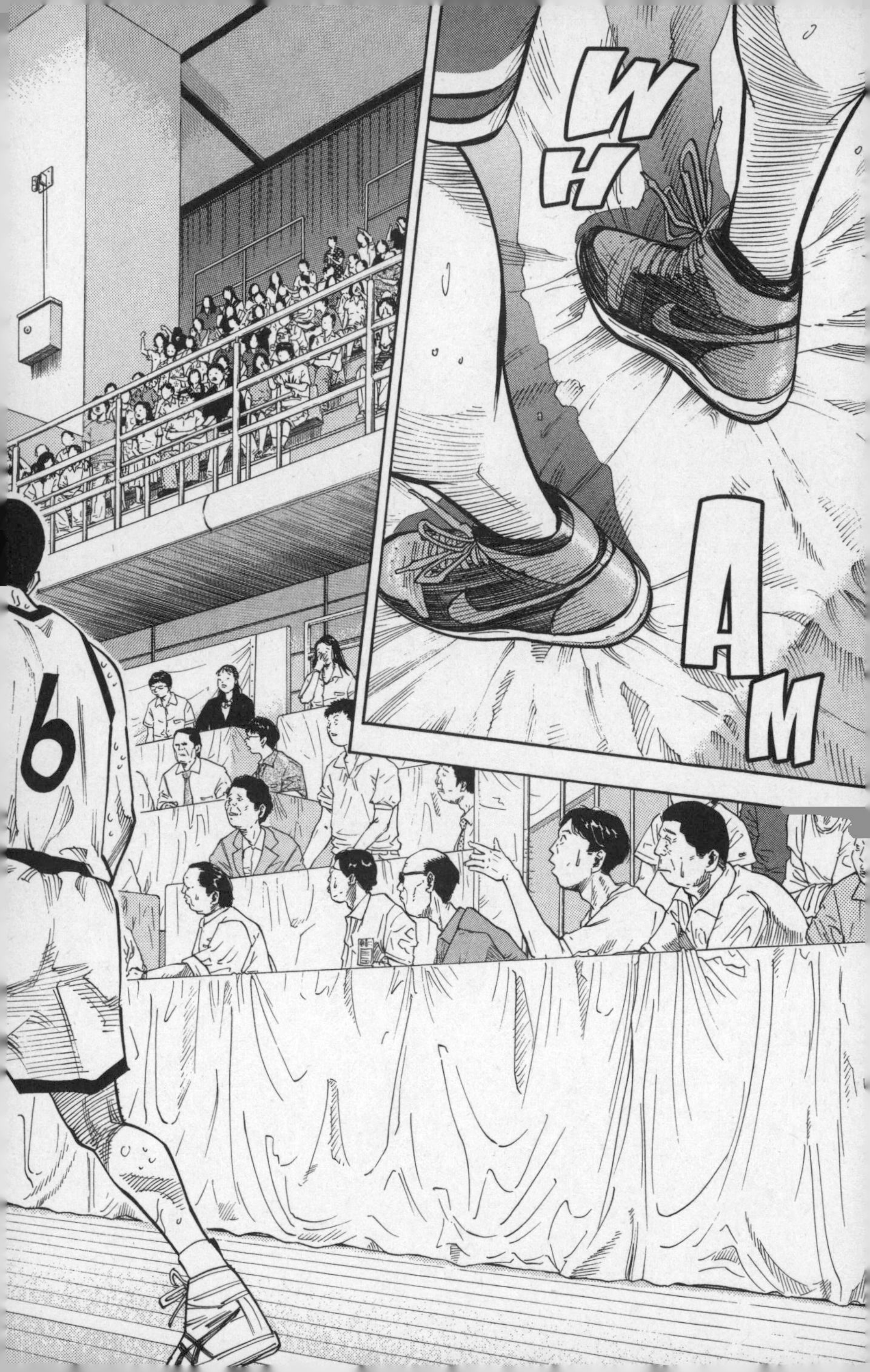
WHAM

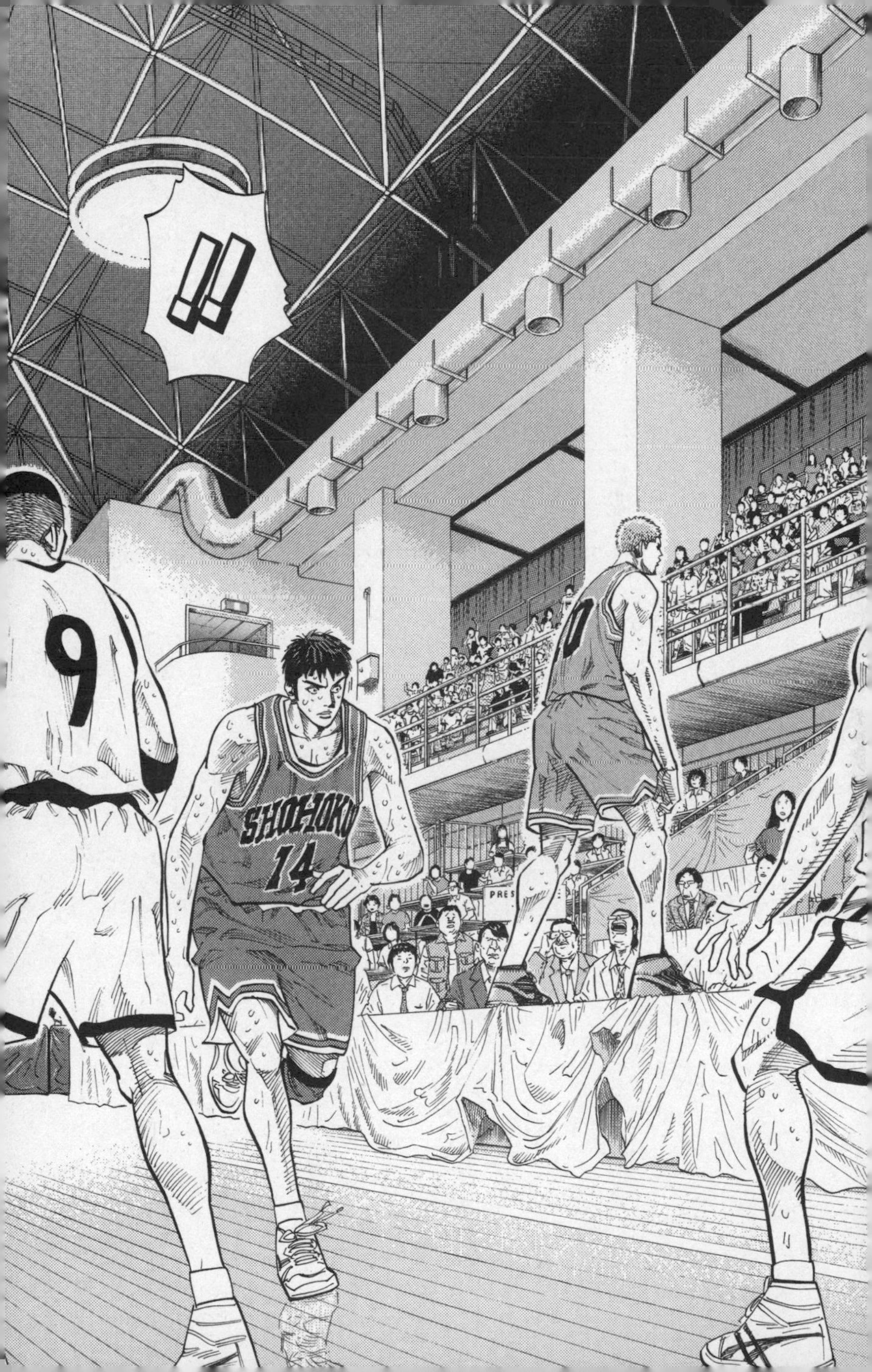
!!

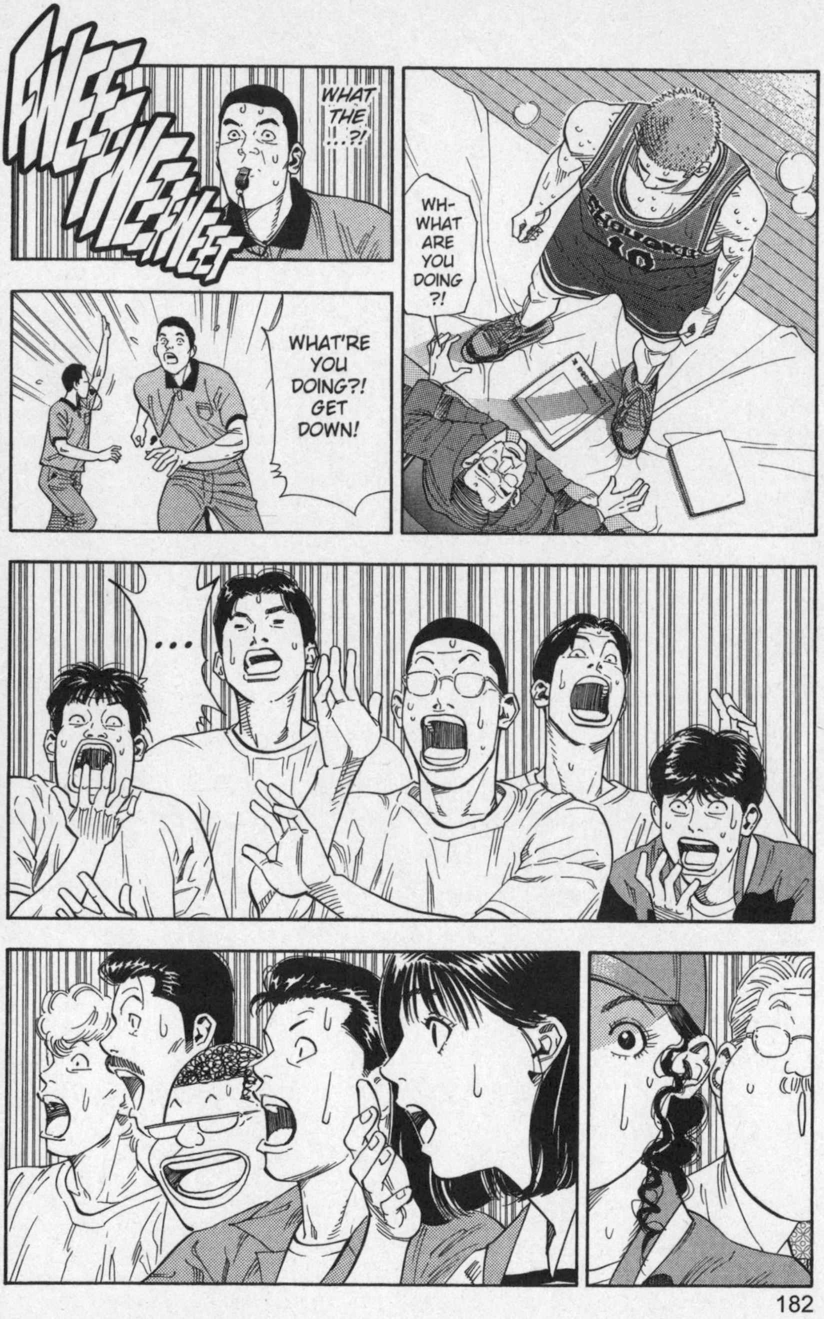
WH-WHAT ARE YOU DOING?!
FWEE FWEE FWEET
WHAT THE...?!
WHAT'RE YOU DOING?! GET DOWN!
...

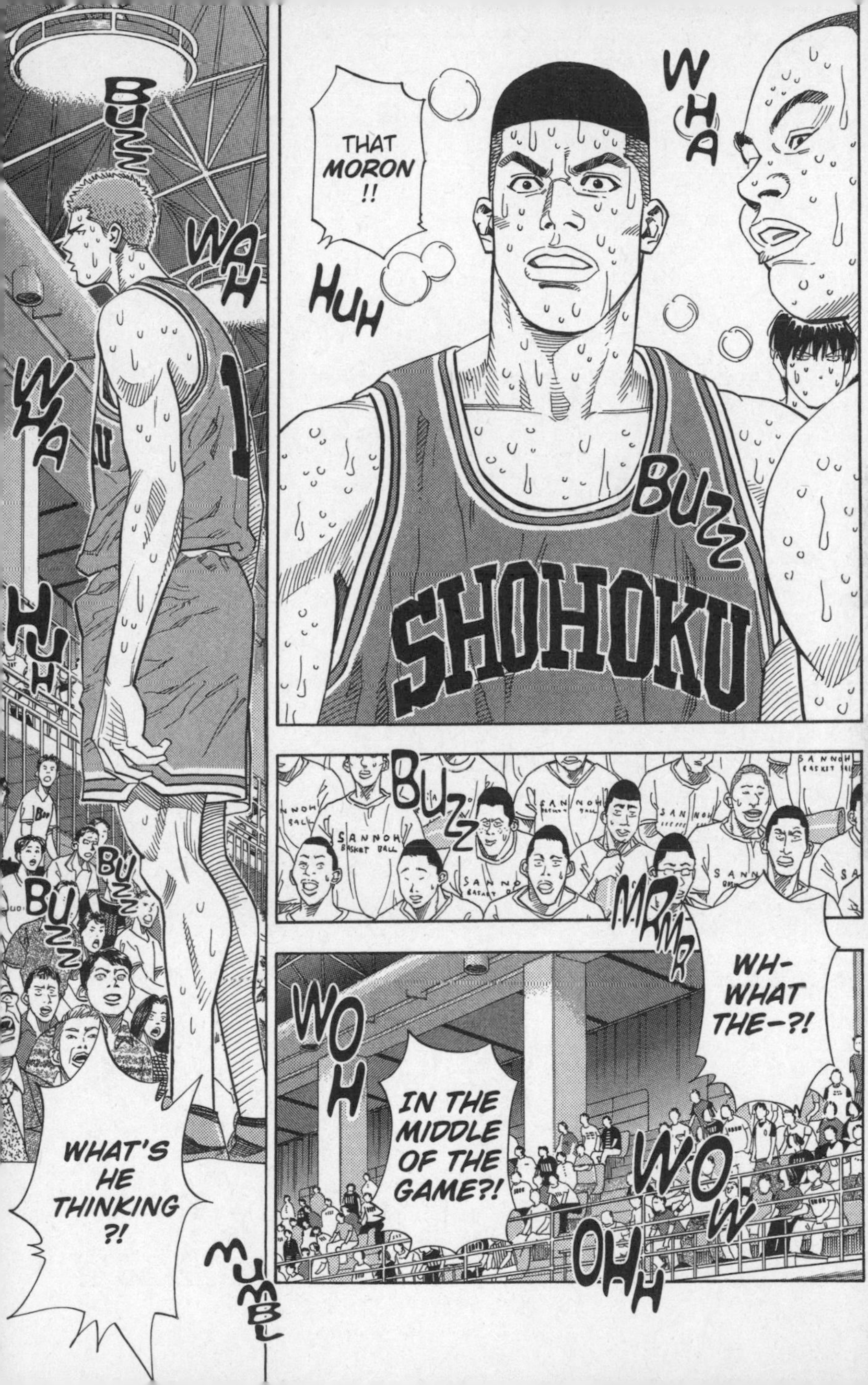
WHA
THAT MORON !!
HUH
BUZZ
BUZZ
MRMR
WH- WHAT THE-?!
WOW
OHH
WOH
IN THE MIDDLE OF THE GAME?!
BUZZ
WAH
WHA
HUH
BUZZ
BUZZ
WHAT'S HE THINKING ?!
MUMBL

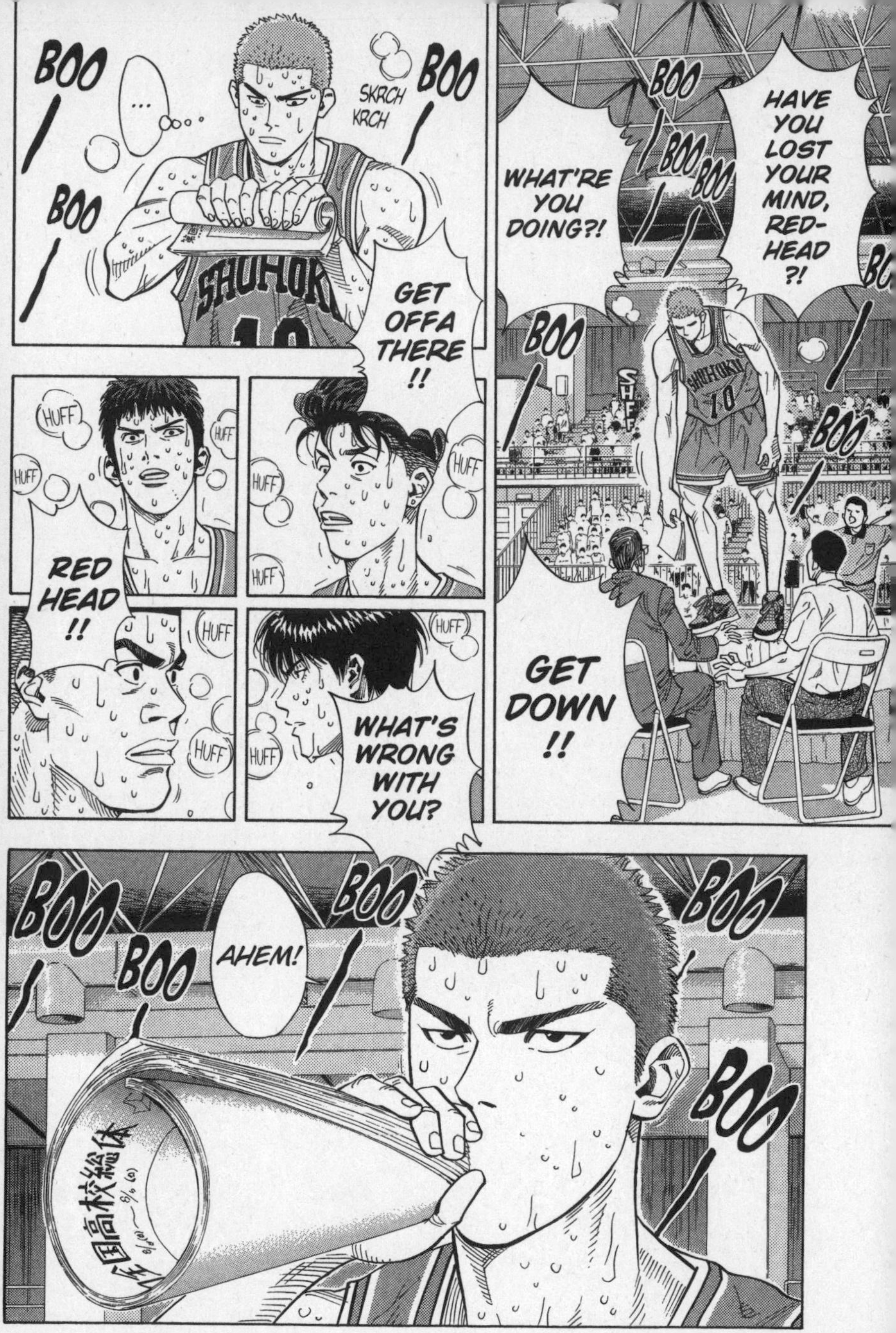
BOO
BOO
BOO
HAVE YOU LOST YOUR MIND, RED-HEAD?!
WHAT'RE YOU DOING?!
BOO
BOO
GET DOWN!!
BOO
SKRCH KRCH
...
BOO
BOO
GET OFFA THERE!!
HUFF
HUFF
HUFF
HUFF
HUFF
HUFF
RED HEAD!!
HUFF
HUFF
WHAT'S WRONG WITH YOU?
HUFF
HUFF
BOO
BOO
BOO
AHEM!
BOO
BOO

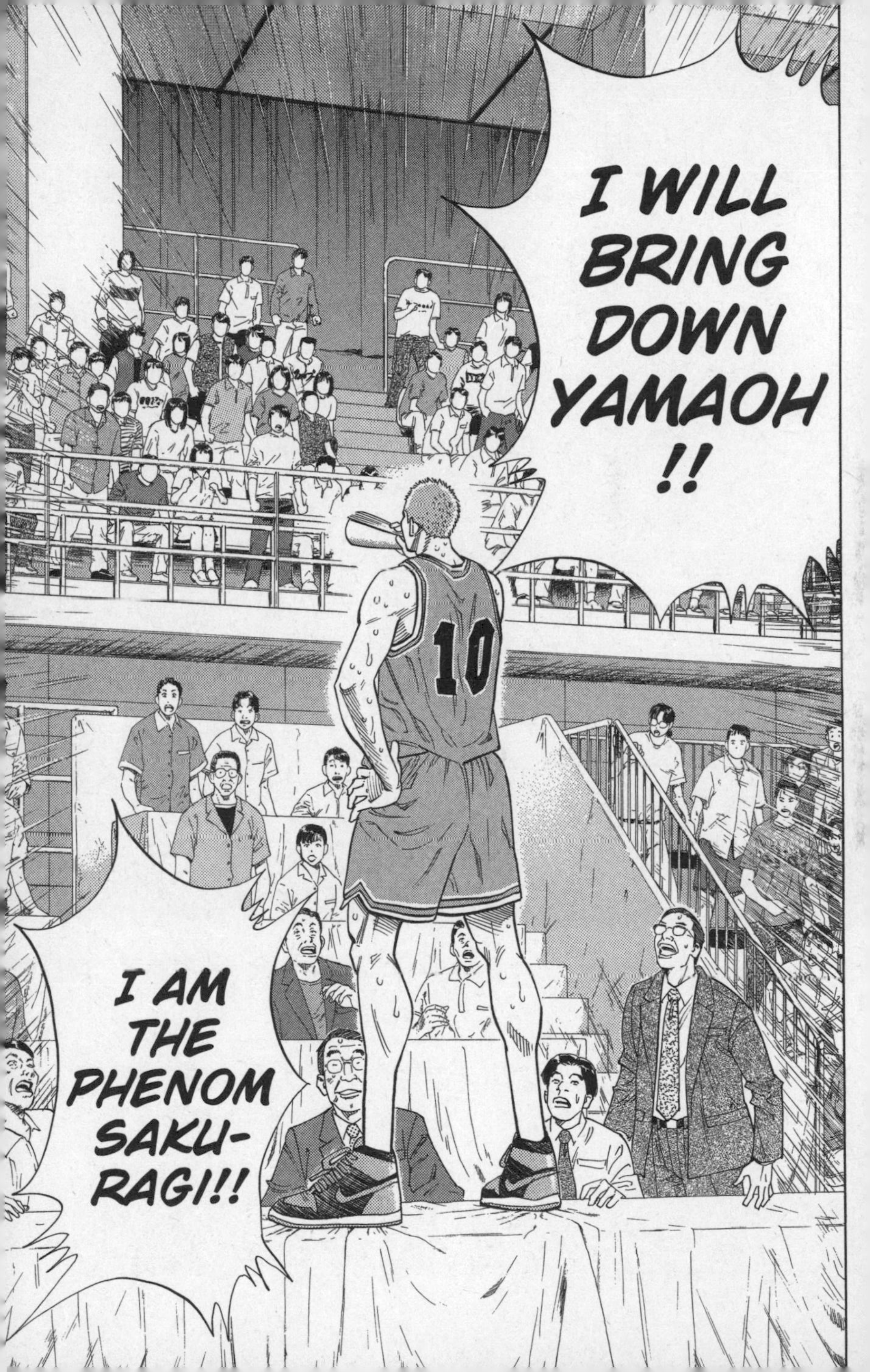
I WILL BRING DOWN YAMAOH !!
I AM THE PHENOM SAKU-RAGI!!

Coming Next Volume

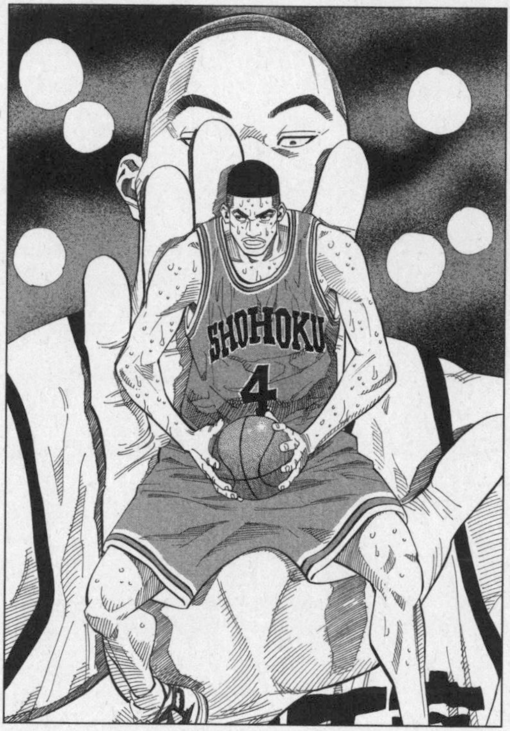
SHOHOKU
4

With Sannoh pulling away with a big lead on the scoreboard in the second half, Shohoku is looking clearly outmatched. With the team foundering, Sakuragi decides he's got to get everyone fired up and boldly declares that he's going to take Sannoh down. Shohoku still has a long way to go, and Akagi himself needs to find a way to overcome Kawata's strong defense. But if Shohoku can find their rhythm, they just might get back in the game.

ON SALE NOW

BAKUMAN.

STORY BY TSUGUMI OHBA
ART BY TAKESHI OBATA

From the creators of *Death Note*

The mystery behind manga making REVEALED!

Average student Moritaka Mashiro enjoys drawing for fun. When his classmate and aspiring writer Akito Takagi discovers his talent, he begs to team up. But what exactly does it take to make it in the manga-publishing world?

Bakuman. Vol. 1
ISBN: 978-1-4215-3513-5
$9.99 US / $12.99 CAN *

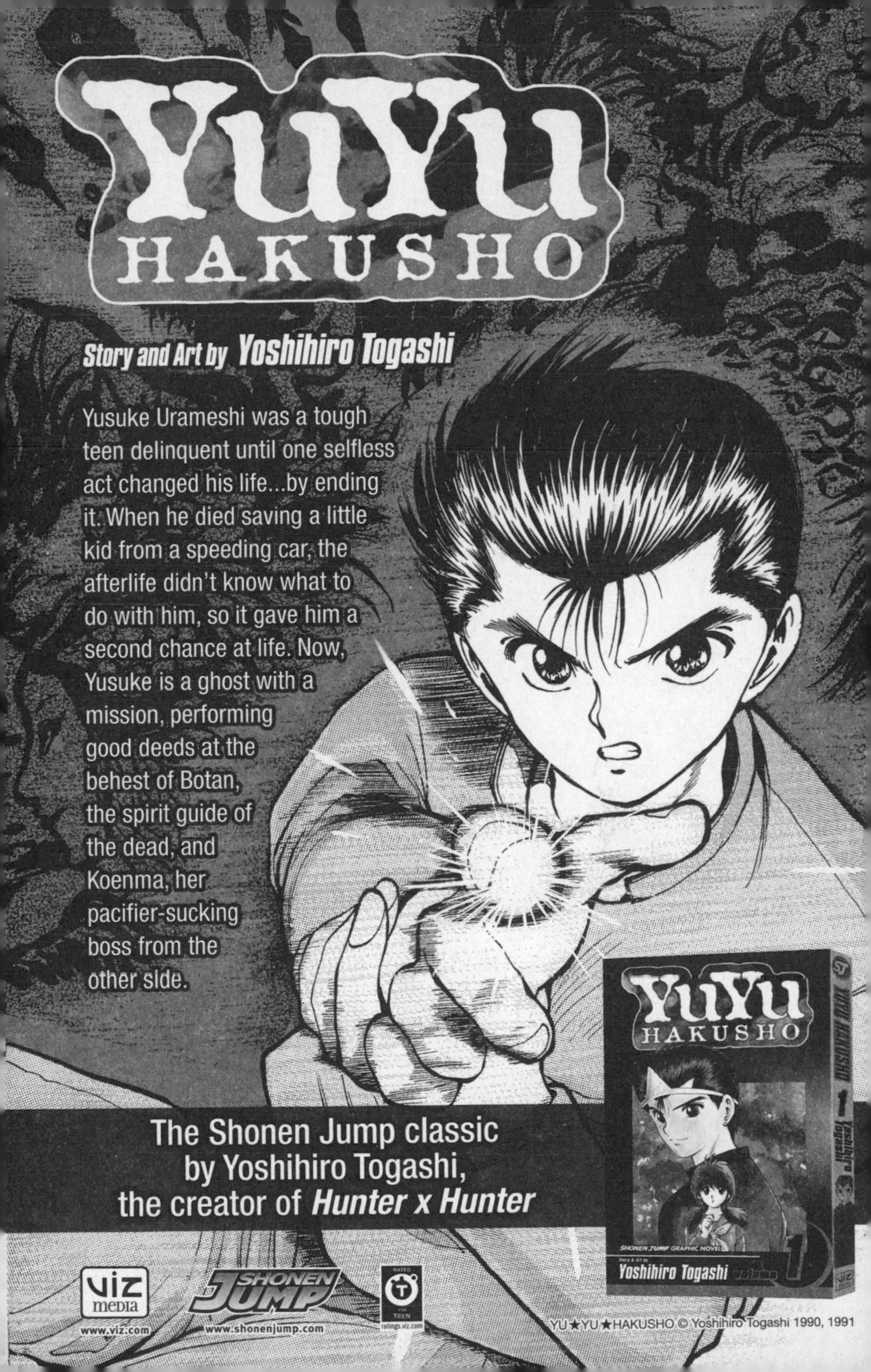
YuYu
HAKUSHO
Story and Art by Yoshihiro Togashi
Yusuke Urameshi was a tough teen delinquent until one selfless act changed his life...by ending it. When he died saving a little kid from a speeding car, the afterlife didn't know what to do with him, so it gave him a second chance at life. Now, Yusuke is a ghost with a mission, performing good deeds at the behest of Botan, the spirit guide of the dead, and Koenma, her pacifier-sucking boss from the other side.
YuYu
HAKUSHO
SHONEN JUMP GRAPHIC NOVEL
Story & Art by
Yoshihiro Togashi
1
The Shonen Jump classic
by Yoshihiro Togashi,
the creator of Hunter x Hunter
viz media
www.viz.com
SHONEN JUMP
www.shonenjump.com
RATED T TEEN
ratings.viz.com
YU★YU★HAKUSHO © Yoshihiro Togashi 1990, 1991

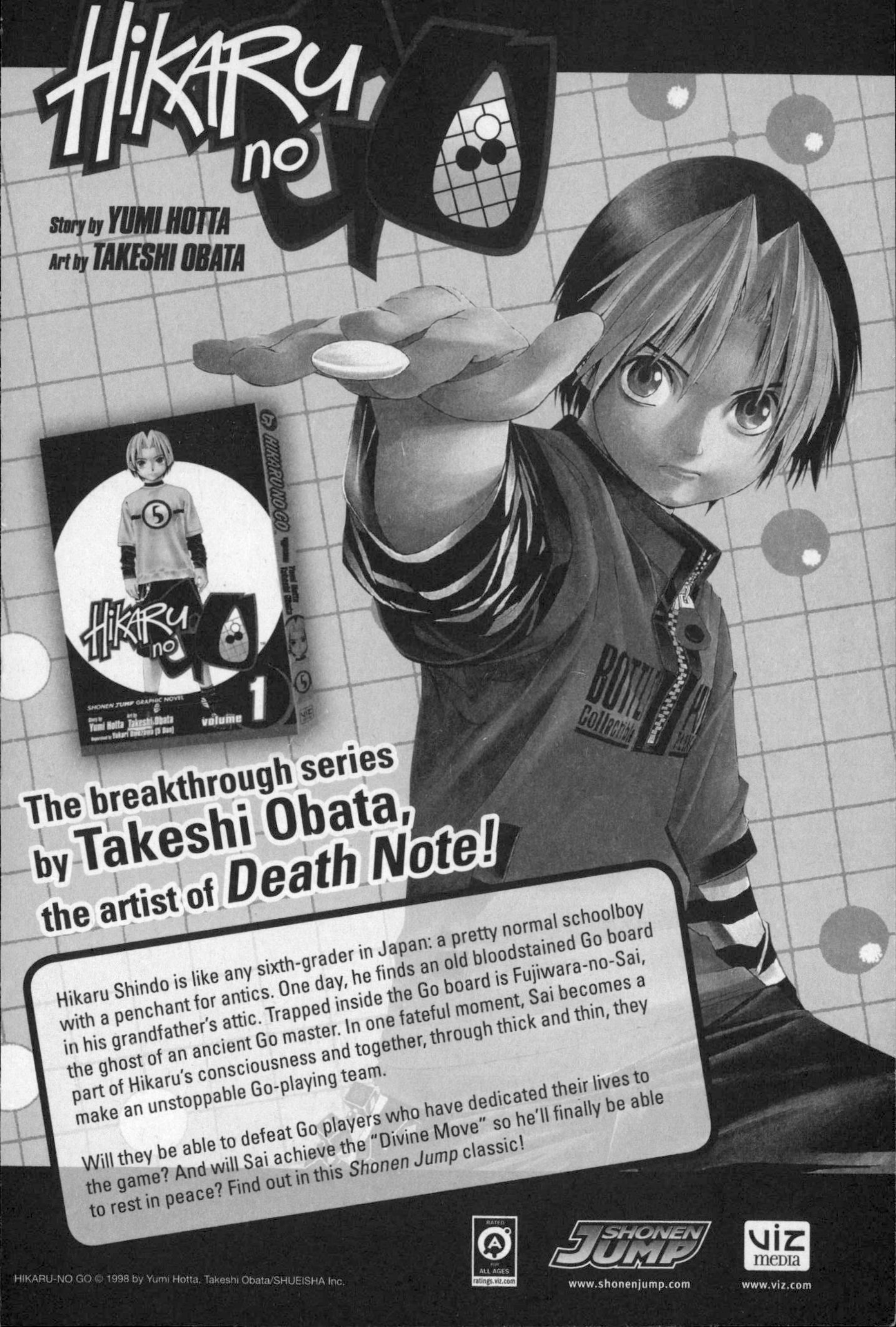
Hikaru no Go
Story by YUMI HOTTA
Art by TAKESHI OBATA
HIKARU NO GO 1 Yumi Hotta Takeshi Obata
SHONEN JUMP GRAPHIC NOVEL
volume 1
The breakthrough series by Takeshi Obata, the artist of Death Note!
Hikaru Shindo is like any sixth-grader in Japan: a pretty normal schoolboy with a penchant for antics. One day, he finds an old bloodstained Go board in his grandfather's attic. Trapped inside the Go board is Fujiwara-no-Sai, the ghost of an ancient Go master. In one fateful moment, Sai becomes a part of Hikaru's consciousness and together, through thick and thin, they make an unstoppable Go-playing team.
Will they be able to defeat Go players who have dedicated their lives to the game? And will Sai achieve the "Divine Move" so he'll finally be able to rest in peace? Find out in this Shonen Jump classic!
RATED A FOR ALL AGES ratings.viz.com
SHONEN JUMP
www.shonenjump.com
viz media
www.viz.com
HIKARU-NO GO © 1998 by Yumi Hotta, Takeshi Obata/SHUEISHA Inc.

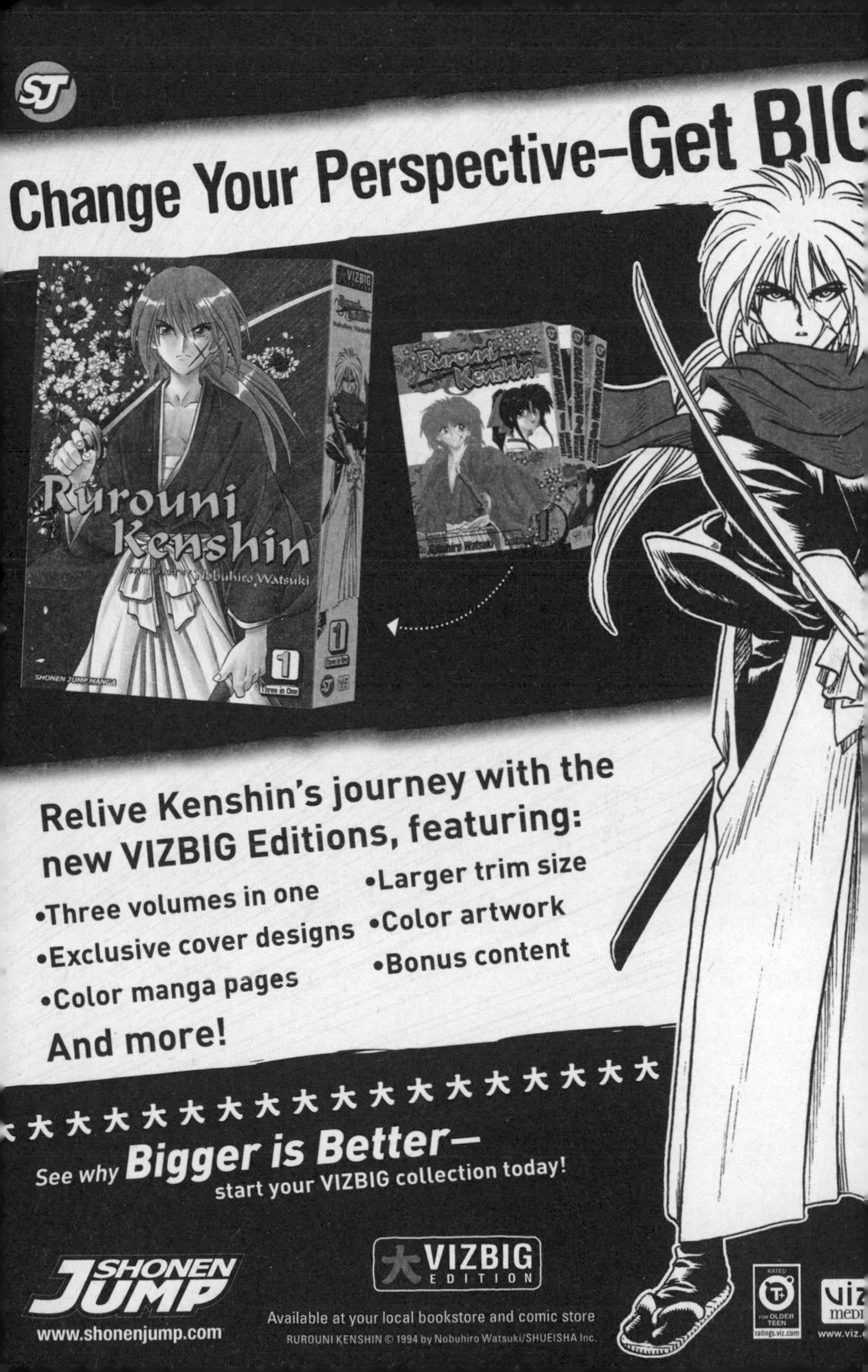
Change Your Perspective–Get BIG
Rurouni Kenshin
Nobuhiro Watsuki
SHONEN JUMP MANGA
1
Three in One
Relive Kenshin's journey with the new VIZBIG Editions, featuring:
•Three volumes in one
•Exclusive cover designs
•Color manga pages
•Larger trim size
•Color artwork
•Bonus content
And more!
See why Bigger is Better—
start your VIZBIG collection today!
SHONEN JUMP
www.shonenjump.com
VIZBIG EDITION
Available at your local bookstore and comic store
RUROUNI KENSHIN © 1994 by Nobuhiro Watsuki/SHUEISHA Inc.
RATED T+ FOR OLDER TEEN
ratings.viz.com

You're Reading in the Wrong Direction!!

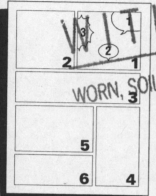

Whoops! Guess what? You're starting at the wrong end of the comic!

…It's true! In keeping with the original Japanese format, **Slam Dunk** is meant to be read from right to left, starting in the upper-right corner.

Unlike English, which is read from left to right, Japanese is read from right to left, meaning that action, sound effects and word-balloon order are completely reversed… something which can make readers unfamiliar with Japanese feel pretty backwards themselves. For this reason, manga or Japanese comics published in the U.S. in English have sometimes been published "flopped"—that is, printed in exact reverse order, as though seen from the other side of a mirror.

By flopping pages, U.S. publishers can avoid confusing readers, but the compromise is not without its downside. For one thing, a character in a flopped manga series who once wore in the original Japanese version a T-shirt emblazoned with "M A Y" (as in "the merry month of") now wears one which reads "Y A M"! Additionally, many manga creators in Japan are themselves unhappy with the process, as some feel the mirror-imaging of their art alters their original intentions.

We are proud to bring you Takehiko Inoue's **Slam Dunk** in the original unflopped format. For now, though, turn to the other side of the book and let the quest begin…!

–Editor

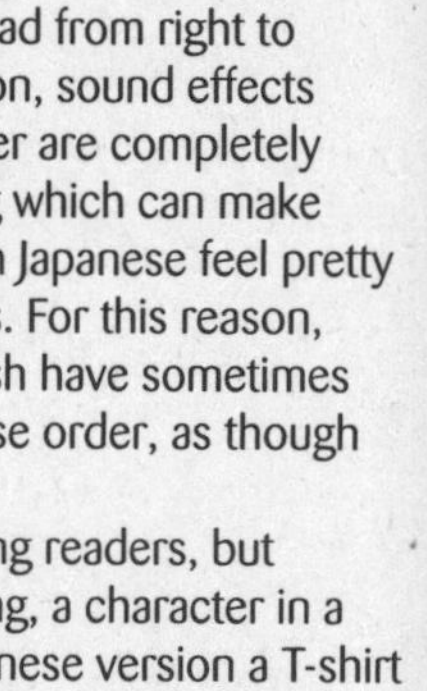